W0017457

2013 | THE LITTLE DATA BOOK ON GENDER

THE WORLD BANK

Contents

Acknowledgments

The Little Data Book on Gender 2013 is a collaborative effort between the Development Data Group of the Development Economics Vice Presidency and the Gender and Development Group of the Poverty Reduction and Economic Management Network.

The Little Data Book on Gender 2013 was prepared by Liu Cui, Vanessa Moreira da Silva, Juan Feng, Masako Hiraga, Hiroko Maeda, Johan Mistiaen, William Prince, and Emi Suzuki of the Development Data Group and Josefina Posadas of the Gender and Development Group. The introduction was written by Masako Hiraga and Josefina Posadas. Production of the book was coordinated by Azita Amjadi and Alison Kwong; Barton Matheson Willse & Worthington typeset the book. The work was carried out under the direction of Shaida Badiee and Jeni Klugman. Staff from The World Bank's Office of the Publisher oversaw publication and dissemination of the book.

Introduction

The Little Data Book on Gender 2013 is a quick reference for users interested in gender statistics. It presents gender-disaggregated data for more than 200 countries in a straightforward, country-by-country reference on demography, education, health, labor force, political participation, and the Millennium Development Goals. Summary pages that cover regional and income group aggregates are also included.

This third issue of *The Little Data Book on Gender* reflects the structure of the *World Development Report 2012 on Gender Equality and Development*. The report looked at the facts and trends surrounding the various dimensions of gender equality in the context of the development process: although many women around the world continue to struggle with gender-based disadvantages, much has changed for the better and at a more rapid pace than ever before. But that progress needs to be expanded, protected, and deepened. While development has closed some gender gaps, other gaps persist, including excess deaths of girls and women, disparities in girls' schooling, unequal access to economic opportunities, and differences in voice within the household and in society. The report argues that gender equality can enhance productivity, improve development outcomes for the next generation, and make institutions more representative of groups in society. For more information about this landmark report, visit www.worldbank.org/wdr2012.

As part of its strategy to provide content when, where, and how users want it, the World Bank now offers two new electronic products on gender. The Gender Equality Data and Statistics Portal (data.worldbank.org/gender) is a resource center for the latest gender-relevant data, with statistics from various sources, tools, training materials, and reference documents covering employment, education, health, public life and decision making, human rights, and demographic outcomes for women and men, and girls and boys. The Gender Data Finder mobile application for iOS, Android or Blackberry allows users to browse and search gender-relevant and sex disaggregated data by keyword, topic, region, and more. Visit http://data.worldbank.org/apps for more information.

Data notes

The data in this book are for 1990 and 2011 or the most recent year unless otherwise noted in the table or the *Glossary*.

- Growth rates are proportional changes from the previous year unless otherwise noted.

- Regional aggregates include data for low- and middle-income economies only.

- Figures in italics indicate data for years or periods other than those specified.

Symbols used:

..	indicates that data are not available or that aggregates cannot be calculated because of missing data.
0 or 0.0	indicates zero or small enough that the number would round to zero at the displayed number of decimal places.
$	indicates current U.S. dollars.

Lettered notes on some country tables can be found in the *Notes* on page 232.

Data are shown for economies with populations greater than 30,000 or for smaller economies if they are members of the World Bank. The term *country* (used interchangeably with *economy*) does not imply political independence or official recognition by the World Bank but refers to any economy for which the authorities report separate social or economic statistics.

The selection of indicators in these pages includes some of those being used to monitor progress toward the Millennium Development Goals. For more information about the eight goals—halving poverty and increasing well-being by 2015—please see the other books in the *World Development Indicators 2013* family of products.

Regional tables

The country composition of regions is based on the World Bank's analytical regions and may differ from common geographic usage.

East Asia and Pacific

American Samoa, Cambodia, China, Fiji, Indonesia, Kiribati, Democratic People's Republic of Korea, Lao People's Democratic Republic, Malaysia, Marshall Islands, Federated States of Micronesia, Mongolia, Myanmar, Palau, Papua New Guinea, Philippines, Samoa, Solomon Islands, Thailand, Timor-Leste, Tonga, Tuvalu, Vanuatu, Vietnam

Europe and Central Asia

Albania, Armenia, Azerbaijan, Belarus, Bosnia and Herzegovina, Bulgaria, Georgia, Kazakhstan, Kosovo, Kyrgyz Republic, Latvia, Lithuania, Former Yugoslav Republic of Macedonia, Moldova, Montenegro, Romania, Russian Federation, Serbia, Tajikistan, Turkey, Turkmenistan, Ukraine, Uzbekistan

Latin America and the Caribbean

Antigua and Barbuda, Argentina, Belize, Bolivia, Brazil, Chile, Colombia, Costa Rica, Cuba, Dominica, Dominican Republic, Ecuador, El Salvador, Grenada, Guatemala, Guyana, Haiti, Honduras, Jamaica, Mexico, Nicaragua, Panama, Paraguay, Peru, St. Lucia, St. Vincent and the Grenadines, Suriname, Uruguay, República Bolivariana de Venezuela

Middle East and North Africa

Algeria, Djibouti, Arab Republic of Egypt, Islamic Republic of Iran, Iraq, Jordan, Lebanon, Libya, Morocco, Syrian Arab Republic, Tunisia, West Bank and Gaza, Republic of Yemen

South Asia

Afghanistan, Bangladesh, Bhutan, India, Maldives, Nepal, Pakistan, Sri Lanka

Sub-Saharan Africa

Angola, Benin, Botswana, Burkina Faso, Burundi, Cameroon, Cape Verde, Central African Republic, Chad, Comoros, Democratic Republic of the Congo, Republic of Congo, Côte d'Ivoire, Eritrea, Ethiopia, Gabon, The Gambia, Ghana, Guinea, Guinea-Bissau, Kenya, Lesotho, Liberia, Madagascar, Malawi, Mali, Mauritania, Mauritius, , Mozambique, Namibia, Niger, Nigeria, Rwanda, São Tomé and Príncipe, Senegal, Seychelles, Sierra Leone, Somalia, South Africa, South Sudan, Sudan, Swaziland, Tanzania, Togo, Uganda, Zambia, Zimbabwe

World

Population (millions)	6,974.2
GNI, Atlas ($ billions)	66,354.3
GNI per capita, Atlas ($)	9,514
Population living below $1.25 a day (%)	..

	1990		2011	
	Female	Male	Female	Male
Demography				
Sex ratio at birth (boys per girls)	1.07		1.07	
Life expectancy at birth (years)	68	63	72	68
Under-five mortality rate (per 1,000 live births)	85	89	50	53
Female-headed households (%)	..		..	
Education				
Gross primary enrollment ratio (% of relevant age group)	93	106	105	108
Gross secondary enrollment ratio (% of relevant age group)	45	54	69	71
Gross tertiary enrollment ratio (% of relevant age group)	13	14	30	28
Primary completion rate (% of relevant age group)	76	85	89	91
Youth literacy rate (% of population ages 15–24)	79	88	87	92
Health and related services				
Total fertility rate (births per woman)	3.2		2.4	
Adolescent fertility rate (births per 1,000 women ages 15–19)	..		53	
Women first married by age 18 (% of women ages 20–24)	..		..	
Contraceptive prevalence (% of women ages 15–49)	58		..	
Unmet need for contraception (% of women ages 15–49)	..		..	
Pregnant women receiving prenatal care (%)	..		81	
Births attended by skilled health staff (% of total)	..		66	
Maternal mortality ratio (per 100,000 live births)	400		210	
Economic structure, participation, and access to resources				
Labor force participation rate (% of population ages 15+)	52	81	51	77
Wage and salaried workers (% of employed ages 15+)	..	..	..	..
Self-employed workers (% of employed ages 15+)	..	..	..	..
Vulnerable employment (% of employed ages 15+)	..	..	..	..
Unpaid family workers (% of employed ages 15+)	..	..	..	..
Employment in agriculture (% of employed ages 15+)	..	..	..	..
Employment in industry (% of employed ages 15+)	..	..	..	..
Employment in service (% of employed ages 15+)	..	..	..	..
Women in wage employment in the nonagricultural sector (%)	35		..	
Women's share of part-time employment (% of total)	..		..	
Maternity leave (weeks)	..		..	
Maternal leave benefits (% of wages paid)	..		..	
Female legislators, senior officials and managers (% of total)	..		..	
Employment to population ratio, total (% ages 15+)	49	76	48	73
Employment to population ratio, youth (% ages 15–24)	45	59	35	49
Children in employment (% of children ages 7–14)	..	..	..	..
Unemployment rate (% of labor force ages 15+)	..	..	..	..
Long-term unemployment rate (% total unemployment)	..	..	..	..
Youth unemployment rate (% of labor force ages 15–24)	..	..	..	..
Account at a formal financial institution (% age 15+)	..	..	47	54
Public life and decision making				
Seats held by women in national parliament (%)	13		21	

East Asia & Pacific

Population (millions)	1,974.2
GNI, Atlas ($ billions)	8,387.3
GNI per capita, Atlas ($)	4,248
Population living below $1.25 a day (%)	12.5

	1990 Female	1990 Male	2011 Female	2011 Male
Demography				
Sex ratio at birth (boys per girls)	1.10		1.13	
Life expectancy at birth (years)	70	66	74	71
Under-five mortality rate (per 1,000 live births)	53	58	20	22
Female-headed households (%)	..		..	
Education				
Gross primary enrollment ratio (% of relevant age group)	117	127	112	110
Gross secondary enrollment ratio (% of relevant age group)	34	44	80	77
Gross tertiary enrollment ratio (% of relevant age group)	4	6	27	25
Primary completion rate (% of relevant age group)	..	..	99	96
Youth literacy rate (% of population ages 15–24)	92	97	99	99
Health and related services				
Total fertility rate (births per woman)	2.6		1.8	
Adolescent fertility rate (births per 1,000 women ages 15–19)	..		19	
Women first married by age 18 (% of women ages 20–24)	..		..	
Contraceptive prevalence (% of women ages 15–49)	75		..	
Unmet need for contraception (% of women ages 15–49)	..		..	
Pregnant women receiving prenatal care (%)	71		92	
Births attended by skilled health staff (% of total)	84		91	
Maternal mortality ratio (per 100,000 live births)	220		83	
Economic structure, participation, and access to resources				
Labor force participation rate (% of population ages 15+)	69	84	65	81
Wage and salaried workers (% of employed ages 15+)	..	..	..	..
Self-employed workers (% of employed ages 15+)	..	..	..	..
Vulnerable employment (% of employed ages 15+)	..	..	..	..
Unpaid family workers (% of employed ages 15+)	..	..	..	..
Employment in agriculture (% of employed ages 15+)	..	..	..	..
Employment in industry (% of employed ages 15+)	..	..	..	..
Employment in service (% of employed ages 15+)	..	..	..	..
Women in wage employment in the nonagricultural sector (%)	37		..	
Women's share of part-time employment (% of total)	..		..	
Maternity leave (weeks)	..		..	
Maternal leave benefits (% of wages paid)	..		..	
Female legislators, senior officials and managers (% of total)	..		..	
Employment to population ratio, total (% ages 15+)	66	80	63	77
Employment to population ratio, youth (% ages 15–24)	67	67	52	53
Children in employment (% of children ages 7–14)	..	..	..	..
Unemployment rate (% of labor force ages 15+)	..	..	..	..
Long-term unemployment rate (% total unemployment)	..	..	..	..
Youth unemployment rate (% of labor force ages 15–24)	..	..	..	..
Account at a formal financial institution (% age 15+)	..	..	52	58
Public life and decision making				
Seats held by women in national parliament (%)	17		18	

Europe & Central Asia

Population (millions)			408.1
GNI, Atlas ($ billions)			3,156.6
GNI per capita, Atlas ($)			7,734
Population living below $1.25 a day (%)			0.7

	1990		2011	
	Female	Male	Female	Male
Demography				
Sex ratio at birth (boys per girls)	1.06		1.06	
Life expectancy at birth (years)	73	64	75	67
Under-five mortality rate (per 1,000 live births)	43	52	19	23
Female-headed households (%)		..		..
Education				
Gross primary enrollment ratio (% of relevant age group)	103	105	100	100
Gross secondary enrollment ratio (% of relevant age group)	87	91	88	91
Gross tertiary enrollment ratio (% of relevant age group)	37	33	61	51
Primary completion rate (% of relevant age group)	94	96	98	99
Youth literacy rate (% of population ages 15–24)	98	99	99	99
Health and related services				
Total fertility rate (births per woman)	2.3		1.8	
Adolescent fertility rate (births per 1,000 women ages 15–19)		..	26	
Women first married by age 18 (% of women ages 20–24)		..		..
Contraceptive prevalence (% of women ages 15–49)		..	74	
Unmet need for contraception (% of women ages 15–49)		..		..
Pregnant women receiving prenatal care (%)		..		..
Births attended by skilled health staff (% of total)	99		98	
Maternal mortality ratio (per 100,000 live births)	70		32	
Economic structure, participation, and access to resources				
Labor force participation rate (% of population ages 15+)	55	75	50	70
Wage and salaried workers (% of employed ages 15+)	..	..	81	80
Self-employed workers (% of employed ages 15+)	..	..	19	20
Vulnerable employment (% of employed ages 15+)	..	..	18	18
Unpaid family workers (% of employed ages 15+)	..	..	5.3	1.9
Employment in agriculture (% of employed ages 15+)	..	..	16	16
Employment in industry (% of employed ages 15+)	..	..	18	35
Employment in service (% of employed ages 15+)	..	..	66	49
Women in wage employment in the nonagricultural sector (%)	46		47	
Women's share of part-time employment (% of total)	..		..	
Maternity leave (weeks)	..		..	
Maternal leave benefits (% of wages paid)	..		..	
Female legislators, senior officials and managers (% of total)	..		..	
Employment to population ratio, total (% ages 15+)	48	66	46	64
Employment to population ratio, youth (% ages 15–24)	36	45	28	41
Children in employment (% of children ages 7–14)	..	..	..	..
Unemployment rate (% of labor force ages 15+)	..	..	7.5	8.3
Long-term unemployment rate (% total unemployment)	..	..	..	..
Youth unemployment rate (% of labor force ages 15–24)	..	..	18	17
Account at a formal financial institution (% age 15+)	..	..	40	50
Public life and decision making				
Seats held by women in national parliament (%)		..	18	

Latin America & Caribbean

Population (millions)	589.0
GNI, Atlas ($ billions)	5,050.3
GNI per capita, Atlas ($)	8,574
Population living below $1.25 a day (%)	5.5

	1990 Female	1990 Male	2011 Female	2011 Male
Demography				
Sex ratio at birth (boys per girls)	1.05		1.05	
Life expectancy at birth (years)	72	65	78	71
Under-five mortality rate (per 1,000 live births)	48	57	17	21
Female-headed households (%)	..		..	
Education				
Gross primary enrollment ratio (% of relevant age group)	116	117	114	118
Gross secondary enrollment ratio (% of relevant age group)	63	59	93	86
Gross tertiary enrollment ratio (% of relevant age group)	16	17	45	36
Primary completion rate (% of relevant age group)	85	82	102	101
Youth literacy rate (% of population ages 15–24)	93	93	97	97
Health and related services				
Total fertility rate (births per woman)	3.2		2.2	
Adolescent fertility rate (births per 1,000 women ages 15–19)	..		71	
Women first married by age 18 (% of women ages 20–24)	..		..	
Contraceptive prevalence (% of women ages 15–49)	58		..	
Unmet need for contraception (% of women ages 15–49)	..		..	
Pregnant women receiving prenatal care (%)	..		96	
Births attended by skilled health staff (% of total)	75		..	
Maternal mortality ratio (per 100,000 live births)	140		81	
Economic structure, participation, and access to resources				
Labor force participation rate (% of population ages 15+)	40	82	54	80
Wage and salaried workers (% of employed ages 15+)	62	60	66	63
Self-employed workers (% of employed ages 15+)	38	40	32	36
Vulnerable employment (% of employed ages 15+)	29	30	31	30
Unpaid family workers (% of employed ages 15+)	10.5	5.3	7.0	3.7
Employment in agriculture (% of employed ages 15+)	15	21	8	19
Employment in industry (% of employed ages 15+)	14	30	14	28
Employment in service (% of employed ages 15+)	71	49	78	52
Women in wage employment in the nonagricultural sector (%)	37		41	
Women's share of part-time employment (% of total)	..		63	
Maternity leave (weeks)	..		..	
Maternal leave benefits (% of wages paid)	..		..	
Female legislators, senior officials and managers (% of total)	..		..	
Employment to population ratio, total (% ages 15+)	37	77	49	75
Employment to population ratio, youth (% ages 15–24)	32	62	35	56
Children in employment (% of children ages 7–14)	..	..	..	..
Unemployment rate (% of labor force ages 15+)	6.9	6.0	9.7	6.3
Long-term unemployment rate (% total unemployment)	..	..	..	..
Youth unemployment rate (% of labor force ages 15–24)	14	10	19	13
Account at a formal financial institution (% age 15+)	..	..	35	44
Public life and decision making				
Seats held by women in national parliament (%)	12		25	

Middle East & North Africa

Population (millions)	336.5
GNI, Atlas ($ billions)	1,279.5
GNI per capita, Atlas ($)	3,866
Population living below $1.25 a day (%)	2.4

	1990		2011	
	Female	Male	Female	Male
Demography				
Sex ratio at birth (boys per girls)	1.05		1.05	
Life expectancy at birth (years)	66	62	74	70
Under-five mortality rate (per 1,000 live births)	68	72	30	34
Female-headed households (%)	..		..	
Education				
Gross primary enrollment ratio (% of relevant age group)	86	103	101	108
Gross secondary enrollment ratio (% of relevant age group)	47	64	71	78
Gross tertiary enrollment ratio (% of relevant age group)	8	14	30	30
Primary completion rate (% of relevant age group)	68	84	87	93
Youth literacy rate (% of population ages 15–24)	67	85	88	94
Health and related services				
Total fertility rate (births per woman)	4.9		2.7	
Adolescent fertility rate (births per 1,000 women ages 15–19)	..		37	
Women first married by age 18 (% of women ages 20–24)	..		..	
Contraceptive prevalence (% of women ages 15–49)	43		..	
Unmet need for contraception (% of women ages 15–49)	..		..	
Pregnant women receiving prenatal care (%)	..		..	
Births attended by skilled health staff (% of total)	..		..	
Maternal mortality ratio (per 100,000 live births)	220		81	
Economic structure, participation, and access to resources				
Labor force participation rate (% of population ages 15+)	18	76	20	73
Wage and salaried workers (% of employed ages 15+)	..	..	..	..
Self-employed workers (% of employed ages 15+)	..	..	..	..
Vulnerable employment (% of employed ages 15+)	..	..	49	33
Unpaid family workers (% of employed ages 15+)	..	..	..	..
Employment in agriculture (% of employed ages 15+)	..	..	43	23
Employment in industry (% of employed ages 15+)	..	..	14	29
Employment in service (% of employed ages 15+)	..	..	43	48
Women in wage employment in the nonagricultural sector (%)	18		..	
Women's share of part-time employment (% of total)	..		..	
Maternity leave (weeks)	..		..	
Maternal leave benefits (% of wages paid)	..		..	
Female legislators, senior officials and managers (% of total)	..		..	
Employment to population ratio, total (% ages 15+)	13	68	16	65
Employment to population ratio, youth (% ages 15–24)	11	42	8	37
Children in employment (% of children ages 7–14)	..	..	..	..
Unemployment rate (% of labor force ages 15+)	21.5	10.8	19.1	8.6
Long-term unemployment rate (% total unemployment)	..	..	..	..
Youth unemployment rate (% of labor force ages 15–24)	..	..	..	..
Account at a formal financial institution (% age 15+)	..	..	13	23
Public life and decision making				
Seats held by women in national parliament (%)	4		14	

South Asia

Population (millions)	1,656.5
GNI, Atlas ($ billions)	2,174.5
GNI per capita, Atlas ($)	1,313
Population living below $1.25 a day (%)	*31.0*

	1990		2011	
	Female	Male	Female	Male
Demography				
Sex ratio at birth (boys per girls)	1.07		1.07	
Life expectancy at birth (years)	59	58	67	64
Under-five mortality rate (per 1,000 live births)	122	116	63	61
Female-headed households (%)	..		..	
Education				
Gross primary enrollment ratio (% of relevant age group)	72	99	105	107
Gross secondary enrollment ratio (% of relevant age group)	26	44	55	61
Gross tertiary enrollment ratio (% of relevant age group)	3	7	13	17
Primary completion rate (% of relevant age group)	51	72	87	89
Youth literacy rate (% of population ages 15–24)	47	69	73	86
Health and related services				
Total fertility rate (births per woman)	4.2		2.7	
Adolescent fertility rate (births per 1,000 women ages 15–19)	..		71	
Women first married by age 18 (% of women ages 20–24)	..		..	
Contraceptive prevalence (% of women ages 15–49)	41		51	
Unmet need for contraception (% of women ages 15–49)	..		..	
Pregnant women receiving prenatal care (%)	..		70	
Births attended by skilled health staff (% of total)	..		48	
Maternal mortality ratio (per 100,000 live births)	620		220	
Economic structure, participation, and access to resources				
Labor force participation rate (% of population ages 15+)	36	85	32	81
Wage and salaried workers (% of employed ages 15+)	9	19	15	20
Self-employed workers (% of employed ages 15+)	91	81	85	80
Vulnerable employment (% of employed ages 15+)	..	..	84	77
Unpaid family workers (% of employed ages 15+)	37.5	13.6	33.7	10.9
Employment in agriculture (% of employed ages 15+)	72	55	65	46
Employment in industry (% of employed ages 15+)	13	17	18	24
Employment in service (% of employed ages 15+)	16	28	17	30
Women in wage employment in the nonagricultural sector (%)	12		..	
Women's share of part-time employment (% of total)	..			
Maternity leave (weeks)	..		..	
Maternal leave benefits (% of wages paid)	..		..	
Female legislators, senior officials and managers (% of total)	..		..	
Employment to population ratio, total (% ages 15+)	34	82	30	79
Employment to population ratio, youth (% ages 15–24)	29	64	21	52
Children in employment (% of children ages 7–14)	..	..	..	..
Unemployment rate (% of labor force ages 15+)	4.5	3.7	4.4	3.3
Long-term unemployment rate (% total unemployment)	..	..	41.4	36.6
Youth unemployment rate (% of labor force ages 15–24)	8	8	12	10
Account at a formal financial institution (% age 15+)	..	..	25	41
Public life and decision making				
Seats held by women in national parliament (%)	6		20	

Sub-Saharan Africa

Population (millions)				874.8
GNI, Atlas ($ billions)				1,100.8
GNI per capita, Atlas ($)				1,258
Population living below $1.25 a day (%)				48.5

	1990		2011	
	Female	Male	Female	Male
Demography				
Sex ratio at birth (boys per girls)	1.04		1.04	
Life expectancy at birth (years)	51	48	56	54
Under-five mortality rate (per 1,000 live births)	169	186	103	114
Female-headed households (%)	..		..	
Education				
Gross primary enrollment ratio (% of relevant age group)	65	78	96	103
Gross secondary enrollment ratio (% of relevant age group)	19	26	36	43
Gross tertiary enrollment ratio (% of relevant age group)	2	4	5	8
Primary completion rate (% of relevant age group)	46	57	67	74
Youth literacy rate (% of population ages 15–24)	59	73	67	76
Health and related services				
Total fertility rate (births per woman)	6.3		4.9	
Adolescent fertility rate (births per 1,000 women ages 15–19)	..		106	
Women first married by age 18 (% of women ages 20–24)	..		..	
Contraceptive prevalence (% of women ages 15–49)	16		25	
Unmet need for contraception (% of women ages 15–49)	..		..	
Pregnant women receiving prenatal care (%)	..		76	
Births attended by skilled health staff (% of total)	..		48	
Maternal mortality ratio (per 100,000 live births)	850		500	
Economic structure, participation, and access to resources				
Labor force participation rate (% of population ages 15+)	58	80	63	76
Wage and salaried workers (% of employed ages 15+)	..	..	..	..
Self-employed workers (% of employed ages 15+)	..	..	..	..
Vulnerable employment (% of employed ages 15+)	..	..	..	..
Unpaid family workers (% of employed ages 15+)	..	..	..	..
Employment in agriculture (% of employed ages 15+)	..	..	..	..
Employment in industry (% of employed ages 15+)	..	..	..	..
Employment in service (% of employed ages 15+)	..	..	..	..
Women in wage employment in the nonagricultural sector (%)	..		..	
Women's share of part-time employment (% of total)	..		..	
Maternity leave (weeks)	..		..	
Maternal leave benefits (% of wages paid)	..		..	
Female legislators, senior officials and managers (% of total)	..		..	
Employment to population ratio, total (% ages 15+)	53	73	58	71
Employment to population ratio, youth (% ages 15–24)	42	51	44	49
Children in employment (% of children ages 7–14)	..	..	..	..
Unemployment rate (% of labor force ages 15+)	..	..	..	..
Long-term unemployment rate (% total unemployment)	..	..	..	..
Youth unemployment rate (% of labor force ages 15–24)	..	..	..	..
Account at a formal financial institution (% age 15+)	..	..	21	27
Public life and decision making				
Seats held by women in national parliament (%)	..		22	

Income group tables

For operational and analytical purposes the World Bank's main criterion for classifying economies is gross national income (GNI) per capita. Each economy in *The Little Data Book on Gender* is classified as low income, middle income, or high income. Low- and middle-income economies are sometimes referred to as developing economies. The use of the term is convenient; it is not intended to imply that all economies in the group are experiencing similar development or that other economies have reached a preferred or final stage of development. Classification by income does not necessarily reflect development status. Note: Classifications are fixed during the World Bank's fiscal year (ending on June 30), thus countries remain in the categories in which they are classified irrespective of any revisions to their per capita income data.

Low-income economies are those with a GNI per capita of $1,025 or less in 2011.

Middle-income economies are those with a GNI per capita of more than $1,025 but less than $12,476. Lower-middle-income and upper-middle-income economies are separated at a GNI per capita of $4,036.

High-income economies are those with a GNI per capita of $12,496 or more.

Euro area includes the member states of the Economic and Monetary Union of the European Union that have adopted the euro as their currency: Austria, Belgium, Cyprus, Estonia, Finland, France, Germany, Greece, Ireland, Italy, Luxembourg, Malta, Netherlands, Portugal, Slovak Republic, Slovenia, and Spain.

Low income

Population (millions)				816.8
GNI, Atlas ($ billions)				466.0
GNI per capita, Atlas ($)				571
Population living below $1.25 a day (%)				*48.0*

	1990		2011	
	Female	Male	Female	Male
Demography				
Sex ratio at birth (boys per girls)	1.04		1.04	
Life expectancy at birth (years)	54	52	60	58
Under-five mortality rate (per 1,000 live births)	156	171	90	100
Female-headed households (%)	..		..	
Education				
Gross primary enrollment ratio (% of relevant age group)	63	78	103	108
Gross secondary enrollment ratio (% of relevant age group)	17	26	38	44
Gross tertiary enrollment ratio (% of relevant age group)	2	5	6	9
Primary completion rate (% of relevant age group)	40	52	65	70
Youth literacy rate (% of population ages 15–24)	53	67	*70*	*77*
Health and related services				
Total fertility rate (births per woman)	5.7		4.0	
Adolescent fertility rate (births per 1,000 women ages 15–19)	..		92	
Women first married by age 18 (% of women ages 20–24)	..		..	
Contraceptive prevalence (% of women ages 15–49)	23		*37*	
Unmet need for contraception (% of women ages 15–49)	..		..	
Pregnant women receiving prenatal care (%)	..		75	
Births attended by skilled health staff (% of total)	..		47	
Maternal mortality ratio (per 100,000 live births)	810		*410*	
Economic structure, participation, and access to resources				
Labor force participation rate (% of population ages 15+)	67	84	68	83
Wage and salaried workers (% of employed ages 15+)	..	..	..	..
Self-employed workers (% of employed ages 15+)	..	..	..	..
Vulnerable employment (% of employed ages 15+)	..	..	..	..
Unpaid family workers (% of employed ages 15+)	..	..	..	..
Employment in agriculture (% of employed ages 15+)	..	..	..	..
Employment in industry (% of employed ages 15+)	..	..	..	..
Employment in service (% of employed ages 15+)	..	..	..	..
Women in wage employment in the nonagricultural sector (%)	..		..	
Women's share of part-time employment (% of total)	..		..	
Maternity leave (weeks)	..		..	
Maternal leave benefits (% of wages paid)	..		..	
Female legislators, senior officials and managers (% of total)	..		..	
Employment to population ratio, total (% ages 15+)	*63*	*80*	64	78
Employment to population ratio, youth (% ages 15–24)	*54*	*63*	51	58
Children in employment (% of children ages 7–14)	..	..	..	..
Unemployment rate (% of labor force ages 15+)	..	..	..	..
Long-term unemployment rate (% total unemployment)	..	..	..	..
Youth unemployment rate (% of labor force ages 15–24)	..	..	..	..
Account at a formal financial institution (% age 15+)	..	..	20	27
Public life and decision making				
Seats held by women in national parliament (%)	..		21	

Middle income

Population (millions)			5,022.4
GNI, Atlas ($ billions)			20,835.4
GNI per capita, Atlas ($)			4,148
Population living below $1.25 a day (%)			*17.4*

	1990		2011	
	Female	Male	Female	Male
Demography				
Sex ratio at birth (boys per girls)	1.08		1.08	
Life expectancy at birth (years)	66	63	71	67
Under-five mortality rate (per 1,000 live births)	81	83	46	47
Female-headed households (%)	..		..	
Education				
Gross primary enrollment ratio (% of relevant age group)	97	112	106	108
Gross secondary enrollment ratio (% of relevant age group)	41	51	70	72
Gross tertiary enrollment ratio (% of relevant age group)	8	10	27	26
Primary completion rate (% of relevant age group)	78	88	93	94
Youth literacy rate (% of population ages 15-24)	79	88	*88*	*94*
Health and related services				
Total fertility rate (births per woman)	3.3		2.3	
Adolescent fertility rate (births per 1,000 women ages 15-19)	..		50	
Women first married by age 18 (% of women ages 20-24)	..		..	
Contraceptive prevalence (% of women ages 15-49)	60		..	
Unmet need for contraception (% of women ages 15-49)	..		..	
Pregnant women receiving prenatal care (%)	..		*82*	
Births attended by skilled health staff (% of total)	..		*70*	
Maternal mortality ratio (per 100,000 live births)	370		*190*	
Economic structure, participation, and access to resources				
Labor force participation rate (% of population ages 15+)	51	82	49	79
Wage and salaried workers (% of employed ages 15+)	..	..	..	..
Self-employed workers (% of employed ages 15+)	..	..	..	..
Vulnerable employment (% of employed ages 15+)	..	..	..	..
Unpaid family workers (% of employed ages 15+)	..	..	..	..
Employment in agriculture (% of employed ages 15+)	..	..	..	..
Employment in industry (% of employed ages 15+)	..	..	..	..
Employment in service (% of employed ages 15+)	..	..	..	..
Women in wage employment in the nonagricultural sector (%)	32		..	
Women's share of part-time employment (% of total)	..		..	
Maternity leave (weeks)	..		..	
Maternal leave benefits (% of wages paid)	..		..	
Female legislators, senior officials and managers (% of total)	..		..	
Employment to population ratio, total (% ages 15+)	48	77	46	74
Employment to population ratio, youth (% ages 15-24)	44	61	32	50
Children in employment (% of children ages 7-14)	..	..	..	..
Unemployment rate (% of labor force ages 15+)	..	..	..	..
Long-term unemployment rate (% total unemployment)	..	..	..	..
Youth unemployment rate (% of labor force ages 15-24)	..	..	..	..
Account at a formal financial institution (% age 15+)	..	..	39	48
Public life and decision making				
Seats held by women in national parliament (%)	13		19	

Lower middle income

Population (millions)			2,532.7
GNI, Atlas ($ billions)			4,488.5
GNI per capita, Atlas ($)			1,772
Population living below $1.25 a day (%)			26.7

	1990		2011	
	Female	Male	Female	Male
Demography				
Sex ratio at birth (boys per girls)	1.06		1.06	
Life expectancy at birth (years)	61	58	68	64
Under-five mortality rate (per 1,000 live births)	109	110	62	63
Female-headed households (%)	..		..	
Education				
Gross primary enrollment ratio (% of relevant age group)	81	101	102	106
Gross secondary enrollment ratio (% of relevant age group)	33	48	59	64
Gross tertiary enrollment ratio (% of relevant age group)	7	9	17	20
Primary completion rate (% of relevant age group)	62	78	89	92
Youth literacy rate (% of population ages 15–24)	63	78	79	89
Health and related services				
Total fertility rate (births per woman)	4.2		2.9	
Adolescent fertility rate (births per 1,000 women ages 15–19)	..		66	
Women first married by age 18 (% of women ages 20–24)	..		..	
Contraceptive prevalence (% of women ages 15–49)	40		51	
Unmet need for contraception (% of women ages 15–49)	..		..	
Pregnant women receiving prenatal care (%)	..		76	
Births attended by skilled health staff (% of total)	..		57	
Maternal mortality ratio (per 100,000 live births)	560		260	
Economic structure, participation, and access to resources				
Labor force participation rate (% of population ages 15+)	39	82	37	79
Wage and salaried workers (% of employed ages 15+)	..	..	..	..
Self-employed workers (% of employed ages 15+)	..	..	..	..
Vulnerable employment (% of employed ages 15+)	..	..	76	70
Unpaid family workers (% of employed ages 15+)	..	..	..	..
Employment in agriculture (% of employed ages 15+)	62	52	..	..
Employment in industry (% of employed ages 15+)	13	18	..	..
Employment in service (% of employed ages 15+)	24	30	..	..
Women in wage employment in the nonagricultural sector (%)	20		..	
Women's share of part-time employment (% of total)	..		..	
Maternity leave (weeks)	..		..	
Maternal leave benefits (% of wages paid)	..		..	
Female legislators, senior officials and managers (% of total)	..		..	
Employment to population ratio, total (% ages 15+)	37	78	34	75
Employment to population ratio, youth (% ages 15–24)	29	58	23	49
Children in employment (% of children ages 7–14)	..	..	..	..
Unemployment rate (% of labor force ages 15+)	..	..	6.4	4.2
Long-term unemployment rate (% total unemployment)	..	..	..	..
Youth unemployment rate (% of labor force ages 15–24)	..	..	..	..
Account at a formal financial institution (% age 15+)	..	..	23	34
Public life and decision making				
Seats held by women in national parliament (%)	11		16	

Upper middle income

Population (millions)		2,489.7
GNI, Atlas ($ billions)		16,340.5
GNI per capita, Atlas ($)		6,563
Population living below $1.25 a day (%)		8.1

	1990 Female	1990 Male	2011 Female	2011 Male
Demography				
Sex ratio at birth (boys per girls)	1.09		1.11	
Life expectancy at birth (years)	71	66	75	71
Under-five mortality rate (per 1,000 live births)	48	53	19	21
Female-headed households (%)	..		..	
Education				
Gross primary enrollment ratio (% of relevant age group)	117	125	111	111
Gross secondary enrollment ratio (% of relevant age group)	47	54	87	83
Gross tertiary enrollment ratio (% of relevant age group)	9	10	38	32
Primary completion rate (% of relevant age group)	96	99	99	97
Youth literacy rate (% of population ages 15–24)	92	96	99	99
Health and related services				
Total fertility rate (births per woman)	2.6		1.8	
Adolescent fertility rate (births per 1,000 women ages 15–19)	..		30	
Women first married by age 18 (% of women ages 20–24)			..	
Contraceptive prevalence (% of women ages 15–49)	76		..	
Unmet need for contraception (% of women ages 15–49)	..		..	
Pregnant women receiving prenatal care (%)	..		94	
Births attended by skilled health staff (% of total)	90		97	
Maternal mortality ratio (per 100,000 live births)	130		62	
Economic structure, participation, and access to resources				
Labor force participation rate (% of population ages 15+)	60	82	59	78
Wage and salaried workers (% of employed ages 15+)	..	..	..	..
Self-employed workers (% of employed ages 15+)	..	..	..	..
Vulnerable employment (% of employed ages 15+)	..	..	..	..
Unpaid family workers (% of employed ages 15+)	..	..	..	..
Employment in agriculture (% of employed ages 15+)	..	..	..	..
Employment in industry (% of employed ages 15+)	..	..	..	..
Employment in service (% of employed ages 15+)	..	..	..	..
Women in wage employment in the nonagricultural sector (%)	38		..	
Women's share of part-time employment (% of total)	..		..	
Maternity leave (weeks)	..			
Maternal leave benefits (% of wages paid)	..			
Female legislators, senior officials and managers (% of total)	..		..	
Employment to population ratio, total (% ages 15+)	57	77	56	74
Employment to population ratio, youth (% ages 15–24)	57	63	44	51
Children in employment (% of children ages 7–14)	..	..	..	..
Unemployment rate (% of labor force ages 15+)	..	..	..	..
Long-term unemployment rate (% total unemployment)	..		..	
Youth unemployment rate (% of labor force ages 15–24)	..	..	..	..
Account at a formal financial institution (% age 15+)	..	..	53	62
Public life and decision making				
Seats held by women in national parliament (%)	14		22	

Low and middle income

Population (millions)			5,839.2
GNI, Atlas ($ billions)			21,324.4
GNI per capita, Atlas ($)			3,652
Population living below $1.25 a day (%)			20.6

	1990		2011	
	Female	Male	Female	Male
Demography				
Sex ratio at birth (boys per girls)	1.07		1.07	
Life expectancy at birth (years)	65	61	70	66
Under-five mortality rate (per 1,000 live births)	93	97	55	58
Female-headed households (%)	..		..	
Education				
Gross primary enrollment ratio (% of relevant age group)	92	107	105	108
Gross secondary enrollment ratio (% of relevant age group)	38	48	65	67
Gross tertiary enrollment ratio (% of relevant age group)	7	9	24	23
Primary completion rate (% of relevant age group)	73	83	88	90
Youth literacy rate (% of population ages 15–24)	76	86	85	91
Health and related services				
Total fertility rate (births per woman)	3.6		2.5	
Adolescent fertility rate (births per 1,000 women ages 15–19)	..		57	
Women first married by age 18 (% of women ages 20–24)	..		..	
Contraceptive prevalence (% of women ages 15–49)	56		..	
Unmet need for contraception (% of women ages 15–49)	..		..	
Pregnant women receiving prenatal care (%)	..		80	
Births attended by skilled health staff (% of total)	..		65	
Maternal mortality ratio (per 100,000 live births)	440		230	
Economic structure, participation, and access to resources				
Labor force participation rate (% of population ages 15+)	53	83	51	79
Wage and salaried workers (% of employed ages 15+)	..	..	..	..
Self-employed workers (% of employed ages 15+)	..	..	..	..
Vulnerable employment (% of employed ages 15+)	..	..	..	..
Unpaid family workers (% of employed ages 15+)	..	..	..	..
Employment in agriculture (% of employed ages 15+)	..	..	..	..
Employment in industry (% of employed ages 15+)	..	..	..	..
Employment in service (% of employed ages 15+)	..	..	..	..
Women in wage employment in the nonagricultural sector (%)	32		..	
Women's share of part-time employment (% of total)	..		..	
Maternity leave (weeks)	..		..	
Maternal leave benefits (% of wages paid)	..		..	
Female legislators, senior officials and managers (% of total)	..		..	
Employment to population ratio, total (% ages 15+)	50	78	48	75
Employment to population ratio, youth (% ages 15–24)	45	61	35	51
Children in employment (% of children ages 7–14)	..	..	..	..
Unemployment rate (% of labor force ages 15+)	..	..	..	..
Long-term unemployment rate (% total unemployment)	..	..	..	..
Youth unemployment rate (% of labor force ages 15–24)	..	..	..	..
Account at a formal financial institution (% age 15+)	..	..	37	46
Public life and decision making				
Seats held by women in national parliament (%)	13		20	

High income

Population (millions)				1,135.0
GNI, Atlas ($ billions)				45,242.5
GNI per capita, Atlas ($)				39,860
Population living below $1.25 a day (%)				..

	1990		2011	
	Female	Male	Female	Male
Demography				
Sex ratio at birth (boys per girls)	1.06		1.05	
Life expectancy at birth (years)	79	72	83	77
Under-five mortality rate (per 1,000 live births)	11	13	5	6
Female-headed households (%)	..		..	
Education				
Gross primary enrollment ratio (% of relevant age group)	102	103	103	103
Gross secondary enrollment ratio (% of relevant age group)	92	92	101	102
Gross tertiary enrollment ratio (% of relevant age group)	43	42	80	64
Primary completion rate (% of relevant age group)	98	96	101	100
Youth literacy rate (% of population ages 15-24)	..	..	100	100
Health and related services				
Total fertility rate (births per woman)	1.8		1.7	
Adolescent fertility rate (births per 1,000 women ages 15-19)	..		17	
Women first married by age 18 (% of women ages 20-24)	..		..	
Contraceptive prevalence (% of women ages 15-49)	70		..	
Unmet need for contraception (% of women ages 15-49)	..		..	
Pregnant women receiving prenatal care (%)	..		..	
Births attended by skilled health staff (% of total)	..		..	
Maternal mortality ratio (per 100,000 live births)	16		14	
Economic structure, participation, and access to resources				
Labor force participation rate (% of population ages 15+)	49	73	52	69
Wage and salaried workers (% of employed ages 15+)	86	82	90	87
Self-employed workers (% of employed ages 15+)	14	17	10	15
Vulnerable employment (% of employed ages 15+)	..	..	..	..
Unpaid family workers (% of employed ages 15+)	5.5	1.0	1.9	0.6
Employment in agriculture (% of employed ages 15+)	5	6	3	4
Employment in industry (% of employed ages 15+)	19	39	11	31
Employment in service (% of employed ages 15+)	76	55	86	64
Women in wage employment in the nonagricultural sector (%)	43		47	
Women's share of part-time employment (% of total)	..		..	
Maternity leave (weeks)	..		..	
Maternal leave benefits (% of wages paid)	..		..	
Female legislators, senior officials and managers (% of total)	..		..	
Employment to population ratio, total (% ages 15+)	46	68	48	63
Employment to population ratio, youth (% ages 15-24)	43	49	36	39
Children in employment (% of children ages 7-14)	..	..	..	..
Unemployment rate (% of labor force ages 15+)	6.9	5.4	8.0	8.2
Long-term unemployment rate (% total unemployment)	20.7	27.2	31.5	35.9
Youth unemployment rate (% of labor force ages 15-24)	14	12	17	19
Account at a formal financial institution (% age 15+)	..	..	87	92
Public life and decision making				
Seats held by women in national parliament (%)	12		24	

Euro area

Population (millions)				332.9
GNI, Atlas ($ billions)				12,871.5
GNI per capita, Atlas ($)				38,661
Population living below $1.25 a day (%)				..

	1990		2011	
	Female	Male	Female	Male
Demography				
Sex ratio at birth (boys per girls)	1.06		1.06	
Life expectancy at birth (years)	80	73	84	79
Under-five mortality rate (per 1,000 live births)	9	11	4	4
Female-headed households (%)	..		..	
Education				
Gross primary enrollment ratio (% of relevant age group)	104	104	105	106
Gross secondary enrollment ratio (% of relevant age group)	94	93	107	109
Gross tertiary enrollment ratio (% of relevant age group)	32	34	65	55
Primary completion rate (% of relevant age group)	99	98	100	98
Youth literacy rate (% of population ages 15–24)	..	..	100	100
Health and related services				
Total fertility rate (births per woman)	1.5		1.6	
Adolescent fertility rate (births per 1,000 women ages 15–19)	..		8	
Women first married by age 18 (% of women ages 20–24)	..		..	
Contraceptive prevalence (% of women ages 15–49)	..		..	
Unmet need for contraception (% of women ages 15–49)	..		..	
Pregnant women receiving prenatal care (%)	..		..	
Births attended by skilled health staff (% of total)	..		..	
Maternal mortality ratio (per 100,000 live births)	11		6	
Economic structure, participation, and access to resources				
Labor force participation rate (% of population ages 15+)	41	68	50	65
Wage and salaried workers (% of employed ages 15+)	84	80	88	80
Self-employed workers (% of employed ages 15+)	16	20	12	20
Vulnerable employment (% of employed ages 15+)	14	16	9	12
Unpaid family workers (% of employed ages 15+)	5.5	1.4	1.4	0.7
Employment in agriculture (% of employed ages 15+)	7	8	2	4
Employment in industry (% of employed ages 15+)	21	42	12	35
Employment in service (% of employed ages 15+)	72	50	85	60
Women in wage employment in the nonagricultural sector (%)	40		48	
Women's share of part-time employment (% of total)	79		76	
Maternity leave (weeks)	..		..	
Maternal leave benefits (% of wages paid)	..		..	
Female legislators, senior officials and managers (% of total)	..		..	
Employment to population ratio, total (% ages 15+)	38	64	44	58
Employment to population ratio, youth (% ages 15–24)	38	46	31	37
Children in employment (% of children ages 7–14)	..	..	..	..
Unemployment rate (% of labor force ages 15+)	13.6	7.0	10.3	9.8
Long-term unemployment rate (% total unemployment)	51.6	50.4	43.9	45.2
Youth unemployment rate (% of labor force ages 15–24)	27	18	23	23
Account at a formal financial institution (% age 15+)	..	..	89	93
Public life and decision making				
Seats held by women in national parliament (%)	12		28	

Country tables

China

Unless otherwise noted, data for China do not include data for Hong Kong SAR, China; Macao SAR, China; or Taiwan, China.

Cyprus

GNI and data calculated using GNI refer to the area controlled by the government of the Republic of Cyprus.

France

Data for Mayotte, to which a reference appeared in previous editions, are included in data for France.

Georgia

GNI and population data and data calculated using GNI and population exclude Abkhazia and South Ossetia.

Kosovo, Montenegro, and Serbia

Data for each country are shown separately where available. However, some indicators for Serbia prior to 2006 include data for Montenegro; these data are noted in the tables. Moreover, data for most indicators for Serbia from 1999 onward exclude data for Kosovo, which in 1999 became a territory under international administration pursuant to UN Security Council Resolution 1244 (1999). Kosovo became a member of the World Bank on June 29, 2009, and its data are shown where available.

Moldova

GNI and population data and data calculated using GNI and population exclude Transnistria.

Morocco

GNI and data calculated using GNI include Former Spanish Sahara.

South Sudan and Sudan

South Sudan declared its independence on July 9, 2011. Data are shown separately for South Sudan where available. However, data reported for Sudan include South Sudan unless otherwise noted.

Tanzania

GNI data and data calculated using GNI refer to mainland Tanzania only.

For more information, see *World Development Indicators 2013* or data .worldbank.org.

Afghanistan

South Asia	Low income
Population (millions)	35.3
GNI, Atlas ($ billions)	16.6
GNI per capita, Atlas ($)	470
Population living below $1.25 a day (%)	..

	1990		2011	
	Female	Male	Female	Male
Demography				
Sex ratio at birth (boys per girls)	1.06		1.06	
Life expectancy at birth (years)	42	42	49	49
Under-five mortality rate (per 1,000 live births)	188	196	99	103
Female-headed households (%)	..		..	
Education				
Gross primary enrollment ratio (% of relevant age group)	21	37	81	114
Gross secondary enrollment ratio (% of relevant age group)	10	20	34	62
Gross tertiary enrollment ratio (% of relevant age group)	1	3	1	5
Primary completion rate (% of relevant age group)	14	39	..	..
Youth literacy rate (% of population ages 15–24)	..	..	..	..
Health and related services				
Total fertility rate (births per woman)	8.0		6.2	
Adolescent fertility rate (births per 1,000 women ages 15–19)	..		103	
Women first married by age 18 (% of women ages 20–24)	..		40	
Contraceptive prevalence (% of women ages 15–49)	..		21	
Unmet need for contraception (% of women ages 15–49)	..		..	
Pregnant women receiving prenatal care (%)	..		48	
Births attended by skilled health staff (% of total)	..		39	
Maternal mortality ratio (per 100,000 live births)	1,300		460	
Economic structure, participation, and access to resources				
Labor force participation rate (% of population ages 15+)	16	82	16	80
Wage and salaried workers (% of employed ages 15+)	..	..	..	..
Self-employed workers (% of employed ages 15+)	..	..	..	..
Vulnerable employment (% of employed ages 15+)	..	..	..	..
Unpaid family workers (% of employed ages 15+)	..	..	..	..
Employment in agriculture (% of employed ages 15+)	..	..	..	..
Employment in industry (% of employed ages 15+)	..	..	..	..
Employment in service (% of employed ages 15+)	..	..	..	..
Women in wage employment in the nonagricultural sector (%)	..		18	
Women's share of part-time employment (% of total)	..		..	
Maternity leave (weeks)	12		13	
Maternal leave benefits (% of wages paid)	100		100	
Female legislators, senior officials and managers (% of total)	..		..	
Employment to population ratio, total (% ages 15+)	14	76	14	74
Employment to population ratio, youth (% ages 15–24)	11	52	10	50
Children in employment (% of children ages 7–14)	..	..	..	..
Unemployment rate (% of labor force ages 15+)	..	..	..	..
Long-term unemployment rate (% total unemployment)	..	..	..	..
Youth unemployment rate (% of labor force ages 15–24)	..	..	..	..
Account at a formal financial institution (% age 15+)	..	..	3	15
Public life and decision making				
Seats held by women in national parliament (%)	4		28	

Albania

Europe & Central Asia			Lower middle income	
Population (millions)				3.2
GNI, Atlas ($ billions)				12.8
GNI per capita, Atlas ($)				3,980
Population living below $1.25 a day (%)				<2

	1990		2011	
	Female	Male	Female	Male
Demography				
Sex ratio at birth (boys per girls)	1.07		1.07	
Life expectancy at birth (years)	75	69	80	74
Under-five mortality rate (per 1,000 live births)	39	43	14	15
Female-headed households (%)	..		16	
Education				
Gross primary enrollment ratio (% of relevant age group)	99	99	..	..
Gross secondary enrollment ratio (% of relevant age group)	85	93	..	..
Gross tertiary enrollment ratio (% of relevant age group)	9	8	50	38
Primary completion rate (% of relevant age group)	..	..	..	..
Youth literacy rate (% of population ages 15–24)	..	..	99	99
Health and related services				
Total fertility rate (births per woman)	3.2		1.5	
Adolescent fertility rate (births per 1,000 women ages 15–19)	..		16	
Women first married by age 18 (% of women ages 20–24)	..		10	
Contraceptive prevalence (% of women ages 15–49)	..		69	
Unmet need for contraception (% of women ages 15–49)	..		13	
Pregnant women receiving prenatal care (%)	..		97	
Births attended by skilled health staff (% of total)	93		99	
Maternal mortality ratio (per 100,000 live births)	48		27	
Economic structure, participation, and access to resources				
Labor force participation rate (% of population ages 15+)	53	75	50	71
Wage and salaried workers (% of employed ages 15+)	..	..	..	..
Self-employed workers (% of employed ages 15+)	..	..	..	..
Vulnerable employment (% of employed ages 15+)	..	..	..	..
Unpaid family workers (% of employed ages 15+)	..	..	..	..
Employment in agriculture (% of employed ages 15+)	..	..	..	..
Employment in industry (% of employed ages 15+)	..	..	..	..
Employment in service (% of employed ages 15+)	..	..	..	..
Women in wage employment in the nonagricultural sector (%)	..			
Women's share of part-time employment (% of total)	..		..	
Maternity leave (weeks)	..		52	
Maternal leave benefits (% of wages paid)	..		80	
Female legislators, senior officials and managers (% of total)	..		..	
Employment to population ratio, total (% ages 15+)	47	68	43	62
Employment to population ratio, youth (% ages 15–24)	39	53	34	43
Children in employment (% of children ages 7–14)	..	..	..	..
Unemployment rate (% of labor force ages 15+)	..	..	15.9	12.2
Long-term unemployment rate (% total unemployment)	..	..	..	..
Youth unemployment rate (% of labor force ages 15–24)	..	..	28	26
Account at a formal financial institution (% age 15+)	..	..	23	34
Public life and decision making				
Seats held by women in national parliament (%)	29		16	

Algeria

Middle East & North Africa | **Upper middle income**

Population (millions)	36.0
GNI, Atlas ($ billions)	160.8
GNI per capita, Atlas ($)	4,470
Population living below $1.25 a day (%)	..

	1990		2011	
	Female	Male	Female	Male
Demography				
Sex ratio at birth (boys per girls)	1.05		1.05	
Life expectancy at birth (years)	68	66	75	72
Under-five mortality rate (per 1,000 live births)	62	70	28	32
Female-headed households (%)	..		..	
Education				
Gross primary enrollment ratio (% of relevant age group)	86	103	106	112
Gross secondary enrollment ratio (% of relevant age group)	54	70	96	94
Gross tertiary enrollment ratio (% of relevant age group)	..	..	38	26
Primary completion rate (% of relevant age group)	73	89	94	95
Youth literacy rate (% of population ages 15–24)	62	86	89	94
Health and related services				
Total fertility rate (births per woman)	4.7		2.2	
Adolescent fertility rate (births per 1,000 women ages 15–19)	..		6	
Women first married by age 18 (% of women ages 20–24)	..		2	
Contraceptive prevalence (% of women ages 15–49)	51		61	
Unmet need for contraception (% of women ages 15–49)	..		11	
Pregnant women receiving prenatal care (%)	58		89	
Births attended by skilled health staff (% of total)	77		95	
Maternal mortality ratio (per 100,000 live births)	220		97	
Economic structure, participation, and access to resources				
Labor force participation rate (% of population ages 15+)	10	74	15	72
Wage and salaried workers (% of employed ages 15+)	..	..	36	32
Self-employed workers (% of employed ages 15+)	..	..	64	68
Vulnerable employment (% of employed ages 15+)	..	..	..	..
Unpaid family workers (% of employed ages 15+)	..	..	8.5	3.4
Employment in agriculture (% of employed ages 15+)	..	..	6	13
Employment in industry (% of employed ages 15+)	..	..	30	34
Employment in service (% of employed ages 15+)	..	..	64	54
Women in wage employment in the nonagricultural sector (%)	..		15	
Women's share of part-time employment (% of total)			..	
Maternity leave (weeks)	14		14	
Maternal leave benefits (% of wages paid)	100		100	
Female legislators, senior officials and managers (% of total)	..		..	
Employment to population ratio, total (% ages 15+)	7	61	12	64
Employment to population ratio, youth (% ages 15–24)	6	37	6	37
Children in employment (% of children ages 7–14)	..	..	..	..
Unemployment rate (% of labor force ages 15+)	17.0	21.7	19.1	8.1
Long-term unemployment rate (% total unemployment)	..	..	..	..
Youth unemployment rate (% of labor force ages 15–24)	..	..	38	19
Account at a formal financial institution (% age 15+)	..	..	20	46
Public life and decision making				
Seats held by women in national parliament (%)	2		32	

American Somoa

East Asia & Pacific	Upper middle income
Population (thousands)	69.5
GNI, Atlas ($ millions)	..
GNI per capita, Atlas ($)	..
Population living below $1.25 a day (%)	..

	1990		2011	
	Female	Male	Female	Male
Demography				
Sex ratio at birth (boys per girls)		..		..
Life expectancy at birth (years)	..	..	..	..
Under-five mortality rate (per 1,000 live births)	..	..	..	..
Female-headed households (%)	..		..	
Education				
Gross primary enrollment ratio (% of relevant age group)	100	98	..	..
Gross secondary enrollment ratio (% of relevant age group)	95	91	..	..
Gross tertiary enrollment ratio (% of relevant age group)	..	..	..	..
Primary completion rate (% of relevant age group)	..	..	..	..
Youth literacy rate (% of population ages 15–24)	..	..	..	..
Health and related services				
Total fertility rate (births per woman)	..		..	
Adolescent fertility rate (births per 1,000 women ages 15–19)	..		..	
Women first married by age 18 (% of women ages 20–24)	..		..	
Contraceptive prevalence (% of women ages 15–49)	..		..	
Unmet need for contraception (% of women ages 15–49)	..		..	
Pregnant women receiving prenatal care (%)	..		..	
Births attended by skilled health staff (% of total)	..		..	
Maternal mortality ratio (per 100,000 live births)	..		..	
Economic structure, participation, and access to resources				
Labor force participation rate (% of population ages 15+)	..	..	..	..
Wage and salaried workers (% of employed ages 15+)	99	97	..	..
Self-employed workers (% of employed ages 15+)	2	3	..	..
Vulnerable employment (% of employed ages 15+)	..	..	..	..
Unpaid family workers (% of employed ages 15+)	0.3	0.1	..	..
Employment in agriculture (% of employed ages 15+)	0	4	..	..
Employment in industry (% of employed ages 15+)	45	43	..	..
Employment in service (% of employed ages 15+)	25	52	..	..
Women in wage employment in the nonagricultural sector (%)	42		..	
Women's share of part-time employment (% of total)	..		..	
Maternity leave (weeks)	..		..	
Maternal leave benefits (% of wages paid)	..		..	
Female legislators, senior officials and managers (% of total)	..		..	
Employment to population ratio, total (% ages 15+)	..	..	..	..
Employment to population ratio, youth (% ages 15–24)	..	..	..	..
Children in employment (% of children ages 7–14)	..	..	..	..
Unemployment rate (% of labor force ages 15+)	1.7	3.6	..	..
Long-term unemployment rate (% total unemployment)	..	..	..	..
Youth unemployment rate (% of labor force ages 15–24)	12	12	..	..
Account at a formal financial institution (% age 15+)	..	..	..	..
Public life and decision making				
Seats held by women in national parliament (%)	..		..	

Andorra

	High income
Population (thousands)	86.2
GNI, Atlas ($ billions)	*3.4*
GNI per capita, Atlas ($)	*41,750*
Population living below $1.25 a day (%)	..

	1990 Female	1990 Male	2011 Female	2011 Male
Demography				
Sex ratio at birth (boys per girls)		..		..
Life expectancy at birth (years)	..	..	..	..
Under-five mortality rate (per 1,000 live births)	8	9	3	4
Female-headed households (%)			..	
Education				
Gross primary enrollment ratio (% of relevant age group)	..	..	82	82
Gross secondary enrollment ratio (% of relevant age group)	..	..	88	86
Gross tertiary enrollment ratio (% of relevant age group)	..	..	*13*	*9*
Primary completion rate (% of relevant age group)	..	..	67	60
Youth literacy rate (% of population ages 15–24)	..	..	..	..
Health and related services				
Total fertility rate (births per woman)		..	*1.2*	
Adolescent fertility rate (births per 1,000 women ages 15–19)		..		..
Women first married by age 18 (% of women ages 20–24)		..		..
Contraceptive prevalence (% of women ages 15–49)		..		..
Unmet need for contraception (% of women ages 15–49)		..		..
Pregnant women receiving prenatal care (%)		..		..
Births attended by skilled health staff (% of total)		..		..
Maternal mortality ratio (per 100,000 live births)		..		..
Economic structure, participation, and access to resources				
Labor force participation rate (% of population ages 15+)	..	..	..	..
Wage and salaried workers (% of employed ages 15+)	..	..	..	..
Self-employed workers (% of employed ages 15+)	..	..	..	..
Vulnerable employment (% of employed ages 15+)	..	..	..	..
Unpaid family workers (% of employed ages 15+)	..	..	..	..
Employment in agriculture (% of employed ages 15+)	..	..	..	..
Employment in industry (% of employed ages 15+)	..	..	..	..
Employment in service (% of employed ages 15+)	..	..	..	..
Women in wage employment in the nonagricultural sector (%)		..	47	
Women's share of part-time employment (% of total)		..		..
Maternity leave (weeks)		..		..
Maternal leave benefits (% of wages paid)		..		..
Female legislators, senior officials and managers (% of total)		..		..
Employment to population ratio, total (% ages 15+)	..	..	..	..
Employment to population ratio, youth (% ages 15–24)	..	..	..	..
Children in employment (% of children ages 7–14)	..	..	..	..
Unemployment rate (% of labor force ages 15+)	..	..	..	..
Long-term unemployment rate (% total unemployment)	..	..	..	..
Youth unemployment rate (% of labor force ages 15–24)	..	..	..	..
Account at a formal financial institution (% age 15+)	..	..	..	..
Public life and decision making				
Seats held by women in national parliament (%)		..	50	

Angola

Sub-Saharan Africa	Upper middle income
Population (millions)	19.6
GNI, Atlas ($ billions)	75.2
GNI per capita, Atlas ($)	3,830
Population living below $1.25 a day (%)	54.3

	1990		2011	
	Female	Male	Female	Male
Demography				
Sex ratio at birth (boys per girls)	1.03		1.03	
Life expectancy at birth (years)	43	39	53	50
Under-five mortality rate (per 1,000 live births)	232	254	150	165
Female-headed households (%)	..		25	
Education				
Gross primary enrollment ratio (% of relevant age group)	81	88	112	137
Gross secondary enrollment ratio (% of relevant age group)	..	..	25	37
Gross tertiary enrollment ratio (% of relevant age group)	0	1	3	4
Primary completion rate (% of relevant age group)	..	..	40	53
Youth literacy rate (% of population ages 15–24)	..	..	66	80
Health and related services				
Total fertility rate (births per woman)	7.2		5.3	
Adolescent fertility rate (births per 1,000 women ages 15–19)	..		153	
Women first married by age 18 (% of women ages 20–24)	..		..	
Contraceptive prevalence (% of women ages 15–49)	..		..	
Unmet need for contraception (% of women ages 15–49)	..		..	
Pregnant women receiving prenatal care (%)	..		80	
Births attended by skilled health staff (% of total)	..		47	
Maternal mortality ratio (per 100,000 live births)	1,200		450	
Economic structure, participation, and access to resources				
Labor force participation rate (% of population ages 15+)	66	76	63	77
Wage and salaried workers (% of employed ages 15+)	..	..	..	..
Self-employed workers (% of employed ages 15+)	..	..	..	..
Vulnerable employment (% of employed ages 15+)	..	..	..	..
Unpaid family workers (% of employed ages 15+)	..	..	..	..
Employment in agriculture (% of employed ages 15+)	..	..	..	..
Employment in industry (% of employed ages 15+)	..	..	..	..
Employment in service (% of employed ages 15+)	..	..	..	..
Women in wage employment in the nonagricultural sector (%)	..		..	
Women's share of part-time employment (% of total)	..		..	
Maternity leave (weeks)	12		12	
Maternal leave benefits (% of wages paid)	100		100	
Female legislators, senior officials and managers (% of total)	..		..	
Employment to population ratio, total (% ages 15+)	62	71	59	72
Employment to population ratio, youth (% ages 15–24)	47	50	45	51
Children in employment (% of children ages 7–14)	..	..	..	..
Unemployment rate (% of labor force ages 15+)	..	..	..	..
Long-term unemployment rate (% total unemployment)	..	..	..	..
Youth unemployment rate (% of labor force ages 15–24)	..	..	..	..
Account at a formal financial institution (% age 15+)	..	..	39	39
Public life and decision making				
Seats held by women in national parliament (%)	15		34	

Antigua and Barbuda

Latin America & the Caribbean	Upper middle income
Population (thousands)	89.6
GNI, Atlas ($ billions)	1.1
GNI per capita, Atlas ($)	11,940
Population living below $1.25 a day (%)	..

	1990 Female	1990 Male	2011 Female	2011 Male
Demography				
Sex ratio at birth (boys per girls)	..		..	
Life expectancy at birth (years)	77	72	..	..
Under-five mortality rate (per 1,000 live births)	23	30	7	9
Female-headed households (%)	..		..	
Education				
Gross primary enrollment ratio (% of relevant age group)	99	104	95	102
Gross secondary enrollment ratio (% of relevant age group)	124	121	104	106
Gross tertiary enrollment ratio (% of relevant age group)	..	..	19	10
Primary completion rate (% of relevant age group)	93	103	92	103
Youth literacy rate (% of population ages 15–24)	..	..	..	..
Health and related services				
Total fertility rate (births per woman)	1.7		..	
Adolescent fertility rate (births per 1,000 women ages 15–19)	..		..	
Women first married by age 18 (% of women ages 20–24)	..		..	
Contraceptive prevalence (% of women ages 15–49)	53		..	
Unmet need for contraception (% of women ages 15–49)	..		..	
Pregnant women receiving prenatal care (%)	..		100	
Births attended by skilled health staff (% of total)	..		100	
Maternal mortality ratio (per 100,000 live births)	..		..	
Economic structure, participation, and access to resources				
Labor force participation rate (% of population ages 15+)	..	..	..	..
Wage and salaried workers (% of employed ages 15+)	83	78	..	..
Self-employed workers (% of employed ages 15+)	16	21	..	..
Vulnerable employment (% of employed ages 15+)	14	15	..	..
Unpaid family workers (% of employed ages 15+)	0.9	0.7	..	..
Employment in agriculture (% of employed ages 15+)	..	..	1	4
Employment in industry (% of employed ages 15+)	..	..	5	26
Employment in service (% of employed ages 15+)	..	..	94	70
Women in wage employment in the nonagricultural sector (%)	..		51	
Women's share of part-time employment (% of total)	..		..	
Maternity leave (weeks)	..		..	
Maternal leave benefits (% of wages paid)	..		..	
Female legislators, senior officials and managers (% of total)	..		..	
Employment to population ratio, total (% ages 15+)	..	..	..	..
Employment to population ratio, youth (% ages 15–24)	..	..	..	..
Children in employment (% of children ages 7–14)	..	..	..	..
Unemployment rate (% of labor force ages 15+)	..	..	..	..
Long-term unemployment rate (% total unemployment)	..	..	..	..
Youth unemployment rate (% of labor force ages 15–24)	..	..	..	..
Account at a formal financial institution (% age 15+)	..	..	..	..
Public life and decision making				
Seats held by women in national parliament (%)	0		11	

Argentina

Latin America & the Caribbean	Upper middle income
Population (millions)	40.8
GNI, Atlas ($ billions)	..
GNI per capita, Atlas ($)	..
Population living below $1.25 a day (%)	<2

	1990		2011	
	Female	Male	Female	Male
Demography				
Sex ratio at birth (boys per girls)	1.04		1.04	
Life expectancy at birth (years)	75	68	80	72
Under-five mortality rate (per 1,000 live births)	25	31	13	16
Female-headed households (%)	..		34	
Education				
Gross primary enrollment ratio (% of relevant age group)	106	107	117	119
Gross secondary enrollment ratio (% of relevant age group)	74	67	95	85
Gross tertiary enrollment ratio (% of relevant age group)	42	36	90	60
Primary completion rate (% of relevant age group)	..	..	108	106
Youth literacy rate (% of population ages 15–24)	99	98	99	99
Health and related services				
Total fertility rate (births per woman)	3.0		2.2	
Adolescent fertility rate (births per 1,000 women ages 15–19)	..		55	
Women first married by age 18 (% of women ages 20–24)	..		..	
Contraceptive prevalence (% of women ages 15–49)	..		..	
Unmet need for contraception (% of women ages 15–49)	..		..	
Pregnant women receiving prenatal care (%)	95		..	
Births attended by skilled health staff (% of total)	96		95	
Maternal mortality ratio (per 100,000 live births)	71		77	
Economic structure, participation, and access to resources				
Labor force participation rate (% of population ages 15+)	41	78	47	75
Wage and salaried workers (% of employed ages 15+)	70	68	81	74
Self-employed workers (% of employed ages 15+)	30	32	19	26
Vulnerable employment (% of employed ages 15+)	27	25	16	20
Unpaid family workers (% of employed ages 15+)	2.5	0.7	1.2	0.4
Employment in agriculture (% of employed ages 15+)	0	1	0	2
Employment in industry (% of employed ages 15+)	18	39	10	33
Employment in service (% of employed ages 15+)	82	60	89	64
Women in wage employment in the nonagricultural sector (%)	37		45	
Women's share of part-time employment (% of total)	..		65	
Maternity leave (weeks)	13		13	
Maternal leave benefits (% of wages paid)	60		100	
Female legislators, senior officials and managers (% of total)	..		23	
Employment to population ratio, total (% ages 15+)	38	74	43	70
Employment to population ratio, youth (% ages 15–24)	36	59	25	43
Children in employment (% of children ages 7–14)	..	..	..	..
Unemployment rate (% of labor force ages 15+)	7.3	7.3	8.5	6.2
Long-term unemployment rate (% total unemployment)	..	..	30.9	21.6
Youth unemployment rate (% of labor force ages 15–24)	16	12	22	17
Account at a formal financial institution (% age 15+)	..	..	32	35
Public life and decision making				
Seats held by women in national parliament (%)	6		37	

Armenia

Europe & Central Asia	Lower middle income
Population (millions)	3.1
GNI, Atlas ($ billions)	10.4
GNI per capita, Atlas ($)	3,360
Population living below $1.25 a day (%)	2.5

	1990		2011	
	Female	Male	Female	Male
Demography				
Sex ratio at birth (boys per girls)	1.07		1.14	
Life expectancy at birth (years)	71	65	77	71
Under-five mortality rate (per 1,000 live births)	43	51	15	19
Female-headed households (%)	..		37	
Education				
Gross primary enrollment ratio (% of relevant age group)	96	93	86	83
Gross secondary enrollment ratio (% of relevant age group)	..	..	90	88
Gross tertiary enrollment ratio (% of relevant age group)	..	..	55	43
Primary completion rate (% of relevant age group)	..	..	85	82
Youth literacy rate (% of population ages 15–24)	100	100	100	100
Health and related services				
Total fertility rate (births per woman)	2.5		1.7	
Adolescent fertility rate (births per 1,000 women ages 15–19)	..		34	
Women first married by age 18 (% of women ages 20–24)	..		7	
Contraceptive prevalence (% of women ages 15–49)	56		55	
Unmet need for contraception (% of women ages 15–49)	..		14	
Pregnant women receiving prenatal care (%)	..		99	
Births attended by skilled health staff (% of total)	100		100	
Maternal mortality ratio (per 100,000 live births)	46		30	
Economic structure, participation, and access to resources				
Labor force participation rate (% of population ages 15+)	61	77	49	70
Wage and salaried workers (% of employed ages 15+)	..	..	60	62
Self-employed workers (% of employed ages 15+)	..	..	40	38
Vulnerable employment (% of employed ages 15+)	..	..	40	36
Unpaid family workers (% of employed ages 15+)	..	..	17.1	7.6
Employment in agriculture (% of employed ages 15+)	..	..	49	39
Employment in industry (% of employed ages 15+)	..	..	8	25
Employment in service (% of employed ages 15+)	..	..	43	35
Women in wage employment in the nonagricultural sector (%)	..		43	
Women's share of part-time employment (% of total)	..		56	
Maternity leave (weeks)	..		20	
Maternal leave benefits (% of wages paid)	..		100	
Female legislators, senior officials and managers (% of total)	..		22	
Employment to population ratio, total (% ages 15+)	36	53	32	52
Employment to population ratio, youth (% ages 15–24)	18	34	14	23
Children in employment (% of children ages 7–14)	..	..	7.5	12.0
Unemployment rate (% of labor force ages 15+)	..	..	35.0	21.9
Long-term unemployment rate (% total unemployment)	..	..	63.8	52.2
Youth unemployment rate (% of labor force ages 15–24)	..	..	55	37
Account at a formal financial institution (% age 15+)	..	..	18	17
Public life and decision making				
Seats held by women in national parliament (%)	36		11	

Aruba

Population (thousands)				108.1
GNI, Atlas ($ billions)				..
GNI per capita, Atlas ($)				..
Population living below $1.25 a day (%)				..

	1990		2011	
	Female	Male	Female	Male
Demography				
Sex ratio at birth (boys per girls)	1.05		1.05	
Life expectancy at birth (years)	76	71	78	73
Under-five mortality rate (per 1,000 live births)	..	..	..	..
Female-headed households (%)	..		..	
Education				
Gross primary enrollment ratio (% of relevant age group)	..	..	106	112
Gross secondary enrollment ratio (% of relevant age group)	..	..	91	90
Gross tertiary enrollment ratio (% of relevant age group)	..	..	37	27
Primary completion rate (% of relevant age group)	..	..	93	88
Youth literacy rate (% of population ages 15–24)	..	..	99	99
Health and related services				
Total fertility rate (births per woman)	2.2		1.7	
Adolescent fertility rate (births per 1,000 women ages 15–19)	..		28	
Women first married by age 18 (% of women ages 20–24)	..		..	
Contraceptive prevalence (% of women ages 15–49)	..		..	
Unmet need for contraception (% of women ages 15–49)	..		..	
Pregnant women receiving prenatal care (%)	..		..	
Births attended by skilled health staff (% of total)	..		..	
Maternal mortality ratio (per 100,000 live births)	..		..	
Economic structure, participation, and access to resources				
Labor force participation rate (% of population ages 15+)	..	..	..	..
Wage and salaried workers (% of employed ages 15+)	95	90	94	88
Self-employed workers (% of employed ages 15+)	5	10	6	12
Vulnerable employment (% of employed ages 15+)	2	5	3	5
Unpaid family workers (% of employed ages 15+)	0.6	0.1	0.4	0.1
Employment in agriculture (% of employed ages 15+)	0	0	0	1
Employment in industry (% of employed ages 15+)	5	28	6	33
Employment in service (% of employed ages 15+)	95	71	93	66
Women in wage employment in the nonagricultural sector (%)	44		49	
Women's share of part-time employment (% of total)	71		..	
Maternity leave (weeks)	..		..	
Maternal leave benefits (% of wages paid)	..		..	
Female legislators, senior officials and managers (% of total)	29		40	
Employment to population ratio, total (% ages 15+)	..	..	..	..
Employment to population ratio, youth (% ages 15–24)	..	..	..	..
Children in employment (% of children ages 7–14)	..	..	..	..
Unemployment rate (% of labor force ages 15+)	6.3	5.9	6.5	5.0
Long-term unemployment rate (% total unemployment)	13.8	16.2	..	..
Youth unemployment rate (% of labor force ages 15–24)	11	13	23	24
Account at a formal financial institution (% age 15+)	..	..	..	..
Public life and decision making				
Seats held by women in national parliament (%)	..		..	

Australia

	High income
Population (millions)	22.3
GNI, Atlas ($ billions)	1,111.4
GNI per capita, Atlas ($)	49,790
Population living below $1.25 a day (%)	..

	1990		2011	
	Female	Male	Female	Male
Demography				
Sex ratio at birth (boys per girls)	1.06		1.06	
Life expectancy at birth (years)	80	74	84	80
Under-five mortality rate (per 1,000 live births)	8	10	4	5
Female-headed households (%)	..		..	
Education				
Gross primary enrollment ratio (% of relevant age group)	106	106	105	105
Gross secondary enrollment ratio (% of relevant age group)	134	134	128	135
Gross tertiary enrollment ratio (% of relevant age group)	38	33	92	68
Primary completion rate (% of relevant age group)	..	..	..	..
Youth literacy rate (% of population ages 15–24)	..	..	..	..
Health and related services				
Total fertility rate (births per woman)	1.9		1.9	
Adolescent fertility rate (births per 1,000 women ages 15–19)	..		13	
Women first married by age 18 (% of women ages 20–24)	..		..	
Contraceptive prevalence (% of women ages 15–49)	76		..	
Unmet need for contraception (% of women ages 15–49)	..		..	
Pregnant women receiving prenatal care (%)	100		98	
Births attended by skilled health staff (% of total)	100		..	
Maternal mortality ratio (per 100,000 live births)	10		7	
Economic structure, participation, and access to resources				
Labor force participation rate (% of population ages 15+)	52	76	59	72
Wage and salaried workers (% of employed ages 15+)	88	83	91	87
Self-employed workers (% of employed ages 15+)	12	17	9	13
Vulnerable employment (% of employed ages 15+)	9	12	7	11
Unpaid family workers (% of employed ages 15+)	1.2	0.5	0.3	0.2
Employment in agriculture (% of employed ages 15+)	4	7	2	4
Employment in industry (% of employed ages 15+)	13	34	9	32
Employment in service (% of employed ages 15+)	83	59	88	64
Women in wage employment in the nonagricultural sector (%)	44		47	
Women's share of part-time employment (% of total)	..		71	
Maternity leave (weeks)	12		52	
Maternal leave benefits (% of wages paid)	..		..	
Female legislators, senior officials and managers (% of total)	..		37	
Employment to population ratio, total (% ages 15+)	47	67	56	69
Employment to population ratio, youth (% ages 15–24)	56	59	60	62
Children in employment (% of children ages 7–14)	..	..	..	..
Unemployment rate (% of labor force ages 15+)	7.2	6.7	5.3	4.9
Long-term unemployment rate (% total unemployment)	17.1	24.1	18.0	19.7
Youth unemployment rate (% of labor force ages 15–24)	13	13	11	12
Account at a formal financial institution (% age 15+)	..	..	99	100
Public life and decision making				
Seats held by women in national parliament (%)	6		25	

Austria

	High income
Population (millions)	8.4
GNI, Atlas ($ billions)	405.7
GNI per capita, Atlas ($)	48,170
Population living below $1.25 a day (%)	..

	1990		2011	
	Female	Male	Female	Male
Demography				
Sex ratio at birth (boys per girls)	1.06		1.06	
Life expectancy at birth (years)	79	72	84	78
Under-five mortality rate (per 1,000 live births)	8	11	4	5
Female-headed households (%)	..		..	
Education				
Gross primary enrollment ratio (% of relevant age group)	102	102	99	100
Gross secondary enrollment ratio (% of relevant age group)	96	105	97	101
Gross tertiary enrollment ratio (% of relevant age group)	30	34	74	63
Primary completion rate (% of relevant age group)	..	..	98	99
Youth literacy rate (% of population ages 15–24)	..	..	..	..
Health and related services				
Total fertility rate (births per woman)	1.5		1.4	
Adolescent fertility rate (births per 1,000 women ages 15–19)	..		10	
Women first married by age 18 (% of women ages 20–24)	..		..	
Contraceptive prevalence (% of women ages 15–49)	..		..	
Unmet need for contraception (% of women ages 15–49)	..		..	
Pregnant women receiving prenatal care (%)	100		..	
Births attended by skilled health staff (% of total)	100		..	
Maternal mortality ratio (per 100,000 live births)	10		4	
Economic structure, participation, and access to resources				
Labor force participation rate (% of population ages 15+)	43	70	54	68
Wage and salaried workers (% of employed ages 15+)	..	..	89	84
Self-employed workers (% of employed ages 15+)	..	..	11	16
Vulnerable employment (% of employed ages 15+)	..	..	9	9
Unpaid family workers (% of employed ages 15+)	..	..	2.3	1.9
Employment in agriculture (% of employed ages 15+)	9	7	5	6
Employment in industry (% of employed ages 15+)	20	49	12	38
Employment in service (% of employed ages 15+)	70	44	82	57
Women in wage employment in the nonagricultural sector (%)	42		48	
Women's share of part-time employment (% of total)	..		80	
Maternity leave (weeks)	16		16	
Maternal leave benefits (% of wages paid)	100		100	
Female legislators, senior officials and managers (% of total)	..		27	
Employment to population ratio, total (% ages 15+)	42	68	52	65
Employment to population ratio, youth (% ages 15–24)	58	64	49	59
Children in employment (% of children ages 7–14)	..	..	..	..
Unemployment rate (% of labor force ages 15+)	3.6	3.0	4.3	4.0
Long-term unemployment rate (% total unemployment)	18.5	18.4	24.2	27.5
Youth unemployment rate (% of labor force ages 15–24)	4	4	9	8
Account at a formal financial institution (% age 15+)	..	..	97	98
Public life and decision making				
Seats held by women in national parliament (%)	12		28	

Azerbaijan

Europe & Central Asia	Upper middle income
Population (millions)	9.2
GNI, Atlas ($ billions)	48.5
GNI per capita, Atlas ($)	5,290
Population living below $1.25 a day (%)	<2

	1990		2011	
	Female	Male	Female	Male
Demography				
Sex ratio at birth (boys per girls)	1.07		1.16	
Life expectancy at birth (years)	69	61	74	68
Under-five mortality rate (per 1,000 live births)	88	100	43	47
Female-headed households (%)	..		25	
Education				
Gross primary enrollment ratio (% of relevant age group)	110	111	95	96
Gross secondary enrollment ratio (% of relevant age group)	88	87	98	100
Gross tertiary enrollment ratio (% of relevant age group)	19	28	20	19
Primary completion rate (% of relevant age group)	95	97	92	93
Youth literacy rate (% of population ages 15–24)	..	..	100	100
Health and related services				
Total fertility rate (births per woman)	2.7		1.9	
Adolescent fertility rate (births per 1,000 women ages 15–19)	..		32	
Women first married by age 18 (% of women ages 20–24)	..		12	
Contraceptive prevalence (% of women ages 15–49)	..		51	
Unmet need for contraception (% of women ages 15–49)	..		23	
Pregnant women receiving prenatal care (%)	..		77	
Births attended by skilled health staff (% of total)	97		88	
Maternal mortality ratio (per 100,000 live births)	56		43	
Economic structure, participation, and access to resources				
Labor force participation rate (% of population ages 15+)	54	71	62	69
Wage and salaried workers (% of employed ages 15+)	..	..	37	48
Self-employed workers (% of employed ages 15+)	..	..	63	52
Vulnerable employment (% of employed ages 15+)	..	..	62	47
Unpaid family workers (% of employed ages 15+)	..	..	..	..
Employment in agriculture (% of employed ages 15+)	..	..	44	32
Employment in industry (% of employed ages 15+)	..	..	6	22
Employment in service (% of employed ages 15+)	..	..	50	47
Women in wage employment in the nonagricultural sector (%)	..		44	
Women's share of part-time employment (% of total)	..		..	
Maternity leave (weeks)	..		18	
Maternal leave benefits (% of wages paid)	..		100	
Female legislators, senior officials and managers (% of total)	..		7	
Employment to population ratio, total (% ages 15+)	50	63	58	64
Employment to population ratio, youth (% ages 15–24)	38	37	31	32
Children in employment (% of children ages 7–14)	..	..	..	..
Unemployment rate (% of labor force ages 15+)	..	..	6.4	4.5
Long-term unemployment rate (% of total unemployment)	..	..	..	..
Youth unemployment rate (% of labor force ages 15–24)	..	..	15	14
Account at a formal financial institution (% age 15+)	..	..	14	16
Public life and decision making				
Seats held by women in national parliament (%)	..		16	

Bahamas, The

High income

Population (thousands)	347.2
GNI, Atlas ($ billions)	7.5
GNI per capita, Atlas ($)	21,970
Population living below $1.25 a day (%)	..

	1990 Female	1990 Male	2011 Female	2011 Male
Demography				
Sex ratio at birth (boys per girls)	1.06		1.06	
Life expectancy at birth (years)	73	66	79	72
Under-five mortality rate (per 1,000 live births)	20	23	15	17
Female-headed households (%)	..		..	
Education				
Gross primary enrollment ratio (% of relevant age group)	95	94	115	113
Gross secondary enrollment ratio (% of relevant age group)	97	95	98	93
Gross tertiary enrollment ratio (% of relevant age group)	29	13	..	..
Primary completion rate (% of relevant age group)	..	..	99	95
Youth literacy rate (% of population ages 15–24)	..	..	..	..
Health and related services				
Total fertility rate (births per woman)	2.6		1.9	
Adolescent fertility rate (births per 1,000 women ages 15–19)	..		29	
Women first married by age 18 (% of women ages 20–24)	..		..	
Contraceptive prevalence (% of women ages 15–49)	62		..	
Unmet need for contraception (% of women ages 15–49)	..		..	
Pregnant women receiving prenatal care (%)	..		98	
Births attended by skilled health staff (% of total)	99		99	
Maternal mortality ratio (per 100,000 live births)	52		47	
Economic structure, participation, and access to resources				
Labor force participation rate (% of population ages 15+)	65	80	69	79
Wage and salaried workers (% of employed ages 15+)	89	84	90	81
Self-employed workers (% of employed ages 15+)	10	15	9	19
Vulnerable employment (% of employed ages 15+)	..	..	..	..
Unpaid family workers (% of employed ages 15+)	0.7	0.3	0.4	0.2
Employment in agriculture (% of employed ages 15+)	2	9	2	6
Employment in industry (% of employed ages 15+)	5	24	4	22
Employment in service (% of employed ages 15+)	93	67	94	72
Women in wage employment in the nonagricultural sector (%)	50		50	
Women's share of part-time employment (% of total)	52		..	
Maternity leave (weeks)	8		13	
Maternal leave benefits (% of wages paid)	100		100	
Female legislators, senior officials and managers (% of total)	33		52	
Employment to population ratio, total (% ages 15+)	58	70	60	71
Employment to population ratio, youth (% ages 15–24)	39	50	36	46
Children in employment (% of children ages 7–14)	..	..	..	..
Unemployment rate (% of labor force ages 15+)	12.2	12.1	13.7	13.6
Long-term unemployment rate (% total unemployment)	40.1	22.6	..	..
Youth unemployment rate (% of labor force ages 15–24)	20	14	22	17
Account at a formal financial institution (% age 15+)	..	..	..	..
Public life and decision making				
Seats held by women in national parliament (%)	4		13	

Bahrain

	High income
Population (millions)	1.3
GNI, Atlas ($ billions)	20.1
GNI per capita, Atlas ($)	15,920
Population living below $1.25 a day (%)	..

	1990 Female	1990 Male	2011 Female	2011 Male
Demography				
Sex ratio at birth (boys per girls)	1.05		1.05	
Life expectancy at birth (years)	74	71	76	75
Under-five mortality rate (per 1,000 live births)	20	21	10	10
Female-headed households (%)	..		..	
Education				
Gross primary enrollment ratio (% of relevant age group)	113	110	107	108
Gross secondary enrollment ratio (% of relevant age group)	89	87	105	101
Gross tertiary enrollment ratio (% of relevant age group)	20	15	44	18
Primary completion rate (% of relevant age group)	106	102	..	..
Youth literacy rate (% of population ages 15–24)	97	97	100	100
Health and related services				
Total fertility rate (births per woman)	3.7		2.5	
Adolescent fertility rate (births per 1,000 women ages 15–19)	..		15	
Women first married by age 18 (% of women ages 20–24)	..		..	
Contraceptive prevalence (% of women ages 15–49)	54		..	
Unmet need for contraception (% of women ages 15–49)	..		..	
Pregnant women receiving prenatal care (%)	..		100	
Births attended by skilled health staff (% of total)	..		97	
Maternal mortality ratio (per 100,000 live births)	23		20	
Economic structure, participation, and access to resources				
Labor force participation rate (% of population ages 15+)	28	88	39	87
Wage and salaried workers (% of employed ages 15+)	..	..	99	96
Self-employed workers (% of employed ages 15+)	..	..	2	4
Vulnerable employment (% of employed ages 15+)	..	..	1	2
Unpaid family workers (% of employed ages 15+)	..	..	0.8	0.5
Employment in agriculture (% of employed ages 15+)	0	3	..	..
Employment in industry (% of employed ages 15+)	7	33	..	..
Employment in service (% of employed ages 15+)	92	64	..	..
Women in wage employment in the nonagricultural sector (%)	8		10	
Women's share of part-time employment (% of total)	..		..	
Maternity leave (weeks)	6		6	
Maternal leave benefits (% of wages paid)	100		100	
Female legislators, senior officials and managers (% of total)	..		..	
Employment to population ratio, total (% ages 15+)	26	83	31	83
Employment to population ratio, youth (% ages 15–24)	15	47	20	38
Children in employment (% of children ages 7–14)	..	..	..	..
Unemployment rate (% of labor force ages 15+)	11.8	5.2	..	..
Long-term unemployment rate (% total unemployment)	..	..	..	..
Youth unemployment rate (% of labor force ages 15–24)	34	22	..	..
Account at a formal financial institution (% age 15+)	..	..	49	79
Public life and decision making				
Seats held by women in national parliament (%)	..		10	

Bangladesh

Population (millions)	150.5
GNI, Atlas ($ billions)	117.8
GNI per capita, Atlas ($)	780
Population living below $1.25 a day (%)	43.3

	1990 Female	1990 Male	2011 Female	2011 Male
Demography				
Sex ratio at birth (boys per girls)	1.05		1.05	
Life expectancy at birth (years)	59	60	70	68
Under-five mortality rate (per 1,000 live births)	138	140	44	48
Female-headed households (%)	9		13	
Education				
Gross primary enrollment ratio (% of relevant age group)	74	88	..	..
Gross secondary enrollment ratio (% of relevant age group)	14	27	55	48
Gross tertiary enrollment ratio (% of relevant age group)	1	7	8	13
Primary completion rate (% of relevant age group)	..	..		
Youth literacy rate (% of population ages 15–24)	38	52	78	75
Health and related services				
Total fertility rate (births per woman)	4.5		2.2	
Adolescent fertility rate (births per 1,000 women ages 15–19)	..		70	
Women first married by age 18 (% of women ages 20–24)	73		66	
Contraceptive prevalence (% of women ages 15–49)	40		61	
Unmet need for contraception (% of women ages 15–49)	18		17	
Pregnant women receiving prenatal care (%)	26		55	
Births attended by skilled health staff (% of total)	10		32	
Maternal mortality ratio (per 100,000 live births)	800		240	
Economic structure, participation, and access to resources				
Labor force participation rate (% of population ages 15+)	62	88	57	84
Wage and salaried workers (% of employed ages 15+)	..	..	..	..
Self-employed workers (% of employed ages 15+)	..	..	..	..
Vulnerable employment (% of employed ages 15+)	..	..	..	..
Unpaid family workers (% of employed ages 15+)	..	..	..	..
Employment in agriculture (% of employed ages 15+)	85	54	..	..
Employment in industry (% of employed ages 15+)	9	16	..	..
Employment in service (% of employed ages 15+)	2	25	..	..
Women in wage employment in the nonagricultural sector (%)	20		..	
Women's share of part-time employment (% of total)	..		..	
Maternity leave (weeks)	12		16	
Maternal leave benefits (% of wages paid)	100		100	
Female legislators, senior officials and managers (% of total)	..		..	
Employment to population ratio, total (% ages 15+)	60	85	54	81
Employment to population ratio, youth (% ages 15–24)	55	72	45	59
Children in employment (% of children ages 7–14)	..	..	6.4	25.7
Unemployment rate (% of labor force ages 15+)	1.9	2.0	7.4	4.2
Long-term unemployment rate (% total unemployment)	..	..		
Youth unemployment rate (% of labor force ages 15–24)	2	3	..	..
Account at a formal financial institution (% age 15+)	..	..	35	44
Public life and decision making				
Seats held by women in national parliament (%)	10		20	

Barbados

	High income
Population (thousands)	273.9
GNI, Atlas ($ billions)	3.5
GNI per capita, Atlas ($)	12,660
Population living below $1.25 a day (%)	..

	1990		2011	
	Female	Male	Female	Male
Demography				
Sex ratio at birth (boys per girls)	1.04		1.04	
Life expectancy at birth (years)	77	72	80	74
Under-five mortality rate (per 1,000 live births)	16	20	18	22
Female-headed households (%)	..		..	
Education				
Gross primary enrollment ratio (% of relevant age group)	115	116	125	126
Gross secondary enrollment ratio (% of relevant age group)	82	91	110	98
Gross tertiary enrollment ratio (% of relevant age group)	20	14	90	36
Primary completion rate (% of relevant age group)	..	..	114	108
Youth literacy rate (% of population ages 15–24)	..	..	..	..
Health and related services				
Total fertility rate (births per woman)	1.7		1.6	
Adolescent fertility rate (births per 1,000 women ages 15–19)	..		41	
Women first married by age 18 (% of women ages 20–24)	..		..	
Contraceptive prevalence (% of women ages 15–49)	55		..	
Unmet need for contraception (% of women ages 15–49)	..		..	
Pregnant women receiving prenatal care (%)	100		100	
Births attended by skilled health staff (% of total)	..		100	
Maternal mortality ratio (per 100,000 live births)	120		51	
Economic structure, participation, and access to resources				
Labor force participation rate (% of population ages 15+)	61	78	65	76
Wage and salaried workers (% of employed ages 15+)	91	85	..	..
Self-employed workers (% of employed ages 15+)	9	15	..	..
Vulnerable employment (% of employed ages 15+)	9	14	..	..
Unpaid family workers (% of employed ages 15+)	0.6	1.0	..	..
Employment in agriculture (% of employed ages 15+)	6	7	2	4
Employment in industry (% of employed ages 15+)	14	29	10	30
Employment in service (% of employed ages 15+)	70	56	87	66
Women in wage employment in the nonagricultural sector (%)	47		51	
Women's share of part-time employment (% of total)	..		..	
Maternity leave (weeks)	12		12	
Maternal leave benefits (% of wages paid)	100		100	
Female legislators, senior officials and managers (% of total)	43		47	
Employment to population ratio, total (% ages 15+)	48	65	56	69
Employment to population ratio, youth (% ages 15–24)	39	44	37	46
Children in employment (% of children ages 7–14)	..	..	..	..
Unemployment rate (% of labor force ages 15+)	20.2	10.3	12.5	9.8
Long-term unemployment rate (% total unemployment)	61.3	55.3	..	..
Youth unemployment rate (% of labor force ages 15–24)	41	22	..	..
Account at a formal financial institution (% age 15+)	..	..	..	..
Public life and decision making				
Seats held by women in national parliament (%)	4		10	

Belarus

Upper middle income

Population (millions)	9.5
GNI, Atlas ($ billions)	55.2
GNI per capita, Atlas ($)	5,830
Population living below $1.25 a day (%)	<2

	1990		2011	
	Female	Male	Female	Male
Demography				
Sex ratio at birth (boys per girls)	1.07		1.06	
Life expectancy at birth (years)	76	66	77	65
Under-five mortality rate (per 1,000 live births)	15	20	5	6
Female-headed households (%)	..		..	
Education				
Gross primary enrollment ratio (% of relevant age group)	96	96	98	98
Gross secondary enrollment ratio (% of relevant age group)	99	95	103	106
Gross tertiary enrollment ratio (% of relevant age group)	..	..	100	71
Primary completion rate (% of relevant age group)	95	95	103	104
Youth literacy rate (% of population ages 15–24)	100	100	100	100
Health and related services				
Total fertility rate (births per woman)	1.9		1.5	
Adolescent fertility rate (births per 1,000 women ages 15–19)	..		21	
Women first married by age 18 (% of women ages 20–24)	..		..	
Contraceptive prevalence (% of women ages 15–49)	..		..	
Unmet need for contraception (% of women ages 15–49)	..		..	
Pregnant women receiving prenatal care (%)	..		..	
Births attended by skilled health staff (% of total)	100		100	
Maternal mortality ratio (per 100,000 live births)	37		4	
Economic structure, participation, and access to resources				
Labor force participation rate (% of population ages 15+)	60	75	50	63
Wage and salaried workers (% of employed ages 15+)	..	..	..	..
Self-employed workers (% of employed ages 15+)	..	..	..	..
Vulnerable employment (% of employed ages 15+)	..	..	..	..
Unpaid family workers (% of employed ages 15+)	..	..	..	..
Employment in agriculture (% of employed ages 15+)	..	..	..	..
Employment in industry (% of employed ages 15+)	..	..	..	..
Employment in service (% of employed ages 15+)	..	..	..	..
Women in wage employment in the nonagricultural sector (%)	55		56	
Women's share of part-time employment (% of total)	..		..	
Maternity leave (weeks)	..		18	
Maternal leave benefits (% of wages paid)	..		100	
Female legislators, senior officials and managers (% of total)	..		..	
Employment to population ratio, total (% ages 15+)	53	66	46	57
Employment to population ratio, youth (% ages 15–24)	38	40	27	35
Children in employment (% of children ages 7–14)	..	..	..	..
Unemployment rate (% of labor force ages 15+)	..	..	..	..
Long-term unemployment rate (% total unemployment)	..	..	..	..
Youth unemployment rate (% of labor force ages 15–24)	..	..	..	..
Account at a formal financial institution (% age 15+)	..	..	58	59
Public life and decision making				
Seats held by women in national parliament (%)	..		27	

Belgium

	High income
Population (millions)	11.0
GNI, Atlas ($ billions)	506.2
GNI per capita, Atlas ($)	45,930
Population living below $1.25 a day (%)	..

	1990		2011	
	Female	Male	Female	Male
Demography				
Sex ratio at birth (boys per girls)	1.05		1.05	
Life expectancy at birth (years)	80	73	83	78
Under-five mortality rate (per 1,000 live births)	9	11	4	5
Female-headed households (%)	..		..	
Education				
Gross primary enrollment ratio (% of relevant age group)	100	99	104	104
Gross secondary enrollment ratio (% of relevant age group)	99	98	109	112
Gross tertiary enrollment ratio (% of relevant age group)	37	38	79	62
Primary completion rate (% of relevant age group)	81	75	93	89
Youth literacy rate (% of population ages 15–24)	..	..	..	..
Health and related services				
Total fertility rate (births per woman)	1.6		1.8	
Adolescent fertility rate (births per 1,000 women ages 15–19)	..		12	
Women first married by age 18 (% of women ages 20–24)	..		..	
Contraceptive prevalence (% of women ages 15–49)	78		..	
Unmet need for contraception (% of women ages 15–49)	..		..	
Pregnant women receiving prenatal care (%)	..		..	
Births attended by skilled health staff (% of total)	100		..	
Maternal mortality ratio (per 100,000 live births)	10		8	
Economic structure, participation, and access to resources				
Labor force participation rate (% of population ages 15+)	36	61	48	61
Wage and salaried workers (% of employed ages 15+)	83	80	90	83
Self-employed workers (% of employed ages 15+)	17	20	11	18
Vulnerable employment (% of employed ages 15+)	17	18	9	12
Unpaid family workers (% of employed ages 15+)	6.2	0.8	1.9	0.5
Employment in agriculture (% of employed ages 15+)	2	4	1	2
Employment in industry (% of employed ages 15+)	16	40	10	35
Employment in service (% of employed ages 15+)	81	56	89	64
Women in wage employment in the nonagricultural sector (%)	39		47	
Women's share of part-time employment (% of total)	80		80	
Maternity leave (weeks)	15		15	
Maternal leave benefits (% of wages paid)	82		82	
Female legislators, senior officials and managers (% of total)	30		30	
Employment to population ratio, total (% ages 15+)	34	58	44	56
Employment to population ratio, youth (% ages 15–24)	29	34	24	29
Children in employment (% of children ages 7–14)	..	..	..	..
Unemployment rate (% of labor force ages 15+)	11.4	4.6	7.2	7.1
Long-term unemployment rate (% total unemployment)	68.4	64.8	49.7	47.1
Youth unemployment rate (% of labor force ages 15–24)	19	10	19	19
Account at a formal financial institution (% age 15+)	..	..	97	95
Public life and decision making				
Seats held by women in national parliament (%)	9		38	

Belize

Latin America & the Caribbean			Lower middle income	
Population (thousands)				356.6
GNI, Atlas ($ billions)				1.3
GNI per capita, Atlas ($)				3,710
Population living below $1.25 a day (%)				..

	1990		2011	
	Female	Male	Female	Male
Demography				
Sex ratio at birth (boys per girls)	1.03		1.03	
Life expectancy at birth (years)	74	71	78	75
Under-five mortality rate (per 1,000 live births)	39	49	15	19
Female-headed households (%)	..		..	
Education				
Gross primary enrollment ratio (% of relevant age group)	106	115	116	126
Gross secondary enrollment ratio (% of relevant age group)	62	62	75	78
Gross tertiary enrollment ratio (% of relevant age group)	..	..	26	16
Primary completion rate (% of relevant age group)	90	95	107	114
Youth literacy rate (% of population ages 15–24)	77	76	..	..
Health and related services				
Total fertility rate (births per woman)	4.5		2.7	
Adolescent fertility rate (births per 1,000 women ages 15–19)	..		72	
Women first married by age 18 (% of women ages 20–24)	..		26	
Contraceptive prevalence (% of women ages 15–49)	47		34	
Unmet need for contraception (% of women ages 15–49)	..		..	
Pregnant women receiving prenatal care (%)	96		99	
Births attended by skilled health staff (% of total)	77		94	
Maternal mortality ratio (per 100,000 live births)	71		53	
Economic structure, participation, and access to resources				
Labor force participation rate (% of population ages 15+)	36	82	48	82
Wage and salaried workers (% of employed ages 15+)	76	68	..	..
Self-employed workers (% of employed ages 15+)	24	32	..	..
Vulnerable employment (% of employed ages 15+)	..	..	..	..
Unpaid family workers (% of employed ages 15+)	2.6	3.3	..	..
Employment in agriculture (% of employed ages 15+)	5	33	..	..
Employment in industry (% of employed ages 15+)	13	23	..	..
Employment in service (% of employed ages 15+)	79	41	..	..
Women in wage employment in the nonagricultural sector (%)	34		38	
Women's share of part-time employment (% of total)	50		..	
Maternity leave (weeks)	12		14	
Maternal leave benefits (% of wages paid)	80		100	
Female legislators, senior officials and managers (% of total)	41		..	
Employment to population ratio, total (% ages 15+)	30	75	42	77
Employment to population ratio, youth (% ages 15–24)	27	59	32	57
Children in employment (% of children ages 7–14)	..	..	..	..
Unemployment rate (% of labor force ages 15+)	2.1	4.4	13.0	5.9
Long-term unemployment rate (% total unemployment)	51.6	30.8	..	..
Youth unemployment rate (% of labor force ages 15–24)	4	7	..	..
Account at a formal financial institution (% age 15+)	..	..	..	..
Public life and decision making				
Seats held by women in national parliament (%)	0		3	

Benin

Sub-Saharan Africa				Low income
Population (millions)				9.1
GNI, Atlas ($ billions)				7.1
GNI per capita, Atlas ($)				780
Population living below $1.25 a day (%)				47.3

	1990		2011	
	Female	Male	Female	Male
Demography				
Sex ratio at birth (boys per girls)	1.04		1.04	
Life expectancy at birth (years)	52	46	58	54
Under-five mortality rate (per 1,000 live births)	171	183	103	109
Female-headed households (%)	..		23	
Education				
Gross primary enrollment ratio (% of relevant age group)	35	71	120	137
Gross secondary enrollment ratio (% of relevant age group)	9	23	39	64
Gross tertiary enrollment ratio (% of relevant age group)	1	5	6	15
Primary completion rate (% of relevant age group)	12	28	66	84
Youth literacy rate (% of population ages 15–24)	27	55	45	66
Health and related services				
Total fertility rate (births per woman)	6.7		5.2	
Adolescent fertility rate (births per 1,000 women ages 15–19)	..		100	
Women first married by age 18 (% of women ages 20–24)	..		34	
Contraceptive prevalence (% of women ages 15–49)	..		17	
Unmet need for contraception (% of women ages 15–49)	..		30	
Pregnant women receiving prenatal care (%)	..		84	
Births attended by skilled health staff (% of total)	..		74	
Maternal mortality ratio (per 100,000 live births)	770		350	
Economic structure, participation, and access to resources				
Labor force participation rate (% of population ages 15+)	57	89	67	78
Wage and salaried workers (% of employed ages 15+)	..	..	..	..
Self-employed workers (% of employed ages 15+)	..	..	..	..
Vulnerable employment (% of employed ages 15+)	..	..	..	..
Unpaid family workers (% of employed ages 15+)	..	..	..	..
Employment in agriculture (% of employed ages 15+)	..	..	..	..
Employment in industry (% of employed ages 15+)	..	..	..	..
Employment in service (% of employed ages 15+)	..	..	..	..
Women in wage employment in the nonagricultural sector (%)	21		..	
Women's share of part-time employment (% of total)	..		..	
Maternity leave (weeks)	14		14	
Maternal leave benefits (% of wages paid)	100		100	
Female legislators, senior officials and managers (% of total)	..		..	
Employment to population ratio, total (% ages 15+)	57	88	67	78
Employment to population ratio, youth (% ages 15–24)	55	79	57	56
Children in employment (% of children ages 7–14)	..	..	76.1	72.8
Unemployment rate (% of labor force ages 15+)	0.6	2.2	..	..
Long-term unemployment rate (% total unemployment)	..	..	..	..
Youth unemployment rate (% of labor force ages 15–24)	1	3	..	..
Account at a formal financial institution (% age 15+)	..	..	10	11
Public life and decision making				
Seats held by women in national parliament (%)	3		8	

Bermuda

South Asia				High income
Population (thousands)				64.7
GNI, Atlas ($ billions)				..
GNI per capita, Atlas ($)				..
Population living below $1.25 a day (%)				..

	1990		2011	
	Female	Male	Female	Male
Demography				
Sex ratio at birth (boys per girls)	..			
Life expectancy at birth (years)	78	70	82	77
Under-five mortality rate (per 1,000 live births)	..	..	..	..
Female-headed households (%)	..		..	
Education				
Gross primary enrollment ratio (% of relevant age group)	..	..	89	91
Gross secondary enrollment ratio (% of relevant age group)	..	..	83	71
Gross tertiary enrollment ratio (% of relevant age group)	..	..	43	20
Primary completion rate (% of relevant age group)	..	..	100	100
Youth literacy rate (% of population ages 15–24)	..	..	..	..
Health and related services				
Total fertility rate (births per woman)		..	1.8	
Adolescent fertility rate (births per 1,000 women ages 15–19)		..		..
Women first married by age 18 (% of women ages 20–24)		..		..
Contraceptive prevalence (% of women ages 15–49)		..		..
Unmet need for contraception (% of women ages 15–49)		..		..
Pregnant women receiving prenatal care (%)		..		..
Births attended by skilled health staff (% of total)		..		..
Maternal mortality ratio (per 100,000 live births)		..		..
Economic structure, participation, and access to resources				
Labor force participation rate (% of population ages 15+)	..	..	..	..
Wage and salaried workers (% of employed ages 15+)	..	..	..	..
Self-employed workers (% of employed ages 15+)	..	..	..	..
Vulnerable employment (% of employed ages 15+)	..	..	..	..
Unpaid family workers (% of employed ages 15+)	..	..	..	..
Employment in agriculture (% of employed ages 15+)	..	..	..	..
Employment in industry (% of employed ages 15+)	..	..	..	..
Employment in service (% of employed ages 15+)	..	..	..	..
Women in wage employment in the nonagricultural sector (%)	49		49	
Women's share of part-time employment (% of total)	..		..	
Maternity leave (weeks)	..		..	
Maternal leave benefits (% of wages paid)	..		..	
Female legislators, senior officials and managers (% of total)	..		..	
Employment to population ratio, total (% ages 15+)	..	..	..	..
Employment to population ratio, youth (% ages 15–24)	..	..	..	..
Children in employment (% of children ages 7–14)	..	..	..	..
Unemployment rate (% of labor force ages 15+)	4.3	7.5	..	..
Long-term unemployment rate (% of total unemployment)	..	..	..	..
Youth unemployment rate (% of labor force ages 15–24)	..	..	..	..
Account at a formal financial institution (% age 15+)	..	..	..	..
Public life and decision making				
Seats held by women in national parliament (%)		..		..

Bhutan

South Asia			Low middle income	
Population (thousands)				738.3
GNI, Atlas ($ billions)				1.6
GNI per capita, Atlas ($)				2,130
Population living below $1.25 a day (%)				10.2

	1990		2011	
	Female	Male	Female	Male
Demography				
Sex ratio at birth (boys per girls)	1.04		1.04	
Life expectancy at birth (years)	54	51	69	65
Under-five mortality rate (per 1,000 live births)	130	147	50	57
Female-headed households (%)	..		..	
Education				
Gross primary enrollment ratio (% of relevant age group)	*41*	*68*	111	110
Gross secondary enrollment ratio (% of relevant age group)	..	..	77	73
Gross tertiary enrollment ratio (% of relevant age group)	..	..	7	10
Primary completion rate (% of relevant age group)	*20*	*27*	105	101
Youth literacy rate (% of population ages 15–24)	..	..	..	..
Health and related services				
Total fertility rate (births per woman)	5.8		2.3	
Adolescent fertility rate (births per 1,000 women ages 15-19)	..		46	
Women first married by age 18 (% of women ages 20–24)	..		26	
Contraceptive prevalence (% of women ages 15–49)	*19*		66	
Unmet need for contraception (% of women ages 15–49)	..		..	
Pregnant women receiving prenatal care (%)	..		97	
Births attended by skilled health staff (% of total)	15		65	
Maternal mortality ratio (per 100,000 live births)	1,000		*180*	
Economic structure, participation, and access to resources				
Labor force participation rate (% of population ages 15+)	50	78	66	77
Wage and salaried workers (% of employed ages 15+)	..	..	17	40
Self-employed workers (% of employed ages 15+)	..	..	83	60
Vulnerable employment (% of employed ages 15+)	..	..	83	60
Unpaid family workers (% of employed ages 15+)	..	..	34.4	24.4
Employment in agriculture (% of employed ages 15+)	..	..	68	53
Employment in industry (% of employed ages 15+)	..	..	9	10
Employment in service (% of employed ages 15+)	..	..	24	37
Women in wage employment in the nonagricultural sector (%)	..		27	
Women's share of part-time employment (% of total)	..		60	
Maternity leave (weeks)	..		..	
Maternal leave benefits (% of wages paid)	..		..	
Female legislators, senior officials and managers (% of total)	..		27	
Employment to population ratio, total (% ages 15+)	48	77	63	75
Employment to population ratio, youth (% ages 15–24)	34	47	44	41
Children in employment (% of children ages 7–14)	..	..	..	..
Unemployment rate (% of labor force ages 15+)	..	..	4.5	1.8
Long-term unemployment rate (% total unemployment)	..	..	..	..
Youth unemployment rate (% of labor force ages 15–24)	..	..	11	7
Account at a formal financial institution (% age 15+)	..	..	..	..
Public life and decision making				
Seats held by women in national parliament (%)	2		9	

Bolivia

Latin America & the Caribbean	Lower middle income
Population (millions)	10.1
GNI, Atlas ($ billions)	20.4
GNI per capita, Atlas ($)	2,020
Population living below $1.25 a day (%)	15.6

	1990		2011	
	Female	Male	Female	Male
Demography				
Sex ratio at birth (boys per girls)	1.05		1.05	
Life expectancy at birth (years)	61	57	69	64
Under-five mortality rate (per 1,000 live births)	112	127	48	54
Female-headed households (%)	19		23	
Education				
Gross primary enrollment ratio (% of relevant age group)	102	110	99	101
Gross secondary enrollment ratio (% of relevant age group)	..	..	80	82
Gross tertiary enrollment ratio (% of relevant age group)	..	..	35	42
Primary completion rate (% of relevant age group)	64	78	95	95
Youth literacy rate (% of population ages 15–24)	92	96	99	100
Health and related services				
Total fertility rate (births per woman)	4.9		3.3	
Adolescent fertility rate (births per 1,000 women ages 15–19)	..		75	
Women first married by age 18 (% of women ages 20–24)	24		22	
Contraceptive prevalence (% of women ages 15–49)	30		61	
Unmet need for contraception (% of women ages 15–49)	23		20	
Pregnant women receiving prenatal care (%)	46		86	
Births attended by skilled health staff (% of total)	43		71	
Maternal mortality ratio (per 100,000 live births)	450		190	
Economic structure, participation, and access to resources				
Labor force participation rate (% of population ages 15+)	50	83	64	81
Wage and salaried workers (% of employed ages 15+)	48	63	33	46
Self-employed workers (% of employed ages 15+)	52	37	67	54
Vulnerable employment (% of employed ages 15+)	50	32	64	47
Unpaid family workers (% of employed ages 15+)	6.7	3.6	32.7	12.6
Employment in agriculture (% of employed ages 15+)	0	2	33	31
Employment in industry (% of employed ages 15+)	12	35	10	28
Employment in service (% of employed ages 15+)	88	63	57	41
Women in wage employment in the nonagricultural sector (%)	35		37	
Women's share of part-time employment (% of total)	..		59	
Maternity leave (weeks)	8		12	
Maternal leave benefits (% of wages paid)	..		100	
Female legislators, senior officials and managers (% of total)	26		29	
Employment to population ratio, total (% ages 15+)	48	79	60	78
Employment to population ratio, youth (% ages 15–24)	39	58	44	55
Children in employment (% of children ages 7–14)	..	..	18.4	21.8
Unemployment rate (% of labor force ages 15+)	12.3	21.1	4.4	2.6
Long-term unemployment rate (% of total unemployment)	..	..	..	..
Youth unemployment rate (% of labor force ages 15–24)	..	..	..	..
Account at a formal financial institution (% age 15+)	..	..	25	31
Public life and decision making				
Seats held by women in national parliament (%)	9		25	

Bosnia and Herzegovina

Europe & Central Asia	Upper middle income
Population (millions)	3.8
GNI, Atlas ($ billions)	18.0
GNI per capita, Atlas ($)	4,780
Population living below $1.25 a day (%)	<2

	1990		2011	
	Female	Male	Female	Male
Demography				
Sex ratio at birth (boys per girls)	1.07		1.07	
Life expectancy at birth (years)	74	62	78	73
Under-five mortality rate (per 1,000 live births)	16	21	7	9
Female-headed households (%)	..		..	
Education				
Gross primary enrollment ratio (% of relevant age group)	..	..	91	90
Gross secondary enrollment ratio (% of relevant age group)	..	..	91	88
Gross tertiary enrollment ratio (% of relevant age group)	..	..	43	33
Primary completion rate (% of relevant age group)	..	..	76	75
Youth literacy rate (% of population ages 15–24)	..	..	100	100
Health and related services				
Total fertility rate (births per woman)	1.7		1.1	
Adolescent fertility rate (births per 1,000 women ages 15–19)	..		14	
Women first married by age 18 (% of women ages 20–24)	..		6	
Contraceptive prevalence (% of women ages 15–49)	..		36	
Unmet need for contraception (% of women ages 15–49)	..		23	
Pregnant women receiving prenatal care (%)	..		99	
Births attended by skilled health staff (% of total)	97		100	
Maternal mortality ratio (per 100,000 live births)	18		8	
Economic structure, participation, and access to resources				
Labor force participation rate (% of population ages 15+)	35	57	35	59
Wage and salaried workers (% of employed ages 15+)	..	..	74	75
Self-employed workers (% of employed ages 15+)	..	..	25	25
Vulnerable employment (% of employed ages 15+)	..	..	25	25
Unpaid family workers (% of employed ages 15+)	..	..	10.2	2.3
Employment in agriculture (% of employed ages 15+)	..	..	21	19
Employment in industry (% of employed ages 15+)	..	..	16	36
Employment in service (% of employed ages 15+)	..	..	63	45
Women in wage employment in the nonagricultural sector (%)	..		41	
Women's share of part-time employment (% of total)	..		..	
Maternity leave (weeks)	..		52	
Maternal leave benefits (% of wages paid)	..		100	
Female legislators, senior officials and managers (% of total)	..		..	
Employment to population ratio, total (% ages 15+)	26	44	25	43
Employment to population ratio, youth (% ages 15–24)	12	20	10	18
Children in employment (% of children ages 7–14)	..	..	9.5	11.7
Unemployment rate (% of labor force ages 15+)	21.6	15.5	29.9	26.0
Long-term unemployment rate (% total unemployment)	..	..	..	..
Youth unemployment rate (% of labor force ages 15–24)	..	..	60	57
Account at a formal financial institution (% age 15+)	..	..	48	67
Public life and decision making				
Seats held by women in national parliament (%)	..		21	

Botswana

Sub-Saharan Africa	Upper middle income
Population (millions)	2.0
GNI, Atlas ($ billions)	15.2
GNI per capita, Atlas ($)	7,470
Population living below $1.25 a day (%)	..

	1990		2011	
	Female	Male	Female	Male
Demography				
Sex ratio at birth (boys per girls)	1.03		1.03	
Life expectancy at birth (years)	66	62	52	54
Under-five mortality rate (per 1,000 live births)	49	57	24	28
Female-headed households (%)	..		..	
Education				
Gross primary enrollment ratio (% of relevant age group)	108	100	108	112
Gross secondary enrollment ratio (% of relevant age group)	42	38	84	79
Gross tertiary enrollment ratio (% of relevant age group)	4	5	8	7
Primary completion rate (% of relevant age group)	97	81	98	97
Youth literacy rate (% of population ages 15–24)	92	86	97	94
Health and related services				
Total fertility rate (births per woman)	4.7		2.7	
Adolescent fertility rate (births per 1,000 women ages 15–19)	..		45	
Women first married by age 18 (% of women ages 20–24)	10		..	
Contraceptive prevalence (% of women ages 15–49)	33		53	
Unmet need for contraception (% of women ages 15–49)	..		..	
Pregnant women receiving prenatal care (%)	92		94	
Births attended by skilled health staff (% of total)	78		95	
Maternal mortality ratio (per 100,000 live births)	140		160	
Economic structure, participation, and access to resources				
Labor force participation rate (% of population ages 15+)	67	81	72	82
Wage and salaried workers (% of employed ages 15+)	65	67	59	62
Self-employed workers (% of employed ages 15+)	35	33	41	38
Vulnerable employment (% of employed ages 15+)	34	31	39	33
Unpaid family workers (% of employed ages 15+)	6.8	1.4	4.4	2.1
Employment in agriculture (% of employed ages 15+)	..	..	24	35
Employment in industry (% of employed ages 15+)	..	..	11	19
Employment in service (% of employed ages 15+)	..	..	65	46
Women in wage employment in the nonagricultural sector (%)	34		41	
Women's share of part-time employment (% of total)	..		55	
Maternity leave (weeks)	12		12	
Maternal leave benefits (% of wages paid)	25		25	
Female legislators, senior officials and managers (% of total)	..		30	
Employment to population ratio, total (% ages 15+)	49	63	57	69
Employment to population ratio, youth (% ages 15–24)	30	41	37	46
Children in employment (% of children ages 7–14)	..	..	..	..
Unemployment rate (% of labor force ages 15+)	17.2	11.7	19.9	15.3
Long-term unemployment rate (% total unemployment)	..	..	60.3	59.2
Youth unemployment rate (% of labor force ages 15–24)	33	20	..	..
Account at a formal financial institution (% age 15+)	..	..	28	32
Public life and decision making				
Seats held by women in national parliament (%)	5		8	

Brazil

Latin America & the Caribbean			Upper middle income	
Population (millions)				196.7
GNI, Atlas ($ billions)				2,107.7
GNI per capita, Atlas ($)				10,720
Population living below $1.25 a day (%)				6.1

	1990		2011	
	Female	Male	Female	Male
Demography				
Sex ratio at birth (boys per girls)	1.05		1.05	
Life expectancy at birth (years)	70	63	77	70
Under-five mortality rate (per 1,000 live births)	52	64	14	17
Female-headed households (%)	21		..	
Education				
Gross primary enrollment ratio (% of relevant age group)	130	131	..	..
Gross secondary enrollment ratio (% of relevant age group)	..	..	..	..
Gross tertiary enrollment ratio (% of relevant age group)	11	10	..	..
Primary completion rate (% of relevant age group)	..	..	..	..
Youth literacy rate (% of population ages 15–24)	..	..	99	97
Health and related services				
Total fertility rate (births per woman)	2.8		1.8	
Adolescent fertility rate (births per 1,000 women ages 15–19)	..		76	
Women first married by age 18 (% of women ages 20–24)	26		36	
Contraceptive prevalence (% of women ages 15–49)	59		81	
Unmet need for contraception (% of women ages 15–49)	18		..	
Pregnant women receiving prenatal care (%)	74		98	
Births attended by skilled health staff (% of total)	70		97	
Maternal mortality ratio (per 100,000 live births)	120		56	
Economic structure, participation, and access to resources				
Labor force participation rate (% of population ages 15+)	45	85	60	81
Wage and salaried workers (% of employed ages 15+)	68	65	69	64
Self-employed workers (% of employed ages 15+)	32	35	25	33
Vulnerable employment (% of employed ages 15+)	30	29	22	27
Unpaid family workers (% of employed ages 15+)	9.4	4.3	6.3	3.4
Employment in agriculture (% of employed ages 15+)	13	28	12	21
Employment in industry (% of employed ages 15+)	13	28	13	29
Employment in service (% of employed ages 15+)	74	44	75	50
Women in wage employment in the nonagricultural sector (%)	35		42	
Women's share of part-time employment (% of total)	..		68	
Maternity leave (weeks)	17		17	
Maternal leave benefits (% of wages paid)	100		100	
Female legislators, senior officials and managers (% of total)	..		36	
Employment to population ratio, total (% ages 15+)	42	79	54	77
Employment to population ratio, youth (% ages 15–24)	38	69	43	62
Children in employment (% of children ages 7–14)	..	..	2.6	5.8
Unemployment rate (% of labor force ages 15+)	3.5	3.8	11.0	6.1
Long-term unemployment rate (% total unemployment)	..	..	..	..
Youth unemployment rate (% of labor force ages 15–24)	7	7	23	14
Account at a formal financial institution (% age 15+)	..	..	51	61
Public life and decision making				
Seats held by women in national parliament (%)	5		9	

Brunei Darussalam

Population (thousands)	405.9
GNI, Atlas ($ billions)	12.5
GNI per capita, Atlas ($)	31,800
Population living below $1.25 a day (%)	..

	1990		2011	
	Female	Male	Female	Male
Demography				
Sex ratio at birth (boys per girls)	1.06		1.06	
Life expectancy at birth (years)	76	72	80	76
Under-five mortality rate (per 1,000 live births)	11	14	7	8
Female-headed households (%)	..		..	
Education				
Gross primary enrollment ratio (% of relevant age group)	113	118	106	104
Gross secondary enrollment ratio (% of relevant age group)	75	69	113	111
Gross tertiary enrollment ratio (% of relevant age group)	8	5	25	15
Primary completion rate (% of relevant age group)	129	115	120	120
Youth literacy rate (% of population ages 15–24)	98	98	100	100
Health and related services				
Total fertility rate (births per woman)	3.5		2.0	
Adolescent fertility rate (births per 1,000 women ages 15–19)	..		23	
Women first married by age 18 (% of women ages 20–24)	..		..	
Contraceptive prevalence (% of women ages 15–49)	..		..	
Unmet need for contraception (% of women ages 15–49)	..		..	
Pregnant women receiving prenatal care (%)	100		99	
Births attended by skilled health staff (% of total)	98		100	
Maternal mortality ratio (per 100,000 live births)	29		24	
Economic structure, participation, and access to resources				
Labor force participation rate (% of population ages 15+)	44	82	56	77
Wage and salaried workers (% of employed ages 15+)	96	94	..	..
Self-employed workers (% of employed ages 15+)	4	6	..	..
Vulnerable employment (% of employed ages 15+)	3	4	..	..
Unpaid family workers (% of employed ages 15+)	0.6	0.4	..	..
Employment in agriculture (% of employed ages 15+)	2	2	..	..
Employment in industry (% of employed ages 15+)	9	31	..	..
Employment in service (% of employed ages 15+)	90	66	..	..
Women in wage employment in the nonagricultural sector (%)	23		..	
Women's share of part-time employment (% of total)	..		..	
Maternity leave (weeks)	..		..	
Maternal leave benefits (% of wages paid)	..		..	
Female legislators, senior officials and managers (% of total)	..		..	
Employment to population ratio, total (% ages 15+)	43	78	53	73
Employment to population ratio, youth (% ages 15–24)	30	46	37	44
Children in employment (% of children ages 7–14)	..	..	..	..
Unemployment rate (% of labor force ages 15+)	6.7	3.7	..	..
Long-term unemployment rate (% total unemployment)	..	..	..	..
Youth unemployment rate (% of labor force ages 15–24)	..	..	..	..
Account at a formal financial institution (% age 15+)	..	..	..	..
Public life and decision making				
Seats held by women in national parliament (%)	..		..	

Bulgaria

Europe & Central Asia	Upper middle income
Population (millions)	7.3
GNI, Atlas ($ billions)	48.8
GNI per capita, Atlas ($)	6,640
Population living below $1.25 a day (%)	<2

	1990		2011	
	Female	Male	Female	Male
Demography				
Sex ratio at birth (boys per girls)	1.06		1.06	
Life expectancy at birth (years)	75	68	78	71
Under-five mortality rate (per 1,000 live births)	20	25	11	13
Female-headed households (%)	..		..	
Education				
Gross primary enrollment ratio (% of relevant age group)	95	96	102	103
Gross secondary enrollment ratio (% of relevant age group)	99	99	87	91
Gross tertiary enrollment ratio (% of relevant age group)	28	24	65	49
Primary completion rate (% of relevant age group)	100	100	106	106
Youth literacy rate (% of population ages 15–24)	..	..	98	98
Health and related services				
Total fertility rate (births per woman)	1.8		1.5	
Adolescent fertility rate (births per 1,000 women ages 15–19)	..		38	
Women first married by age 18 (% of women ages 20–24)	..		..	
Contraceptive prevalence (% of women ages 15–49)	..		..	
Unmet need for contraception (% of women ages 15–49)	..		..	
Pregnant women receiving prenatal care (%)	..		..	
Births attended by skilled health staff (% of total)	99		100	
Maternal mortality ratio (per 100,000 live births)	24		11	
Economic structure, participation, and access to resources				
Labor force participation rate (% of population ages 15+)	55	63	49	60
Wage and salaried workers (% of employed ages 15+)	..	..	91	85
Self-employed workers (% of employed ages 15+)	..	..	10	15
Vulnerable employment (% of employed ages 15+)	..	..	7	10
Unpaid family workers (% of employed ages 15+)	..	..	1.3	0.8
Employment in agriculture (% of employed ages 15+)	..	..	5	8
Employment in industry (% of employed ages 15+)	..	..	25	41
Employment in service (% of employed ages 15+)	..	..	70	51
Women in wage employment in the nonagricultural sector (%)	52		49	
Women's share of part-time employment (% of total)	..		53	
Maternity leave (weeks)	17		19	
Maternal leave benefits (% of wages paid)	100		90	
Female legislators, senior officials and managers (% of total)	..		37	
Employment to population ratio, total (% ages 15+)	45	50	44	53
Employment to population ratio, youth (% ages 15–24)	33	26	20	27
Children in employment (% of children ages 7–14)	..	..	..	..
Unemployment rate (% of labor force ages 15+)	22.0	20.9	10.0	12.3
Long-term unemployment rate (% total unemployment)	52.3	52.6	54.8	57.1
Youth unemployment rate (% of labor force ages 15–24)	..	..	25	28
Account at a formal financial institution (% age 15+)	..	..	55	50
Public life and decision making				
Seats held by women in national parliament (%)	21		23	

Burkina Faso

Sub-Saharan Africa	Low income
Population (millions)	17.0
GNI, Atlas ($ billions)	9.9
GNI per capita, Atlas ($)	580
Population living below $1.25 a day (%)	44.6

	1990		2011	
	Female	Male	Female	Male
Demography				
Sex ratio at birth (boys per girls)	1.05		1.05	
Life expectancy at birth (years)	50	47	56	54
Under-five mortality rate (per 1,000 live births)	202	215	142	151
Female-headed households (%)	7		10	
Education				
Gross primary enrollment ratio (% of relevant age group)	23	37	76	82
Gross secondary enrollment ratio (% of relevant age group)	5	10	20	25
Gross tertiary enrollment ratio (% of relevant age group)	0	1	3	5
Primary completion rate (% of relevant age group)	13	23	42	48
Youth literacy rate (% of population ages 15–24)	14	27	33	47
Health and related services				
Total fertility rate (births per woman)	6.8		5.8	
Adolescent fertility rate (births per 1,000 women ages 15–19)	..		119	
Women first married by age 18 (% of women ages 20–24)	62		52	
Contraceptive prevalence (% of women ages 15–49)	8		16	
Unmet need for contraception (% of women ages 15–49)	25		31	
Pregnant women receiving prenatal care (%)	59		94	
Births attended by skilled health staff (% of total)	42		66	
Maternal mortality ratio (per 100,000 live births)	700		300	
Economic structure, participation, and access to resources				
Labor force participation rate (% of population ages 15+)	77	91	78	90
Wage and salaried workers (% of employed ages 15+)	1	6	4	10
Self-employed workers (% of employed ages 15+)	98	93	94	88
Vulnerable employment (% of employed ages 15+)	98	92	93	87
Unpaid family workers (% of employed ages 15+)	87.3	52.2	69.2	26.5
Employment in agriculture (% of employed ages 15+)	..	..	..	..
Employment in industry (% of employed ages 15+)	..	..	..	..
Employment in service (% of employed ages 15+)	..	..	..	..
Women in wage employment in the nonagricultural sector (%)	23		27	
Women's share of part-time employment (% of total)	..		..	
Maternity leave (weeks)	14		14	
Maternal leave benefits (% of wages paid)	100		100	
Female legislators, senior officials and managers (% of total)	..		31	
Employment to population ratio, total (% ages 15+)	76	88	76	87
Employment to population ratio, youth (% ages 15–24)	72	80	70	76
Children in employment (% of children ages 7–14)	..	..	34.5	49.0
Unemployment rate (% of labor force ages 15+)	..	..	1.7	2.9
Long-term unemployment rate (% total unemployment)	..	..	..	..
Youth unemployment rate (% of labor force ages 15–24)	..	..	3	5
Account at a formal financial institution (% age 15+)	..	..	11	16
Public life and decision making				
Seats held by women in national parliament (%)	..		16	

Burundi

Sub-Saharan Africa				Low income
Population (millions)				8.6
GNI, Atlas ($ billions)				2.2
GNI per capita, Atlas ($)				250
Population living below $1.25 a day (%)				81.3

	1990		2011	
	Female	Male	Female	Male
Demography				
Sex ratio at birth (boys per girls)	1.03		1.03	
Life expectancy at birth (years)	48	45	52	49
Under-five mortality rate (per 1,000 live births)	175	190	133	145
Female-headed households (%)	..		27	
Education				
Gross primary enrollment ratio (% of relevant age group)	63	78	165	164
Gross secondary enrollment ratio (% of relevant age group)	4	6	24	32
Gross tertiary enrollment ratio (% of relevant age group)	0	1	2	4
Primary completion rate (% of relevant age group)	33	48	62	62
Youth literacy rate (% of population ages 15–24)	48	59	78	78
Health and related services				
Total fertility rate (births per woman)	6.5		4.2	
Adolescent fertility rate (births per 1,000 women ages 15–19)	..		20	
Women first married by age 18 (% of women ages 20–24)	17		20	
Contraceptive prevalence (% of women ages 15–49)	9		22	
Unmet need for contraception (% of women ages 15–49)	..		32	
Pregnant women receiving prenatal care (%)	79		99	
Births attended by skilled health staff (% of total)	19		60	
Maternal mortality ratio (per 100,000 live births)	1,100		800	
Economic structure, participation, and access to resources				
Labor force participation rate (% of population ages 15+)	91	90	84	82
Wage and salaried workers (% of employed ages 15+)	..	..	..	..
Self-employed workers (% of employed ages 15+)	..	..	..	..
Vulnerable employment (% of employed ages 15+)	..	..	..	..
Unpaid family workers (% of employed ages 15+)	..	..	..	..
Employment in agriculture (% of employed ages 15+)	..	..	..	..
Employment in industry (% of employed ages 15+)	..	..	..	..
Employment in service (% of employed ages 15+)	..	..	..	..
Women in wage employment in the nonagricultural sector.(%)	14		..	
Women's share of part-time employment (% of total)	..		..	
Maternity leave (weeks)	12		12	
Maternal leave benefits (% of wages paid)	90		50	
Female legislators, senior officials and managers (% of total)	..		..	
Employment to population ratio, total (% ages 15+)	85	84	79	77
Employment to population ratio, youth (% ages 15–24)	75	70	61	56
Children in employment (% of children ages 7–14)	..	..	32.4	31.3
Unemployment rate (% of labor force ages 15+)	0.3	0.7	..	..
Long-term unemployment rate (% total unemployment)	..	..	..	..
Youth unemployment rate (% of labor force ages 15–24)	0	1	..	..
Account at a formal financial institution (% age 15+)	..	..	6	9
Public life and decision making				
Seats held by women in national parliament (%)	..		31	

Cambodia

East Asia & Pacific			Low income	

Population (millions)			14.3
GNI, Atlas ($ billions)			11.7
GNI per capita, Atlas ($)			820
Population living below $1.25 a day (%)			*18.6*

	1990		2011	
	Female	Male	Female	Male
Demography				
Sex ratio at birth (boys per girls)	1.05		1.05	
Life expectancy at birth (years)	57	54	64	62
Under-five mortality rate (per 1,000 live births)	108	125	37	47
Female-headed households (%)	..		27	
Education				
Gross primary enrollment ratio (% of relevant age group)	*124*	*155*	122	129
Gross secondary enrollment ratio (% of relevant age group)	..	..	45	48
Gross tertiary enrollment ratio (% of relevant age group)	0	2	11	18
Primary completion rate (% of relevant age group)	..	..	90	90
Youth literacy rate (% of population ages 15–24)	..	..	86	88
Health and related services				
Total fertility rate (births per woman)	5.7		2.5	
Adolescent fertility rate (births per 1,000 women ages 15–19)	..		35	
Women first married by age 18 (% of women ages 20–24)	..		18	
Contraceptive prevalence (% of women ages 15–49)	..		51	
Unmet need for contraception (% of women ages 15–49)	..		17	
Pregnant women receiving prenatal care (%)	..		89	
Births attended by skilled health staff (% of total)	..		71	
Maternal mortality ratio (per 100,000 live births)	830		*250*	
Economic structure, participation, and access to resources				
Labor force participation rate (% of population ages 15+)	78	84	79	87
Wage and salaried workers (% of employed ages 15+)	..	..	27	36
Self-employed workers (% of employed ages 15+)	..	..	73	64
Vulnerable employment (% of employed ages 15+)	..	..	73	64
Unpaid family workers (% of employed ages 15+)	..	..	13.9	16.2
Employment in agriculture (% of employed ages 15+)	..	..	57	55
Employment in industry (% of employed ages 15+)	..	..	18	16
Employment in service (% of employed ages 15+)	..	..	26	29
Women in wage employment in the nonagricultural sector (%)	..		..	
Women's share of part-time employment (% of total)	..		..	
Maternity leave (weeks)	12		13	
Maternal leave benefits (% of wages paid)	100		50	
Female legislators, senior officials and managers (% of total)	..		21	
Employment to population ratio, total (% ages 15+)	77	84	78	85
Employment to population ratio, youth (% ages 15–24)	73	68	70	69
Children in employment (% of children ages 7–14)	..	..	33.9	35.0
Unemployment rate (% of labor force ages 15+)	..	..	0.1	0.3
Long-term unemployment rate (% total unemployment)	..	..	..	..
Youth unemployment rate (% of labor force ages 15–24)	..	..	3	4
Account at a formal financial institution (% age 15+)	..	..	4	4
Public life and decision making				
Seats held by women in national parliament (%)	..		20	

Cameroon

Sub-Saharan Africa			Lower middle income	
Population (millions)				20.0
GNI, Atlas ($ billions)				24.1
GNI per capita, Atlas ($)				1,210
Population living below $1.25 a day (%)				9.6

	1990		2011	
	Female	Male	Female	Male
Demography				
Sex ratio at birth (boys per girls)	1.03		1.03	
Life expectancy at birth (years)	55	52	53	51
Under-five mortality rate (per 1,000 live births)	137	154	120	135
Female-headed households (%)	18		..	
Education				
Gross primary enrollment ratio (% of relevant age group)	89	104	111	128
Gross secondary enrollment ratio (% of relevant age group)	20	30	47	56
Gross tertiary enrollment ratio (% of relevant age group)	..	..	11	14
Primary completion rate (% of relevant age group)	52	56	72	84
Youth literacy rate (% of population ages 15–24)	..	..	77	89
Health and related services				
Total fertility rate (births per woman)	5.9		4.4	
Adolescent fertility rate (births per 1,000 women ages 15–19)	..		118	
Women first married by age 18 (% of women ages 20–24)	58		38	
Contraceptive prevalence (% of women ages 15–49)	16		23	
Unmet need for contraception (% of women ages 15–49)	22		3	
Pregnant women receiving prenatal care (%)	79		85	
Births attended by skilled health staff (% of total)	64		64	
Maternal mortality ratio (per 100,000 live births)	670		690	
Economic structure, participation, and access to resources				
Labor force participation rate (% of population ages 15+)	55	80	64	77
Wage and salaried workers (% of employed ages 15+)	..	..	11	29
Self-employed workers (% of employed ages 15+)	..	..	89	71
Vulnerable employment (% of employed ages 15+)	..	..	87	67
Unpaid family workers (% of employed ages 15+)	..	..	37.2	22.3
Employment in agriculture (% of employed ages 15+)	..	..	58	49
Employment in industry (% of employed ages 15+)	..	..	12	13
Employment in service (% of employed ages 15+)	..	..	30	38
Women in wage employment in the nonagricultural sector (%)	..		26	
Women's share of part-time employment (% of total)	..		..	
Maternity leave (weeks)	14		14	
Maternal leave benefits (% of wages paid)	100		100	
Female legislators, senior officials and managers (% of total)	..		..	
Employment to population ratio, total (% ages 15+)	53	74	62	74
Employment to population ratio, youth (% ages 15–24)	36	47	40	46
Children in employment (% of children ages 7–14)	..	..	43.4	43.5
Unemployment rate (% of labor force ages 15+)	..	..	4.5	3.1
Long-term unemployment rate (% total unemployment)	..	..	..	..
Youth unemployment rate (% of labor force ages 15–24)	..	..	..	..
Account at a formal financial institution (% age 15+)	..	..	11	19
Public life and decision making				
Seats held by women in national parliament (%)	14		14	

Canada

High income

Population (millions)	34.5
GNI, Atlas ($ billions)	1,570.9
GNI per capita, Atlas ($)	45,550
Population living below $1.25 a day (%)	..

	1990		2011	
	Female	**Male**	**Female**	**Male**
Demography				
Sex ratio at birth (boys per girls)	1.05		1.06	
Life expectancy at birth (years)	81	74	83	79
Under-five mortality rate (per 1,000 live births)	7	9	5	6
Female-headed households (%)	..		..	
Education				
Gross primary enrollment ratio (% of relevant age group)	103	104	100	100
Gross secondary enrollment ratio (% of relevant age group)	100	99	100	103
Gross tertiary enrollment ratio (% of relevant age group)	100	81	..	..
Primary completion rate (% of relevant age group)	..	..	96	96
Youth literacy rate (% of population ages 15–24)	..	..	..	..
Health and related services				
Total fertility rate (births per woman)	1.8		1.6	
Adolescent fertility rate (births per 1,000 women ages 15–19)	..		12	
Women first married by age 18 (% of women ages 20–24)	..		..	
Contraceptive prevalence (% of women ages 15–49)	..		..	
Unmet need for contraception (% of women ages 15–49)	..		..	
Pregnant women receiving prenatal care (%)	..		100	
Births attended by skilled health staff (% of total)	100		100	
Maternal mortality ratio (per 100,000 live births)	6		12	
Economic structure, participation, and access to resources				
Labor force participation rate (% of population ages 15+)	58	76	62	71
Wage and salaried workers (% of employed ages 15+)	90	82	92	90
Self-employed workers (% of employed ages 15+)	10	18	8	10
Vulnerable employment (% of employed ages 15+)	..	..	..	..
Unpaid family workers (% of employed ages 15+)	0.9	0.2	0.1	0.1
Employment in agriculture (% of employed ages 15+)	2	5	1	3
Employment in industry (% of employed ages 15+)	12	34	10	32
Employment in service (% of employed ages 15+)	86	61	89	65
Women in wage employment in the nonagricultural sector (%)	47		50	
Women's share of part-time employment (% of total)	70		67	
Maternity leave (weeks)	17		17	
Maternal leave benefits (% of wages paid)	57		55	
Female legislators, senior officials and managers (% of total)	34		36	
Employment to population ratio, total (% ages 15+)	52	67	58	66
Employment to population ratio, youth (% ages 15–24)	58	57	57	54
Children in employment (% of children ages 7–14)	..	..	..	..
Unemployment rate (% of labor force ages 15+)	8.1	8.2	7.0	7.8
Long-term unemployment rate (% total unemployment)	6.0	7.9	11.8	13.9
Youth unemployment rate (% of labor force ages 15–24)	11	14	12	16
Account at a formal financial institution (% age 15+)	..	..	97	94
Public life and decision making				
Seats held by women in national parliament (%)	13		25	

Cape Verde

Sub-Saharan Africa			Lower middle income	
Population (thousands)				500.6
GNI, Atlas ($ billions)				1.8
GNI per capita, Atlas ($)				3,540
Population living below $1.25 a day (%)				21.0

	1990		2011	
	Female	Male	Female	Male
Demography				
Sex ratio at birth (boys per girls)	1.03		1.03	
Life expectancy at birth (years)	68	62	78	70
Under-five mortality rate (per 1,000 live births)	54	62	20	23
Female-headed households (%)	..		..	
Education				
Gross primary enrollment ratio (% of relevant age group)	119	123	105	114
Gross secondary enrollment ratio (% of relevant age group)	21	20	97	83
Gross tertiary enrollment ratio (% of relevant age group)	0	0	24	17
Primary completion rate (% of relevant age group)	56	58	96	94
Youth literacy rate (% of population ages 15–24)	86	90	99	97
Health and related services				
Total fertility rate (births per woman)	5.3		2.3	
Adolescent fertility rate (births per 1,000 women ages 15–19)	..		72	
Women first married by age 18 (% of women ages 20–24)	..		..	
Contraceptive prevalence (% of women ages 15–49)	24		..	
Unmet need for contraception (% of women ages 15–49)	..		..	
Pregnant women receiving prenatal care (%)	..		..	
Births attended by skilled health staff (% of total)	..		..	
Maternal mortality ratio (per 100,000 live births)	200		79	
Economic structure, participation, and access to resources				
Labor force participation rate (% of population ages 15+)	42	85	51	83
Wage and salaried workers (% of employed ages 15+)	..	..	..	..
Self-employed workers (% of employed ages 15+)	..	..	..	..
Vulnerable employment (% of employed ages 15+)	..	..	..	..
Unpaid family workers (% of employed ages 15+)	..	..	..	..
Employment in agriculture (% of employed ages 15+)	..	..	..	..
Employment in industry (% of employed ages 15+)	..	..	..	..
Employment in service (% of employed ages 15+)	..	..	..	..
Women in wage employment in the nonagricultural sector (%)	..		..	
Women's share of part-time employment (% of total)	..		..	
Maternity leave (weeks)	..		9	
Maternal leave benefits (% of wages paid)	..		90	
Female legislators, senior officials and managers (% of total)	..		..	
Employment to population ratio, total (% ages 15+)	40	79	48	78
Employment to population ratio, youth (% ages 15–24)	43	71	42	65
Children in employment (% of children ages 7–14)	..	..	..	..
Unemployment rate (% of labor force ages 15+)	22.6	23.3	..	..
Long-term unemployment rate (% total unemployment)	..	..	..	..
Youth unemployment rate (% of labor force ages 15–24)	42	41	..	..
Account at a formal financial institution (% age 15+)	..	..	..	..
Public life and decision making				
Seats held by women in national parliament (%)	12		21	

Cayman Islands

Population (thousands)	56.7
GNI, Atlas ($ millions)	..
GNI per capita, Atlas ($)	..
Population living below $1.25 a day (%)	..

	1990		2011	
	Female	Male	Female	Male
Demography				
Sex ratio at birth (boys per girls)	..		..	
Life expectancy at birth (years)	..	..	..	..
Under-five mortality rate (per 1,000 live births)	..	..	..	..
Female-headed households (%)	..		..	
Education				
Gross primary enrollment ratio (% of relevant age group)	..	..	..	..
Gross secondary enrollment ratio (% of relevant age group)	..	..	..	..
Gross tertiary enrollment ratio (% of relevant age group)	..	..	..	..
Primary completion rate (% of relevant age group)	..	..	..	..
Youth literacy rate (% of population ages 15–24)	..	..	99	99
Health and related services				
Total fertility rate (births per woman)	..		..	
Adolescent fertility rate (births per 1,000 women ages 15–19)	..		..	
Women first married by age 18 (% of women ages 20–24)	..		..	
Contraceptive prevalence (% of women ages 15–49)	..		..	
Unmet need for contraception (% of women ages 15–49)	..		..	
Pregnant women receiving prenatal care (%)	..		..	
Births attended by skilled health staff (% of total)	..		..	
Maternal mortality ratio (per 100,000 live births)	..		..	
Economic structure, participation, and access to resources				
Labor force participation rate (% of population ages 15+)	..	..	..	..
Wage and salaried workers (% of employed ages 15+)	..	..	95	87
Self-employed workers (% of employed ages 15+)	..	..	5	12
Vulnerable employment (% of employed ages 15+)	..	..	..	..
Unpaid family workers (% of employed ages 15+)	..	..	..	..
Employment in agriculture (% of employed ages 15+)	0	2	1	3
Employment in industry (% of employed ages 15+)	3	34	4	33
Employment in service (% of employed ages 15+)	98	64	94	63
Women in wage employment in the nonagricultural sector (%)	50		51	
Women's share of part-time employment (% of total)	..		..	
Maternity leave (weeks)	..		..	
Maternal leave benefits (% of wages paid)	..		..	
Female legislators, senior officials and managers (% of total)	..		44	
Employment to population ratio, total (% ages 15+)	..	..	..	..
Employment to population ratio, youth (% ages 15–24)	..	..	..	..
Children in employment (% of children ages 7–14)	..	..	..	..
Unemployment rate (% of labor force ages 15+)	12.2	5.3	4.1	3.8
Long-term unemployment rate (% total unemployment)	..	..	..	..
Youth unemployment rate (% of labor force ages 15–24)	..	..	13	14
Account at a formal financial institution (% age 15+)	..	..	..	..
Public life and decision making				
Seats held by women in national parliament (%)	..		..	

Central African Republic

Sub-Saharan Africa	Low income
Population (millions)	4.5
GNI, Atlas ($ billions)	2.1
GNI per capita, Atlas ($)	480
Population living below $1.25 a day (%)	62.8

	1990		2011	
	Female	Male	Female	Male
Demography				
Sex ratio at birth (boys per girls)	1.03		1.03	
Life expectancy at birth (years)	51	47	50	47
Under-five mortality rate (per 1,000 live births)	163	175	157	170
Female-headed households (%)	..		..	
Education				
Gross primary enrollment ratio (% of relevant age group)	54	86	79	109
Gross secondary enrollment ratio (% of relevant age group)	7	16	13	23
Gross tertiary enrollment ratio (% of relevant age group)	0	2	1	4
Primary completion rate (% of relevant age group)	19	42	33	53
Youth literacy rate (% of population ages 15–24)	35	63	58	72
Health and related services				
Total fertility rate (births per woman)	5.8		4.5	
Adolescent fertility rate (births per 1,000 women ages 15–19)	..		100	
Women first married by age 18 (% of women ages 20–24)	..		68	
Contraceptive prevalence (% of women ages 15–49)	..		15	
Unmet need for contraception (% of women ages 15–49)	..		..	
Pregnant women receiving prenatal care (%)	..		68	
Births attended by skilled health staff (% of total)	..		54	
Maternal mortality ratio (per 100,000 live births)	930		890	
Economic structure, participation, and access to resources				
Labor force participation rate (% of population ages 15+)	69	87	73	85
Wage and salaried workers (% of employed ages 15+)	..	..	..	..
Self-employed workers (% of employed ages 15+)	..	..	..	..
Vulnerable employment (% of employed ages 15+)	..	..	..	..
Unpaid family workers (% of employed ages 15+)	..	..	..	..
Employment in agriculture (% of employed ages 15+)	..	..	..	..
Employment in industry (% of employed ages 15+)	..	..	..	..
Employment in service (% of employed ages 15+)	..	..	..	..
Women in wage employment in the nonagricultural sector (%)	..		..	
Women's share of part-time employment (% of total)	..		..	
Maternity leave (weeks)	14		14	
Maternal leave benefits (% of wages paid)	50		50	
Female legislators, senior officials and managers (% of total)	..		..	
Employment to population ratio, total (% ages 15+)	65	81	68	80
Employment to population ratio, youth (% ages 15–24)	52	64	51	61
Children in employment (% of children ages 7–14)	..	..	..	..
Unemployment rate (% of labor force ages 15+)	..	..	..	..
Long-term unemployment rate (% total unemployment)	..	..	..	..
Youth unemployment rate (% of labor force ages 15–24)	..	..	..	..
Account at a formal financial institution (% age 15+)	..	..	3	3
Public life and decision making				
Seats held by women in national parliament (%)	4		13	

Chad

Sub-Saharan Africa			Low income	

Population (millions)				11.5
GNI, Atlas ($ billions)				8.3
GNI per capita, Atlas ($)				720
Population living below $1.25 a day (%)				*61.9*

	1990		2011	
	Female	Male	Female	Male
Demography				
Sex ratio at birth (boys per girls)	1.03		1.03	
Life expectancy at birth (years)	52	49	51	48
Under-five mortality rate (per 1,000 live births)	198	219	160	177
Female-headed households (%)	..		..	
Education				
Gross primary enrollment ratio (% of relevant age group)	30	69	86	115
Gross secondary enrollment ratio (% of relevant age group)	2	11	15	35
Gross tertiary enrollment ratio (% of relevant age group)	..	..	1	4
Primary completion rate (% of relevant age group)	6	27	29	47
Youth literacy rate (% of population ages 15–24)	*9*	*26*	*41*	*53*
Health and related services				
Total fertility rate (births per woman)	6.7		5.9	
Adolescent fertility rate (births per 1,000 women ages 15–19)	..		143	
Women first married by age 18 (% of women ages 20–24)	..		*68*	
Contraceptive prevalence (% of women ages 15–49)	..		5	
Unmet need for contraception (% of women ages 15–49)	..		..	
Pregnant women receiving prenatal care (%)	..		53	
Births attended by skilled health staff (% of total)	..		23	
Maternal mortality ratio (per 100,000 live births)	920		*1,100*	
Economic structure, participation, and access to resources				
Labor force participation rate (% of population ages 15+)	64	81	64	80
Wage and salaried workers (% of employed ages 15+)	*1*	*9*	..	..
Self-employed workers (% of employed ages 15+)	*98*	*90*	..	..
Vulnerable employment (% of employed ages 15+)	*98*	*90*	..	..
Unpaid family workers (% of employed ages 15+)	*44.4*	*13.2*	..	..
Employment in agriculture (% of employed ages 15+)	86	80	..	..
Employment in industry (% of employed ages 15+)	1	3	..	..
Employment in service (% of employed ages 15+)	13	16	..	..
Women in wage employment in the nonagricultural sector (%)	4		..	
Women's share of part-time employment (% of total)	..		..	
Maternity leave (weeks)	14		*14*	
Maternal leave benefits (% of wages paid)	50		*50*	
Female legislators, senior officials and managers (% of total)	..		..	
Employment to population ratio, total (% ages 15+)	60	76	60	75
Employment to population ratio, youth (% ages 15–24)	*51*	*51*	*50*	*51*
Children in employment (% of children ages 7–14)	..	..	..	..
Unemployment rate (% of labor force ages 15+)	*0.3*	*1.1*	..	..
Long-term unemployment rate (% total unemployment)	..	..	..	..
Youth unemployment rate (% of labor force ages 15–24)	..	..	..	..
Account at a formal financial institution (% age 15+)	..	..	7	11
Public life and decision making				
Seats held by women in national parliament (%)	..		15	

Channel Islands

Population (thousands)		153.9
GNI, Atlas ($ billions)		..
GNI per capita, Atlas ($)		..
Population living below $1.25 a day (%)		..

	1990		2011	
	Female	Male	Female	Male
Demography				
Sex ratio at birth (boys per girls)	1.06		1.06	
Life expectancy at birth (years)	78	73	82	78
Under-five mortality rate (per 1,000 live births)	..	..	..	..
Female-headed households (%)	..		..	
Education				
Gross primary enrollment ratio (% of relevant age group)	..	..	..	..
Gross secondary enrollment ratio (% of relevant age group)	..	..	..	..
Gross tertiary enrollment ratio (% of relevant age group)	..	..	..	..
Primary completion rate (% of relevant age group)	..	..	..	..
Youth literacy rate (% of population ages 15–24)	..	..	..	..
Health and related services				
Total fertility rate (births per woman)	1.5		1.5	
Adolescent fertility rate (births per 1,000 women ages 15–19)	..		9	
Women first married by age 18 (% of women ages 20–24)	..		..	
Contraceptive prevalence (% of women ages 15–49)	..		..	
Unmet need for contraception (% of women ages 15–49)	..		..	
Pregnant women receiving prenatal care (%)	..		..	
Births attended by skilled health staff (% of total)	..		..	
Maternal mortality ratio (per 100,000 live births)	..		..	
Economic structure, participation, and access to resources				
Labor force participation rate (% of population ages 15+)	..	..	..	..
Wage and salaried workers (% of employed ages 15+)	..	..	..	..
Self-employed workers (% of employed ages 15+)	..	..	..	..
Vulnerable employment (% of employed ages 15+)	..	..	..	..
Unpaid family workers (% of employed ages 15+)	..	..	..	..
Employment in agriculture (% of employed ages 15+)	..	..	..	..
Employment in industry (% of employed ages 15+)	..	..	..	..
Employment in service (% of employed ages 15+)	..	..	..	..
Women in wage employment in the nonagricultural sector (%)	..		..	
Women's share of part-time employment (% of total)	..		..	
Maternity leave (weeks)	..		18	
Maternal leave benefits (% of wages paid)	..		..	
Female legislators, senior officials and managers (% of total)	..		..	
Employment to population ratio, total (% ages 15+)	..	..	..	..
Employment to population ratio, youth (% ages 15–24)	..	..	..	..
Children in employment (% of children ages 7–14)	..	..	..	..
Unemployment rate (% of labor force ages 15+)	..	..	..	..
Long-term unemployment rate (% total unemployment)	..	..	..	..
Youth unemployment rate (% of labor force ages 15–24)	..	..	..	..
Account at a formal financial institution (% age 15+)	..	..	..	..
Public life and decision making				
Seats held by women in national parliament (%)	..		..	

Chile

Latin America & the Caribbean	Upper middle income
Population (millions)	17.3
GNI, Atlas ($ billions)	212.0
GNI per capita, Atlas ($)	12,280
Population living below $1.25 a day (%)	<2

	1990		2011	
	Female	Male	Female	Male
Demography				
Sex ratio at birth (boys per girls)	1.04		1.04	
Life expectancy at birth (years)	77	71	82	76
Under-five mortality rate (per 1,000 live births)	17	21	8	10
Female-headed households (%)	..		..	
Education				
Gross primary enrollment ratio (% of relevant age group)	104	106	101	104
Gross secondary enrollment ratio (% of relevant age group)	80	76	91	88
Gross tertiary enrollment ratio (% of relevant age group)	24	28	68	64
Primary completion rate (% of relevant age group)	..	..	99	99
Youth literacy rate (% of population ages 15–24)	99	98	99	99
Health and related services				
Total fertility rate (births per woman)	2.6		1.8	
Adolescent fertility rate (births per 1,000 women ages 15–19)	..		56	
Women first married by age 18 (% of women ages 20–24)	..		..	
Contraceptive prevalence (% of women ages 15–49)	56		58	
Unmet need for contraception (% of women ages 15–49)	..		..	
Pregnant women receiving prenatal care (%)	95		..	
Births attended by skilled health staff (% of total)	99		100	
Maternal mortality ratio (per 100,000 live births)	56		25	
Economic structure, participation, and access to resources				
Labor force participation rate (% of population ages 15+)	32	77	47	74
Wage and salaried workers (% of employed ages 15+)	77	71	62	73
Self-employed workers (% of employed ages 15+)	20	28	26	27
Vulnerable employment (% of employed ages 15+)	..	..	24	25
Unpaid family workers (% of employed ages 15+)	..	..	2.2	0.9
Employment in agriculture (% of employed ages 15+)	6	25	5	14
Employment in industry (% of employed ages 15+)	14	30	10	31
Employment in service (% of employed ages 15+)	80	44	85	55
Women in wage employment in the nonagricultural sector (%)	37		38	
Women's share of part-time employment (% of total)	50		59	
Maternity leave (weeks)	18		18	
Maternal leave benefits (% of wages paid)	100		100	
Female legislators, senior officials and managers (% of total)	..		..	
Employment to population ratio, total (% ages 15+)	29	71	43	70
Employment to population ratio, youth (% ages 15–24)	19	43	25	38
Children in employment (% of children ages 7–14)	..	..	..	..
Unemployment rate (% of labor force ages 15+)	5.7	5.7	8.7	6.1
Long-term unemployment rate (% total unemployment)	27.2	14.7	..	..
Youth unemployment rate (% of labor force ages 15–24)	12	13	21	15
Account at a formal financial institution (% age 15+)	..	..	41	43
Public life and decision making				
Seats held by women in national parliament (%)	..		14	

China

East Asia & Pacific	Upper middle income
Population (millions)	1,344.1
GNI, Atlas ($ billions)	6,643.2
GNI per capita, Atlas ($)	4,940
Population living below $1.25 a day (%)	*11.8*

	1990		2011	
	Female	Male	Female	Male
Demography				
Sex ratio at birth (boys per girls)	1.13		1.18	
Life expectancy at birth (years)[b]	71	68	75	72
Under-five mortality rate (per 1,000 live births)	48	50	14	15
Female-headed households (%)	..		..	
Education				
Gross primary enrollment ratio (% of relevant age group)	126	139	115	111
Gross secondary enrollment ratio (% of relevant age group)	32	43	83	80
Gross tertiary enrollment ratio (% of relevant age group)	3	5	28	25
Primary completion rate (% of relevant age group)	..	..	..	..
Youth literacy rate (% of population ages 15–24)	91	97	99	99
Health and related services				
Total fertility rate (births per woman)	2.3		1.6	
Adolescent fertility rate (births per 1,000 women ages 15–19)	..		9	
Women first married by age 18 (% of women ages 20–24)	..		..	
Contraceptive prevalence (% of women ages 15–49)	85		85	
Unmet need for contraception (% of women ages 15–49)	..		..	
Pregnant women receiving prenatal care (%)	70		94	
Births attended by skilled health staff (% of total)	94		*100*	
Maternal mortality ratio (per 100,000 live births)	120		37	
Economic structure, participation, and access to resources				
Labor force participation rate (% of population ages 15+)	72	85	68	80
Wage and salaried workers (% of employed ages 15+)	..	..	..	..
Self-employed workers (% of employed ages 15+)	..	..	..	..
Vulnerable employment (% of employed ages 15+)	..	..	..	..
Unpaid family workers (% of employed ages 15+)	..	..	..	..
Employment in agriculture (% of employed ages 15+)	..	..	..	..
Employment in industry (% of employed ages 15+)	..	..	..	..
Employment in service (% of employed ages 15+)	..	..	..	..
Women in wage employment in the nonagricultural sector (%)	38		..	
Women's share of part-time employment (% of total)	..		..	
Maternity leave (weeks)	8		*13*	
Maternal leave benefits (% of wages paid)	100		*100*	
Female legislators, senior officials and managers (% of total)	..		..	
Employment to population ratio, total (% ages 15+)	70	80	65	76
Employment to population ratio, youth (% ages 15–24)	74	69	59	54
Children in employment (% of children ages 7–14)	..	..	..	..
Unemployment rate (% of labor force ages 15+)	..	..	..	..
Long-term unemployment rate (% total unemployment)	..	..	..	..
Youth unemployment rate (% of labor force ages 15–24)	..	..	..	..
Account at a formal financial institution (% age 15+)	..	..	60	68
Public life and decision making				
Seats held by women in national parliament (%)	21		21	

Colombia

Latin America & the Caribbean			Upper middle income	
Population (millions)				46.9
GNI, Atlas ($ billions)				284.9
GNI per capita, Atlas ($)				6,070
Population living below $1.25 a day (%)				8.2

	1990		2011	
	Female	Male	Female	Male
Demography				
Sex ratio at birth (boys per girls)	1.05		1.05	
Life expectancy at birth (years)	72	64	77	70
Under-five mortality rate (per 1,000 live births)	31	38	16	20
Female-headed households (%)	23		34	
Education				
Gross primary enrollment ratio (% of relevant age group)	113	99	110	114
Gross secondary enrollment ratio (% of relevant age group)	57	48	102	93
Gross tertiary enrollment ratio (% of relevant age group)	16	15	45	41
Primary completion rate (% of relevant age group)	86	63	111	112
Youth literacy rate (% of population ages 15–24)	92	89	99	98
Health and related services				
Total fertility rate (births per woman)	3.1		2.1	
Adolescent fertility rate (births per 1,000 women ages 15–19)	..		69	
Women first married by age 18 (% of women ages 20–24)	22		23	
Contraceptive prevalence (% of women ages 15–49)	66		79	
Unmet need for contraception (% of women ages 15–49)	11		7	
Pregnant women receiving prenatal care (%)	83		97	
Births attended by skilled health staff (% of total)	94		99	
Maternal mortality ratio (per 100,000 live births)	170		92	
Economic structure, participation, and access to resources				
Labor force participation rate (% of population ages 15+)	32	77	56	80
Wage and salaried workers (% of employed ages 15+)	72	65	48	45
Self-employed workers (% of employed ages 15+)	28	35	52	55
Vulnerable employment (% of employed ages 15+)	26	30	49	48
Unpaid family workers (% of employed ages 15+)	2.4	0.8	7.1	3.7
Employment in agriculture (% of employed ages 15+)	1	2	5	26
Employment in industry (% of employed ages 15+)	25	35	16	23
Employment in service (% of employed ages 15+)	74	63	79	51
Women in wage employment in the nonagricultural sector (%)	42		46	
Women's share of part-time employment (% of total)	..		60	
Maternity leave (weeks)	12		12	
Maternal leave benefits (% of wages paid)	100		100	
Female legislators, senior officials and managers (% of total)	..		..	
Employment to population ratio, total (% ages 15+)	25	69	48	73
Employment to population ratio, youth (% ages 15–24)	18	51	28	44
Children in employment (% of children ages 7–14)	..	..	4.4	8.3
Unemployment rate (% of labor force ages 15+)	13.2	8.1	15.0	9.1
Long-term unemployment rate (% total unemployment)	..	..	..	..
Youth unemployment rate (% of labor force ages 15–24)	25	15	30	18
Account at a formal financial institution (% age 15+)	..	..	25	36
Public life and decision making				
Seats held by women in national parliament (%)	5		12	

Comoros

Sub-Saharan Africa			Low income	
Population (thousands)				753.9
GNI, Atlas ($ millions)				581.0
GNI per capita, Atlas ($)				770
Population living below $1.25 a day (%)				46.1

	1990		2011	
	Female	Male	Female	Male
Demography				
Sex ratio at birth (boys per girls)	1.05		1.05	
Life expectancy at birth (years)	58	54	62	60
Under-five mortality rate (per 1,000 live births)	113	130	74	85
Female-headed households (%)	..		..	
Education				
Gross primary enrollment ratio (% of relevant age group)	71	101	90	106
Gross secondary enrollment ratio (% of relevant age group)	28	41	..	..
Gross tertiary enrollment ratio (% of relevant age group)	0	1	9	10
Primary completion rate (% of relevant age group)	37	43	65	84
Youth literacy rate (% of population ages 15–24)	..	..	85	86
Health and related services				
Total fertility rate (births per woman)	5.6		4.9	
Adolescent fertility rate (births per 1,000 women ages 15–19)	..		52	
Women first married by age 18 (% of women ages 20–24)	..		..	
Contraceptive prevalence (% of women ages 15–49)	..		..	
Unmet need for contraception (% of women ages 15–49)	..		..	
Pregnant women receiving prenatal care (%)	..		..	
Births attended by skilled health staff (% of total)	..		..	
Maternal mortality ratio (per 100,000 live births)	440		280	
Economic structure, participation, and access to resources				
Labor force participation rate (% of population ages 15+)	27	80	35	80
Wage and salaried workers (% of employed ages 15+)	..	..	..	..
Self-employed workers (% of employed ages 15+)	..	..	..	..
Vulnerable employment (% of employed ages 15+)	..	..	..	..
Unpaid family workers (% of employed ages 15+)	..	..	..	..
Employment in agriculture (% of employed ages 15+)	..	..	..	..
Employment in industry (% of employed ages 15+)	..	..	..	..
Employment in service (% of employed ages 15+)	..	..	..	..
Women in wage employment in the nonagricultural sector (%)	..			
Women's share of part-time employment (% of total)	..			
Maternity leave (weeks)	14		14	
Maternal leave benefits (% of wages paid)	100		100	
Female legislators, senior officials and managers (% of total)	..		..	
Employment to population ratio, total (% ages 15+)	26	75	33	75
Employment to population ratio, youth (% ages 15–24)	21	51	22	48
Children in employment (% of children ages 7–14)	..	..	..	..
Unemployment rate (% of labor force ages 15+)	16.9	21.3	..	..
Long-term unemployment rate (% total unemployment)	..	..	..	..
Youth unemployment rate (% of labor force ages 15–24)	..	..	..	..
Account at a formal financial institution (% age 15+)	..	..	18	26
Public life and decision making				
Seats held by women in national parliament (%)	0		3	

Congo, Dem. Rep.

Sub-Saharan Africa			Low income	
Population (millions)				67.8
GNI, Atlas ($ billions)				13.1
GNI per capita, Atlas ($)				190
Population living below $1.25 a day (%)				87.7

	1990		2011	
	Female	Male	Female	Male
Demography				
Sex ratio at birth (boys per girls)	1.03		1.03	
Life expectancy at birth (years)	48	45	50	47
Under-five mortality rate (per 1,000 live births)	171	192	158	178
Female-headed households (%)	..		21	
Education				
Gross primary enrollment ratio (% of relevant age group)	48	67	89	103
Gross secondary enrollment ratio (% of relevant age group)	14	29	29	50
Gross tertiary enrollment ratio (% of relevant age group)	..	..	3	9
Primary completion rate (% of relevant age group)	37	62	50	67
Youth literacy rate (% of population ages 15–24)	..	..	62	68
Health and related services				
Total fertility rate (births per woman)	7.1		5.7	
Adolescent fertility rate (births per 1,000 women ages 15–19)	..		177	
Women first married by age 18 (% of women ages 20–24)	..		39	
Contraceptive prevalence (% of women ages 15–49)	8		17	
Unmet need for contraception (% of women ages 15–49)	..		24	
Pregnant women receiving prenatal care (%)	..		89	
Births attended by skilled health staff (% of total)	..		80	
Maternal mortality ratio (per 100,000 live births)	930		540	
Economic structure, participation, and access to resources				
Labor force participation rate (% of population ages 15+)	67	75	70	73
Wage and salaried workers (% of employed ages 15+)	..	..	..	..
Self-employed workers (% of employed ages 15+)	..	..	..	..
Vulnerable employment (% of employed ages 15+)	..	..	..	..
Unpaid family workers (% of employed ages 15+)	..	..	..	..
Employment in agriculture (% of employed ages 15+)	..	..	..	..
Employment in industry (% of employed ages 15+)	..	..	..	..
Employment in service (% of employed ages 15+)	..	..	..	..
Women in wage employment in the nonagricultural sector (%)	26		..	
Women's share of part-time employment (% of total)	..		..	
Maternity leave (weeks)	14		14	
Maternal leave benefits (% of wages paid)	67		67	
Female legislators, senior officials and managers (% of total)	..		..	
Employment to population ratio, total (% ages 15+)	64	70	66	68
Employment to population ratio, youth (% ages 15–24)	45	37	44	38
Children in employment (% of children ages 7–14)	..	..	21.4	19.5
Unemployment rate (% of labor force ages 15+)	..	..	..	..
Long-term unemployment rate (% total unemployment)	..	..	..	..
Youth unemployment rate (% of labor force ages 15–24)	..	..	..	..
Account at a formal financial institution (% age 15+)	..	..	3	5
Public life and decision making				
Seats held by women in national parliament (%)	5		9	

Congo, Rep.

Sub-Saharan Africa			Lower middle income	
Population (millions)				4.1
GNI, Atlas ($ billions)				9.3
GNI per capita, Atlas ($)				2,250
Population living below $1.25 a day (%)				*54.1*

	1990		2011	
	Female	Male	Female	Male
Demography				
Sex ratio at birth (boys per girls)	1.03		1.03	
Life expectancy at birth (years)	58	55	59	56
Under-five mortality rate (per 1,000 live births)	113	124	94	103
Female-headed households (%)	..		..	
Education				
Gross primary enrollment ratio (% of relevant age group)	122	130	113	119
Gross secondary enrollment ratio (% of relevant age group)	42	55	..	..
Gross tertiary enrollment ratio (% of relevant age group)	2	8	7	11
Primary completion rate (% of relevant age group)	60	61	69	73
Youth literacy rate (% of population ages 15–24)	..	..	..	..
Health and related services				
Total fertility rate (births per woman)	5.4		4.5	
Adolescent fertility rate (births per 1,000 women ages 15–19)	..		114	
Women first married by age 18 (% of women ages 20–24)	..		*33*	
Contraceptive prevalence (% of women ages 15–49)	..		..	
Unmet need for contraception (% of women ages 15–49)	..		..	
Pregnant women receiving prenatal care (%)	..		..	
Births attended by skilled health staff (% of total)	..		..	
Maternal mortality ratio (per 100,000 live births)	420		*560*	
Economic structure, participation, and access to resources				
Labor force participation rate (% of population ages 15+)	60	73	68	73
Wage and salaried workers (% of employed ages 15+)	..	..	..	..
Self-employed workers (% of employed ages 15+)	..	..	..	..
Vulnerable employment (% of employed ages 15+)	..	..	..	..
Unpaid family workers (% of employed ages 15+)	..	..	..	..
Employment in agriculture (% of employed ages 15+)	..	..	..	..
Employment in industry (% of employed ages 15+)	..	..	..	..
Employment in service (% of employed ages 15+)	..	..	..	..
Women in wage employment in the nonagricultural sector (%)	26		..	
Women's share of part-time employment (% of total)	..		..	
Maternity leave (weeks)	15		*15*	
Maternal leave benefits (% of wages paid)	100		*100*	
Female legislators, senior officials and managers (% of total)	..		..	
Employment to population ratio, total (% ages 15+)	57	68	64	68
Employment to population ratio, youth (% ages 15–24)	*40*	*42*	*40*	*41*
Children in employment (% of children ages 7–14)	..	..	..	..
Unemployment rate (% of labor force ages 15+)	..	..	..	..
Long-term unemployment rate (% total unemployment)	..	..	..	..
Youth unemployment rate (% of labor force ages 15–24)	..	..	..	..
Account at a formal financial institution (% age 15+)	..	..	7	11
Public life and decision making				
Seats held by women in national parliament (%)	14		7	

Costa Rica

Latin America & the Caribbean	Upper middle income
Population (millions)	4.7
GNI, Atlas ($ billions)	36.1
GNI per capita, Atlas ($)	7,640
Population living below $1.25 a day (%)	*3.1*

	1990		2011	
	Female	Male	Female	Male
Demography				
Sex ratio at birth (boys per girls)	1.05		1.05	
Life expectancy at birth (years)	78	73	82	77
Under-five mortality rate (per 1,000 live births)	15	19	9	11
Female-headed households (%)	..		..	
Education				
Gross primary enrollment ratio (% of relevant age group)	102	103	107	108
Gross secondary enrollment ratio (% of relevant age group)	45	42	104	99
Gross tertiary enrollment ratio (% of relevant age group)	..	..	49	38
Primary completion rate (% of relevant age group)	*81*	*78*	101	97
Youth literacy rate (% of population ages 15–24)	..	..	99	98
Health and related services				
Total fertility rate (births per woman)	3.2		1.8	
Adolescent fertility rate (births per 1,000 women ages 15–19)	..		63	
Women first married by age 18 (% of women ages 20–24)	..		..	
Contraceptive prevalence (% of women ages 15–49)	75		82	
Unmet need for contraception (% of women ages 15–49)	..		..	
Pregnant women receiving prenatal care (%)	*95*		*90*	
Births attended by skilled health staff (% of total)	*98*		*99*	
Maternal mortality ratio (per 100,000 live births)	38		*40*	
Economic structure, participation, and access to resources				
Labor force participation rate (% of population ages 15+)	33	84	46	79
Wage and salaried workers (% of employed ages 15+)	78	67	79	74
Self-employed workers (% of employed ages 15+)	22	33	21	26
Vulnerable employment (% of employed ages 15+)	21	26	19	21
Unpaid family workers (% of employed ages 15+)	6.3	4.7	1.7	1.0
Employment in agriculture (% of employed ages 15+)	6	34	4	20
Employment in industry (% of employed ages 15+)	24	27	11	25
Employment in service (% of employed ages 15+)	69	39	84	55
Women in wage employment in the nonagricultural sector (%)	37		43	
Women's share of part-time employment (% of total)	53		60	
Maternity leave (weeks)	17		17	
Maternal leave benefits (% of wages paid)	100		*100*	
Female legislators, senior officials and managers (% of total)	..		35	
Employment to population ratio, total (% ages 15+)	*31*	*79*	44	76
Employment to population ratio, youth (% ages 15–24)	*31*	*65*	32	52
Children in employment (% of children ages 7–14)	..		1.6	3.4
Unemployment rate (% of labor force ages 15+)	5.9	4.1	10.3	6.0
Long-term unemployment rate (% total unemployment)	13.9	8.4	..	..
Youth unemployment rate (% of labor force ages 15–24)	10	8	22	14
Account at a formal financial institution (% age 15+)	..	..	41	60
Public life and decision making				
Seats held by women in national parliament (%)	11		39	

Côte d'Ivoire

Sub-Saharan Africa	Lower middle income
Population (millions)	20.2
GNI, Atlas ($ billions)	22.1
GNI per capita, Atlas ($)	1,090
Population living below $1.25 a day (%)	23.8

	1990		2011	
	Female	Male	Female	Male
Demography				
Sex ratio at birth (boys per girls)	1.02		1.02	
Life expectancy at birth (years)	54	51	57	54
Under-five mortality rate (per 1,000 live births)	138	164	105	125
Female-headed households (%)	15		..	
Education				
Gross primary enrollment ratio (% of relevant age group)	56	79	80	96
Gross secondary enrollment ratio (% of relevant age group)	..	..	..	..
Gross tertiary enrollment ratio (% of relevant age group)	1	4	6	11
Primary completion rate (% of relevant age group)	30	50	52	65
Youth literacy rate (% of population ages 15–24)	38	60	62	72
Health and related services				
Total fertility rate (births per woman)	6.3		4.3	
Adolescent fertility rate (births per 1,000 women ages 15–19)	..		110	
Women first married by age 18 (% of women ages 20–24)	44		..	
Contraceptive prevalence (% of women ages 15–49)	11		13	
Unmet need for contraception (% of women ages 15–49)	27		29	
Pregnant women receiving prenatal care (%)	83		85	
Births attended by skilled health staff (% of total)	45		57	
Maternal mortality ratio (per 100,000 live births)	710		400	
Economic structure, participation, and access to resources				
Labor force participation rate (% of population ages 15+)	43	88	52	81
Wage and salaried workers (% of employed ages 15+)	..	..	..	..
Self-employed workers (% of employed ages 15+)	..	..	..	..
Vulnerable employment (% of employed ages 15+)	..	..	..	..
Unpaid family workers (% of employed ages 15+)	..	..	..	..
Employment in agriculture (% of employed ages 15+)	..	..	..	..
Employment in industry (% of employed ages 15+)	..	..	..	..
Employment in service (% of employed ages 15+)	..	..	..	..
Women in wage employment in the nonagricultural sector (%)	..		..	
Women's share of part-time employment (% of total)	..		..	
Maternity leave (weeks)	14		14	
Maternal leave benefits (% of wages paid)	100		100	
Female legislators, senior officials and managers (% of total)	..		..	
Employment to population ratio, total (% ages 15+)	42	82	50	77
Employment to population ratio, youth (% ages 15–24)	35	64	39	57
Children in employment (% of children ages 7–14)	..	..	43.6	47.7
Unemployment rate (% of labor force ages 15+)	..	..	..	..
Long-term unemployment rate (% total unemployment)	..	..	..	..
Youth unemployment rate (% of labor force ages 15–24)	..	..	..	..
Account at a formal financial institution (% age 15+)	..	..	..	..
Public life and decision making				
Seats held by women in national parliament (%)	6		10	

Croatia

High income

Population (millions)	4.4
GNI, Atlas ($ billions)	59.6
GNI per capita, Atlas ($)	13,540
Population living below $1.25 a day (%)	<2

	1990		2011	
	Female	Male	Female	Male
Demography				
Sex ratio at birth (boys per girls)	1.06		1.06	
Life expectancy at birth (years)	76	69	80	74
Under-five mortality rate (per 1,000 live births)	11	14	5	6
Female-headed households (%)	..		24	
Education				
Gross primary enrollment ratio (% of relevant age group)	81	81	93	93
Gross secondary enrollment ratio (% of relevant age group)	84	81	99	93
Gross tertiary enrollment ratio (% of relevant age group)	25	26	62	46
Primary completion rate (% of relevant age group)	..	..	93	93
Youth literacy rate (% of population ages 15–24)	100	100	100	100
Health and related services				
Total fertility rate (births per woman)	1.6		1.5	
Adolescent fertility rate (births per 1,000 women ages 15–19)	..		13	
Women first married by age 18 (% of women ages 20–24)	..		..	
Contraceptive prevalence (% of women ages 15–49)	..		..	
Unmet need for contraception (% of women ages 15–49)	..		..	
Pregnant women receiving prenatal care (%)	..		100	
Births attended by skilled health staff (% of total)	100		100	
Maternal mortality ratio (per 100,000 live births)	8		17	
Economic structure, participation, and access to resources				
Labor force participation rate (% of population ages 15+)	47	69	46	60
Wage and salaried workers (% of employed ages 15+)	..	..	78	77
Self-employed workers (% of employed ages 15+)	..	..	22	23
Vulnerable employment (% of employed ages 15+)	..	..	19	17
Unpaid family workers (% of employed ages 15+)	..	..	5.5	1.2
Employment in agriculture (% of employed ages 15+)	..	..	16	15
Employment in industry (% of employed ages 15+)	..	..	16	37
Employment in service (% of employed ages 15+)	..	..	67	48
Women in wage employment in the nonagricultural sector (%)	43		47	
Women's share of part-time employment (% of total)	..		58	
Maternity leave (weeks)	..		52	
Maternal leave benefits (% of wages paid)	..		100	
Female legislators, senior officials and managers (% of total)	..		25	
Employment to population ratio, total (% ages 15+)	41	62	40	52
Employment to population ratio, youth (% ages 15–24)	25	29	20	27
Children in employment (% of children ages 7–14)	..	..	..	..
Unemployment rate (% of labor force ages 15+)	11.2	11.1	13.2	13.7
Long-term unemployment rate (% total unemployment)	..	..	65.2	62.7
Youth unemployment rate (% of labor force ages 15–24)	39	42	37	36
Account at a formal financial institution (% age 15+)	..	..	87	90
Public life and decision making				
Seats held by women in national parliament (%)	..		24	

Cuba

Latin America & the Caribbean	Upper middle income
Population (millions)	11.3
GNI, Atlas ($ billions)	61.5
GNI per capita, Atlas ($)	5,460
Population living below $1.25 a day (%)	..

	1990		2011	
	Female	Male	Female	Male
Demography				
Sex ratio at birth (boys per girls)	1.06		1.06	
Life expectancy at birth (years)	76	73	81	77
Under-five mortality rate (per 1,000 live births)	12	15	5	6
Female-headed households (%)	..		46	
Education				
Gross primary enrollment ratio (% of relevant age group)	98	102	100	102
Gross secondary enrollment ratio (% of relevant age group)	95	84	90	91
Gross tertiary enrollment ratio (% of relevant age group)	25	18	101	61
Primary completion rate (% of relevant age group)	..	..	99	98
Youth literacy rate (% of population ages 15–24)	..	..	100	100
Health and related services				
Total fertility rate (births per woman)	1.8		1.5	
Adolescent fertility rate (births per 1,000 women ages 15–19)	..		44	
Women first married by age 18 (% of women ages 20–24)	..		40	
Contraceptive prevalence (% of women ages 15–49)	70		74	
Unmet need for contraception (% of women ages 15–49)	..		8	
Pregnant women receiving prenatal care (%)	..		100	
Births attended by skilled health staff (% of total)	100		100	
Maternal mortality ratio (per 100,000 live births)	63		73	
Economic structure, participation, and access to resources				
Labor force participation rate (% of population ages 15+)	35	72	43	70
Wage and salaried workers (% of employed ages 15+)	..	..	94	78
Self-employed workers (% of employed ages 15+)	..	..	6	23
Vulnerable employment (% of employed ages 15+)	..	..	..	..
Unpaid family workers (% of employed ages 15+)	..	..	..	..
Employment in agriculture (% of employed ages 15+)	..	..	8	25
Employment in industry (% of employed ages 15+)	..	..	12	20
Employment in service (% of employed ages 15+)	..	..	80	55
Women in wage employment in the nonagricultural sector (%)	..		45	
Women's share of part-time employment (% of total)	..		..	
Maternity leave (weeks)	18		18	
Maternal leave benefits (% of wages paid)	100		100	
Female legislators, senior officials and managers (% of total)	..		..	
Employment to population ratio, total (% ages 15+)	35	71	42	69
Employment to population ratio, youth (% ages 15–24)	28	53	35	45
Children in employment (% of children ages 7–14)	..	..	..	..
Unemployment rate (% of labor force ages 15+)	..	..	2.7	2.4
Long-term unemployment rate (% total unemployment)	..	..	..	..
Youth unemployment rate (% of labor force ages 15–24)	..	..	4	3
Account at a formal financial institution (% age 15+)	..	..	..	..
Public life and decision making				
Seats held by women in national parliament (%)	34		45	

Curaçao

High income

Population (thousands)	145.6
GNI, Atlas ($ millions)	..
GNI per capita, Atlas ($)	..
Population living below $1.25 a day (%)	..

	1990		2011	
	Female	Male	Female	Male
Demography				
Sex ratio at birth (boys per girls)	..		..	
Life expectancy at birth (years)	..	..	80	72
Under-five mortality rate (per 1,000 live births)	..	..	..	..
Female-headed households (%)	..		..	
Education				
Gross primary enrollment ratio (% of relevant age group)	..	..	..	..
Gross secondary enrollment ratio (% of relevant age group)	..	..	..	..
Gross tertiary enrollment ratio (% of relevant age group)	..	..	..	..
Primary completion rate (% of relevant age group)	..	..	..	..
Youth literacy rate (% of population ages 15–24)	..	..	..	..
Health and related services				
Total fertility rate (births per woman)	..		2.2	
Adolescent fertility rate (births per 1,000 women ages 15–19)	..		..	
Women first married by age 18 (% of women ages 20–24)	..		..	
Contraceptive prevalence (% of women ages 15–49)	..		..	
Unmet need for contraception (% of women ages 15–49)	..		..	
Pregnant women receiving prenatal care (%)	..		..	
Births attended by skilled health staff (% of total)	..		..	
Maternal mortality ratio (per 100,000 live births)	..		..	
Economic structure, participation, and access to resources				
Labor force participation rate (% of population ages 15+)	..	..	..	..
Wage and salaried workers (% of employed ages 15+)	..	..	..	..
Self-employed workers (% of employed ages 15+)	..	..	..	..
Vulnerable employment (% of employed ages 15+)	..	..	..	..
Unpaid family workers (% of employed ages 15+)	..	..	..	..
Employment in agriculture (% of employed ages 15+)	..	..	..	..
Employment in industry (% of employed ages 15+)	..	..	..	..
Employment in service (% of employed ages 15+)	..	..	..	..
Women in wage employment in the nonagricultural sector (%)	..		..	
Women's share of part-time employment (% of total)	..		..	
Maternity leave (weeks)	..		..	
Maternal leave benefits (% of wages paid)	..		..	
Female legislators, senior officials and managers (% of total)	..		..	
Employment to population ratio, total (% ages 15+)	..	..	..	..
Employment to population ratio, youth (% ages 15–24)	..	..	..	..
Children in employment (% of children ages 7–14)	..	..	..	..
Unemployment rate (% of labor force ages 15+)	..	..	..	..
Long-term unemployment rate (% total unemployment)	..	..	..	..
Youth unemployment rate (% of labor force ages 15–24)	..	..	..	..
Account at a formal financial institution (% age 15+)	..	..	..	..
Public life and decision making				
Seats held by women in national parliament (%)	..		..	

Cyprus

	High income
Population (millions)	1.1
GNI, Atlas ($ billions)	23.7
GNI per capita, Atlas ($)	29,450
Population living below $1.25 a day (%)	..

	1990		2011	
	Female	Male	Female	Male
Demography				
Sex ratio at birth (boys per girls)	1.07		1.07	
Life expectancy at birth (years)	79	75	82	77
Under-five mortality rate (per 1,000 live births)	10	12	3	3
Female-headed households (%)	..		..	
Education				
Gross primary enrollment ratio (% of relevant age group)	101	101	102	102
Gross secondary enrollment ratio (% of relevant age group)	94	92	92	91
Gross tertiary enrollment ratio (% of relevant age group)	14	14	46	51
Primary completion rate (% of relevant age group)	101	101	101	98
Youth literacy rate (% of population ages 15–24)	100	100	100	100
Health and related services				
Total fertility rate (births per woman)	2.4		1.5	
Adolescent fertility rate (births per 1,000 women ages 15–19)	..		6	
Women first married by age 18 (% of women ages 20–24)	..		..	
Contraceptive prevalence (% of women ages 15–49)	..		..	
Unmet need for contraception (% of women ages 15–49)	..		..	
Pregnant women receiving prenatal care (%)	..		99	
Births attended by skilled health staff (% of total)	..		..	
Maternal mortality ratio (per 100,000 live births)	17		10	
Economic structure, participation, and access to resources				
Labor force participation rate (% of population ages 15+)	46	74	57	72
Wage and salaried workers (% of employed ages 15+)	..	..	88	77
Self-employed workers (% of employed ages 15+)	..	..	12	23
Vulnerable employment (% of employed ages 15+)	..	..	11	16
Unpaid family workers (% of employed ages 15+)	..	..	2.4	1.4
Employment in agriculture (% of employed ages 15+)	16	12	3	5
Employment in industry (% of employed ages 15+)	25	31	9	32
Employment in service (% of employed ages 15+)	59	55	89	63
Women in wage employment in the nonagricultural sector (%)	..		49	
Women's share of part-time employment (% of total)	..		61	
Maternity leave (weeks)	..		18	
Maternal leave benefits (% of wages paid)	..		75	
Female legislators, senior officials and managers (% of total)	..		14	
Employment to population ratio, total (% ages 15+)	43	69	53	66
Employment to population ratio, youth (% ages 15–24)	37	40	31	31
Children in employment (% of children ages 7–14)	..	..	..	..
Unemployment rate (% of labor force ages 15+)	2.2	2.0	7.7	7.8
Long-term unemployment rate (% total unemployment)	..	..	20.1	21.6
Youth unemployment rate (% of labor force ages 15–24)	..	..	22	23
Account at a formal financial institution (% age 15+)	..	..	83	88
Public life and decision making				
Seats held by women in national parliament (%)	2		11	

Czech Republic

High income

Population (millions)	10.5
GNI, Atlas ($ billions)	196.3
GNI per capita, Atlas ($)	18,700
Population living below $1.25 a day (%)	..

	1990		2011	
	Female	Male	Female	Male
Demography				
Sex ratio at birth (boys per girls)	1.06		1.06	
Life expectancy at birth (years)	75	68	81	75
Under-five mortality rate (per 1,000 live births)	12	16	4	4
Female-headed households (%)	..		..	
Education				
Gross primary enrollment ratio (% of relevant age group)	92	92	106	106
Gross secondary enrollment ratio (% of relevant age group)	89	97	90	90
Gross tertiary enrollment ratio (% of relevant age group)	14	18	75	53
Primary completion rate (% of relevant age group)	96	94	105	105
Youth literacy rate (% of population ages 15–24)	..	..	..	..
Health and related services				
Total fertility rate (births per woman)	1.9		1.4	
Adolescent fertility rate (births per 1,000 women ages 15–19)	..		10	
Women first married by age 18 (% of women ages 20–24)	..		..	
Contraceptive prevalence (% of women ages 15–49)	78		..	
Unmet need for contraception (% of women ages 15–49)	..		..	
Pregnant women receiving prenatal care (%)	99		..	
Births attended by skilled health staff (% of total)	100		100	
Maternal mortality ratio (per 100,000 live births)	15		5	
Economic structure, participation, and access to resources				
Labor force participation rate (% of population ages 15+)	52	71	50	68
Wage and salaried workers (% of employed ages 15+)	90	84	87	78
Self-employed workers (% of employed ages 15+)	10	16	13	22
Vulnerable employment (% of employed ages 15+)	5	8	11	17
Unpaid family workers (% of employed ages 15+)	0.4	0.2	1.0	0.2
Employment in agriculture (% of employed ages 15+)	6	9	2	4
Employment in industry (% of employed ages 15+)	33	51	24	49
Employment in service (% of employed ages 15+)	61	40	74	47
Women in wage employment in the nonagricultural sector (%)	51		46	
Women's share of part-time employment (% of total)	69		73	
Maternity leave (weeks)	..		28	
Maternal leave benefits (% of wages paid)	..		69	
Female legislators, senior officials and managers (% of total)	25		26	
Employment to population ratio, total (% ages 15+)	51	70	46	64
Employment to population ratio, youth (% ages 15–24)	41	57	21	29
Children in employment (% of children ages 7–14)	..	..	..	..
Unemployment rate (% of labor force ages 15+)	2.1	2.4	7.9	5.8
Long-term unemployment rate (% total unemployment)	16.4	17.9	41.4	41.7
Youth unemployment rate (% of labor force ages 15–24)	4	5	18	18
Account at a formal financial institution (% age 15+)	..	..	81	81
Public life and decision making				
Seats held by women in national parliament (%)	..		22	

Denmark

	High income
Population (millions)	5.6
GNI, Atlas ($ billions)	335.1
GNI per capita, Atlas ($)	60,160
Population living below $1.25 a day (%)	..

	1990		2011	
	Female	Male	Female	Male
Demography				
Sex ratio at birth (boys per girls)	1.06		1.06	
Life expectancy at birth (years)	78	72	82	78
Under-five mortality rate (per 1,000 live births)	8	10	3	4
Female-headed households (%)	..		..	
Education				
Gross primary enrollment ratio (% of relevant age group)	98	97	99	99
Gross secondary enrollment ratio (% of relevant age group)	111	108	119	118
Gross tertiary enrollment ratio (% of relevant age group)	36	32	88	61
Primary completion rate (% of relevant age group)	95	95	99	98
Youth literacy rate (% of population ages 15–24)	..	..	..	..
Health and related services				
Total fertility rate (births per woman)	1.7		1.8	
Adolescent fertility rate (births per 1,000 women ages 15–19)	..		5	
Women first married by age 18 (% of women ages 20–24)	..		..	
Contraceptive prevalence (% of women ages 15–49)	78		..	
Unmet need for contraception (% of women ages 15–49)	..		..	
Pregnant women receiving prenatal care (%)	..		..	
Births attended by skilled health staff (% of total)	100		..	
Maternal mortality ratio (per 100,000 live births)	13		12	
Economic structure, participation, and access to resources				
Labor force participation rate (% of population ages 15+)	62	75	60	69
Wage and salaried workers (% of employed ages 15+)	93	85	95	88
Self-employed workers (% of employed ages 15+)	7	15	5	12
Vulnerable employment (% of employed ages 15+)	6	8	4	7
Unpaid family workers (% of employed ages 15+)	4.0	0.1	0.4	0.2
Employment in agriculture (% of employed ages 15+)	3	8	1	4
Employment in industry (% of employed ages 15+)	16	37	9	29
Employment in service (% of employed ages 15+)	81	55	89	67
Women in wage employment in the nonagricultural sector (%)	48		50	
Women's share of part-time employment (% of total)	71		62	
Maternity leave (weeks)	18		7	
Maternal leave benefits (% of wages paid)	..		100	
Female legislators, senior officials and managers (% of total)	18		28	
Employment to population ratio, total (% ages 15+)	56	68	56	64
Employment to population ratio, youth (% ages 15–24)	63	68	59	57
Children in employment (% of children ages 7–14)	..	..	..	..
Unemployment rate (% of labor force ages 15+)	8.9	7.8	7.5	7.7
Long-term unemployment rate (% total unemployment)	31.3	27.5	22.3	26.2
Youth unemployment rate (% of labor force ages 15–24)	12	11	13	16
Account at a formal financial institution (% age 15+)	..	..	99	100
Public life and decision making				
Seats held by women in national parliament (%)	31		39	

Djibouti

Middle East & North Africa			Lower middle income	
Population (thousands)				905.6
GNI, Atlas ($ billions)				1.1
GNI per capita, Atlas ($)				1,270
Population living below $1.25 a day (%)				18.8

	1990		2011	
	Female	Male	Female	Male
Demography				
Sex ratio at birth (boys per girls)	1.04		1.04	
Life expectancy at birth (years)	53	50	59	56
Under-five mortality rate (per 1,000 live births)	114	129	84	95
Female-headed households (%)	..		..	
Education				
Gross primary enrollment ratio (% of relevant age group)	30	41	58[a]	64[a]
Gross secondary enrollment ratio (% of relevant age group)	9	13	34[a]	44[a]
Gross tertiary enrollment ratio (% of relevant age group)	0	0	4	6
Primary completion rate (% of relevant age group)	..	..	54[a]	59[a]
Youth literacy rate (% of population ages 15–24)	..	..	..	..
Health and related services				
Total fertility rate (births per woman)	6.2		3.7	
Adolescent fertility rate (births per 1,000 women ages 15–19)	..		20	
Women first married by age 18 (% of women ages 20–24)	..		5	
Contraceptive prevalence (% of women ages 15–49)	..		23	
Unmet need for contraception (% of women ages 15–49)	..		22	
Pregnant women receiving prenatal care (%)	..		92	
Births attended by skilled health staff (% of total)	..		93	
Maternal mortality ratio (per 100,000 live births)	290		200	
Economic structure, participation, and access to resources				
Labor force participation rate (% of population ages 15+)	27	67	36	67
Wage and salaried workers (% of employed ages 15+)	..	..	..	..
Self-employed workers (% of employed ages 15+)	..	..	..	..
Vulnerable employment (% of employed ages 15+)	..	..	..	..
Unpaid family workers (% of employed ages 15+)	..	..	..	..
Employment in agriculture (% of employed ages 15+)	..	..	..	..
Employment in industry (% of employed ages 15+)	..	..	..	..
Employment in service (% of employed ages 15+)	..	..	..	..
Women in wage employment in the nonagricultural sector (%)	..		..	
Women's share of part-time employment (% of total)	..		..	
Maternity leave (weeks)	14		14	
Maternal leave benefits (% of wages paid)	50		100	
Female legislators, senior officials and managers (% of total)	..		..	
Employment to population ratio, total (% ages 15+)	..	..	..	..
Employment to population ratio, youth (% ages 15–24)	..	..	..	..
Children in employment (% of children ages 7–14)	..	..	..	..
Unemployment rate (% of labor force ages 15+)	46.7	41.9	..	..
Long-term unemployment rate (% total unemployment)	..	..	..	..
Youth unemployment rate (% of labor force ages 15–24)	..	..	..	..
Account at a formal financial institution (% age 15+)	..	..	9	17
Public life and decision making				
Seats held by women in national parliament (%)	0		14	

Dominica

Latin America & the Caribbean				Upper middle income
Population (thousands)				67.7
GNI, Atlas ($ millions)				475.5
GNI per capita, Atlas ($)				7,030
Population living below $1.25 a day (%)				..

	1990		2011	
	Female	Male	Female	Male
Demography				
Sex ratio at birth (boys per girls)	..		..	
Life expectancy at birth (years)	76	72	..	..
Under-five mortality rate (per 1,000 live births)	16	19	11	13
Female-headed households (%)	..		..	
Education				
Gross primary enrollment ratio (% of relevant age group)	100	107	118	119
Gross secondary enrollment ratio (% of relevant age group)	77	64	102	95
Gross tertiary enrollment ratio (% of relevant age group)	5	6	..	..
Primary completion rate (% of relevant age group)	112	89	101	87
Youth literacy rate (% of population ages 15–24)	..	..	..	..
Health and related services				
Total fertility rate (births per woman)	2.5		..	
Adolescent fertility rate (births per 1,000 women ages 15–19)	..		..	
Women first married by age 18 (% of women ages 20–24)	..		..	
Contraceptive prevalence (% of women ages 15–49)	50		..	
Unmet need for contraception (% of women ages 15–49)	..		..	
Pregnant women receiving prenatal care (%)	90		100	
Births attended by skilled health staff (% of total)	..		100	
Maternal mortality ratio (per 100,000 live births)	..		..	
Economic structure, participation, and access to resources				
Labor force participation rate (% of population ages 15+)	..	..	..	..
Wage and salaried workers (% of employed ages 15+)	70	57	..	..
Self-employed workers (% of employed ages 15+)	28	41	..	..
Vulnerable employment (% of employed ages 15+)	23	32	..	..
Unpaid family workers (% of employed ages 15+)	2.9	3.0	..	..
Employment in agriculture (% of employed ages 15+)	13	40	..	..
Employment in industry (% of employed ages 15+)	13	27	..	..
Employment in service (% of employed ages 15+)	71	31	..	..
Women in wage employment in the nonagricultural sector (%)	40		..	
Women's share of part-time employment (% of total)	..		..	
Maternity leave (weeks)	9		..	
Maternal leave benefits (% of wages paid)	..		..	
Female legislators, senior officials and managers (% of total)	55		..	
Employment to population ratio, total (% ages 15+)	..	..	..	..
Employment to population ratio, youth (% ages 15–24)	..	..	..	..
Children in employment (% of children ages 7–14)	..	..	..	..
Unemployment rate (% of labor force ages 15+)	9.8	9.9	..	..
Long-term unemployment rate (% total unemployment)	..	..	..	..
Youth unemployment rate (% of labor force ages 15–24)	29	14	..	..
Account at a formal financial institution (% age 15+)	..	..	..	..
Public life and decision making				
Seats held by women in national parliament (%)	10		13	

Dominican Republic

Latin America & the Caribbean	Upper middle income
Population (millions)	10.1
GNI, Atlas ($ billions)	52.6
GNI per capita, Atlas ($)	5,240
Population living below $1.25 a day (%)	2.2

	1990		2011	
	Female	Male	Female	Male
Demography				
Sex ratio at birth (boys per girls)	1.05		1.05	
Life expectancy at birth (years)	70	65	76	71
Under-five mortality rate (per 1,000 live births)	54	62	23	27
Female-headed households (%)	25		35	
Education				
Gross primary enrollment ratio (% of relevant age group)	125	120	102	112
Gross secondary enrollment ratio (% of relevant age group)	..	..	81	72
Gross tertiary enrollment ratio (% of relevant age group)	..	..	..	..
Primary completion rate (% of relevant age group)	..	..	93	91
Youth literacy rate (% of population ages 15–24)	..	..	98	96
Health and related services				
Total fertility rate (births per woman)	3.5		2.5	
Adolescent fertility rate (births per 1,000 women ages 15–19)	..		105	
Women first married by age 18 (% of women ages 20–24)	30		41	
Contraceptive prevalence (% of women ages 15–49)	56		73	
Unmet need for contraception (% of women ages 15–49)	17		11	
Pregnant women receiving prenatal care (%)	97		99	
Births attended by skilled health staff (% of total)	92		98	
Maternal mortality ratio (per 100,000 live births)	220		150	
Economic structure, participation, and access to resources				
Labor force participation rate (% of population ages 15+)	44	84	51	79
Wage and salaried workers (% of employed ages 15+)	69	53	45	39
Self-employed workers (% of employed ages 15+)	31	47	24	52
Vulnerable employment (% of employed ages 15+)	30	42	22	48
Unpaid family workers (% of employed ages 15+)	3.7	6.2	2.1	1.6
Employment in agriculture (% of employed ages 15+)	3	27	2	19
Employment in industry (% of employed ages 15+)	24	23	7	21
Employment in service (% of employed ages 15+)	74	50	60	47
Women in wage employment in the nonagricultural sector (%)	32		42	
Women's share of part-time employment (% of total)	..		51	
Maternity leave (weeks)	12		12	
Maternal leave benefits (% of wages paid)	100		100	
Female legislators, senior officials and managers (% of total)	..		31	
Employment to population ratio, total (% ages 15+)	29	74	39	73
Employment to population ratio, youth (% ages 15–24)	21	54	24	50
Children in employment (% of children ages 7–14)	..	..	7.9	19.9
Unemployment rate (% of labor force ages 15+)	33.3	12.8	16.4	9.3
Long-term unemployment rate (% total unemployment)	..		..	..
Youth unemployment rate (% of labor force ages 15–24)	48	25	45	21
Account at a formal financial institution (% age 15+)	..	..	37	39
Public life and decision making				
Seats held by women in national parliament (%)	8		21	

Ecuador

Latin America & the Caribbean			Upper middle income	
Population (millions)				14.7
GNI, Atlas ($ billions)				61.7
GNI per capita, Atlas ($)				4,200
Population living below $1.25 a day (%)				4.6

	1990		2011	
	Female	Male	Female	Male
Demography				
Sex ratio at birth (boys per girls)	1.05		1.05	
Life expectancy at birth (years)	71	66	79	73
Under-five mortality rate (per 1,000 live births)	49	56	21	25
Female-headed households (%)	..		..	
Education				
Gross primary enrollment ratio (% of relevant age group)	120	121	120	121
Gross secondary enrollment ratio (% of relevant age group)	60	57	88	87
Gross tertiary enrollment ratio (% of relevant age group)	23	34	43	37
Primary completion rate (% of relevant age group)	92	92	113	111
Youth literacy rate (% of population ages 15–24)	96	97	99	98
Health and related services				
Total fertility rate (births per woman)	3.7		2.4	
Adolescent fertility rate (births per 1,000 women ages 15–19)	..		81	
Women first married by age 18 (% of women ages 20–24)	26		..	
Contraceptive prevalence (% of women ages 15–49)	53		..	
Unmet need for contraception (% of women ages 15–49)	..		..	
Pregnant women receiving prenatal care (%)	75		..	
Births attended by skilled health staff (% of total)	61		..	
Maternal mortality ratio (per 100,000 live births)	180		110	
Economic structure, participation, and access to resources				
Labor force participation rate (% of population ages 15+)	39	84	54	83
Wage and salaried workers (% of employed ages 15+)	45	60	49	59
Self-employed workers (% of employed ages 15+)	44	40	51	41
Vulnerable employment (% of employed ages 15+)	41	33	50	37
Unpaid family workers (% of employed ages 15+)	11.3	3.9	17.5	6.2
Employment in agriculture (% of employed ages 15+)	3	10	21	33
Employment in industry (% of employed ages 15+)	17	30	11	23
Employment in service (% of employed ages 15+)	81	60	68	44
Women in wage employment in the nonagricultural sector (%)	31		39	
Women's share of part-time employment (% of total)	60		53	
Maternity leave (weeks)	12		12	
Maternal leave benefits (% of wages paid)	100		100	
Female legislators, senior officials and managers (% of total)	..		28	
Employment to population ratio, total (% ages 15+)	36	79	50	79
Employment to population ratio, youth (% ages 15–24)	29	59	34	54
Children in employment (% of children ages 7–14)	..	..	2.5	3.8
Unemployment rate (% of labor force ages 15+)	9.1	4.3	6.4	4.1
Long-term unemployment rate (% total unemployment)	..	..	..	..
Youth unemployment rate (% of labor force ages 15–24)	17	11	18	12
Account at a formal financial institution (% age 15+)	..	..	33	40
Public life and decision making				
Seats held by women in national parliament (%)	5		32	

Egypt, Arab Rep.

Middle East & North Africa	Lower middle income
Population (millions)	82.5
GNI, Atlas ($ billions)	214.7
GNI per capita, Atlas ($)	2,600
Population living below $1.25 a day (%)	<2

	1990		2011	
	Female	Male	Female	Male
Demography				
Sex ratio at birth (boys per girls)	1.05		1.05	
Life expectancy at birth (years)	64	60	75	71
Under-five mortality rate (per 1,000 live births)	86	86	20	22
Female-headed households (%)	12		13	
Education				
Gross primary enrollment ratio (% of relevant age group)	79	95	104	108
Gross secondary enrollment ratio (% of relevant age group)	59	77	71	74
Gross tertiary enrollment ratio (% of relevant age group)	10	18	31	34
Primary completion rate (% of relevant age group)	57	79	99	102
Youth literacy rate (% of population ages 15–24)	54	71	84	91
Health and related services				
Total fertility rate (births per woman)	4.4		2.7	
Adolescent fertility rate (births per 1,000 women ages 15–19)	..		42	
Women first married by age 18 (% of women ages 20–24)	27		17	
Contraceptive prevalence (% of women ages 15–49)	48		60	
Unmet need for contraception (% of women ages 15–49)	20		9	
Pregnant women receiving prenatal care (%)	52		74	
Births attended by skilled health staff (% of total)	37		79	
Maternal mortality ratio (per 100,000 live births)	230		66	
Economic structure, participation, and access to resources				
Labor force participation rate (% of population ages 15+)	27	74	24	74
Wage and salaried workers (% of employed ages 15+)	50	57	48	61
Self-employed workers (% of employed ages 15+)	51	43	52	39
Vulnerable employment (% of employed ages 15+)	46	24	49	22
Unpaid family workers (% of employed ages 15+)	32.8	9.6	33.9	8.7
Employment in agriculture (% of employed ages 15+)	52	35	46	28
Employment in industry (% of employed ages 15+)	10	24	6	27
Employment in service (% of employed ages 15+)	38	41	49	44
Women in wage employment in the nonagricultural sector (%)	21		18	
Women's share of part-time employment (% of total)	..		..	
Maternity leave (weeks)	7		13	
Maternal leave benefits (% of wages paid)	100		100	
Female legislators, senior officials and managers (% of total)	..		11	
Employment to population ratio, total (% ages 15+)	17	69	17	69
Employment to population ratio, youth (% ages 15–24)	12	32	8	36
Children in employment (% of children ages 7–14)	..	..	..	..
Unemployment rate (% of labor force ages 15+)	17.9	5.2	22.6	4.9
Long-term unemployment rate (% total unemployment)	..	..	..	..
Youth unemployment rate (% of labor force ages 15–24)	..	..	54	15
Account at a formal financial institution (% age 15+)	..	..	7	13
Public life and decision making				
Seats held by women in national parliament (%)	4		2	

El Salvador

Latin America & the Caribbean	Lower middle income
Population (millions)	6.2
GNI, Atlas ($ billions)	21.7
GNI per capita, Atlas ($)	3,480
Population living below $1.25 a day (%)	9.0

	1990		2011	
	Female	Male	Female	Male
Demography				
Sex ratio at birth (boys per girls)	1.05		1.05	
Life expectancy at birth (years)	71	61	77	67
Under-five mortality rate (per 1,000 live births)	55	65	14	17
Female-headed households (%)	..		..	
Education				
Gross primary enrollment ratio (% of relevant age group)	94	95	112	117
Gross secondary enrollment ratio (% of relevant age group)	40	36	68	68
Gross tertiary enrollment ratio (% of relevant age group)	19	21	26	23
Primary completion rate (% of relevant age group)	65	62	101	100
Youth literacy rate (% of population ages 15–24)	85	85	96	96
Health and related services				
Total fertility rate (births per woman)	4.0		2.2	
Adolescent fertility rate (births per 1,000 women ages 15–19)	..		77	
Women first married by age 18 (% of women ages 20–24)	..		25	
Contraceptive prevalence (% of women ages 15–49)	47		73	
Unmet need for contraception (% of women ages 15–49)	..		..	
Pregnant women receiving prenatal care (%)	69		94	
Births attended by skilled health staff (% of total)	90		96	
Maternal mortality ratio (per 100,000 live births)	150		81	
Economic structure, participation, and access to resources				
Labor force participation rate (% of population ages 15+)	41	83	47	79
Wage and salaried workers (% of employed ages 15+)	50	62	51	63
Self-employed workers (% of employed ages 15+)	49	37	49	37
Vulnerable employment (% of employed ages 15+)	46	27	46	32
Unpaid family workers (% of employed ages 15+)	8.6	7.4	7.6	6.5
Employment in agriculture (% of employed ages 15+)	3	11	5	32
Employment in industry (% of employed ages 15+)	22	35	18	24
Employment in service (% of employed ages 15+)	75	54	76	44
Women in wage employment in the nonagricultural sector (%)	46		48	
Women's share of part-time employment (% of total)	54		54	
Maternity leave (weeks)	12		12	
Maternal leave benefits (% of wages paid)	75		75	
Female legislators, senior officials and managers (% of total)	44		29	
Employment to population ratio, total (% ages 15+)	39	76	45	72
Employment to population ratio, youth (% ages 15–24)	30	62	30	54
Children in employment (% of children ages 7–14)	..	..	4.4	10.4
Unemployment rate (% of labor force ages 15+)	9.8	10.1	5.1	8.4
Long-term unemployment rate (% total unemployment)	..	..	..	..
Youth unemployment rate (% of labor force ages 15–24)	14	15	8	13
Account at a formal financial institution (% age 15+)	..	..	10	18
Public life and decision making				
Seats held by women in national parliament (%)	12		26	

Equatorial Guinea

Population (thousands)	720.2
GNI, Atlas ($ billions)	11.3
GNI per capita, Atlas ($)	15,670
Population living below $1.25 a day (%)	..

	1990		2011	
	Female	Male	Female	Male
Demography				
Sex ratio at birth (boys per girls)	1.03		1.03	
Life expectancy at birth (years)	48	45	52	50
Under-five mortality rate (per 1,000 live births)	180	199	112	124
Female-headed households (%)	..		..	
Education				
Gross primary enrollment ratio (% of relevant age group)	148	157	86	88
Gross secondary enrollment ratio (% of relevant age group)	26	59	..	..
Gross tertiary enrollment ratio (% of relevant age group)	0	3	..	..
Primary completion rate (% of relevant age group)	50	56	52	51
Youth literacy rate (% of population ages 15–24)	..	..	98	98
Health and related services				
Total fertility rate (births per woman)	5.9		5.1	
Adolescent fertility rate (births per 1,000 women ages 15–19)	..		116	
Women first married by age 18 (% of women ages 20–24)	..		..	
Contraceptive prevalence (% of women ages 15–49)	..		..	
Unmet need for contraception (% of women ages 15–49)	..		..	
Pregnant women receiving prenatal care (%)	37		..	
Births attended by skilled health staff (% of total)	5		..	
Maternal mortality ratio (per 100,000 live births)	1,200		240	
Economic structure, participation, and access to resources				
Labor force participation rate (% of population ages 15+)	80	92	81	92
Wage and salaried workers (% of employed ages 15+)	..	..	..	..
Self-employed workers (% of employed ages 15+)	..	..	..	..
Vulnerable employment (% of employed ages 15+)	..	..	..	..
Unpaid family workers (% of employed ages 15+)	..	..	..	..
Employment in agriculture (% of employed ages 15+)	..	..	..	..
Employment in industry (% of employed ages 15+)	..	..	..	..
Employment in service (% of employed ages 15+)	..	..	..	..
Women in wage employment in the nonagricultural sector (%)	11		..	
Women's share of part-time employment (% of total)	..		..	
Maternity leave (weeks)	12		12	
Maternal leave benefits (% of wages paid)	75		75	
Female legislators, senior officials and managers (% of total)	..		..	
Employment to population ratio, total (% ages 15+)	76	86	75	85
Employment to population ratio, youth (% ages 15–24)	58	80	56	78
Children in employment (% of children ages 7–14)	..	..	..	..
Unemployment rate (% of labor force ages 15+)	..	..	..	..
Long-term unemployment rate (% total unemployment)	..	..	..	..
Youth unemployment rate (% of labor force ages 15–24)	..	..	..	..
Account at a formal financial institution (% age 15+)	..	..	..	..
Public life and decision making				
Seats held by women in national parliament (%)	13		10	

Eritrea

Sub-Saharan Africa	Low income
Population (millions)	5.4
GNI, Atlas ($ billions)	2.3
GNI per capita, Atlas ($)	430
Population living below $1.25 a day (%)	..

	1990		2011	
	Female	Male	Female	Male
Demography				
Sex ratio at birth (boys per girls)	1.03		1.03	
Life expectancy at birth (years)	50	46	64	59
Under-five mortality rate (per 1,000 live births)	125	151	61	74
Female-headed households (%)	..		..	
Education				
Gross primary enrollment ratio (% of relevant age group)	20	21	42	51
Gross secondary enrollment ratio (% of relevant age group)	11	12	29	37
Gross tertiary enrollment ratio (% of relevant age group)	..	..	1	3
Primary completion rate (% of relevant age group)	16	21	36	43
Youth literacy rate (% of population ages 15–24)	..	..	87	92
Health and related services				
Total fertility rate (births per woman)	6.2		4.4	
Adolescent fertility rate (births per 1,000 women ages 15–19)	..		56	
Women first married by age 18 (% of women ages 20–24)	..		..	
Contraceptive prevalence (% of women ages 15–49)	..		..	
Unmet need for contraception (% of women ages 15–49)	..		..	
Pregnant women receiving prenatal care (%)	..		..	
Births attended by skilled health staff (% of total)	..		..	
Maternal mortality ratio (per 100,000 live births)	880		240	
Economic structure, participation, and access to resources				
Labor force participation rate (% of population ages 15+)	74	91	80	90
Wage and salaried workers (% of employed ages 15+)	..	..	..	..
Self-employed workers (% of employed ages 15+)	..	..	..	..
Vulnerable employment (% of employed ages 15+)	..	..	..	..
Unpaid family workers (% of employed ages 15+)	..	..	..	..
Employment in agriculture (% of employed ages 15+)	..	..	..	..
Employment in industry (% of employed ages 15+)	..	..	..	..
Employment in service (% of employed ages 15+)	..	..	..	..
Women in wage employment in the nonagricultural sector (%)	..		..	
Women's share of part-time employment (% of total)	..		..	
Maternity leave (weeks)	..		9	
Maternal leave benefits (% of wages paid)	..		..	
Female legislators, senior officials and managers (% of total)	..		..	
Employment to population ratio, total (% ages 15+)	69	84	75	84
Employment to population ratio, youth (% ages 15–24)	67	75	66	72
Children in employment (% of children ages 7–14)	..	..	..	..
Unemployment rate (% of labor force ages 15+)	..	..	..	..
Long-term unemployment rate (% total unemployment)	..	..	..	..
Youth unemployment rate (% of labor force ages 15–24)	..	..	..	..
Account at a formal financial institution (% age 15+)	..	..	..	..
Public life and decision making				
Seats held by women in national parliament (%)	..		22	

Estonia

High income

Population (millions)	1.3
GNI, Atlas ($ billions)	20.4
GNI per capita, Atlas ($)	15,260
Population living below $1.25 a day (%)	<2

	1990		2011	
	Female	Male	Female	Male
Demography				
Sex ratio at birth (boys per girls)	1.06		1.06	
Life expectancy at birth (years)	75	65	81	71
Under-five mortality rate (per 1,000 live births)	17	23	3	4
Female-headed households (%)	..		..	
Education				
Gross primary enrollment ratio (% of relevant age group)	93	95	98	99
Gross secondary enrollment ratio (% of relevant age group)	104	97	107	107
Gross tertiary enrollment ratio (% of relevant age group)	25	23	80	49
Primary completion rate (% of relevant age group)	..	..	95	98
Youth literacy rate (% of population ages 15–24)	100	100	100	100
Health and related services				
Total fertility rate (births per woman)	2.0		1.5	
Adolescent fertility rate (births per 1,000 women ages 15–19)	..		18	
Women first married by age 18 (% of women ages 20–24)	..		..	
Contraceptive prevalence (% of women ages 15–49)	70		..	
Unmet need for contraception (% of women ages 15–49)	..		..	
Pregnant women receiving prenatal care (%)	..		..	
Births attended by skilled health staff (% of total)	99		100	
Maternal mortality ratio (per 100,000 live births)	48		2	
Economic structure, participation, and access to resources				
Labor force participation rate (% of population ages 15+)	63	77	57	68
Wage and salaried workers (% of employed ages 15+)	97	97	95	88
Self-employed workers (% of employed ages 15+)	3	3	5	12
Vulnerable employment (% of employed ages 15+)	3	2	4	6
Unpaid family workers (% of employed ages 15+)	2.3	0.9	0.2	0.3
Employment in agriculture (% of employed ages 15+)	15	27	2	6
Employment in industry (% of employed ages 15+)	31	42	19	45
Employment in service (% of employed ages 15+)	53	31	78	47
Women in wage employment in the nonagricultural sector (%)	52		54	
Women's share of part-time employment (% of total)	..		72	
Maternity leave (weeks)	..		20	
Maternal leave benefits (% of wages paid)	..		100	
Female legislators, senior officials and managers (% of total)	39		36	
Employment to population ratio, total (% ages 15+)	60	74	51	59
Employment to population ratio, youth (% ages 15–24)	47	54	29	34
Children in employment (% of children ages 7–14)	..	..	..	..
Unemployment rate (% of labor force ages 15+)	0.7	0.6	11.8	13.1
Long-term unemployment rate (% total unemployment)	28.3	37.1	53.6	59.7
Youth unemployment rate (% of labor force ages 15–24)	..	..	21	24
Account at a formal financial institution (% age 15+)	..	..	97	96
Public life and decision making				
Seats held by women in national parliament (%)	..		21	

Ethiopia

Sub-Saharan Africa				Low income

Population (millions)				84.7
GNI, Atlas ($ billions)				31.0
GNI per capita, Atlas ($)				370
Population living below $1.25 a day (%)				30.7

	1990		2011	
	Female	Male	Female	Male
Demography				
Sex ratio at birth (boys per girls)	1.03		1.03	
Life expectancy at birth (years)	49	46	61	58
Under-five mortality rate (per 1,000 live births)	184	212	72	82
Female-headed households (%)	..		26	
Education				
Gross primary enrollment ratio (% of relevant age group)	29	44	101	111
Gross secondary enrollment ratio (% of relevant age group)	12	16	35	40
Gross tertiary enrollment ratio (% of relevant age group)	0	1	5	11
Primary completion rate (% of relevant age group)	18	29	55	61
Youth literacy rate (% of population ages 15–24)	28	39	47	63
Health and related services				
Total fertility rate (births per woman)	7.1		4.0	
Adolescent fertility rate (births per 1,000 women ages 15–19)	..		53	
Women first married by age 18 (% of women ages 20–24)	..		41	
Contraceptive prevalence (% of women ages 15–49)	5		29	
Unmet need for contraception (% of women ages 15–49)	..		26	
Pregnant women receiving prenatal care (%)	..		43	
Births attended by skilled health staff (% of total)	..		10	
Maternal mortality ratio (per 100,000 live births)	950		350	
Economic structure, participation, and access to resources				
Labor force participation rate (% of population ages 15+)	72	91	78	90
Wage and salaried workers (% of employed ages 15+)	2	4	..	..
Self-employed workers (% of employed ages 15+)	97	91	..	..
Vulnerable employment (% of employed ages 15+)	96	89	..	..
Unpaid family workers (% of employed ages 15+)	72.6	20.5	..	..
Employment in agriculture (% of employed ages 15+)	..	..	..	..
Employment in industry (% of employed ages 15+)	..	..	..	..
Employment in service (% of employed ages 15+)	..	..	..	..
Women in wage employment in the nonagricultural sector (%)	..		42	
Women's share of part-time employment (% of total)	..		..	
Maternity leave (weeks)	12		13	
Maternal leave benefits (% of wages paid)	100		100	
Female legislators, senior officials and managers (% of total)	..		16	
Employment to population ratio, total (% ages 15+)	64	87	72	87
Employment to population ratio, youth (% ages 15–24)	62	79	66	76
Children in employment (% of children ages 7–14)	..	..	19.5	32.5
Unemployment rate (% of labor force ages 15+)	1.6	1.1	22.6	11.7
Long-term unemployment rate (% total unemployment)	..	..	..	..
Youth unemployment rate (% of labor force ages 15–24)	3	2	29	20
Account at a formal financial institution (% age 15+)	..	..	..	..
Public life and decision making				
Seats held by women in national parliament (%)	..		28	

Faeroe Islands

Population (thousands)	48.9
GNI, Atlas ($ millions)	..
GNI per capita, Atlas ($)	..
Population living below $1.25 a day (%)	..

	1990		2011	
	Female	Male	Female	Male
Demography				
Sex ratio at birth (boys per girls)	..		..	
Life expectancy at birth (years)	80	73	85	79
Under-five mortality rate (per 1,000 live births)	..	..	..	..
Female-headed households (%)	..		..	
Education				
Gross primary enrollment ratio (% of relevant age group)	..	..	..	..
Gross secondary enrollment ratio (% of relevant age group)	..	..	..	..
Gross tertiary enrollment ratio (% of relevant age group)	..	..	..	..
Primary completion rate (% of relevant age group)	..	..	..	..
Youth literacy rate (% of population ages 15–24)	..	..	..	..
Health and related services				
Total fertility rate (births per woman)	..		..	
Adolescent fertility rate (births per 1,000 women ages 15–19)	..		..	
Women first married by age 18 (% of women ages 20–24)	..		..	
Contraceptive prevalence (% of women ages 15–49)	..		..	
Unmet need for contraception (% of women ages 15–49)	..		..	
Pregnant women receiving prenatal care (%)	..		..	
Births attended by skilled health staff (% of total)	..		..	
Maternal mortality ratio (per 100,000 live births)	..		..	
Economic structure, participation, and access to resources				
Labor force participation rate (% of population ages 15+)	..	..	..	..
Wage and salaried workers (% of employed ages 15+)	..	..	..	..
Self-employed workers (% of employed ages 15+)	..	..	..	..
Vulnerable employment (% of employed ages 15+)	..	..	..	..
Unpaid family workers (% of employed ages 15+)	..	..	..	..
Employment in agriculture (% of employed ages 15+)	..	..	..	..
Employment in industry (% of employed ages 15+)	..	..	..	..
Employment in service (% of employed ages 15+)	..	..	..	..
Women in wage employment in the nonagricultural sector (%)	..		..	
Women's share of part-time employment (% of total)	..		..	
Maternity leave (weeks)	..		..	
Maternal leave benefits (% of wages paid)	..		..	
Female legislators, senior officials and managers (% of total)	..		..	
Employment to population ratio, total (% ages 15+)	..	..	..	..
Employment to population ratio, youth (% ages 15–24)	..	..	..	..
Children in employment (% of children ages 7–14)	..	..	..	..
Unemployment rate (% of labor force ages 15+)	..	..	..	..
Long-term unemployment rate (% total unemployment)	..	..	..	..
Youth unemployment rate (% of labor force ages 15–24)	..	..	..	..
Account at a formal financial institution (% age 15+)	..	..	..	..
Public life and decision making				
Seats held by women in national parliament (%)	..		..	

Fiji

East Asia & Pacific   **Lower middle income**

Population (thousands)	868.4
GNI, Atlas ($ billions)	3.2
GNI per capita, Atlas ($)	3,720
Population living below $1.25 a day (%)	5.9

	1990		2011	
	Female	Male	Female	Male
Demography				
Sex ratio at birth (boys per girls)	1.06		1.06	
Life expectancy at birth (years)	68	64	72	67
Under-five mortality rate (per 1,000 live births)	27	32	15	18
Female-headed households (%)	..		..	
Education				
Gross primary enrollment ratio (% of relevant age group)	109	109	105	105
Gross secondary enrollment ratio (% of relevant age group)	75	78	94	87
Gross tertiary enrollment ratio (% of relevant age group)	2	4	..	..
Primary completion rate (% of relevant age group)	95	95	103	104
Youth literacy rate (% of population ages 15–24)	..	..	..	..
Health and related services				
Total fertility rate (births per woman)	3.4		2.6	
Adolescent fertility rate (births per 1,000 women ages 15–19)	..		43	
Women first married by age 18 (% of women ages 20–24)	..		..	
Contraceptive prevalence (% of women ages 15–49)	..		32	
Unmet need for contraception (% of women ages 15–49)	..		..	
Pregnant women receiving prenatal care (%)	..		100	
Births attended by skilled health staff (% of total)	..		100	
Maternal mortality ratio (per 100,000 live births)	32		26	
Economic structure, participation, and access to resources				
Labor force participation rate (% of population ages 15+)	29	83	39	80
Wage and salaried workers (% of employed ages 15+)	..	..	..	..
Self-employed workers (% of employed ages 15+)	..	..	..	..
Vulnerable employment (% of employed ages 15+)	..	..	..	..
Unpaid family workers (% of employed ages 15+)	..	..	..	..
Employment in agriculture (% of employed ages 15+)	..	..	..	..
Employment in industry (% of employed ages 15+)	..	..	..	..
Employment in service (% of employed ages 15+)	..	..	..	..
Women in wage employment in the nonagricultural sector (%)	30		..	
Women's share of part-time employment (% of total)	..		..	
Maternity leave (weeks)	12		12	
Maternal leave benefits (% of wages paid)	..		..	
Female legislators, senior officials and managers (% of total)	..		..	
Employment to population ratio, total (% ages 15+)	28	79	37	76
Employment to population ratio, youth (% ages 15–24)	24	59	26	52
Children in employment (% of children ages 7–14)	..	..	..	..
Unemployment rate (% of labor force ages 15+)	..	..	12.9	6.4
Long-term unemployment rate (% total unemployment)	..	..	..	..
Youth unemployment rate (% of labor force ages 15–24)	..	..	..	..
Account at a formal financial institution (% age 15+)	..	..	..	..
Public life and decision making				
Seats held by women in national parliament (%)	..		9	

Finland

High income

Population (millions)	5.4
GNI, Atlas ($ billions)	257.3
GNI per capita, Atlas ($)	47,760
Population living below $1.25 a day (%)	..

	1990		2011	
	Female	**Male**	**Female**	**Male**
Demography				
Sex ratio at birth (boys per girls)	1.05		1.05	
Life expectancy at birth (years)	79	71	84	77
Under-five mortality rate (per 1,000 live births)	6	7	3	3
Female-headed households (%)	..		..	
Education				
Gross primary enrollment ratio (% of relevant age group)	98	99	99	99
Gross secondary enrollment ratio (% of relevant age group)	124	105	110	105
Gross tertiary enrollment ratio (% of relevant age group)	47	42	103	85
Primary completion rate (% of relevant age group)	102	102	99	98
Youth literacy rate (% of population ages 15–24)	..	..	..	..
Health and related services				
Total fertility rate (births per woman)	1.8		1.8	
Adolescent fertility rate (births per 1,000 women ages 15–19)	..		9	
Women first married by age 18 (% of women ages 20–24)	..		..	
Contraceptive prevalence (% of women ages 15–49)	77		..	
Unmet need for contraception (% of women ages 15–49)	..		..	
Pregnant women receiving prenatal care (%)	100		..	
Births attended by skilled health staff (% of total)	100		..	
Maternal mortality ratio (per 100,000 live births)	7		5	
Economic structure, participation, and access to resources				
Labor force participation rate (% of population ages 15+)	59	72	56	64
Wage and salaried workers (% of employed ages 15+)	89	81	91	82
Self-employed workers (% of employed ages 15+)	11	20	9	18
Vulnerable employment (% of employed ages 15+)	..	..	7	12
Unpaid family workers (% of employed ages 15+)	1.1	1.7	0.4	0.6
Employment in agriculture (% of employed ages 15+)	7	11	2	6
Employment in industry (% of employed ages 15+)	17	42	9	36
Employment in service (% of employed ages 15+)	76	48	88	58
Women in wage employment in the nonagricultural sector (%)	51		51	
Women's share of part-time employment (% of total)	67		61	
Maternity leave (weeks)	15		15	
Maternal leave benefits (% of wages paid)	80		70	
Female legislators, senior officials and managers (% of total)	..		32	
Employment to population ratio, total (% ages 15+)	55	65	52	59
Employment to population ratio, youth (% ages 15–24)	46	51	41	41
Children in employment (% of children ages 7–14)	..	..	..	..
Unemployment rate (% of labor force ages 15+)	2.6	3.5	7.1	8.3
Long-term unemployment rate (% total unemployment)	8.4	9.7	17.3	26.4
Youth unemployment rate (% of labor force ages 15–24)	8	9	18	19
Account at a formal financial institution (% age 15+)	..	..	100	99
Public life and decision making				
Seats held by women in national parliament (%)	32		43	

France

				High income
Population (millions)				65.4
GNI, Atlas ($ billions)				2,775.7
GNI per capita, Atlas ($)				42,420
Population living below $1.25 a day (%)				..

	1990		2011	
	Female	Male	Female	Male
Demography				
Sex ratio at birth (boys per girls)	1.05		1.05	
Life expectancy at birth (years)	81	73	85	78
Under-five mortality rate (per 1,000 live births)	8	10	4	5
Female-headed households (%)	..		..	
Education				
Gross primary enrollment ratio (% of relevant age group)	110	112	109	111
Gross secondary enrollment ratio (% of relevant age group)	98	92	114	113
Gross tertiary enrollment ratio (% of relevant age group)	40	35	64	50
Primary completion rate (% of relevant age group)	..	..	..	..
Youth literacy rate (% of population ages 15–24)	..	..	..	..
Health and related services				
Total fertility rate (births per woman)	1.8		2.0	
Adolescent fertility rate (births per 1,000 women ages 15–19)	..		6	
Women first married by age 18 (% of women ages 20–24)	..		..	
Contraceptive prevalence (% of women ages 15–49)	81		..	
Unmet need for contraception (% of women ages 15–49)	..		..	
Pregnant women receiving prenatal care (%)	99		..	
Births attended by skilled health staff (% of total)	99		..	
Maternal mortality ratio (per 100,000 live births)	13		8	
Economic structure, participation, and access to resources				
Labor force participation rate (% of population ages 15+)	46	65	51	62
Wage and salaried workers (% of employed ages 15+)	87	82	92	85
Self-employed workers (% of employed ages 15+)	13	18	8	15
Vulnerable employment (% of employed ages 15+)	11	11	6	9
Unpaid family workers (% of employed ages 15+)	5.5	0.9	0.8	0.3
Employment in agriculture (% of employed ages 15+)	5	6	2	4
Employment in industry (% of employed ages 15+)	17	39	11	33
Employment in service (% of employed ages 15+)	78	55	87	63
Women in wage employment in the nonagricultural sector (%)	45		50	
Women's share of part-time employment (% of total)	79		77	
Maternity leave (weeks)	16		16	
Maternal leave benefits (% of wages paid)	84		100	
Female legislators, senior officials and managers (% of total)	32		39	
Employment to population ratio, total (% ages 15+)	41	60	46	56
Employment to population ratio, youth (% ages 15–24)	29	36	27	34
Children in employment (% of children ages 7–14)	..	..	..	..
Unemployment rate (% of labor force ages 15+)	12.2	7.2	9.7	8.8
Long-term unemployment rate (% total unemployment)	43.5	38.6	40.3	41.8
Youth unemployment rate (% of labor force ages 15–24)	23	17	23	21
Account at a formal financial institution (% age 15+)	..	..	97	97
Public life and decision making				
Seats held by women in national parliament (%)	7		27	

French Polynesia

High income

Population (thousands)	273.8
GNI, Atlas ($ billions)	..
GNI per capita, Atlas ($)	..
Population living below $1.25 a day (%)	..

	1990		2011	
	Female	Male	Female	Male
Demography				
Sex ratio at birth (boys per girls)	1.05		1.05	
Life expectancy at birth (years)	72	67	78	73
Under-five mortality rate (per 1,000 live births)	..	..	..	..
Female-headed households (%)		..		..
Education				
Gross primary enrollment ratio (% of relevant age group)	125	130	..	..
Gross secondary enrollment ratio (% of relevant age group)	78	57	..	..
Gross tertiary enrollment ratio (% of relevant age group)	..	..	..	..
Primary completion rate (% of relevant age group)	..	..	..	..
Youth literacy rate (% of population ages 15–24)	..	..	..	..
Health and related services				
Total fertility rate (births per woman)	3.3		2.1	
Adolescent fertility rate (births per 1,000 women ages 15–19)	..		49	
Women first married by age 18 (% of women ages 20–24)	..		..	
Contraceptive prevalence (% of women ages 15–49)	..		..	
Unmet need for contraception (% of women ages 15–49)	..		..	
Pregnant women receiving prenatal care (%)	..		..	
Births attended by skilled health staff (% of total)	..		..	
Maternal mortality ratio (per 100,000 live births)	..		..	
Economic structure, participation, and access to resources				
Labor force participation rate (% of population ages 15+)	49	74	48	67
Wage and salaried workers (% of employed ages 15+)	..	..	..	..
Self-employed workers (% of employed ages 15+)	..	..	..	..
Vulnerable employment (% of employed ages 15+)	..	..	..	..
Unpaid family workers (% of employed ages 15+)	..	..	..	..
Employment in agriculture (% of employed ages 15+)	..	..	..	..
Employment in industry (% of employed ages 15+)	..	..	..	..
Employment in service (% of employed ages 15+)	..	..	..	..
Women in wage employment in the nonagricultural sector (%)	..		43	
Women's share of part-time employment (% of total)	..		..	
Maternity leave (weeks)	..		..	
Maternal leave benefits (% of wages paid)	..		..	
Female legislators, senior officials and managers (% of total)	..		..	
Employment to population ratio, total (% ages 15+)	..	..	..	..
Employment to population ratio, youth (% ages 15–24)	..	..	..	..
Children in employment (% of children ages 7–14)	..	..	..	..
Unemployment rate (% of labor force ages 15+)	..	..	..	..
Long-term unemployment rate (% total unemployment)	..	..	..	..
Youth unemployment rate (% of labor force ages 15–24)	..	..	..	..
Account at a formal financial institution (% age 15+)	..	..	..	..
Public life and decision making				
Seats held by women in national parliament (%)		..		..

Gabon

Sub-Saharan Africa   **Upper middle income**

Population (millions)	1.5
GNI, Atlas ($ billions)	12.4
GNI per capita, Atlas ($)	8,080
Population living below $1.25 a day (%)	*4.8*

	1990 Female	1990 Male	2011 Female	2011 Male
Demography				
Sex ratio at birth (boys per girls)	1.03		1.03	
Life expectancy at birth (years)	63	60	64	62
Under-five mortality rate (per 1,000 live births)	86	103	59	72
Female-headed households (%)	..		..	
Education				
Gross primary enrollment ratio (% of relevant age group)	*155*	*155*	*179*	*184*
Gross secondary enrollment ratio (% of relevant age group)	*37*	*43*	..	..
Gross tertiary enrollment ratio (% of relevant age group)	*3*	*8*	..	..
Primary completion rate (% of relevant age group)	*69*	*70*	..	..
Youth literacy rate (% of population ages 15–24)	*92*	*94*	*97*	*99*
Health and related services				
Total fertility rate (births per woman)	5.2		3.2	
Adolescent fertility rate (births per 1,000 women ages 15–19)	..		83	
Women first married by age 18 (% of women ages 20–24)	..		..	
Contraceptive prevalence (% of women ages 15–49)	..		..	
Unmet need for contraception (% of women ages 15–49)	..		..	
Pregnant women receiving prenatal care (%)	..		..	
Births attended by skilled health staff (% of total)	..		..	
Maternal mortality ratio (per 100,000 live births)	270		*230*	
Economic structure, participation, and access to resources				
Labor force participation rate (% of population ages 15+)	56	71	56	65
Wage and salaried workers (% of employed ages 15+)	29	59	..	..
Self-employed workers (% of employed ages 15+)	63	38	..	..
Vulnerable employment (% of employed ages 15+)	63	37	..	..
Unpaid family workers (% of employed ages 15+)	5.3	2.0	..	..
Employment in agriculture (% of employed ages 15+)	61	26	..	..
Employment in industry (% of employed ages 15+)	3	19	..	..
Employment in service (% of employed ages 15+)	36	56	..	..
Women in wage employment in the nonagricultural sector (%)	29		35	
Women's share of part-time employment (% of total)	..			
Maternity leave (weeks)	..		*14*	
Maternal leave benefits (% of wages paid)	..		*100*	
Female legislators, senior officials and managers (% of total)	..		..	
Employment to population ratio, total (% ages 15+)	47	57	48	53
Employment to population ratio, youth (% ages 15–24)	19	22	14	16
Children in employment (% of children ages 7–14)	..	..	..	..
Unemployment rate (% of labor force ages 15+)	16.1	19.1	..	..
Long-term unemployment rate (% total unemployment)	..	..	..	..
Youth unemployment rate (% of labor force ages 15–24)	40	42	..	..
Account at a formal financial institution (% age 15+)	..	..	17	21
Public life and decision making				
Seats held by women in national parliament (%)	13		16	

Gambia, The

Sub-Saharan Africa				Low income
Population (millions)				1.8
GNI, Atlas ($ millions)				889.3
GNI per capita, Atlas ($)				500
Population living below $1.25 a day (%)				29.8

	1990		2011	
	Female	Male	Female	Male
Demography				
Sex ratio at birth (boys per girls)	1.03		1.03	
Life expectancy at birth (years)	54	52	60	57
Under-five mortality rate (per 1,000 live births)	154	175	94	107
Female-headed households (%)	..		..	
Education				
Gross primary enrollment ratio (% of relevant age group)	41	65	82	79
Gross secondary enrollment ratio (% of relevant age group)	10	22	53	56
Gross tertiary enrollment ratio (% of relevant age group)	..	..	..	..
Primary completion rate (% of relevant age group)	29	54	67	65
Youth literacy rate (% of population ages 15–24)	..	..	62	72
Health and related services				
Total fertility rate (births per woman)	6.1		4.8	
Adolescent fertility rate (births per 1,000 women ages 15–19)	..		69	
Women first married by age 18 (% of women ages 20–24)	..		36	
Contraceptive prevalence (% of women ages 15–49)	12		13	
Unmet need for contraception (% of women ages 15–49)	..		..	
Pregnant women receiving prenatal care (%)	..		98	
Births attended by skilled health staff (% of total)	44		57	
Maternal mortality ratio (per 100,000 live births)	700		360	
Economic structure, participation, and access to resources				
Labor force participation rate (% of population ages 15+)	70	85	72	83
Wage and salaried workers (% of employed ages 15+)	..	..	..	..
Self-employed workers (% of employed ages 15+)	..	..	..	..
Vulnerable employment (% of employed ages 15+)	..	..	..	..
Unpaid family workers (% of employed ages 15+)	..	..	..	..
Employment in agriculture (% of employed ages 15+)	77	54	..	..
Employment in industry (% of employed ages 15+)	1	11	..	..
Employment in service (% of employed ages 15+)	20	35	..	..
Women in wage employment in the nonagricultural sector (%)	..		..	
Women's share of part-time employment (% of total)	..		..	
Maternity leave (weeks)	..		12	
Maternal leave benefits (% of wages paid)	..		100	
Female legislators, senior officials and managers (% of total)	..		..	
Employment to population ratio, total (% ages 15+)	65	80	68	78
Employment to population ratio, youth (% ages 15–24)	58	62	57	58
Children in employment (% of children ages 7–14)	..	..	34.3	37.6
Unemployment rate (% of labor force ages 15+)	..	..	..	..
Long-term unemployment rate (% total unemployment)	..	..	..	..
Youth unemployment rate (% of labor force ages 15–24)	..	..	..	..
Account at a formal financial institution (% age 15+)	..	..	..	..
Public life and decision making				
Seats held by women in national parliament (%)	8		8	

Georgia

Europe & Central Asia	Lower middle income
Population (millions)	4.5
GNI, Atlas ($ billions)	12.8
GNI per capita, Atlas ($)	2,860
Population living below $1.25 a day (%)	18.0

	1990		2011	
	Female	Male	Female	Male
Demography				
Sex ratio at birth (boys per girls)	1.08		1.11	
Life expectancy at birth (years)	74	67	77	70
Under-five mortality rate (per 1,000 live births)	42	52	18	23
Female-headed households (%)	..		..	
Education				
Gross primary enrollment ratio (% of relevant age group)	97	97	108	105
Gross secondary enrollment ratio (% of relevant age group)	94	96	87	91
Gross tertiary enrollment ratio (% of relevant age group)	35	38	33	27
Primary completion rate (% of relevant age group)	..	..	116	116
Youth literacy rate (% of population ages 15–24)	..	..	100	100
Health and related services				
Total fertility rate (births per woman)	2.2		1.6	
Adolescent fertility rate (births per 1,000 women ages 15–19)			41	
Women first married by age 18 (% of women ages 20–24)			14	
Contraceptive prevalence (% of women ages 15–49)			53	
Unmet need for contraception (% of women ages 15–49)			..	
Pregnant women receiving prenatal care (%)	..		98	
Births attended by skilled health staff (% of total)	97		100	
Maternal mortality ratio (per 100,000 live births)	63		67	
Economic structure, participation, and access to resources				
Labor force participation rate (% of population ages 15+)	55	75	56	74
Wage and salaried workers (% of employed ages 15+)	..	..	35	37
Self-employed workers (% of employed ages 15+)	..	..	65	63
Vulnerable employment (% of employed ages 15+)	..	..	65	62
Unpaid family workers (% of employed ages 15+)	..	..	37.9	19.6
Employment in agriculture (% of employed ages 15+)	..	..	57	51
Employment in industry (% of employed ages 15+)	..	..	4	17
Employment in service (% of employed ages 15+)	..	..	40	33
Women in wage employment in the nonagricultural sector (%)	..		49	
Women's share of part-time employment (% of total)	..		..	
Maternity leave (weeks)	..		..	
Maternal leave benefits (% of wages paid)	..		..	
Female legislators, senior officials and managers (% of total)	..		34	
Employment to population ratio, total (% ages 15+)	48	63	48	63
Employment to population ratio, youth (% ages 15–24)	18	27	15	28
Children in employment (% of children ages 7–14)	..	..	29.9	33.6
Unemployment rate (% of labor force ages 15+)	..	..	13.1	16.7
Long-term unemployment rate (% total unemployment)	..	..	..	..
Youth unemployment rate (% of labor force ages 15–24)	..	..	41	32
Account at a formal financial institution (% age 15+)	..	..	35	31
Public life and decision making				
Seats held by women in national parliament (%)	..		12	

Germany

High income

Population (millions)	81.8
GNI, Atlas ($ billions)	3,617.7
GNI per capita, Atlas ($)	44,230
Population living below $1.25 a day (%)	..

	1990		2011	
	Female	Male	Female	Male
Demography				
Sex ratio at birth (boys per girls)	1.06		1.06	
Life expectancy at birth (years)	79	72	83	78
Under-five mortality rate (per 1,000 live births)	7	10	4	4
Female-headed households (%)	..		..	
Education				
Gross primary enrollment ratio (% of relevant age group)	99	98	102	103
Gross secondary enrollment ratio (% of relevant age group)	99	101	100	106
Gross tertiary enrollment ratio (% of relevant age group)	29	40	..	..
Primary completion rate (% of relevant age group)	101	101	101	101
Youth literacy rate (% of population ages 15–24)	..	..	..	..
Health and related services				
Total fertility rate (births per woman)	1.5		1.4	
Adolescent fertility rate (births per 1,000 women ages 15–19)	..		7	
Women first married by age 18 (% of women ages 20–24)	..		..	
Contraceptive prevalence (% of women ages 15–49)	70		..	
Unmet need for contraception (% of women ages 15–49)	..		..	
Pregnant women receiving prenatal care (%)	..		..	
Births attended by skilled health staff (% of total)	100		100	
Maternal mortality ratio (per 100,000 live births)	13		7	
Economic structure, participation, and access to resources				
Labor force participation rate (% of population ages 15+)	43	70	53	67
Wage and salaried workers (% of employed ages 15+)	92	89	92	86
Self-employed workers (% of employed ages 15+)	8	11	9	14
Vulnerable employment (% of employed ages 15+)	6	5	6	8
Unpaid family workers (% of employed ages 15+)	2.9	0.4	0.9	0.3
Employment in agriculture (% of employed ages 15+)	4	4	1	2
Employment in industry (% of employed ages 15+)	26	50	14	40
Employment in service (% of employed ages 15+)	70	45	85	58
Women in wage employment in the nonagricultural sector (%)	43		48	
Women's share of part-time employment (% of total)	89		79	
Maternity leave (weeks)	14		14	
Maternal leave benefits (% of wages paid)	100		100	
Female legislators, senior officials and managers (% of total)	26		30	
Employment to population ratio, total (% ages 15+)	45	69	50	62
Employment to population ratio, youth (% ages 15–24)	55	61	45	50
Children in employment (% of children ages 7–14)	..	..	..	..
Unemployment rate (% of labor force ages 15+)	7.0	4.5	5.6	6.2
Long-term unemployment rate (% total unemployment)	44.5	49.1	45.9	49.0
Youth unemployment rate (% of labor force ages 15–24)	6	5	8	9
Account at a formal financial institution (% age 15+)	..	..	99	98
Public life and decision making				
Seats held by women in national parliament (%)	..		33	

Ghana

Sub-Saharan Africa			Lower middle income	
Population (millions)				25.0
GNI, Atlas ($ billions)				35.1
GNI per capita, Atlas ($)				1,410
Population living below $1.25 a day (%)				28.6

	1990		2011	
	Female	Male	Female	Male
Demography				
Sex ratio at birth (boys per girls)	1.06		1.06	
Life expectancy at birth (years)	58	56	65	63
Under-five mortality rate (per 1,000 live births)	114	128	72	83
Female-headed households (%)	37		34	
Education				
Gross primary enrollment ratio (% of relevant age group)	65	76	107[a]	113[a]
Gross secondary enrollment ratio (% of relevant age group)	28	43	56[a]	62[a]
Gross tertiary enrollment ratio (% of relevant age group)	0	1	9	15
Primary completion rate (% of relevant age group)	57	72	88[a]	110[a]
Youth literacy rate (% of population ages 15–24)	..	..	80	82
Health and related services				
Total fertility rate (births per woman)	5.6		4.1	
Adolescent fertility rate (births per 1,000 women ages 15–19)	..		64	
Women first married by age 18 (% of women ages 20–24)	41		21	
Contraceptive prevalence (% of women ages 15–49)	17		34	
Unmet need for contraception (% of women ages 15–49)	37		35	
Pregnant women receiving prenatal care (%)	82		96	
Births attended by skilled health staff (% of total)	40		68	
Maternal mortality ratio (per 100,000 live births)	580		350	
Economic structure, participation, and access to resources				
Labor force participation rate (% of population ages 15+)	70	73	67	72
Wage and salaried workers (% of employed ages 15+)	..	..	11	30
Self-employed workers (% of employed ages 15+)	..	..	89	70
Vulnerable employment (% of employed ages 15+)	..	..	85	65
Unpaid family workers (% of employed ages 15+)	..	..	28.5	11.7
Employment in agriculture (% of employed ages 15+)	59	66	53	61
Employment in industry (% of employed ages 15+)	10	10	14	13
Employment in service (% of employed ages 15+)	32	23	33	25
Women in wage employment in the nonagricultural sector (%)	..		..	
Women's share of part-time employment (% of total)	..		..	
Maternity leave (weeks)	12		12	
Maternal leave benefits (% of wages paid)	50		100	
Female legislators, senior officials and managers (% of total)	..		..	
Employment to population ratio, total (% ages 15+)	64	69	64	69
Employment to population ratio, youth (% ages 15–24)	44	37	36	36
Children in employment (% of children ages 7–14)	..		48.0	49.9
Unemployment rate (% of labor force ages 15+)	5.5	3.7	3.6	3.5
Long-term unemployment rate (% total unemployment)	..	..	..	..
Youth unemployment rate (% of labor force ages 15–24)	19	15	..	..
Account at a formal financial institution (% age 15+)	..	..	27	32
Public life and decision making				
Seats held by women in national parliament (%)	..		8	

Greece

High income

Population (millions)	11.3
GNI, Atlas ($ billions)	276.7
GNI per capita, Atlas ($)	24,490
Population living below $1.25 a day (%)	..

	1990		2011	
	Female	Male	Female	Male
Demography				
Sex ratio at birth (boys per girls)	1.07		1.07	
Life expectancy at birth (years)	80	75	83	79
Under-five mortality rate (per 1,000 live births)	12	14	4	5
Female-headed households (%)	..		..	
Education				
Gross primary enrollment ratio (% of relevant age group)	98	99	101	101
Gross secondary enrollment ratio (% of relevant age group)	93	95	107	112
Gross tertiary enrollment ratio (% of relevant age group)	25	25	94	85
Primary completion rate (% of relevant age group)	98	98	99	99
Youth literacy rate (% of population ages 15–24)	99	99	99	99
Health and related services				
Total fertility rate (births per woman)	1.4		1.4	
Adolescent fertility rate (births per 1,000 women ages 15–19)	..		10	
Women first married by age 18 (% of women ages 20–24)	..		..	
Contraceptive prevalence (% of women ages 15–49)	..		..	
Unmet need for contraception (% of women ages 15–49)	..		..	
Pregnant women receiving prenatal care (%)	..		..	
Births attended by skilled health staff (% of total)	..		..	
Maternal mortality ratio (per 100,000 live births)	6		3	
Economic structure, participation, and access to resources				
Labor force participation rate (% of population ages 15+)	36	67	45	65
Wage and salaried workers (% of employed ages 15+)	52	53	68	60
Self-employed workers (% of employed ages 15+)	48	47	32	40
Vulnerable employment (% of employed ages 15+)	46	40	27	30
Unpaid family workers (% of employed ages 15+)	27.7	4.8	8.5	3.3
Employment in agriculture (% of employed ages 15+)	30	20	13	12
Employment in industry (% of employed ages 15+)	17	33	8	25
Employment in service (% of employed ages 15+)	52	46	80	63
Women in wage employment in the nonagricultural sector (%)	35		43	
Women's share of part-time employment (% of total)	61		63	
Maternity leave (weeks)	15		17	
Maternal leave benefits (% of wages paid)	100		50	
Female legislators, senior officials and managers (% of total)	23		23	
Employment to population ratio, total (% ages 15+)	30	63	35	56
Employment to population ratio, youth (% ages 15–24)	24	38	14	21
Children in employment (% of children ages 7–14)	..	..	..	..
Unemployment rate (% of labor force ages 15+)	11.7	4.2	21.4	14.9
Long-term unemployment rate (% total unemployment)	55.8	39.9	54.0	45.0
Youth unemployment rate (% of labor force ages 15–24)	33	15	52	39
Account at a formal financial institution (% age 15+)	..	..	76	80
Public life and decision making				
Seats held by women in national parliament (%)	7		21	

Greenland

	High income
Population (thousands)	56.8
GNI, Atlas ($ billions)	1.5
GNI per capita, Atlas ($)	26,020
Population living below $1.25 a day (%)	..

	1990		2011	
	Female	Male	Female	Male
Demography				
Sex ratio at birth (boys per girls)	..		..	
Life expectancy at birth (years)	68	63	73	68
Under-five mortality rate (per 1,000 live births)	..	..	..	..
Female-headed households (%)	..		..	
Education				
Gross primary enrollment ratio (% of relevant age group)	..	..	..	..
Gross secondary enrollment ratio (% of relevant age group)	..	..	..	..
Gross tertiary enrollment ratio (% of relevant age group)	..	..	..	..
Primary completion rate (% of relevant age group)	..	..	..	..
Youth literacy rate (% of population ages 15–24)	..	..	..	..
Health and related services				
Total fertility rate (births per woman)	2.4		2.1	
Adolescent fertility rate (births per 1,000 women ages 15–19)	..		..	
Women first married by age 18 (% of women ages 20–24)	..		..	
Contraceptive prevalence (% of women ages 15–49)	..		..	
Unmet need for contraception (% of women ages 15–49)	..		..	
Pregnant women receiving prenatal care (%)	..		..	
Births attended by skilled health staff (% of total)	..		..	
Maternal mortality ratio (per 100,000 live births)	..		..	
Economic structure, participation, and access to resources				
Labor force participation rate (% of population ages 15+)	..	..	..	..
Wage and salaried workers (% of employed ages 15+)	..	..	..	..
Self-employed workers (% of employed ages 15+)	..	..	..	..
Vulnerable employment (% of employed ages 15+)	..	..	..	..
Unpaid family workers (% of employed ages 15+)	..	..	..	..
Employment in agriculture (% of employed ages 15+)	..	..	..	..
Employment in industry (% of employed ages 15+)	..	..	..	..
Employment in service (% of employed ages 15+)	..	..	..	..
Women in wage employment in the nonagricultural sector (%)	..		..	
Women's share of part-time employment (% of total)	..		..	
Maternity leave (weeks)	..		..	
Maternal leave benefits (% of wages paid)	..		..	
Female legislators, senior officials and managers (% of total)	..		..	
Employment to population ratio, total (% ages 15+)	..	..	..	..
Employment to population ratio, youth (% ages 15–24)	..	..	..	..
Children in employment (% of children ages 7–14)	..	..	..	..
Unemployment rate (% of labor force ages 15+)	..	..	6.7	10.0
Long-term unemployment rate (% total unemployment)	..	..	..	..
Youth unemployment rate (% of labor force ages 15–24)	..	..	..	..
Account at a formal financial institution (% age 15+)	..	..	..	..
Public life and decision making				
Seats held by women in national parliament (%)	..		..	

Grenada

Latin America & the Caribbean	High income
Population (thousands)	104.9
GNI, Atlas ($ millions)	770.9
GNI per capita, Atlas ($)	7,350
Population living below $1.25 a day (%)	..

	1990		2011	
	Female	Male	Female	Male
Demography				
Sex ratio at birth (boys per girls)	1.05		1.05	
Life expectancy at birth (years)	71	67	77	74
Under-five mortality rate (per 1,000 live births)	20	22	12	13
Female-headed households (%)	..		..	
Education				
Gross primary enrollment ratio (% of relevant age group)	*110*	*120*	*102*	*105*
Gross secondary enrollment ratio (% of relevant age group)	96	86	*109*	*106*
Gross tertiary enrollment ratio (% of relevant age group)	..	..	61	45
Primary completion rate (% of relevant age group)	..	..	103	120
Youth literacy rate (% of population ages 15–24)	..	..	..	..
Health and related services				
Total fertility rate (births per woman)	3.8		2.2	
Adolescent fertility rate (births per 1,000 women ages 15–19)	..		37	
Women first married by age 18 (% of women ages 20–24)	..		..	
Contraceptive prevalence (% of women ages 15–49)	54		54	
Unmet need for contraception (% of women ages 15–49)	..		..	
Pregnant women receiving prenatal care (%)	100		100	
Births attended by skilled health staff (% of total)	..		99	
Maternal mortality ratio (per 100,000 live births)	34		24	
Economic structure, participation, and access to resources				
Labor force participation rate (% of population ages 15+)	..	..	..	..
Wage and salaried workers (% of employed ages 15+)	84	74	..	..
Self-employed workers (% of employed ages 15+)	17	18	..	..
Vulnerable employment (% of employed ages 15+)	15	14	..	..
Unpaid family workers (% of employed ages 15+)	5.5	1.4	..	..
Employment in agriculture (% of employed ages 15+)	15	24	..	..
Employment in industry (% of employed ages 15+)	17	30	..	..
Employment in service (% of employed ages 15+)	62	40	..	..
Women in wage employment in the nonagricultural sector (%)	40		..	
Women's share of part-time employment (% of total)	43		..	
Maternity leave (weeks)	12		13	
Maternal leave benefits (% of wages paid)	60		100	
Female legislators, senior officials and managers (% of total)	30		..	
Employment to population ratio, total (% ages 15+)	..	..	..	..
Employment to population ratio, youth (% ages 15–24)	..	..	..	..
Children in employment (% of children ages 7–14)	..	..	..	..
Unemployment rate (% of labor force ages 15+)	37.0	18.5	..	..
Long-term unemployment rate (% of total unemployment)	..	..	..	..
Youth unemployment rate (% of labor force ages 15–24)	27	28	..	..
Account at a formal financial institution (% age 15+)	..	..	..	..
Public life and decision making				
Seats held by women in national parliament (%)	..		13	

Guam

	High income
Population (thousands)	182.1
GNI, Atlas ($ millions)	..
GNI per capita, Atlas ($)	..
Population living below $1.25 a day (%)	..

	1990		2011	
	Female	Male	Female	Male
Demography				
Sex ratio at birth (boys per girls)	1.06		1.06	
Life expectancy at birth (years)	74	70	79	74
Under-five mortality rate (per 1,000 live births)	..	..	..	..
Female-headed households (%)	..		..	
Education				
Gross primary enrollment ratio (% of relevant age group)	..	..	..	..
Gross secondary enrollment ratio (% of relevant age group)	..	..	..	..
Gross tertiary enrollment ratio (% of relevant age group)	..	..	..	..
Primary completion rate (% of relevant age group)	..	..	..	..
Youth literacy rate (% of population ages 15–24)	..	..	..	..
Health and related services				
Total fertility rate (births per woman)	3.1		2.4	
Adolescent fertility rate (births per 1,000 women ages 15–19)	..		50	
Women first married by age 18 (% of women ages 20–24)	..		..	
Contraceptive prevalence (% of women ages 15–49)	..		..	
Unmet need for contraception (% of women ages 15–49)	..		..	
Pregnant women receiving prenatal care (%)	..		..	
Births attended by skilled health staff (% of total)	..		..	
Maternal mortality ratio (per 100,000 live births)	..		..	
Economic structure, participation, and access to resources				
Labor force participation rate (% of population ages 15+)	51	78	47	74
Wage and salaried workers (% of employed ages 15+)	..	..	..	..
Self-employed workers (% of employed ages 15+)	..	..	..	..
Vulnerable employment (% of employed ages 15+)	..	..	..	..
Unpaid family workers (% of employed ages 15+)	..	..	..	..
Employment in agriculture (% of employed ages 15+)	..	..	..	..
Employment in industry (% of employed ages 15+)	..	..	..	..
Employment in service (% of employed ages 15+)	..	..	..	..
Women in wage employment in the nonagricultural sector (%)	..		43	
Women's share of part-time employment (% of total)	..		..	
Maternity leave (weeks)	..		..	
Maternal leave benefits (% of wages paid)	..		..	
Female legislators, senior officials and managers (% of total)	..		..	
Employment to population ratio, total (% ages 15+)	..	..	..	..
Employment to population ratio, youth (% ages 15–24)	..	..	..	..
Children in employment (% of children ages 7–14)	..	..	..	..
Unemployment rate (% of labor force ages 15+)	4.5	4.3	..	..
Long-term unemployment rate (% total unemployment)	..	..	..	..
Youth unemployment rate (% of labor force ages 15–24)	16	16	..	..
Account at a formal financial institution (% age 15+)	..	..	..	..
Public life and decision making				
Seats held by women in national parliament (%)	..		..	

Guatemala

Latin America & the Caribbean			Lower middle income	
Population (millions)				14.8
GNI, Atlas ($ billions)				42.4
GNI per capita, Atlas ($)				2,870
Population living below $1.25 a day (%)				13.5

	1990		2011	
	Female	Male	Female	Male
Demography				
Sex ratio at birth (boys per girls)	1.05		1.05	
Life expectancy at birth (years)	65	59	75	68
Under-five mortality rate (per 1,000 live births)	74	82	28	33
Female-headed households (%)	..		..	
Education				
Gross primary enrollment ratio (% of relevant age group)	75	86	114	118
Gross secondary enrollment ratio (% of relevant age group)	24	27	62	67
Gross tertiary enrollment ratio (% of relevant age group)	..	..	18	18
Primary completion rate (% of relevant age group)	..	..	83	88
Youth literacy rate (% of population ages 15–24)	71	82	85	89
Health and related services				
Total fertility rate (births per woman)	5.6		3.9	
Adolescent fertility rate (births per 1,000 women ages 15–19)	..		103	
Women first married by age 18 (% of women ages 20–24)	41		30	
Contraceptive prevalence (% of women ages 15–49)	23		54	
Unmet need for contraception (% of women ages 15–49)	..		..	
Pregnant women receiving prenatal care (%)	35		93	
Births attended by skilled health staff (% of total)	29		52	
Maternal mortality ratio (per 100,000 live births)	160		120	
Economic structure, participation, and access to resources				
Labor force participation rate (% of population ages 15+)	41	88	49	88
Wage and salaried workers (% of employed ages 15+)	68	46	..	..
Self-employed workers (% of employed ages 15+)	32	54	..	..
Vulnerable employment (% of employed ages 15+)	30	53	..	..
Unpaid family workers (% of employed ages 15+)	9.1	14.4	..	..
Employment in agriculture (% of employed ages 15+)	3	18	16	44
Employment in industry (% of employed ages 15+)	22	34	21	24
Employment in service (% of employed ages 15+)	75	49	63	32
Women in wage employment in the nonagricultural sector (%)	37		30	
Women's share of part-time employment (% of total)	..		..	
Maternity leave (weeks)	11		12	
Maternal leave benefits (% of wages paid)	100		100	
Female legislators, senior officials and managers (% of total)	..		..	
Employment to population ratio, total (% ages 15+)	39	85	47	86
Employment to population ratio, youth (% ages 15–24)	32	76	40	76
Children in employment (% of children ages 7–14)	..	..	11.7	24.5
Unemployment rate (% of labor force ages 15+)	3.1	1.6	6.6	2.9
Long-term unemployment rate (% total unemployment)	..	..	..	..
Youth unemployment rate (% of labor force ages 15–24)	6	3	..	..
Account at a formal financial institution (% age 15+)	..	..	16	30
Public life and decision making				
Seats held by women in national parliament (%)	7		13	

Guinea

Sub-Saharan Africa	Low income
Population (millions)	10.2
GNI, Atlas ($ billions)	4.4
GNI per capita, Atlas ($)	430
Population living below $1.25 a day (%)	43.3

	1990		2011	
	Female	Male	Female	Male
Demography				
Sex ratio at birth (boys per girls)	1.06		1.06	
Life expectancy at birth (years)	45	42	56	53
Under-five mortality rate (per 1,000 live births)	224	232	123	128
Female-headed households (%)	..		..	
Education				
Gross primary enrollment ratio (% of relevant age group)	23	49	91	105
Gross secondary enrollment ratio (% of relevant age group)	6	17	32	51
Gross tertiary enrollment ratio (% of relevant age group)	0	2	6	16
Primary completion rate (% of relevant age group)	9	31	53	75
Youth literacy rate (% of population ages 15–24)	..	..	57	70
Health and related services				
Total fertility rate (births per woman)	6.7		5.2	
Adolescent fertility rate (births per 1,000 women ages 15–19)	..		138	
Women first married by age 18 (% of women ages 20–24)	67		..	
Contraceptive prevalence (% of women ages 15–49)	2		..	
Unmet need for contraception (% of women ages 15–49)	..		..	
Pregnant women receiving prenatal care (%)	58		88	
Births attended by skilled health staff (% of total)	31		46	
Maternal mortality ratio (per 100,000 live births)	1,200		610	
Economic structure, participation, and access to resources				
Labor force participation rate (% of population ages 15+)	64	79	65	78
Wage and salaried workers (% of employed ages 15+)	..	..	..	..
Self-employed workers (% of employed ages 15+)	..	..	..	..
Vulnerable employment (% of employed ages 15+)	..	..	..	..
Unpaid family workers (% of employed ages 15+)	..	..	..	..
Employment in agriculture (% of employed ages 15+)	79	73	..	..
Employment in industry (% of employed ages 15+)	3	9	..	..
Employment in service (% of employed ages 15+)	18	18	..	..
Women in wage employment in the nonagricultural sector (%)	..		29	
Women's share of part-time employment (% of total)	..		..	
Maternity leave (weeks)	14		14	
Maternal leave benefits (% of wages paid)	100		100	
Female legislators, senior officials and managers (% of total)	..		..	
Employment to population ratio, total (% ages 15+)	63	76	64	76
Employment to population ratio, youth (% ages 15–24)	48	54	50	54
Children in employment (% of children ages 7–14)	49.5	47.2	..	..
Unemployment rate (% of labor force ages 15+)	1.7	4.6	..	..
Long-term unemployment rate (% total unemployment)	..	..	..	..
Youth unemployment rate (% of labor force ages 15–24)	..	..	..	..
Account at a formal financial institution (% age 15+)	..	..	3	4
Public life and decision making				
Seats held by women in national parliament (%)	..		19	

Guinea-Bissau

Sub-Saharan Africa			Low income	

Population (millions)				1.5
GNI, Atlas ($ millions)				925.5
GNI per capita, Atlas ($)				600
Population living below $1.25 a day (%)				48.9

	1990		2011	
	Female	Male	Female	Male
Demography				
Sex ratio at birth (boys per girls)	1.03		1.03	
Life expectancy at birth (years)	44	41	50	47
Under-five mortality rate (per 1,000 live births)	193	227	147	174
Female-headed households (%)	..		..	
Education				
Gross primary enrollment ratio (% of relevant age group)	39	69	119	127
Gross secondary enrollment ratio (% of relevant age group)	3	7	..	..
Gross tertiary enrollment ratio (% of relevant age group)	0	1	..	..
Primary completion rate (% of relevant age group)	4	8	60	75
Youth literacy rate (% of population ages 15–24)	..	..	65	79
Health and related services				
Total fertility rate (births per woman)	6.6		5.0	
Adolescent fertility rate (births per 1,000 women ages 15–19)	..		99	
Women first married by age 18 (% of women ages 20–24)	..		22	
Contraceptive prevalence (% of women ages 15–49)	..		14	
Unmet need for contraception (% of women ages 15–49)	..		25	
Pregnant women receiving prenatal care (%)	..		93	
Births attended by skilled health staff (% of total)	..		44	
Maternal mortality ratio (per 100,000 live births)	1,100		790	
Economic structure, participation, and access to resources				
Labor force participation rate (% of population ages 15+)	60	78	68	78
Wage and salaried workers (% of employed ages 15+)	..	..	..	..
Self-employed workers (% of employed ages 15+)	..	..	..	..
Vulnerable employment (% of employed ages 15+)	..	..	..	..
Unpaid family workers (% of employed ages 15+)	..	..	..	..
Employment in agriculture (% of employed ages 15+)	..	..	..	..
Employment in industry (% of employed ages 15+)	..	..	..	..
Employment in service (% of employed ages 15+)	..	..	..	..
Women in wage employment in the nonagricultural sector (%)	11		..	
Women's share of part-time employment (% of total)	..		..	
Maternity leave (weeks)	8		9	
Maternal leave benefits (% of wages paid)	100		100	
Female legislators, senior officials and managers (% of total)	..		..	
Employment to population ratio, total (% ages 15+)	57	73	64	73
Employment to population ratio, youth (% ages 15–24)	41	49	48	51
Children in employment (% of children ages 7–14)	..	..	48.1	52.8
Unemployment rate (% of labor force ages 15+)	..	..	..	..
Long-term unemployment rate (% total unemployment)	..	..	..	..
Youth unemployment rate (% of labor force ages 15–24)	..	..	..	..
Account at a formal financial institution (% age 15+)	..	..	..	..
Public life and decision making				
Seats held by women in national parliament (%)	20		14	

Guyana

Latin America & the Caribbean	Lower middle income
Population (thousands)	756.0
GNI, Atlas ($ billions)	2.2
GNI per capita, Atlas ($)	2,900
Population living below $1.25 a day (%)	..

	1990		2011	
	Female	Male	Female	Male
Demography				
Sex ratio at birth (boys per girls)	1.05		1.05	
Life expectancy at birth (years)	64	58	73	67
Under-five mortality rate (per 1,000 live births)	55	70	32	40
Female-headed households (%)	..		34	
Education				
Gross primary enrollment ratio (% of relevant age group)	106	110	89	85
Gross secondary enrollment ratio (% of relevant age group)	83	81	98	89
Gross tertiary enrollment ratio (% of relevant age group)	5	7	17	7
Primary completion rate (% of relevant age group)	97	97	87	84
Youth literacy rate (% of population ages 15–24)	..	..	..	..
Health and related services				
Total fertility rate (births per woman)	2.6		2.2	
Adolescent fertility rate (births per 1,000 women ages 15–19)	..		57	
Women first married by age 18 (% of women ages 20–24)	..		23	
Contraceptive prevalence (% of women ages 15–49)	38		43	
Unmet need for contraception (% of women ages 15–49)	..		29	
Pregnant women receiving prenatal care (%)	..		92	
Births attended by skilled health staff (% of total)	..		92	
Maternal mortality ratio (per 100,000 live births)	180		280	
Economic structure, participation, and access to resources				
Labor force participation rate (% of population ages 15+)	36	83	42	79
Wage and salaried workers (% of employed ages 15+)	53	52	..	..
Self-employed workers (% of employed ages 15+)	47	48	..	..
Vulnerable employment (% of employed ages 15+)	..	..	..	..
Unpaid family workers (% of employed ages 15+)	..	..	..	..
Employment in agriculture (% of employed ages 15+)	..	..	..	..
Employment in industry (% of employed ages 15+)	..	..	..	..
Employment in service (% of employed ages 15+)	..	..	..	..
Women in wage employment in the nonagricultural sector (%)	..		..	
Women's share of part-time employment (% of total)	..		55	
Maternity leave (weeks)	13		13	
Maternal leave benefits (% of wages paid)	..		70	
Female legislators, senior officials and managers (% of total)	..		..	
Employment to population ratio, total (% ages 15+)	31	76	36	72
Employment to population ratio, youth (% ages 15–24)	22	58	21	48
Children in employment (% of children ages 7–14)	..	..	..	..
Unemployment rate (% of labor force ages 15+)	18.1	8.4	25.7	17.2
Long-term unemployment rate (% total unemployment)	..	..	..	..
Youth unemployment rate (% of labor force ages 15–24)	38	21	50	44
Account at a formal financial institution (% age 15+)	..	..	..	..
Public life and decision making				
Seats held by women in national parliament (%)	37		31	

Haiti

Latin America & the Caribbean				Low income
Population (millions)				10.1
GNI, Atlas ($ billions)				7.1
GNI per capita, Atlas ($)				700
Population living below $1.25 a day (%)				61.7

	1990		2011	
	Female	Male	Female	Male
Demography				
Sex ratio at birth (boys per girls)	1.05		1.05	
Life expectancy at birth (years)	56	54	63	61
Under-five mortality rate (per 1,000 live births)	134	152	66	74
Female-headed households (%)	..		44	
Education				
Gross primary enrollment ratio (% of relevant age group)	73	76	..	..
Gross secondary enrollment ratio (% of relevant age group)	..	..	..	..
Gross tertiary enrollment ratio (% of relevant age group)	1	2	..	..
Primary completion rate (% of relevant age group)	35	41	..	..
Youth literacy rate (% of population ages 15–24)	..	..	70	74
Health and related services				
Total fertility rate (births per woman)	5.4		3.3	
Adolescent fertility rate (births per 1,000 women ages 15–19)	..		42	
Women first married by age 18 (% of women ages 20–24)	..		30	
Contraceptive prevalence (% of women ages 15–49)	10		32	
Unmet need for contraception (% of women ages 15–49)	..		38	
Pregnant women receiving prenatal care (%)	71		85	
Births attended by skilled health staff (% of total)	23		26	
Maternal mortality ratio (per 100,000 live births)	620		350	
Economic structure, participation, and access to resources				
Labor force participation rate (% of population ages 15+)	57	78	60	71
Wage and salaried workers (% of employed ages 15+)	21	17	..	..
Self-employed workers (% of employed ages 15+)	77	81	..	..
Vulnerable employment (% of employed ages 15+)	..	..	..	..
Unpaid family workers (% of employed ages 15+)	11.2	12.3	..	..
Employment in agriculture (% of employed ages 15+)	50	76	..	..
Employment in industry (% of employed ages 15+)	9	9	..	..
Employment in service (% of employed ages 15+)	38	13	..	..
Women in wage employment in the nonagricultural sector (%)	44		..	
Women's share of part-time employment (% of total)	..		..	
Maternity leave (weeks)	12		12	
Maternal leave benefits (% of wages paid)	100		100	
Female legislators, senior officials and managers (% of total)	..		..	
Employment to population ratio, total (% ages 15+)	48	70	54	66
Employment to population ratio, youth (% ages 15–24)	27	40	26	33
Children in employment (% of children ages 7–14)	..	..	..	..
Unemployment rate (% of labor force ages 15+)	13.8	11.9	..	..
Long-term unemployment rate (% total unemployment)	..	..	..	..
Youth unemployment rate (% of labor force ages 15–24)	24	23	..	..
Account at a formal financial institution (% age 15+)	..	..	21	23
Public life and decision making				
Seats held by women in national parliament (%)	..		4	

Honduras

Latin America & the Caribbean			Lower middle income	
Population (millions)				7.8
GNI, Atlas ($ billions)				15.4
GNI per capita, Atlas ($)				1,980
Population living below $1.25 a day (%)				*17.9*

	1990		2011	
	Female	Male	Female	Male
Demography				
Sex ratio at birth (boys per girls)	1.05		1.05	
Life expectancy at birth (years)	69	64	75	71
Under-five mortality rate (per 1,000 live births)	52	58	20	23
Female-headed households (%)	..		*26*	
Education				
Gross primary enrollment ratio (% of relevant age group)	108	107	114	114
Gross secondary enrollment ratio (% of relevant age group)	*37*	*30*	82	67
Gross tertiary enrollment ratio (% of relevant age group)	8	10	*22*	*19*
Primary completion rate (% of relevant age group)	*61*	*68*	105	98
Youth literacy rate (% of population ages 15–24)	..	..	96	94
Health and related services				
Total fertility rate (births per woman)	5.1		3.1	
Adolescent fertility rate (births per 1,000 women ages 15–19)	..		87	
Women first married by age 18 (% of women ages 20–24)	..		*39*	
Contraceptive prevalence (% of women ages 15–49)	47		65	
Unmet need for contraception (% of women ages 15–49)	..		*17*	
Pregnant women receiving prenatal care (%)	88		*92*	
Births attended by skilled health staff (% of total)	47		*67*	
Maternal mortality ratio (per 100,000 live births)	220		*100*	
Economic structure, participation, and access to resources				
Labor force participation rate (% of population ages 15+)	33	86	42	83
Wage and salaried workers (% of employed ages 15+)	49	50	*41*	*46*
Self-employed workers (% of employed ages 15+)	51	50	59	54
Vulnerable employment (% of employed ages 15+)	50	48	57	51
Unpaid family workers (% of employed ages 15+)	6.3	11.3	*11.9*	*13.3*
Employment in agriculture (% of employed ages 15+)	6	65	*12*	*50*
Employment in industry (% of employed ages 15+)	23	15	*21*	*19*
Employment in service (% of employed ages 15+)	71	20	*67*	*31*
Women in wage employment in the nonagricultural sector (%)	41		42	
Women's share of part-time employment (% of total)	59		..	
Maternity leave (weeks)	10		*12*	
Maternal leave benefits (% of wages paid)	100		*100*	
Female legislators, senior officials and managers (% of total)	..		..	
Employment to population ratio, total (% ages 15+)	*31*	*83*	41	81
Employment to population ratio, youth (% ages 15–24)	*26*	*71*	29	64
Children in employment (% of children ages 7–14)	..	..	*4.1*	*13.3*
Unemployment rate (% of labor force ages 15+)	6.2	4.4	5.6	4.3
Long-term unemployment rate (% total unemployment)	..	..	..	..
Youth unemployment rate (% of labor force ages 15–24)	9	11	..	..
Account at a formal financial institution (% age 15+)	..	..	15	26
Public life and decision making				
Seats held by women in national parliament (%)	10		20	

Hong Kong SAR, China

High income

Population (millions)	7.1
GNI, Atlas ($ billions)	254.6
GNI per capita, Atlas ($)	36,010
Population living below $1.25 a day (%)	..

	1990 Female	1990 Male	2011 Female	2011 Male
Demography				
Sex ratio at birth (boys per girls)	1.07		1.07	
Life expectancy at birth (years)	80	75	87	80
Under-five mortality rate (per 1,000 live births)	..	..	..	..
Female-headed households (%)	..		..	
Education				
Gross primary enrollment ratio (% of relevant age group)	*106*	*107*	*110*	*106*
Gross secondary enrollment ratio (% of relevant age group)	*78*	*74*	*81*	*79*
Gross tertiary enrollment ratio (% of relevant age group)	*15*	*22*	*63*	*57*
Primary completion rate (% of relevant age group)	..	..	92	90
Youth literacy rate (% of population ages 15–24)	..	..	..	..
Health and related services				
Total fertility rate (births per woman)	1.3		1.2	
Adolescent fertility rate (births per 1,000 women ages 15–19)	..		4	
Women first married by age 18 (% of women ages 20–24)	..		..	
Contraceptive prevalence (% of women ages 15–49)	*86*		*80*	
Unmet need for contraception (% of women ages 15–49)	..		..	
Pregnant women receiving prenatal care (%)	..		..	
Births attended by skilled health staff (% of total)	..		..	
Maternal mortality ratio (per 100,000 live births)	..		..	
Economic structure, participation, and access to resources				
Labor force participation rate (% of population ages 15+)	47	79	51	68
Wage and salaried workers (% of employed ages 15+)	95	85	94	86
Self-employed workers (% of employed ages 15+)	5	15	6	14
Vulnerable employment (% of employed ages 15+)	*4*	*7*	*4*	*9*
Unpaid family workers (% of employed ages 15+)	*2.0*	*0.2*	*0.7*	*0.1*
Employment in agriculture (% of employed ages 15+)	*1*	*1*	*0*	*0*
Employment in industry (% of employed ages 15+)	*33*	*39*	*4*	*19*
Employment in service (% of employed ages 15+)	*66*	*60*	*96*	*80*
Women in wage employment in the nonagricultural sector (%)	41		50	
Women's share of part-time employment (% of total)	..		56	
Maternity leave (weeks)	10		10	
Maternal leave benefits (% of wages paid)	67		80	
Female legislators, senior officials and managers (% of total)	17		32	
Employment to population ratio, total (% ages 15+)	*47*	*78*	*50*	*65*
Employment to population ratio, youth (% ages 15–24)	*54*	*55*	*33*	*32*
Children in employment (% of children ages 7–14)	..	..	..	..
Unemployment rate (% of labor force ages 15+)	1.3	1.3	2.8	3.9
Long-term unemployment rate (% total unemployment)	..	..	..	..
Youth unemployment rate (% of labor force ages 15–24)	3	4	8	11
Account at a formal financial institution (% age 15+)	..	..	89	88
Public life and decision making				
Seats held by women in national parliament (%)	..		..	

Hungary

	High income
Population (millions)	10.0
GNI, Atlas ($ billions)	126.9
GNI per capita, Atlas ($)	12,730
Population living below $1.25 a day (%)	<2

	1990		2011	
	Female	Male	Female	Male
Demography				
Sex ratio at birth (boys per girls)	1.06		1.06	
Life expectancy at birth (years)	74	65	79	71
Under-five mortality rate (per 1,000 live births)	17	21	6	7
Female-headed households (%)	..		..	
Education				
Gross primary enrollment ratio (% of relevant age group)	87	88	101	102
Gross secondary enrollment ratio (% of relevant age group)	88	87	99	101
Gross tertiary enrollment ratio (% of relevant age group)	15	14	70	52
Primary completion rate (% of relevant age group)	86	85	97	98
Youth literacy rate (% of population ages 15–24)	99	99	99	99
Health and related services				
Total fertility rate (births per woman)	1.8		1.2	
Adolescent fertility rate (births per 1,000 women ages 15–19)	..		14	
Women first married by age 18 (% of women ages 20–24)	..		..	
Contraceptive prevalence (% of women ages 15–49)	81		..	
Unmet need for contraception (% of women ages 15–49)	..		..	
Pregnant women receiving prenatal care (%)	..		..	
Births attended by skilled health staff (% of total)	99		100	
Maternal mortality ratio (per 100,000 live births)	23		21	
Economic structure, participation, and access to resources				
Labor force participation rate (% of population ages 15+)	46	65	44	58
Wage and salaried workers (% of employed ages 15+)	89	81	92	85
Self-employed workers (% of employed ages 15+)	11	16	9	15
Vulnerable employment (% of employed ages 15+)	7	8	5	8
Unpaid family workers (% of employed ages 15+)	1.8	0.7	0.6	0.3
Employment in agriculture (% of employed ages 15+)	15	21	3	7
Employment in industry (% of employed ages 15+)	30	43	20	40
Employment in service (% of employed ages 15+)	55	36	77	53
Women in wage employment in the nonagricultural sector (%)	49		49	
Women's share of part-time employment (% of total)	..		62	
Maternity leave (weeks)	24		24	
Maternal leave benefits (% of wages paid)	100		70	
Female legislators, senior officials and managers (% of total)	..		40	
Employment to population ratio, total (% ages 15+)	42	56	39	52
Employment to population ratio, youth (% ages 15–24)	34	41	17	21
Children in employment (% of children ages 7–14)	..	..	..	..
Unemployment rate (% of labor force ages 15+)	8.7	11.0	10.9	11.0
Long-term unemployment rate (% total unemployment)	19.8	20.9	49.2	48.9
Youth unemployment rate (% of labor force ages 15–24)	15	22	25	27
Account at a formal financial institution (% age 15+)	..	..	73	72
Public life and decision making				
Seats held by women in national parliament (%)	21		9	

Iceland

	High income
Population (thousands)	319.0
GNI, Atlas ($ billions)	11.1
GNI per capita, Atlas ($)	34,820
Population living below $1.25 a day (%)	..

	1990		2011	
	Female	Male	Female	Male
Demography				
Sex ratio at birth (boys per girls)	1.04		1.05	
Life expectancy at birth (years)	81	75	84	81
Under-five mortality rate (per 1,000 live births)	6	7	2	3
Female-headed households (%)	..		..	
Education				
Gross primary enrollment ratio (% of relevant age group)	102	101	99	99
Gross secondary enrollment ratio (% of relevant age group)	98	101	109	107
Gross tertiary enrollment ratio (% of relevant age group)	29	22	101	57
Primary completion rate (% of relevant age group)	..	..	97	99
Youth literacy rate (% of population ages 15–24)	..	..	..	..
Health and related services				
Total fertility rate (births per woman)	2.3		2.0	
Adolescent fertility rate (births per 1,000 women ages 15–19)	..		12	
Women first married by age 18 (% of women ages 20–24)	..		..	
Contraceptive prevalence (% of women ages 15–49)	..		..	
Unmet need for contraception (% of women ages 15–49)	..		..	
Pregnant women receiving prenatal care (%)	..		..	
Births attended by skilled health staff (% of total)	..		..	
Maternal mortality ratio (per 100,000 live births)	8		5	
Economic structure, participation, and access to resources				
Labor force participation rate (% of population ages 15+)	68	82	71	78
Wage and salaried workers (% of employed ages 15+)	88	73	91	83
Self-employed workers (% of employed ages 15+)	12	27	8	16
Vulnerable employment (% of employed ages 15+)	9	17	6	10
Unpaid family workers (% of employed ages 15+)	3.0	2.1	0.0	0.1
Employment in agriculture (% of employed ages 15+)	5	14	2	9
Employment in industry (% of employed ages 15+)	18	33	8	28
Employment in service (% of employed ages 15+)	77	53	90	62
Women in wage employment in the nonagricultural sector (%)	53		52	
Women's share of part-time employment (% of total)	82		68	
Maternity leave (weeks)	8		13	
Maternal leave benefits (% of wages paid)	..		80	
Female legislators, senior officials and managers (% of total)	27		40	
Employment to population ratio, total (% ages 15+)	66	80	67	72
Employment to population ratio, youth (% ages 15–24)	57	57	64	53
Children in employment (% of children ages 7–14)	..	..	..	..
Unemployment rate (% of labor force ages 15+)	2.9	2.3	6.2	7.8
Long-term unemployment rate (% total unemployment)	10.4	1.1	24.5	25.6
Youth unemployment rate (% of labor force ages 15–24)	4	6	11	18
Account at a formal financial institution (% age 15+)	..	..	..	..
Public life and decision making				
Seats held by women in national parliament (%)	21		40	

India

South Asia			Lower middle income	
Population (millions)				1,241.5
GNI, Atlas ($ billions)				1,766.2
GNI per capita, Atlas ($)				1,420
Population living below $1.25 a day (%)				32.7

	1990		2011	
	Female	Male	Female	Male
Demography				
Sex ratio at birth (boys per girls)	1.08		1.08	
Life expectancy at birth (years)	59	58	67	64
Under-five mortality rate (per 1,000 live births)	119	110	64	59
Female-headed households (%)	9		14	
Education				
Gross primary enrollment ratio (% of relevant age group)	77	104	116	116
Gross secondary enrollment ratio (% of relevant age group)	27	46	60	66
Gross tertiary enrollment ratio (% of relevant age group)	4	8	15	21
Primary completion rate (% of relevant age group)	51	74	95	96
Youth literacy rate (% of population ages 15–24)	49	74	74	88
Health and related services				
Total fertility rate (births per woman)	3.9		2.6	
Adolescent fertility rate (births per 1,000 women ages 15–19)	..		77	
Women first married by age 18 (% of women ages 20–24)	54		47	
Contraceptive prevalence (% of women ages 15–49)	45		55	
Unmet need for contraception (% of women ages 15–49)	17		13	
Pregnant women receiving prenatal care (%)	62		75	
Births attended by skilled health staff (% of total)	34		52	
Maternal mortality ratio (per 100,000 live births)	600		200	
Economic structure, participation, and access to resources				
Labor force participation rate (% of population ages 15+)	35	85	29	81
Wage and salaried workers (% of employed ages 15+)	8	18	15	19
Self-employed workers (% of employed ages 15+)	92	82	86	81
Vulnerable employment (% of employed ages 15+)	91	80	85	79
Unpaid family workers (% of employed ages 15+)	37.8	13.7	33.9	11.0
Employment in agriculture (% of employed ages 15+)	72	56	65	46
Employment in industry (% of employed ages 15+)	12	17	18	24
Employment in service (% of employed ages 15+)	15	27	17	30
Women in wage employment in the nonagricultural sector (%)	13		..	
Women's share of part-time employment (% of total)	..		..	
Maternity leave (weeks)	12		12	
Maternal leave benefits (% of wages paid)	100		100	
Female legislators, senior officials and managers (% of total)	15		14	
Employment to population ratio, total (% ages 15+)	34	82	28	78
Employment to population ratio, youth (% ages 15–24)	28	63	17	49
Children in employment (% of children ages 7–14)	..	..	2.1	2.8
Unemployment rate (% of labor force ages 15+)	3.9	3.6	4.3	3.3
Long-term unemployment rate (% total unemployment)	..	..	41.4	36.6
Youth unemployment rate (% of labor force ages 15–24)	8	8	12	10
Account at a formal financial institution (% age 15+)	..	..	26	44
Public life and decision making				
Seats held by women in national parliament (%)	5		11	

Indonesia

East Asia & Pacific	Lower middle income
Population (millions)	242.3
GNI, Atlas ($ billions)	712.7
GNI per capita, Atlas ($)	2,940
Population living below $1.25 a day (%)	18.1

	1990		2011	
	Female	Male	Female	Male
Demography				
Sex ratio at birth (boys per girls)	1.05		1.05	
Life expectancy at birth (years)	64	60	71	68
Under-five mortality rate (per 1,000 live births)	75	88	29	34
Female-headed households (%)	13		13	
Education				
Gross primary enrollment ratio (% of relevant age group)	110	115	119	117
Gross secondary enrollment ratio (% of relevant age group)	41	50	77	77
Gross tertiary enrollment ratio (% of relevant age group)	7	11	22	24
Primary completion rate (% of relevant age group)	..	..	105	104
Youth literacy rate (% of population ages 15–24)	95	97	99	100
Health and related services				
Total fertility rate (births per woman)	3.1		2.1	
Adolescent fertility rate (births per 1,000 women ages 15–19)	..		43	
Women first married by age 18 (% of women ages 20–24)	34		22	
Contraceptive prevalence (% of women ages 15–49)	50		61	
Unmet need for contraception (% of women ages 15–49)	14		15	
Pregnant women receiving prenatal care (%)	76		93	
Births attended by skilled health staff (% of total)	41		82	
Maternal mortality ratio (per 100,000 live births)	600		220	
Economic structure, participation, and access to resources				
Labor force participation rate (% of population ages 15+)	50	81	51	84
Wage and salaried workers (% of employed ages 15+)	..	..	32	34
Self-employed workers (% of employed ages 15+)	..	..	68	66
Vulnerable employment (% of employed ages 15+)	..	..	67	62
Unpaid family workers (% of employed ages 15+)	..	..	32.4	8.1
Employment in agriculture (% of employed ages 15+)	56	56	35	37
Employment in industry (% of employed ages 15+)	12	15	15	24
Employment in service (% of employed ages 15+)	31	30	50	40
Women in wage employment in the nonagricultural sector (%)	29		32	
Women's share of part-time employment (% of total)	..		..	
Maternity leave (weeks)	12		13	
Maternal leave benefits (% of wages paid)	100		100	
Female legislators, senior officials and managers (% of total)	..		22	
Employment to population ratio, total (% ages 15+)	48	79	47	79
Employment to population ratio, youth (% ages 15–24)	37	55	31	49
Children in employment (% of children ages 7–14)	..	..	3.2	4.2
Unemployment rate (% of labor force ages 15+)	2.7	2.8	7.6	5.9
Long-term unemployment rate (% total unemployment)	..	..	..	..
Youth unemployment rate (% of labor force ages 15–24)	9	9	21	19
Account at a formal financial institution (% age 15+)	..	..	19	20
Public life and decision making				
Seats held by women in national parliament (%)	12		19	

Iran, Islamic Rep.

Middle East & North Africa	Upper middle income
Population (millions)	74.8
GNI, Atlas ($ billions)	330.4
GNI per capita, Atlas ($)	4,520
Population living below $1.25 a day (%)	<2

	1990		2011	
	Female	Male	Female	Male
Demography				
Sex ratio at birth (boys per girls)	1.05		1.05	
Life expectancy at birth (years)	66	58	75	71
Under-five mortality rate (per 1,000 live births)	60	62	25	25
Female-headed households (%)	..		..	
Education				
Gross primary enrollment ratio (% of relevant age group)	101	115	107	108
Gross secondary enrollment ratio (% of relevant age group)	45	63	84	87
Gross tertiary enrollment ratio (% of relevant age group)	3	9	49	48
Primary completion rate (% of relevant age group)	81	93	106	106
Youth literacy rate (% of population ages 15–24)	81	92	99	99
Health and related services				
Total fertility rate (births per woman)	4.8		1.6	
Adolescent fertility rate (births per 1,000 women ages 15–19)	..		26	
Women first married by age 18 (% of women ages 20–24)	..		..	
Contraceptive prevalence (% of women ages 15–49)	49		..	
Unmet need for contraception (% of women ages 15–49)	..		..	
Pregnant women receiving prenatal care (%)	..		..	
Births attended by skilled health staff (% of total)	..		..	
Maternal mortality ratio (per 100,000 live births)	120		21	
Economic structure, participation, and access to resources				
Labor force participation rate (% of population ages 15+)	10	80	16	73
Wage and salaried workers (% of employed ages 15+)	..	..	47	54
Self-employed workers (% of employed ages 15+)	..	..	53	46
Vulnerable employment (% of employed ages 15+)	..	..	52	40
Unpaid family workers (% of employed ages 15+)	..	..	29.7	4.8
Employment in agriculture (% of employed ages 15+)	..	..	31	19
Employment in industry (% of employed ages 15+)	..	..	27	33
Employment in service (% of employed ages 15+)	..	..	42	47
Women in wage employment in the nonagricultural sector (%)	11		15	
Women's share of part-time employment (% of total)	..		..	
Maternity leave (weeks)	12		13	
Maternal leave benefits (% of wages paid)	67		67	
Female legislators, senior officials and managers (% of total)	..		13	
Employment to population ratio, total (% ages 15+)	8	72	14	66
Employment to population ratio, youth (% ages 15–24)	9	48	9	39
Children in employment (% of children ages 7–14)	..	..	..	..
Unemployment rate (% of labor force ages 15+)	24.4	9.5	16.8	9.1
Long-term unemployment rate (% total unemployment)	..	..	..	..
Youth unemployment rate (% of labor force ages 15–24)	..	..	34	20
Account at a formal financial institution (% age 15+)	..	..	62	85
Public life and decision making				
Seats held by women in national parliament (%)	2		3	

Iraq

Middle East & North Africa			Lower middle income	
Population (millions)				33.0
GNI, Atlas ($ billions)				87.0
GNI per capita, Atlas ($)				2,640
Population living below $1.25 a day (%)				2.8

	1990		2011	
	Female	Male	Female	Male
Demography				
Sex ratio at birth (boys per girls)	1.07		1.07	
Life expectancy at birth (years)	72	63	72	66
Under-five mortality rate (per 1,000 live births)	42	50	35	41
Female-headed households (%)	..		11	
Education				
Gross primary enrollment ratio (% of relevant age group)	99	117	95	113
Gross secondary enrollment ratio (% of relevant age group)	36	57	45	60
Gross tertiary enrollment ratio (% of relevant age group)	9	16	..	..
Primary completion rate (% of relevant age group)	53	64	55	74
Youth literacy rate (% of population ages 15–24)	..	..	81	85
Health and related services				
Total fertility rate (births per woman)	6.0		4.6	
Adolescent fertility rate (births per 1,000 women ages 15–19)	..		88	
Women first married by age 18 (% of women ages 20–24)	..		17	
Contraceptive prevalence (% of women ages 15–49)	14		50	
Unmet need for contraception (% of women ages 15–49)	..		..	
Pregnant women receiving prenatal care (%)	..		84	
Births attended by skilled health staff (% of total)	54		80	
Maternal mortality ratio (per 100,000 live births)	89		63	
Economic structure, participation, and access to resources				
Labor force participation rate (% of population ages 15+)	11	71	15	69
Wage and salaried workers (% of employed ages 15+)	..	..	..	..
Self-employed workers (% of employed ages 15+)	..	..	..	..
Vulnerable employment (% of employed ages 15+)	..	..	..	..
Unpaid family workers (% of employed ages 15+)	..	..	..	..
Employment in agriculture (% of employed ages 15+)	..	..	51	17
Employment in industry (% of employed ages 15+)	..	..	4	22
Employment in service (% of employed ages 15+)	..	..	46	61
Women in wage employment in the nonagricultural sector (%)	..		12	
Women's share of part-time employment (% of total)	..		..	
Maternity leave (weeks)	8		9	
Maternal leave benefits (% of wages paid)	100		100	
Female legislators, senior officials and managers (% of total)	..		..	
Employment to population ratio, total (% ages 15+)	7	59	10	58
Employment to population ratio, youth (% ages 15–24)	3	38	2	31
Children in employment (% of children ages 7–14)	..	..	11.3	17.9
Unemployment rate (% of labor force ages 15+)	..	..	22.5	16.2
Long-term unemployment rate (% total unemployment)	..	..	..	..
Youth unemployment rate (% of labor force ages 15–24)	..	..	..	..
Account at a formal financial institution (% age 15+)	..	..	8	13
Public life and decision making				
Seats held by women in national parliament (%)	11		25	

Ireland

	High income
Population (millions)	4.6
GNI, Atlas ($ billions)	179.2
GNI per capita, Atlas ($)	39,150
Population living below $1.25 a day (%)	..

	1990		2011	
	Female	Male	Female	Male
Demography				
Sex ratio at birth (boys per girls)	1.07		1.07	
Life expectancy at birth (years)	78	72	83	78
Under-five mortality rate (per 1,000 live births)	8	10	4	4
Female-headed households (%)	..		..	
Education				
Gross primary enrollment ratio (% of relevant age group)	104	103	108	108
Gross secondary enrollment ratio (% of relevant age group)	104	95	124	118
Gross tertiary enrollment ratio (% of relevant age group)	26	30	71	62
Primary completion rate (% of relevant age group)	103	103	104	102
Youth literacy rate (% of population ages 15–24)	..	..	..	..
Health and related services				
Total fertility rate (births per woman)	2.1		2.1	
Adolescent fertility rate (births per 1,000 women ages 15–19)	..		11	
Women first married by age 18 (% of women ages 20–24)	..		..	
Contraceptive prevalence (% of women ages 15–49)	..		..	
Unmet need for contraception (% of women ages 15–49)	..		..	
Pregnant women receiving prenatal care (%)	..		..	
Births attended by skilled health staff (% of total)	..		..	
Maternal mortality ratio (per 100,000 live births)	6		6	
Economic structure, participation, and access to resources				
Labor force participation rate (% of population ages 15+)	36	71	53	69
Wage and salaried workers (% of employed ages 15+)	89	68	93	75
Self-employed workers (% of employed ages 15+)	12	32	8	25
Vulnerable employment (% of employed ages 15+)	10	25	5	18
Unpaid family workers (% of employed ages 15+)	3.5	2.0	0.7	0.5
Employment in agriculture (% of employed ages 15+)	4	18	1	8
Employment in industry (% of employed ages 15+)	17	34	9	28
Employment in service (% of employed ages 15+)	79	48	90	64
Women in wage employment in the nonagricultural sector (%)	42		52	
Women's share of part-time employment (% of total)	70		75	
Maternity leave (weeks)	14		26	
Maternal leave benefits (% of wages paid)	70		80	
Female legislators, senior officials and managers (% of total)	18		33	
Employment to population ratio, total (% ages 15+)	30	60	47	56
Employment to population ratio, youth (% ages 15–24)	36	40	32	29
Children in employment (% of children ages 7–14)	..	..	..	..
Unemployment rate (% of labor force ages 15+)	15.0	13.6	10.6	17.4
Long-term unemployment rate (% total unemployment)	56.2	70.5	46.7	64.7
Youth unemployment rate (% of labor force ages 15–24)	18	21	23	35
Account at a formal financial institution (% age 15+)	..	..	92	96
Public life and decision making				
Seats held by women in national parliament (%)	8		15	

Isle of Man

Population (thousands)	83.3
GNI, Atlas ($ billions)	..
GNI per capita, Atlas ($)	..
Population living below $1.25 a day (%)	..

	1990		2011	
	Female	Male	Female	Male
Demography				
Sex ratio at birth (boys per girls)	..		..	
Life expectancy at birth (years)	80	74	..	..
Under-five mortality rate (per 1,000 live births)	..	..	..	..
Female-headed households (%)	..		..	
Education				
Gross primary enrollment ratio (% of relevant age group)	..	..	..	..
Gross secondary enrollment ratio (% of relevant age group)	..	..	..	..
Gross tertiary enrollment ratio (% of relevant age group)	..	..	..	..
Primary completion rate (% of relevant age group)	..	..	..	..
Youth literacy rate (% of population ages 15–24)	..	..	..	..
Health and related services				
Total fertility rate (births per woman)	1.8		..	
Adolescent fertility rate (births per 1,000 women ages 15–19)	..		..	
Women first married by age 18 (% of women ages 20–24)	..		..	
Contraceptive prevalence (% of women ages 15–49)	..		..	
Unmet need for contraception (% of women ages 15–49)	..		..	
Pregnant women receiving prenatal care (%)	..		..	
Births attended by skilled health staff (% of total)	..		..	
Maternal mortality ratio (per 100,000 live births)	..		..	
Economic structure, participation, and access to resources				
Labor force participation rate (% of population ages 15+)	..	..	..	..
Wage and salaried workers (% of employed ages 15+)	..	..	..	..
Self-employed workers (% of employed ages 15+)	..	..	..	..
Vulnerable employment (% of employed ages 15+)	..	..	..	..
Unpaid family workers (% of employed ages 15+)	..	..	..	..
Employment in agriculture (% of employed ages 15+)	..	..	1	3
Employment in industry (% of employed ages 15+)	..	..	4	24
Employment in service (% of employed ages 15+)	..	..	95	73
Women in wage employment in the nonagricultural sector (%)	..		..	
Women's share of part-time employment (% of total)	..		..	
Maternity leave (weeks)	..		..	
Maternal leave benefits (% of wages paid)	..		..	
Female legislators, senior officials and managers (% of total)	..		..	
Employment to population ratio, total (% ages 15+)	..	..	..	..
Employment to population ratio, youth (% ages 15–24)	..	..	..	..
Children in employment (% of children ages 7–14)	..	..	..	..
Unemployment rate (% of labor force ages 15+)	3.3	4.7	2.0	2.8
Long-term unemployment rate (% total unemployment)	..	..	..	..
Youth unemployment rate (% of labor force ages 15–24)	6	9	5	10
Account at a formal financial institution (% age 15+)	..	..	..	..
Public life and decision making				
Seats held by women in national parliament (%)	..		..	

Israel

	High income
Population (millions)	7.8
GNI, Atlas ($ billions)	224.7
GNI per capita, Atlas ($)	28,930
Population living below $1.25 a day (%)	..

	1990		2011	
	Female	Male	Female	Male
Demography				
Sex ratio at birth (boys per girls)	1.05		1.05	
Life expectancy at birth (years)	78	75	84	80
Under-five mortality rate (per 1,000 live births)	11	12	4	5
Female-headed households (%)	..		..	
Education				
Gross primary enrollment ratio (% of relevant age group)	97	94	105	104
Gross secondary enrollment ratio (% of relevant age group)	91	86	103	101
Gross tertiary enrollment ratio (% of relevant age group)	33	34	71	55
Primary completion rate (% of relevant age group)	..	..	102	101
Youth literacy rate (% of population ages 15–24)	..	..	..	..
Health and related services				
Total fertility rate (births per woman)	2.8		3.0	
Adolescent fertility rate (births per 1,000 women ages 15–19)	..		14	
Women first married by age 18 (% of women ages 20–24)	..		..	
Contraceptive prevalence (% of women ages 15–49)	68		..	
Unmet need for contraception (% of women ages 15–49)	..		..	
Pregnant women receiving prenatal care (%)	..		..	
Births attended by skilled health staff (% of total)	99		..	
Maternal mortality ratio (per 100,000 live births)	12		7	
Economic structure, participation, and access to resources				
Labor force participation rate (% of population ages 15+)	41	63	53	62
Wage and salaried workers (% of employed ages 15+)	..	..	92	84
Self-employed workers (% of employed ages 15+)	..	..	8	17
Vulnerable employment (% of employed ages 15+)	..	..	5	9
Unpaid family workers (% of employed ages 15+)	..	..	0.2	0.1
Employment in agriculture (% of employed ages 15+)	2	5	1	3
Employment in industry (% of employed ages 15+)	15	36	10	30
Employment in service (% of employed ages 15+)	82	58	89	67
Women in wage employment in the nonagricultural sector (%)	43		50	
Women's share of part-time employment (% of total)	..		74	
Maternity leave (weeks)	12		14	
Maternal leave benefits (% of wages paid)	75		100	
Female legislators, senior officials and managers (% of total)	..		32	
Employment to population ratio, total (% ages 15+)	36	57	50	59
Employment to population ratio, youth (% ages 15–24)	23	26	30	26
Children in employment (% of children ages 7–14)	..	..	..	..
Unemployment rate (% of labor force ages 15+)	11.3	8.4	5.6	5.6
Long-term unemployment rate (% total unemployment)	..	..	17.4	19.8
Youth unemployment rate (% of labor force ages 15–24)	23	21	11	12
Account at a formal financial institution (% age 15+)	..	..	92	88
Public life and decision making				
Seats held by women in national parliament (%)	7		20	

Italy

High income

Population (millions)	60.7
GNI, Atlas ($ billions)	2,144.7
GNI per capita, Atlas ($)	35,320
Population living below $1.25 a day (%)	..

	1990		2011	
	Female	Male	Female	Male
Demography				
Sex ratio at birth (boys per girls)	1.06		1.06	
Life expectancy at birth (years)	80	74	85	80
Under-five mortality rate (per 1,000 live births)	9	11	3	4
Female-headed households (%)	..		..	
Education				
Gross primary enrollment ratio (% of relevant age group)	98	99	101	102
Gross secondary enrollment ratio (% of relevant age group)	79	79	100	101
Gross tertiary enrollment ratio (% of relevant age group)	29	30	76	54
Primary completion rate (% of relevant age group)	100	100	104	103
Youth literacy rate (% of population ages 15–24)	..	..	100	100
Health and related services				
Total fertility rate (births per woman)	1.3		1.4	
Adolescent fertility rate (births per 1,000 women ages 15–19)	..		5	
Women first married by age 18 (% of women ages 20–24)	..			
Contraceptive prevalence (% of women ages 15–49)	..		..	
Unmet need for contraception (% of women ages 15–49)	..		..	
Pregnant women receiving prenatal care (%)	..		..	
Births attended by skilled health staff (% of total)	..		..	
Maternal mortality ratio (per 100,000 live births)	10		4	
Economic structure, participation, and access to resources				
Labor force participation rate (% of population ages 15+)	35	67	38	60
Wage and salaried workers (% of employed ages 15+)	76	70	82	71
Self-employed workers (% of employed ages 15+)	24	31	18	30
Vulnerable employment (% of employed ages 15+)	24	29	15	21
Unpaid family workers (% of employed ages 15+)	7.4	2.2	2.2	1.1
Employment in agriculture (% of employed ages 15+)	9	9	3	4
Employment in industry (% of employed ages 15+)	23	37	14	38
Employment in service (% of employed ages 15+)	68	55	83	57
Women in wage employment in the nonagricultural sector (%)	36		44	
Women's share of part-time employment (% of total)	71		77	
Maternity leave (weeks)	21		22	
Maternal leave benefits (% of wages paid)	80		80	
Female legislators, senior officials and managers (% of total)	16		25	
Employment to population ratio, total (% ages 15+)	30	62	34	55
Employment to population ratio, youth (% ages 15–24)	28	38	16	25
Children in employment (% of children ages 7–14)	..	..	..	..
Unemployment rate (% of labor force ages 15+)	15.7	6.4	9.6	7.6
Long-term unemployment rate (% total unemployment)	70.5	68.5	51.9	50.7
Youth unemployment rate (% of labor force ages 15–24)	35	23	32	27
Account at a formal financial institution (% age 15+)	..	..	64	79
Public life and decision making				
Seats held by women in national parliament (%)	13		21	

Jamaica

Latin America & the Caribbean	Upper middle income
Population (millions)	2.7
GNI, Atlas ($ billions)	..
GNI per capita, Atlas ($)	..
Population living below $1.25 a day (%)	<2

	1990		2011	
	Female	Male	Female	Male
Demography				
Sex ratio at birth (boys per girls)	1.05		1.05	
Life expectancy at birth (years)	73	68	76	71
Under-five mortality rate (per 1,000 live births)	29	39	16	21
Female-headed households (%)	..		..	
Education				
Gross primary enrollment ratio (% of relevant age group)	104	105	87	91
Gross secondary enrollment ratio (% of relevant age group)	72	68	94	91
Gross tertiary enrollment ratio (% of relevant age group)	..	..	35	15
Primary completion rate (% of relevant age group)	100	94	73	74
Youth literacy rate (% of population ages 15–24)	..	..	98	93
Health and related services				
Total fertility rate (births per woman)	2.9		2.3	
Adolescent fertility rate (births per 1,000 women ages 15–19)	..		71	
Women first married by age 18 (% of women ages 20–24)	..		..	
Contraceptive prevalence (% of women ages 15–49)	55		72	
Unmet need for contraception (% of women ages 15–49)	..		..	
Pregnant women receiving prenatal care (%)	98		99	
Births attended by skilled health staff (% of total)	92		98	
Maternal mortality ratio (per 100,000 live births)	59		110	
Economic structure, participation, and access to resources				
Labor force participation rate (% of population ages 15+)	66	82	56	72
Wage and salaried workers (% of employed ages 15+)	61	52	67	55
Self-employed workers (% of employed ages 15+)	38	47	33	45
Vulnerable employment (% of employed ages 15+)	37	46	31	41
Unpaid family workers (% of employed ages 15+)	4.5	2.1	2.1	0.4
Employment in agriculture (% of employed ages 15+)	16	36	8	25
Employment in industry (% of employed ages 15+)	12	25	7	23
Employment in service (% of employed ages 15+)	72	39	85	52
Women in wage employment in the nonagricultural sector (%)	47		48	
Women's share of part-time employment (% of total)	60		..	
Maternity leave (weeks)	12		12	
Maternal leave benefits (% of wages paid)	100		..	
Female legislators, senior officials and managers (% of total)	..		..	
Employment to population ratio, total (% ages 15+)	52	74	46	66
Employment to population ratio, youth (% ages 15–24)	31	55	19	32
Children in employment (% of children ages 7–14)	..	..	..	..
Unemployment rate (% of labor force ages 15+)	23.1	9.3	17.2	9.6
Long-term unemployment rate (% total unemployment)	27.8	21.4	..	..
Youth unemployment rate (% of labor force ages 15–24)	47	19	38	24
Account at a formal financial institution (% age 15+)	..	..	67	75
Public life and decision making				
Seats held by women in national parliament (%)	5		13	

Japan

High income

Population (millions)	127.8
GNI, Atlas ($ billions)	5,739.5
GNI per capita, Atlas ($)	44,900
Population living below $1.25 a day (%)	..

	1990		2011	
	Female	Male	Female	Male
Demography				
Sex ratio at birth (boys per girls)	1.06		1.06	
Life expectancy at birth (years)	82	76	86	79
Under-five mortality rate (per 1,000 live births)	6	7	3	4
Female-headed households (%)	..		..	
Education				
Gross primary enrollment ratio (% of relevant age group)	102	102	103	103
Gross secondary enrollment ratio (% of relevant age group)	97	95	102	102
Gross tertiary enrollment ratio (% of relevant age group)	23	36	56	63
Primary completion rate (% of relevant age group)	104	103	102	102
Youth literacy rate (% of population ages 15–24)	..	..	..	..
Health and related services				
Total fertility rate (births per woman)	1.5		1.4	
Adolescent fertility rate (births per 1,000 women ages 15–19)	..		6	
Women first married by age 18 (% of women ages 20–24)	..		..	
Contraceptive prevalence (% of women ages 15–49)	58		..	
Unmet need for contraception (% of women ages 15–49)	..		..	
Pregnant women receiving prenatal care (%)	..		..	
Births attended by skilled health staff (% of total)	100		..	
Maternal mortality ratio (per 100,000 live births)	12		5	
Economic structure, participation, and access to resources				
Labor force participation rate (% of population ages 15+)	50	77	49	72
Wage and salaried workers (% of employed ages 15+)	72	81	89	87
Self-employed workers (% of employed ages 15+)	27	19	11	13
Vulnerable employment (% of employed ages 15+)	26	15	11	10
Unpaid family workers (% of employed ages 15+)	16.7	2.5	5.6	1.0
Employment in agriculture (% of employed ages 15+)	9	6	4	4
Employment in industry (% of employed ages 15+)	27	39	15	33
Employment in service (% of employed ages 15+)	64	55	80	62
Women in wage employment in the nonagricultural sector (%)	38		43	
Women's share of part-time employment (% of total)	..		71	
Maternity leave (weeks)	14		14	
Maternal leave benefits (% of wages paid)	60		67	
Female legislators, senior officials and managers (% of total)	..		..	
Employment to population ratio, total (% ages 15+)	50	76	47	68
Employment to population ratio, youth (% ages 15–24)	44	43	40	38
Children in employment (% of children ages 7–14)	..	..	..	..
Unemployment rate (% of labor force ages 15+)	2.2	2.0	4.1	4.8
Long-term unemployment rate (% total unemployment)	8.5	25.9	26.7	47.3
Youth unemployment rate (% of labor force ages 15–24)	4	5	7	9
Account at a formal financial institution (% age 15+)	..	..	97	96
Public life and decision making				
Seats held by women in national parliament (%)	1		8	

Jordan

Middle East & North Africa			Upper middle income	
Population (millions)				6.2
GNI, Atlas ($ billions)				27.1
GNI per capita, Atlas ($)				4,380
Population living below $1.25 a day (%)				<2

	1990		2011	
	Female	Male	Female	Male
Demography				
Sex ratio at birth (boys per girls)	1.05		1.05	
Life expectancy at birth (years)	72	69	75	72
Under-five mortality rate (per 1,000 live births)	36	37	19	22
Female-headed households (%)	6		11	
Education				
Gross primary enrollment ratio (% of relevant age group)	101	102	92	92
Gross secondary enrollment ratio (% of relevant age group)	77	75	89	85
Gross tertiary enrollment ratio (% of relevant age group)	23	18	41	35
Primary completion rate (% of relevant age group)	95	95	101	101
Youth literacy rate (% of population ages 15–24)	..	..	99	99
Health and related services				
Total fertility rate (births per woman)	5.8		3.7	
Adolescent fertility rate (births per 1,000 women ages 15–19)	..		24	
Women first married by age 18 (% of women ages 20–24)	16		10	
Contraceptive prevalence (% of women ages 15–49)	40		59	
Unmet need for contraception (% of women ages 15–49)	22		11	
Pregnant women receiving prenatal care (%)	80		99	
Births attended by skilled health staff (% of total)	87		99	
Maternal mortality ratio (per 100,000 live births)	110		63	
Economic structure, participation, and access to resources				
Labor force participation rate (% of population ages 15+)	9	65	16	66
Wage and salaried workers (% of employed ages 15+)	..	..	95	82
Self-employed workers (% of employed ages 15+)	..	..	5	18
Vulnerable employment (% of employed ages 15+)	..	..	3	11
Unpaid family workers (% of employed ages 15+)	..	..	0.3	0.4
Employment in agriculture (% of employed ages 15+)	4	7	1	2
Employment in industry (% of employed ages 15+)	8	18	8	20
Employment in service (% of employed ages 15+)	87	75	91	78
Women in wage employment in the nonagricultural sector (%)	11		16	
Women's share of part-time employment (% of total)	..		..	
Maternity leave (weeks)	6		10	
Maternal leave benefits (% of wages paid)	50		100	
Female legislators, senior officials and managers (% of total)	..		..	
Employment to population ratio, total (% ages 15+)	6	55	12	59
Employment to population ratio, youth (% ages 15–24)	2	31	6	31
Children in employment (% of children ages 7–14)	..		0.4	1.6
Unemployment rate (% of labor force ages 15+)	30.0	18.1	21.2	11.0
Long-term unemployment rate (% total unemployment)	..	..	..	..
Youth unemployment rate (% of labor force ages 15–24)	..	..	47	26
Account at a formal financial institution (% age 15+)	..	..	17	34
Public life and decision making				
Seats held by women in national parliament (%)	0		11	

Kazakhstan

Europe & Central Asia				Upper middle income
Population (millions)				16.6
GNI, Atlas ($ billions)				136.7
GNI per capita, Atlas ($)				8,260
Population living below $1.25 a day (%)				<2

	1990		2011	
	Female	Male	Female	Male
Demography				
Sex ratio at birth (boys per girls)	1.07		1.07	
Life expectancy at birth (years)	73	64	74	64
Under-five mortality rate (per 1,000 live births)	50	64	24	32
Female-headed households (%)	..		..	
Education				
Gross primary enrollment ratio (% of relevant age group)	120	120	110[a]	110[a]
Gross secondary enrollment ratio (% of relevant age group)	96	94	100[a]	103[a]
Gross tertiary enrollment ratio (% of relevant age group)	39	31	51[a]	35[a]
Primary completion rate (% of relevant age group)	105	105	109[a]	108[a]
Youth literacy rate (% of population ages 15–24)	100	100	100	100
Health and related services				
Total fertility rate (births per woman)	2.7		2.6	
Adolescent fertility rate (births per 1,000 women ages 15–19)			26	
Women first married by age 18 (% of women ages 20–24)	..		6	
Contraceptive prevalence (% of women ages 15–49)	..		51	
Unmet need for contraception (% of women ages 15–49)	..		..	
Pregnant women receiving prenatal care (%)	..		100	
Births attended by skilled health staff (% of total)	99		100	
Maternal mortality ratio (per 100,000 live births)	92		51	
Economic structure, participation, and access to resources				
Labor force participation rate (% of population ages 15+)	62	78	67	77
Wage and salaried workers (% of employed ages 15+)	..	..	67	68
Self-employed workers (% of employed ages 15+)	..	..	34	32
Vulnerable employment (% of employed ages 15+)	..	..	32	29
Unpaid family workers (% of employed ages 15+)	..	..	0.8	0.8
Employment in agriculture (% of employed ages 15+)	..	..	29	31
Employment in industry (% of employed ages 15+)	..	..	12	26
Employment in service (% of employed ages 15+)	..	..	59	43
Women in wage employment in the nonagricultural sector (%)	..		50	
Women's share of part-time employment (% of total)	..		..	
Maternity leave (weeks)	..		18	
Maternal leave benefits (% of wages paid)	..		100	
Female legislators, senior officials and managers (% of total)	..		38	
Employment to population ratio, total (% ages 15+)	56	72	62	74
Employment to population ratio, youth (% ages 15–24)	41	50	41	48
Children in employment (% of children ages 7–14)	..	..	2.8	4.4
Unemployment rate (% of labor force ages 15+)	..	..	6.2	4.6
Long-term unemployment rate (% total unemployment)	..	..	..	..
Youth unemployment rate (% of labor force ages 15–24)	..	..	5	4
Account at a formal financial institution (% age 15+)	..	..	44	40
Public life and decision making				
Seats held by women in national parliament (%)	..		24	

Kenya

Sub-Saharan Africa			Low income	
Population (millions)				41.6
GNI, Atlas ($ billions)				34.1
GNI per capita, Atlas ($)				820
Population living below $1.25 a day (%)				43.4

	1990		2011	
	Female	Male	Female	Male
Demography				
Sex ratio at birth (boys per girls)	1.03		1.03	
Life expectancy at birth (years)	61	58	58	56
Under-five mortality rate (per 1,000 live births)	92	104	67	78
Female-headed households (%)	33		34	
Education				
Gross primary enrollment ratio (% of relevant age group)	99	102	112	115
Gross secondary enrollment ratio (% of relevant age group)	36	45	57	63
Gross tertiary enrollment ratio (% of relevant age group)	1	2	3	5
Primary completion rate (% of relevant age group)	..	..	..	..
Youth literacy rate (% of population ages 15–24)	..	..	94	92
Health and related services				
Total fertility rate (births per woman)	6.0		4.7	
Adolescent fertility rate (births per 1,000 women ages 15–19)	..		99	
Women first married by age 18 (% of women ages 20–24)	32		26	
Contraceptive prevalence (% of women ages 15–49)	27		46	
Unmet need for contraception (% of women ages 15–49)	36		26	
Pregnant women receiving prenatal care (%)	77		92	
Births attended by skilled health staff (% of total)	50		44	
Maternal mortality ratio (per 100,000 live births)	400		360	
Economic structure, participation, and access to resources				
Labor force participation rate (% of population ages 15+)	70	80	62	72
Wage and salaried workers (% of employed ages 15+)	..	..	..	..
Self-employed workers (% of employed ages 15+)	..	..	..	..
Vulnerable employment (% of employed ages 15+)	..	..	..	..
Unpaid family workers (% of employed ages 15+)	..	..	..	..
Employment in agriculture (% of employed ages 15+)	..	..	..	..
Employment in industry (% of employed ages 15+)	..	..	..	..
Employment in service (% of employed ages 15+)	..	..	..	..
Women in wage employment in the nonagricultural sector (%)	21		..	
Women's share of part-time employment (% of total)	..		..	
Maternity leave (weeks)	8		13	
Maternal leave benefits (% of wages paid)	..		100	
Female legislators, senior officials and managers (% of total)	..		..	
Employment to population ratio, total (% ages 15+)	62	72	55	66
Employment to population ratio, youth (% ages 15–24)	44	47	29	36
Children in employment (% of children ages 7–14)	..	..	..	..
Unemployment rate (% of labor force ages 15+)	..	..	..	..
Long-term unemployment rate (% total unemployment)	..	..	..	..
Youth unemployment rate (% of labor force ages 15–24)	..	..	..	..
Account at a formal financial institution (% age 15+)	..	..	39	46
Public life and decision making				
Seats held by women in national parliament (%)	1		10	

Kiribati

East Asia & Pacific **Lower middle income**

Population (thousands)	101.1
GNI, Atlas ($ millions)	204.8
GNI per capita, Atlas ($)	2,030
Population living below $1.25 a day (%)	..

	1990		2011	
	Female	Male	Female	Male
Demography				
Sex ratio at birth (boys per girls)		..		..
Life expectancy at birth (years)	61	56	..	..
Under-five mortality rate (per 1,000 live births)	83	92	45	50
Female-headed households (%)		..		..
Education				
Gross primary enrollment ratio (% of relevant age group)	116	114	115	111
Gross secondary enrollment ratio (% of relevant age group)	36	39	90	81
Gross tertiary enrollment ratio (% of relevant age group)	..	..		
Primary completion rate (% of relevant age group)	102	100	113	111
Youth literacy rate (% of population ages 15–24)	..	..		
Health and related services				
Total fertility rate (births per woman)	3.8		..	
Adolescent fertility rate (births per 1,000 women ages 15–19)	..		..	
Women first married by age 18 (% of women ages 20–24)			20	
Contraceptive prevalence (% of women ages 15–49)	..		22	
Unmet need for contraception (% of women ages 15–49)	..		..	
Pregnant women receiving prenatal care (%)	88		88	
Births attended by skilled health staff (% of total)	72		80	
Maternal mortality ratio (per 100,000 live births)	..		..	
Economic structure, participation, and access to resources				
Labor force participation rate (% of population ages 15+)	..	..	..	..
Wage and salaried workers (% of employed ages 15+)	..	..	..	..
Self-employed workers (% of employed ages 15+)	..	..	..	..
Vulnerable employment (% of employed ages 15+)	..	..	..	..
Unpaid family workers (% of employed ages 15+)	..	..	..	..
Employment in agriculture (% of employed ages 15+)	..	..	..	..
Employment in industry (% of employed ages 15+)	..	..	..	..
Employment in service (% of employed ages 15+)	..	..	..	..
Women in wage employment in the nonagricultural sector (%)	..		..	
Women's share of part-time employment (% of total)	..		..	
Maternity leave (weeks)	..		..	
Maternal leave benefits (% of wages paid)	..		..	
Female legislators, senior officials and managers (% of total)	..		..	
Employment to population ratio, total (% ages 15+)	..	..	..	..
Employment to population ratio, youth (% ages 15–24)	..	..	..	..
Children in employment (% of children ages 7–14)	..	..	..	..
Unemployment rate (% of labor force ages 15+)	..	..	..	..
Long-term unemployment rate (% total unemployment)	..	..	..	..
Youth unemployment rate (% of labor force ages 15–24)	..	..	..	..
Account at a formal financial institution (% age 15+)	..	..	..	..
Public life and decision making				
Seats held by women in national parliament (%)	0		9	

Korea, Dem. People's Rep.

East Asia & Pacific	Low income
Population (millions)	24.5
GNI, Atlas ($ millions)	..
GNI per capita, Atlas ($)	..
Population living below $1.25 a day (%)	..

	1990		2011	
	Female	Male	Female	Male
Demography				
Sex ratio at birth (boys per girls)	1.05		1.05	
Life expectancy at birth (years)	74	67	72	66
Under-five mortality rate (per 1,000 live births)	43	47	32	35
Female-headed households (%)	..			
Education				
Gross primary enrollment ratio (% of relevant age group)	..	..	..	..
Gross secondary enrollment ratio (% of relevant age group)	..	..	..	..
Gross tertiary enrollment ratio (% of relevant age group)	..	..	..	..
Primary completion rate (% of relevant age group)	..	..	..	..
Youth literacy rate (% of population ages 15–24)	..	..	100	100
Health and related services				
Total fertility rate (births per woman)	2.4		2.0	
Adolescent fertility rate (births per 1,000 women ages 15–19)	..		1	
Women first married by age 18 (% of women ages 20–24)	..		..	
Contraceptive prevalence (% of women ages 15–49)	62		..	
Unmet need for contraception (% of women ages 15–49)	..		..	
Pregnant women receiving prenatal care (%)	..		100	
Births attended by skilled health staff (% of total)	..		100	
Maternal mortality ratio (per 100,000 live births)	97		81	
Economic structure, participation, and access to resources				
Labor force participation rate (% of population ages 15+)	76	88	72	84
Wage and salaried workers (% of employed ages 15+)	..	..	..	..
Self-employed workers (% of employed ages 15+)	..	..	..	..
Vulnerable employment (% of employed ages 15+)	..	..	..	..
Unpaid family workers (% of employed ages 15+)	..	..	..	..
Employment in agriculture (% of employed ages 15+)	..	..	..	..
Employment in industry (% of employed ages 15+)	..	..	..	..
Employment in service (% of employed ages 15+)	..	..	..	..
Women in wage employment in the nonagricultural sector (%)	41		..	
Women's share of part-time employment (% of total)	..		..	
Maternity leave (weeks)	..		..	
Maternal leave benefits (% of wages paid)	..		..	
Female legislators, senior officials and managers (% of total)	..		..	
Employment to population ratio, total (% ages 15+)	74	85	69	79
Employment to population ratio, youth (% ages 15–24)	74	72	59	53
Children in employment (% of children ages 7–14)	..	..	..	..
Unemployment rate (% of labor force ages 15+)	..	..	..	..
Long-term unemployment rate (% total unemployment)	..	..	..	..
Youth unemployment rate (% of labor force ages 15–24)	..	..	..	..
Account at a formal financial institution (% age 15+)	..	..	..	..
Public life and decision making				
Seats held by women in national parliament (%)	21		16	

Korea, Rep.

High income

Population (millions)	49.8
GNI, Atlas ($ billions)	1,039.0
GNI per capita, Atlas ($)	20,870
Population living below $1.25 a day (%)	..

	1990		2011	
	Female	Male	Female	Male
Demography				
Sex ratio at birth (boys per girls)	1.12		1.10	
Life expectancy at birth (years)	76	67	84	78
Under-five mortality rate (per 1,000 live births)	7	8	4	5
Female-headed households (%)	..		..	
Education				
Gross primary enrollment ratio (% of relevant age group)	107	105	105	106
Gross secondary enrollment ratio (% of relevant age group)	90	95	96	98
Gross tertiary enrollment ratio (% of relevant age group)	23	49	86	119
Primary completion rate (% of relevant age group)	100	99	101	102
Youth literacy rate (% of population ages 15–24)	..	..	..	..
Health and related services				
Total fertility rate (births per woman)	1.6		1.2	
Adolescent fertility rate (births per 1,000 women ages 15–19)	..		5	
Women first married by age 18 (% of women ages 20–24)	..		..	
Contraceptive prevalence (% of women ages 15–49)	79		80	
Unmet need for contraception (% of women ages 15–49)	..		..	
Pregnant women receiving prenatal care (%)	..		..	
Births attended by skilled health staff (% of total)	..		..	
Maternal mortality ratio (per 100,000 live births)	18		16	
Economic structure, participation, and access to resources				
Labor force participation rate (% of population ages 15+)	47	73	49	71
Wage and salaried workers (% of employed ages 15+)	57	63	74	70
Self-employed workers (% of employed ages 15+)	43	37	26	30
Vulnerable employment (% of employed ages 15+)	..	..	27	23
Unpaid family workers (% of employed ages 15+)	24.5	2.5	10.7	1.2
Employment in agriculture (% of employed ages 15+)	20	16	7	6
Employment in industry (% of employed ages 15+)	30	39	13	20
Employment in service (% of employed ages 15+)	50	45	81	73
Women in wage employment in the nonagricultural sector (%)	38		43	
Women's share of part-time employment (% of total)	59		57	
Maternity leave (weeks)	..		13	
Maternal leave benefits (% of wages paid)	..		100	
Female legislators, senior officials and managers (% of total)	6		10	
Employment to population ratio, total (% ages 15+)	46	72	48	69
Employment to population ratio, youth (% ages 15–24)	40	32	27	20
Children in employment (% of children ages 7–14)	..	..	..	..
Unemployment rate (% of labor force ages 15+)	1.8	2.9	3.1	3.6
Long-term unemployment rate (% total unemployment)	0.9	3.3	0.2	0.5
Youth unemployment rate (% of labor force ages 15–24)	6	10	8	12
Account at a formal financial institution (% age 15+)	..	..	93	93
Public life and decision making				
Seats held by women in national parliament (%)	2		16	

Kosovo

Europe & Central Asia			Lower middle income	

Population (millions)	1.8
GNI, Atlas ($ billions)	6.3
GNI per capita, Atlas ($)	3,510
Population living below $1.25 a day (%)	..

	1990		2011	
	Female	Male	Female	Male
Demography				
Sex ratio at birth (boys per girls)	..		..	
Life expectancy at birth (years)	70	66	72	68
Under-five mortality rate (per 1,000 live births)	..	..	..	..
Female-headed households (%)	..		..	
Education				
Gross primary enrollment ratio (% of relevant age group)	..	..	..	..
Gross secondary enrollment ratio (% of relevant age group)	..	..	..	..
Gross tertiary enrollment ratio (% of relevant age group)	..	..	..	..
Primary completion rate (% of relevant age group)	..	..	..	..
Youth literacy rate (% of population ages 15–24)	..	..	..	..
Health and related services				
Total fertility rate (births per woman)	3.9		2.2	
Adolescent fertility rate (births per 1,000 women ages 15–19)	..		..	
Women first married by age 18 (% of women ages 20–24)	..		..	
Contraceptive prevalence (% of women ages 15–49)	..		..	
Unmet need for contraception (% of women ages 15–49)	..		..	
Pregnant women receiving prenatal care (%)	..		..	
Births attended by skilled health staff (% of total)	..		..	
Maternal mortality ratio (per 100,000 live births)	..		..	
Economic structure, participation, and access to resources				
Labor force participation rate (% of population ages 15+)	..	..	..	..
Wage and salaried workers (% of employed ages 15+)	..	..	..	..
Self-employed workers (% of employed ages 15+)	..	..	..	..
Vulnerable employment (% of employed ages 15+)	..	..	..	..
Unpaid family workers (% of employed ages 15+)	..	..	..	..
Employment in agriculture (% of employed ages 15+)	..	..	..	..
Employment in industry (% of employed ages 15+)	..	..	..	..
Employment in service (% of employed ages 15+)	..	..	..	..
Women in wage employment in the nonagricultural sector (%)	..		..	
Women's share of part-time employment (% of total)	..		..	
Maternity leave (weeks)	..		..	
Maternal leave benefits (% of wages paid)	..		..	
Female legislators, senior officials and managers (% of total)	..		..	
Employment to population ratio, total (% ages 15+)	..	..	..	..
Employment to population ratio, youth (% ages 15–24)	..	..	..	..
Children in employment (% of children ages 7–14)	..	..	..	..
Unemployment rate (% of labor force ages 15+)	..	..	40.7	56.4
Long-term unemployment rate (% total unemployment)	..	..	..	..
Youth unemployment rate (% of labor force ages 15–24)	..	..	82	69
Account at a formal financial institution (% age 15+)	..	..	31	57
Public life and decision making				
Seats held by women in national parliament (%)	..		..	

Kuwait

High income

Population (millions)	2.8
GNI, Atlas ($ billions)	133.8
GNI per capita, Atlas ($)	48,900
Population living below $1.25 a day (%)	..

	1990 Female	1990 Male	2011 Female	2011 Male
Demography				
Sex ratio at birth (boys per girls)	1.03		1.03	
Life expectancy at birth (years)	74	72	76	74
Under-five mortality rate (per 1,000 live births)	15	18	10	12
Female-headed households (%)	..		..	
Education				
Gross primary enrollment ratio (% of relevant age group)	90	92	107	104
Gross secondary enrollment ratio (% of relevant age group)	72	80	104	98
Gross tertiary enrollment ratio (% of relevant age group)	14	10	..	..
Primary completion rate (% of relevant age group)	55	57	114	110
Youth literacy rate (% of population ages 15–24)	..	..	99	99
Health and related services				
Total fertility rate (births per woman)	2.6		2.3	
Adolescent fertility rate (births per 1,000 women ages 15–19)	..		14	
Women first married by age 18 (% of women ages 20–24)	..		..	
Contraceptive prevalence (% of women ages 15–49)	35		..	
Unmet need for contraception (% of women ages 15–49)	..		..	
Pregnant women receiving prenatal care (%)	..		100	
Births attended by skilled health staff (% of total)	96		100	
Maternal mortality ratio (per 100,000 live births)	11		14	
Economic structure, participation, and access to resources				
Labor force participation rate (% of population ages 15+)	35	78	43	82
Wage and salaried workers (% of employed ages 15+)	..	..	..	..
Self-employed workers (% of employed ages 15+)	..	..	..	..
Vulnerable employment (% of employed ages 15+)	..	..	..	..
Unpaid family workers (% of employed ages 15+)	..	..	..	..
Employment in agriculture (% of employed ages 15+)	0	2	..	..
Employment in industry (% of employed ages 15+)	2	33	..	..
Employment in service (% of employed ages 15+)	98	65	..	..
Women in wage employment in the nonagricultural sector (%)	..		..	
Women's share of part-time employment (% of total)	..		..	
Maternity leave (weeks)	10		10	
Maternal leave benefits (% of wages paid)	100		100	
Female legislators, senior officials and managers (% of total)	..		..	
Employment to population ratio, total (% ages 15+)	35	78	43	81
Employment to population ratio, youth (% ages 15–24)	22	37	22	38
Children in employment (% of children ages 7–14)	..	..	..	..
Unemployment rate (% of labor force ages 15+)	2.6	1.7	..	..
Long-term unemployment rate (% total unemployment)	..	..	..	..
Youth unemployment rate (% of labor force ages 15–24)	..	..	..	..
Account at a formal financial institution (% age 15+)	..	..	80	93
Public life and decision making				
Seats held by women in national parliament (%)	..		6	

Kyrgyz Republic

Europe & Central Asia			Low income	
Population (millions)				5.5
GNI, Atlas ($ billions)				5.0
GNI per capita, Atlas ($)				900
Population living below $1.25 a day (%)				6.7

	1990		2011	
	Female	Male	Female	Male
Demography				
Sex ratio at birth (boys per girls)	1.06		1.06	
Life expectancy at birth (years)	73	64	74	66
Under-five mortality rate (per 1,000 live births)	63	77	28	34
Female-headed households (%)	..		25	
Education				
Gross primary enrollment ratio (% of relevant age group)	111	109	100	102
Gross secondary enrollment ratio (% of relevant age group)	102	103	88	88
Gross tertiary enrollment ratio (% of relevant age group)	26	19	46	37
Primary completion rate (% of relevant age group)	..	..	95	96
Youth literacy rate (% of population ages 15–24)	..	..	100	100
Health and related services				
Total fertility rate (births per woman)	3.7		3.1	
Adolescent fertility rate (births per 1,000 women ages 15–19)	..		33	
Women first married by age 18 (% of women ages 20–24)	..		10	
Contraceptive prevalence (% of women ages 15–49)	..		48	
Unmet need for contraception (% of women ages 15–49)	..		1	
Pregnant women receiving prenatal care (%)	..		97	
Births attended by skilled health staff (% of total)	99		99	
Maternal mortality ratio (per 100,000 live births)	73		71	
Economic structure, participation, and access to resources				
Labor force participation rate (% of population ages 15+)	58	74	56	79
Wage and salaried workers (% of employed ages 15+)	..	..	52	50
Self-employed workers (% of employed ages 15+)	..	..	48	50
Vulnerable employment (% of employed ages 15+)	..	..	47	47
Unpaid family workers (% of employed ages 15+)	..	..	19.3	8.8
Employment in agriculture (% of employed ages 15+)	..	..	35	37
Employment in industry (% of employed ages 15+)	..	..	11	26
Employment in service (% of employed ages 15+)	..	..	54	37
Women in wage employment in the nonagricultural sector (%)	..		51	
Women's share of part-time employment (% of total)	..		..	
Maternity leave (weeks)	..		18	
Maternal leave benefits (% of wages paid)	..		100	
Female legislators, senior officials and managers (% of total)	..		35	
Employment to population ratio, total (% ages 15+)	52	68	50	72
Employment to population ratio, youth (% ages 15–24)	37	45	31	50
Children in employment (% of children ages 7–14)	..	..	35.6	37.5
Unemployment rate (% of labor force ages 15+)	..	..	9.4	7.3
Long-term unemployment rate (% total unemployment)	..	..	..	..
Youth unemployment rate (% of labor force ages 15–24)	..	..	16	14
Account at a formal financial institution (% age 15+)	..	..	4	4
Public life and decision making				
Seats held by women in national parliament (%)	..		23	

Lao PDR

Population (millions)	6.3
GNI, Atlas ($ billions)	7.1
GNI per capita, Atlas ($)	1,130
Population living below $1.25 a day (%)	33.9

	1990		2011	
	Female	Male	Female	Male
Demography				
Sex ratio at birth (boys per girls)	1.05		1.05	
Life expectancy at birth (years)	56	53	69	66
Under-five mortality rate (per 1,000 live births)	139	156	39	44
Female-headed households (%)	..		..	
Education				
Gross primary enrollment ratio (% of relevant age group)	89	112	122	130
Gross secondary enrollment ratio (% of relevant age group)	19	28	42	49
Gross tertiary enrollment ratio (% of relevant age group)	1	2	15	20
Primary completion rate (% of relevant age group)	36	46	90	95
Youth literacy rate (% of population ages 15–24)	..	..	86	92
Health and related services				
Total fertility rate (births per woman)	6.2		2.7	
Adolescent fertility rate (births per 1,000 women ages 15–19)	..		32	
Women first married by age 18 (% of women ages 20–24)	..		..	
Contraceptive prevalence (% of women ages 15–49)	19		..	
Unmet need for contraception (% of women ages 15–49)	..		..	
Pregnant women receiving prenatal care (%)	..		71	
Births attended by skilled health staff (% of total)	..		37	
Maternal mortality ratio (per 100,000 live births)	1,600		470	
Economic structure, participation, and access to resources				
Labor force participation rate (% of population ages 15+)	80	83	77	80
Wage and salaried workers (% of employed ages 15+)	..	..	..	..
Self-employed workers (% of employed ages 15+)	..	..	..	..
Vulnerable employment (% of employed ages 15+)	..	..	..	..
Unpaid family workers (% of employed ages 15+)	..	..	..	..
Employment in agriculture (% of employed ages 15+)	..	..	..	..
Employment in industry (% of employed ages 15+)	..	..	..	..
Employment in service (% of employed ages 15+)	..	..	..	..
Women in wage employment in the nonagricultural sector (%)	20		..	
Women's share of part-time employment (% of total)	..		..	
Maternity leave (weeks)	12		13	
Maternal leave benefits (% of wages paid)	100		100	
Female legislators, senior officials and managers (% of total)	..		..	
Employment to population ratio, total (% ages 15+)	79	81	76	78
Employment to population ratio, youth (% ages 15–24)	80	65	67	56
Children in employment (% of children ages 7–14)	..	..	19.2	17.9
Unemployment rate (% of labor force ages 15+)	..	..	..	..
Long-term unemployment rate (% of total unemployment)	..	..	..	..
Youth unemployment rate (% of labor force ages 15–24)	..	..	..	..
Account at a formal financial institution (% age 15+)	..	..	26	27
Public life and decision making				
Seats held by women in national parliament (%)	6		25	

Latvia

Europe & Central Asia			Upper middle income	
Population (millions)				2.1
GNI, Atlas ($ billions)				27.4
GNI per capita, Atlas ($)				13,320
Population living below $1.25 a day (%)				<2

	1990		2011	
	Female	Male	Female	Male
Demography				
Sex ratio at birth (boys per girls)	1.05		1.05	
Life expectancy at birth (years)	75	64	79	69
Under-five mortality rate (per 1,000 live births)	18	23	8	9
Female-headed households (%)	..		..	
Education				
Gross primary enrollment ratio (% of relevant age group)	98	91	100	100
Gross secondary enrollment ratio (% of relevant age group)	93	92	94	98
Gross tertiary enrollment ratio (% of relevant age group)	29	21	71	44
Primary completion rate (% of relevant age group)	..	..	92	93
Youth literacy rate (% of population ages 15–24)	100	100	100	100
Health and related services				
Total fertility rate (births per woman)	2.0		1.3	
Adolescent fertility rate (births per 1,000 women ages 15–19)	..		14	
Women first married by age 18 (% of women ages 20–24)	..		..	
Contraceptive prevalence (% of women ages 15–49)	..		..	
Unmet need for contraception (% of women ages 15–49)	..		..	
Pregnant women receiving prenatal care (%)	..		..	
Births attended by skilled health staff (% of total)	100		100	
Maternal mortality ratio (per 100,000 live births)	57		34	
Economic structure, participation, and access to resources				
Labor force participation rate (% of population ages 15+)	63	77	55	67
Wage and salaried workers (% of employed ages 15+)	..	..	91	86
Self-employed workers (% of employed ages 15+)	..	..	9	14
Vulnerable employment (% of employed ages 15+)	..	..	7	9
Unpaid family workers (% of employed ages 15+)	..	..	1.1	1.1
Employment in agriculture (% of employed ages 15+)	..	..	6	13
Employment in industry (% of employed ages 15+)	..	..	15	32
Employment in service (% of employed ages 15+)	..	..	80	53
Women in wage employment in the nonagricultural sector (%)	52		54	
Women's share of part-time employment (% of total)	..		60	
Maternity leave (weeks)	..		16	
Maternal leave benefits (% of wages paid)	..		100	
Female legislators, senior officials and managers (% of total)	..		45	
Employment to population ratio, total (% ages 15+)	54	65	48	55
Employment to population ratio, youth (% ages 15–24)	40	44	28	32
Children in employment (% of children ages 7–14)	..	..	..	..
Unemployment rate (% of labor force ages 15+)	..	..	13.1	17.6
Long-term unemployment rate (% total unemployment)	..	..	48.6	59.0
Youth unemployment rate (% of labor force ages 15–24)	..		29	30
Account at a formal financial institution (% age 15+)	..	..	92	87
Public life and decision making				
Seats held by women in national parliament (%)	..		23	

Lebanon

Middle East & North Africa   **Upper middle income**

Population (millions)	4.3
GNI, Atlas ($ billions)	38.9
GNI per capita, Atlas ($)	9,140
Population living below $1.25 a day (%)	..

	1990 Female	1990 Male	2011 Female	2011 Male
Demography				
Sex ratio at birth (boys per girls)	1.05		1.05	
Life expectancy at birth (years)	71	66	75	70
Under-five mortality rate (per 1,000 live births)	32	34	9	10
Female-headed households (%)	..		..	
Education				
Gross primary enrollment ratio (% of relevant age group)	96	100	106	109
Gross secondary enrollment ratio (% of relevant age group)	63	59	88	79
Gross tertiary enrollment ratio (% of relevant age group)	27	29	62	54
Primary completion rate (% of relevant age group)	..	..	89	85
Youth literacy rate (% of population ages 15–24)	..	..	99	98
Health and related services				
Total fertility rate (births per woman)	3.1		1.8	
Adolescent fertility rate (births per 1,000 women ages 15–19)	..		16	
Women first married by age 18 (% of women ages 20–24)	..		6	
Contraceptive prevalence (% of women ages 15–49)	..		54	
Unmet need for contraception (% of women ages 15–49)	..		..	
Pregnant women receiving prenatal care (%)	..		..	
Births attended by skilled health staff (% of total)	..		..	
Maternal mortality ratio (per 100,000 live births)	52		25	
Economic structure, participation, and access to resources				
Labor force participation rate (% of population ages 15+)	17	70	23	71
Wage and salaried workers (% of employed ages 15+)	..	..	82	56
Self-employed workers (% of employed ages 15+)	..	..	18	44
Vulnerable employment (% of employed ages 15+)	..	..	16	32
Unpaid family workers (% of employed ages 15+)	..	..	5.9	4.0
Employment in agriculture (% of employed ages 15+)	..	..	..	..
Employment in industry (% of employed ages 15+)	..	..	..	..
Employment in service (% of employed ages 15+)	..	..	..	..
Women in wage employment in the nonagricultural sector (%)	..		..	
Women's share of part-time employment (% of total)	..		..	
Maternity leave (weeks)	5		7	
Maternal leave benefits (% of wages paid)	100		100	
Female legislators, senior officials and managers (% of total)	..		8	
Employment to population ratio, total (% ages 15+)	16	65	20	65
Employment to population ratio, youth (% ages 15–24)	14	36	14	31
Children in employment (% of children ages 7–14)	..	..	..	..
Unemployment rate (% of labor force ages 15+)	..	..	10.1	8.6
Long-term unemployment rate (% total unemployment)	..	..	..	..
Youth unemployment rate (% of labor force ages 15–24)	..	..	22	22
Account at a formal financial institution (% age 15+)	..	..	26	49
Public life and decision making				
Seats held by women in national parliament (%)	0		3	

Lesotho

Sub-Saharan Africa			Lower middle income	
Population (millions)				2.2
GNI, Atlas ($ billions)				2.7
GNI per capita, Atlas ($)				1,210
Population living below $1.25 a day (%)				43.4

	1990		2011	
	Female	Male	Female	Male
Demography				
Sex ratio at birth (boys per girls)	1.03		1.03	
Life expectancy at birth (years)	61	58	47	49
Under-five mortality rate (per 1,000 live births)	80	95	79	93
Female-headed households (%)	..		36	
Education				
Gross primary enrollment ratio (% of relevant age group)	119	98	101	104
Gross secondary enrollment ratio (% of relevant age group)	29	20	57	41
Gross tertiary enrollment ratio (% of relevant age group)	1	1	4	3
Primary completion rate (% of relevant age group)	75	41	76	60
Youth literacy rate (% of population ages 15–24)	..	..	98	86
Health and related services				
Total fertility rate (births per woman)	4.9		3.1	
Adolescent fertility rate (births per 1,000 women ages 15–19)	..		63	
Women first married by age 18 (% of women ages 20–24)	..		19	
Contraceptive prevalence (% of women ages 15–49)	23		47	
Unmet need for contraception (% of women ages 15–49)	..		23	
Pregnant women receiving prenatal care (%)	91		92	
Births attended by skilled health staff (% of total)	61		62	
Maternal mortality ratio (per 100,000 live births)	520		620	
Economic structure, participation, and access to resources				
Labor force participation rate (% of population ages 15+)	67	83	59	73
Wage and salaried workers (% of employed ages 15+)	..	..	..	..
Self-employed workers (% of employed ages 15+)	..	..	..	..
Vulnerable employment (% of employed ages 15+)	..	..	..	..
Unpaid family workers (% of employed ages 15+)	..	..	..	..
Employment in agriculture (% of employed ages 15+)	..	..	..	..
Employment in industry (% of employed ages 15+)	..	..	..	..
Employment in service (% of employed ages 15+)	..	..	..	..
Women in wage employment in the nonagricultural sector (%)	..		..	
Women's share of part-time employment (% of total)	..		..	
Maternity leave (weeks)	..		12	
Maternal leave benefits (% of wages paid)	..			
Female legislators, senior officials and managers (% of total)	..		..	
Employment to population ratio, total (% ages 15+)	39	60	41	56
Employment to population ratio, youth (% ages 15–24)	28	49	21	37
Children in employment (% of children ages 7–14)	..	..	..	..
Unemployment rate (% of labor force ages 15+)	7.8	11.1	28.0	23.0
Long-term unemployment rate (% total unemployment)	..	..	..	..
Youth unemployment rate (% of labor force ages 15–24)	..	..	42	29
Account at a formal financial institution (% age 15+)	..	..	17	20
Public life and decision making				
Seats held by women in national parliament (%)	..		27	

Liberia

Sub-Saharan Africa   **Low income**

Population (millions)	4.1
GNI, Atlas ($ billions)	1.4
GNI per capita, Atlas ($)	330
Population living below $1.25 a day (%)	83.8

	1990		2011	
	Female	Male	Female	Male
Demography				
Sex ratio at birth (boys per girls)	1.06		1.06	
Life expectancy at birth (years)	44	41	58	56
Under-five mortality rate (per 1,000 live births)	227	255	74	83
Female-headed households (%)	..		30	
Education				
Gross primary enrollment ratio (% of relevant age group)	..	..	98	108
Gross secondary enrollment ratio (% of relevant age group)	..	..	40	49
Gross tertiary enrollment ratio (% of relevant age group)	1	4	..	..
Primary completion rate (% of relevant age group)	..	..	60	72
Youth literacy rate (% of population ages 15–24)	54	66	82	71
Health and related services				
Total fertility rate (births per woman)	6.5		5.2	
Adolescent fertility rate (births per 1,000 women ages 15–19)	..		127	
Women first married by age 18 (% of women ages 20–24)	48		38	
Contraceptive prevalence (% of women ages 15–49)	6		11	
Unmet need for contraception (% of women ages 15–49)	..		36	
Pregnant women receiving prenatal care (%)	83		79	
Births attended by skilled health staff (% of total)	58		46	
Maternal mortality ratio (per 100,000 live births)	1,200		770	
Economic structure, participation, and access to resources				
Labor force participation rate (% of population ages 15+)	56	64	58	64
Wage and salaried workers (% of employed ages 15+)	..	..	9	28
Self-employed workers (% of employed ages 15+)	..	..	91	72
Vulnerable employment (% of employed ages 15+)	..	..	89	69
Unpaid family workers (% of employed ages 15+)	..	..	19.7	12.5
Employment in agriculture (% of employed ages 15+)	..	..	48	50
Employment in industry (% of employed ages 15+)	..	..	5	14
Employment in service (% of employed ages 15+)	..	..	47	37
Women in wage employment in the nonagricultural sector (%)	..		..	
Women's share of part-time employment (% of total)	..		..	
Maternity leave (weeks)	..		..	
Maternal leave benefits (% of wages paid)	..		..	
Female legislators, senior officials and managers (% of total)	..		..	
Employment to population ratio, total (% ages 15+)	54	61	56	62
Employment to population ratio, youth (% ages 15–24)	33	36	33	34
Children in employment (% of children ages 7–14)	..	..	15.0	21.7
Unemployment rate (% of labor force ages 15+)	..	..	4.1	3.4
Long-term unemployment rate (% total unemployment)	..	..	..	..
Youth unemployment rate (% of labor force ages 15–24)	..	..	7	3
Account at a formal financial institution (% age 15+)	..	..	15	23
Public life and decision making				
Seats held by women in national parliament (%)	..		11	

Libya

Middle East & North Africa		Upper middle income
Population (millions)		6.4
GNI, Atlas ($ billions)		77.1
GNI per capita, Atlas ($)		12,320
Population living below $1.25 a day (%)		..

	1990		2011	
	Female	Male	Female	Male
Demography				
Sex ratio at birth (boys per girls)	1.06		1.06	
Life expectancy at birth (years)	70	66	78	72
Under-five mortality rate (per 1,000 live births)	42	46	16	17
Female-headed households (%)	..		..	
Education				
Gross primary enrollment ratio (% of relevant age group)	105	112	112	117
Gross secondary enrollment ratio (% of relevant age group)	68	79	119	102
Gross tertiary enrollment ratio (% of relevant age group)	14	17	..	..
Primary completion rate (% of relevant age group)	..	..	..	..
Youth literacy rate (% of population ages 15–24)	96	99	100	100
Health and related services				
Total fertility rate (births per woman)	4.8		2.5	
Adolescent fertility rate (births per 1,000 women ages 15–19)	..		3	
Women first married by age 18 (% of women ages 20–24)	..		..	
Contraceptive prevalence (% of women ages 15–49)	..		..	
Unmet need for contraception (% of women ages 15–49)	..		..	
Pregnant women receiving prenatal care (%)	..		93	
Births attended by skilled health staff (% of total)	..		100	
Maternal mortality ratio (per 100,000 live births)	99		58	
Economic structure, participation, and access to resources				
Labor force participation rate (% of population ages 15+)	18	73	30	77
Wage and salaried workers (% of employed ages 15+)	..	..	..	..
Self-employed workers (% of employed ages 15+)	..	..	..	..
Vulnerable employment (% of employed ages 15+)	..	..	..	..
Unpaid family workers (% of employed ages 15+)	..	..	..	..
Employment in agriculture (% of employed ages 15+)	..	..	..	..
Employment in industry (% of employed ages 15+)	..	..	..	..
Employment in service (% of employed ages 15+)	..	..	..	..
Women in wage employment in the nonagricultural sector (%)	..		..	
Women's share of part-time employment (% of total)	..		..	
Maternity leave (weeks)	7		7	
Maternal leave benefits (% of wages paid)	50		100	
Female legislators, senior officials and managers (% of total)	..		..	
Employment to population ratio, total (% ages 15+)	16	68	24	69
Employment to population ratio, youth (% ages 15–24)	11	40	13	36
Children in employment (% of children ages 7–14)	..	..	..	..
Unemployment rate (% of labor force ages 15+)	..	..	..	..
Long-term unemployment rate (% total unemployment)	..	..	..	..
Youth unemployment rate (% of labor force ages 15–24)	..	..	..	..
Account at a formal financial institution (% age 15+)	..	..	..	..
Public life and decision making				
Seats held by women in national parliament (%)	..		17	

Liechtenstein

South Asia				High income

Population (thousands)	36.3
GNI, Atlas ($ billions)	4.9
GNI per capita, Atlas ($)	137,070
Population living below $1.25 a day (%)	..

	1990		2011	
	Female	Male	Female	Male
Demography				
Sex ratio at birth (boys per girls)	..		..	
Life expectancy at birth (years)	..	..	..	..
Under-five mortality rate (per 1,000 live births)	..	..	..	..
Female-headed households (%)	..		..	
Education				
Gross primary enrollment ratio (% of relevant age group)	..	..	105	105
Gross secondary enrollment ratio (% of relevant age group)	..	..	101	122
Gross tertiary enrollment ratio (% of relevant age group)	..	..	30	56
Primary completion rate (% of relevant age group)	..	..	100	101
Youth literacy rate (% of population ages 15–24)	..	..	..	..
Health and related services				
Total fertility rate (births per woman)		..	1.7	
Adolescent fertility rate (births per 1,000 women ages 15–19)		..	..	
Women first married by age 18 (% of women ages 20–24)		..	..	
Contraceptive prevalence (% of women ages 15–49)		..	..	
Unmet need for contraception (% of women ages 15–49)		..	..	
Pregnant women receiving prenatal care (%)		..	..	
Births attended by skilled health staff (% of total)		..	..	
Maternal mortality ratio (per 100,000 live births)		..	..	
Economic structure, participation, and access to resources				
Labor force participation rate (% of population ages 15+)	..	..	..	..
Wage and salaried workers (% of employed ages 15+)	..	..	..	..
Self-employed workers (% of employed ages 15+)	..	..	..	..
Vulnerable employment (% of employed ages 15+)	..	..	..	..
Unpaid family workers (% of employed ages 15+)	..	..	..	..
Employment in agriculture (% of employed ages 15+)	..	..	..	..
Employment in industry (% of employed ages 15+)	..	..	..	..
Employment in service (% of employed ages 15+)	..	..	..	..
Women in wage employment in the nonagricultural sector (%)		..	44	
Women's share of part-time employment (% of total)		..	..	
Maternity leave (weeks)	8		..	
Maternal leave benefits (% of wages paid)	80		..	
Female legislators, senior officials and managers (% of total)		..	..	
Employment to population ratio, total (% ages 15+)	..	..	..	..
Employment to population ratio, youth (% ages 15–24)	..	..	..	..
Children in employment (% of children ages 7–14)	..	..	..	..
Unemployment rate (% of labor force ages 15+)	..	..	..	..
Long-term unemployment rate (% total unemployment)	..	..	..	..
Youth unemployment rate (% of labor force ages 15–24)	..	..	..	..
Account at a formal financial institution (% age 15+)	..	..	..	..
Public life and decision making				
Seats held by women in national parliament (%)	4		24	

Lithuania

Europe & Central Asia			Upper middle income	
Population (millions)				3.0
GNI, Atlas ($ billions)				39.3
GNI per capita, Atlas ($)				12,980
Population living below $1.25 a day (%)				<2

	1990		2011	
	Female	Male	Female	Male
Demography				
Sex ratio at birth (boys per girls)	1.05		1.05	
Life expectancy at birth (years)	76	66	79	68
Under-five mortality rate (per 1,000 live births)	15	19	5	6
Female-headed households (%)	..		..	
Education				
Gross primary enrollment ratio (% of relevant age group)	89	95	93	95
Gross secondary enrollment ratio (% of relevant age group)	83	86	97	100
Gross tertiary enrollment ratio (% of relevant age group)	27	39	83	56
Primary completion rate (% of relevant age group)	..	..	94	97
Youth literacy rate (% of population ages 15–24)	100	100	100	100
Health and related services				
Total fertility rate (births per woman)	2.0		1.8	
Adolescent fertility rate (births per 1,000 women ages 15–19)	..		17	
Women first married by age 18 (% of women ages 20–24)	..		..	
Contraceptive prevalence (% of women ages 15–49)	..		..	
Unmet need for contraception (% of women ages 15–49)	..		..	
Pregnant women receiving prenatal care (%)	..		..	
Births attended by skilled health staff (% of total)	100		100	
Maternal mortality ratio (per 100,000 live births)	34		8	
Economic structure, participation, and access to resources				
Labor force participation rate (% of population ages 15+)	59	74	54	64
Wage and salaried workers (% of employed ages 15+)	..	..	91	88
Self-employed workers (% of employed ages 15+)	..	..	9	12
Vulnerable employment (% of employed ages 15+)	..	..	8	9
Unpaid family workers (% of employed ages 15+)	..	..	1.5	1.3
Employment in agriculture (% of employed ages 15+)	..	..	7	11
Employment in industry (% of employed ages 15+)	..	..	16	33
Employment in service (% of employed ages 15+)	..	..	77	56
Women in wage employment in the nonagricultural sector (%)	55		54	
Women's share of part-time employment (% of total)			62	
Maternity leave (weeks)	..		18	
Maternal leave benefits (% of wages paid)	..		100	
Female legislators, senior officials and managers (% of total)	..		38	
Employment to population ratio, total (% ages 15+)	50	61	47	53
Employment to population ratio, youth (% ages 15–24)	31	36	19	22
Children in employment (% of children ages 7–14)	..	..	..	..
Unemployment rate (% of labor force ages 15+)	..	..	13.0	17.8
Long-term unemployment rate (% total unemployment)	..	..	51.4	52.2
Youth unemployment rate (% of labor force ages 15–24)	..	..	31	35
Account at a formal financial institution (% age 15+)	..	..	76	71
Public life and decision making				
Seats held by women in national parliament (%)	..		25	

Luxembourg

High income

Population (thousands)	518.3
GNI, Atlas ($ billions)	40.1
GNI per capita, Atlas ($)	77,390
Population living below $1.25 a day (%)	..

	1990		2011	
	Female	Male	Female	Male
Demography				
Sex ratio at birth (boys per girls)	1.06		1.06	
Life expectancy at birth (years)	78	72	84	79
Under-five mortality rate (per 1,000 live births)	7	9	3	3
Female-headed households (%)	..		..	
Education				
Gross primary enrollment ratio (% of relevant age group)	94	87	98	96
Gross secondary enrollment ratio (% of relevant age group)	70	68	103	100
Gross tertiary enrollment ratio (% of relevant age group)	1	3	10	11
Primary completion rate (% of relevant age group)	..	..	84	83
Youth literacy rate (% of population ages 15–24)	..	..	..	..
Health and related services				
Total fertility rate (births per woman)	1.6		1.5	
Adolescent fertility rate (births per 1,000 women ages 15–19)	..		9	
Women first married by age 18 (% of women ages 20–24)	..		..	
Contraceptive prevalence (% of women ages 15–49)	..		..	
Unmet need for contraception (% of women ages 15–49)	..		..	
Pregnant women receiving prenatal care (%)	..		..	
Births attended by skilled health staff (% of total)	100		..	
Maternal mortality ratio (per 100,000 live births)	6		20	
Economic structure, participation, and access to resources				
Labor force participation rate (% of population ages 15+)	34	68	49	65
Wage and salaried workers (% of employed ages 15+)	90	89	93	90
Self-employed workers (% of employed ages 15+)	11	11	7	10
Vulnerable employment (% of employed ages 15+)	9	8	6	6
Unpaid family workers (% of employed ages 15+)	4.1	0.5	0.4	0.4
Employment in agriculture (% of employed ages 15+)	3	3	1	2
Employment in industry (% of employed ages 15+)	8	42	4	19
Employment in service (% of employed ages 15+)	89	55	92	75
Women in wage employment in the nonagricultural sector (%)	..		44	
Women's share of part-time employment (% of total)	87		82	
Maternity leave (weeks)	14		16	
Maternal leave benefits (% of wages paid)	100		100	
Female legislators, senior officials and managers (% of total)	40		24	
Employment to population ratio, total (% ages 15+)	35	68	46	63
Employment to population ratio, youth (% ages 15–24)	49	55	19	24
Children in employment (% of children ages 7–14)	..	..	..	..
Unemployment rate (% of labor force ages 15+)	2.4	1.2	6.3	3.8
Long-term unemployment rate (% total unemployment)	21.4	46.2	25.4	33.1
Youth unemployment rate (% of labor force ages 15–24)	5	3	21	13
Account at a formal financial institution (% age 15+)	..	..	95	94
Public life and decision making				
Seats held by women in national parliament (%)	13		22	

Macao SAR, China

	High income
Population (thousands)	555.7
GNI, Atlas ($ billions)	24.7
GNI per capita, Atlas ($)	45,460
Population living below $1.25 a day (%)	..

	1990 Female	1990 Male	2011 Female	2011 Male
Demography				
Sex ratio at birth (boys per girls)	1.05		1.05	
Life expectancy at birth (years)	79	74	83	79
Under-five mortality rate (per 1,000 live births)	..	..	..	..
Female-headed households (%)	..		..	
Education				
Gross primary enrollment ratio (% of relevant age group)	104	109	99	102
Gross secondary enrollment ratio (% of relevant age group)	63	58	92	99
Gross tertiary enrollment ratio (% of relevant age group)	18	47	67	69
Primary completion rate (% of relevant age group)	97	97	98	97
Youth literacy rate (% of population ages 15–24)	..	..	100	100
Health and related services				
Total fertility rate (births per woman)	1.7		1.1	
Adolescent fertility rate (births per 1,000 women ages 15–19)	..		4	
Women first married by age 18 (% of women ages 20–24)	..		..	
Contraceptive prevalence (% of women ages 15–49)	..		..	
Unmet need for contraception (% of women ages 15–49)	..		..	
Pregnant women receiving prenatal care (%)	..		..	
Births attended by skilled health staff (% of total)	..		..	
Maternal mortality ratio (per 100,000 live births)	..		..	
Economic structure, participation, and access to resources				
Labor force participation rate (% of population ages 15+)	45	72	67	77
Wage and salaried workers (% of employed ages 15+)	..	..	96	90
Self-employed workers (% of employed ages 15+)	..	..	4	11
Vulnerable employment (% of employed ages 15+)	..	..	3	6
Unpaid family workers (% of employed ages 15+)	..	..	0.6	0.1
Employment in agriculture (% of employed ages 15+)	0	0	0	0
Employment in industry (% of employed ages 15+)	50	37	12	27
Employment in service (% of employed ages 15+)	49	63	88	73
Women in wage employment in the nonagricultural sector (%)	43		50	
Women's share of part-time employment (% of total)	..		..	
Maternity leave (weeks)	..		..	
Maternal leave benefits (% of wages paid)	..		..	
Female legislators, senior officials and managers (% of total)	..		31	
Employment to population ratio, total (% ages 15+)	44	70	65	75
Employment to population ratio, youth (% ages 15–24)	45	46	46	43
Children in employment (% of children ages 7–14)	..	..	..	..
Unemployment rate (% of labor force ages 15+)	4.0	2.5	2.1	3.0
Long-term unemployment rate (% of total unemployment)	..	..	..	..
Youth unemployment rate (% of labor force ages 15–24)	3	4	5	7
Account at a formal financial institution (% age 15+)	..	..	..	..
Public life and decision making				
Seats held by women in national parliament (%)	..		..	

Macedonia, FYR

Europe & Central Asia			Upper middle income	
Population (millions)				2.1
GNI, Atlas ($ billions)				9.9
GNI per capita, Atlas ($)				4,810
Population living below $1.25 a day (%)				<2

	1990		2011	
	Female	Male	Female	Male
Demography				
Sex ratio at birth (boys per girls)	1.08		1.08	
Life expectancy at birth (years)	73	69	77	73
Under-five mortality rate (per 1,000 live births)	36	39	9	11
Female-headed households (%)	..		8	
Education				
Gross primary enrollment ratio (% of relevant age group)	99	100	91	89
Gross secondary enrollment ratio (% of relevant age group)	75	77	83	84
Gross tertiary enrollment ratio (% of relevant age group)	18	19	42	36
Primary completion rate (% of relevant age group)	..	..	93	92
Youth literacy rate (% of population ages 15–24)	99	99	99	99
Health and related services				
Total fertility rate (births per woman)	2.1		1.4	
Adolescent fertility rate (births per 1,000 women ages 15–19)	..		19	
Women first married by age 18 (% of women ages 20–24)	..		7	
Contraceptive prevalence (% of women ages 15–49)	..		..	
Unmet need for contraception (% of women ages 15–49)	..		34	
Pregnant women receiving prenatal care (%)	..		99	
Births attended by skilled health staff (% of total)	89		100	
Maternal mortality ratio (per 100,000 live births)	16		10	
Economic structure, participation, and access to resources				
Labor force participation rate (% of population ages 15+)	43	67	43	69
Wage and salaried workers (% of employed ages 15+)	..	..	76	69
Self-employed workers (% of employed ages 15+)	..	..	24	31
Vulnerable employment (% of employed ages 15+)	..	..	21	24
Unpaid family workers (% of employed ages 15+)	..	..	14.9	6.1
Employment in agriculture (% of employed ages 15+)	..	..	20	20
Employment in industry (% of employed ages 15+)	..	..	28	33
Employment in service (% of employed ages 15+)	..	..	52	47
Women in wage employment in the nonagricultural sector (%)	38		42	
Women's share of part-time employment (% of total)	..		45	
Maternity leave (weeks)	..		39	
Maternal leave benefits (% of wages paid)	..		..	
Female legislators, senior officials and managers (% of total)	..		28	
Employment to population ratio, total (% ages 15+)	29	47	29	48
Employment to population ratio, youth (% ages 15–24)	14	20	11	19
Children in employment (% of children ages 7–14)	..	..	..	..
Unemployment rate (% of labor force ages 15+)	..	..	30.8	31.8
Long-term unemployment rate (% total unemployment)	..	..	81.0	83.6
Youth unemployment rate (% of labor force ages 15–24)	..	..	55	56
Account at a formal financial institution (% age 15+)	..	..	72	76
Public life and decision making				
Seats held by women in national parliament (%)	..		33	

Madagascar

Population (millions)	21.3
GNI, Atlas ($ billions)	9.1
GNI per capita, Atlas ($)	430
Population living below $1.25 a day (%)	81.3

	1990		2011	
	Female	Male	Female	Male
Demography				
Sex ratio at birth (boys per girls)	1.02		1.03	
Life expectancy at birth (years)	52	50	68	65
Under-five mortality rate (per 1,000 live births)	152	171	58	65
Female-headed households (%)	22		22	
Education				
Gross primary enrollment ratio (% of relevant age group)	98	102	147	150
Gross secondary enrollment ratio (% of relevant age group)	18	19	30	32
Gross tertiary enrollment ratio (% of relevant age group)	3	4	4	4
Primary completion rate (% of relevant age group)	37	35	74	72
Youth literacy rate (% of population ages 15–24)	..	..	64	66
Health and related services				
Total fertility rate (births per woman)	6.3		4.6	
Adolescent fertility rate (births per 1,000 women ages 15–19)	..		125	
Women first married by age 18 (% of women ages 20–24)	37		48	
Contraceptive prevalence (% of women ages 15–49)	17		40	
Unmet need for contraception (% of women ages 15–49)	32		19	
Pregnant women receiving prenatal care (%)	78		86	
Births attended by skilled health staff (% of total)	57		44	
Maternal mortality ratio (per 100,000 live births)	640		240	
Economic structure, participation, and access to resources				
Labor force participation rate (% of population ages 15+)	83	89	83	89
Wage and salaried workers (% of employed ages 15+)	11	15	..	..
Self-employed workers (% of employed ages 15+)	87	84	..	..
Vulnerable employment (% of employed ages 15+)	87	83	..	..
Unpaid family workers (% of employed ages 15+)	41.6	24.3	..	..
Employment in agriculture (% of employed ages 15+)	..	..	..	..
Employment in industry (% of employed ages 15+)	..	..	..	..
Employment in service (% of employed ages 15+)	..	..	..	..
Women in wage employment in the nonagricultural sector (%)	31		..	
Women's share of part-time employment (% of total)	..		..	
Maternity leave (weeks)	14		14	
Maternal leave benefits (% of wages paid)	50		100	
Female legislators, senior officials and managers (% of total)	..		..	
Employment to population ratio, total (% ages 15+)	80	86	80	87
Employment to population ratio, youth (% ages 15–24)	70	72	69	72
Children in employment (% of children ages 7–14)	..	..	24.2	27.7
Unemployment rate (% of labor force ages 15+)	..	..	..	..
Long-term unemployment rate (% total unemployment)	..	..	..	..
Youth unemployment rate (% of labor force ages 15–24)	..	..	..	..
Account at a formal financial institution (% age 15+)	..	..	5	6
Public life and decision making				
Seats held by women in national parliament (%)	7		18	

Malawi

Sub-Saharan Africa			Low income	
Population (millions)				15.4
GNI, Atlas ($ billions)				5.6
GNI per capita, Atlas ($)				360
Population living below $1.25 a day (%)				73.9

	1990		2011	
	Female	Male	Female	Male
Demography				
Sex ratio at birth (boys per girls)	1.03		1.03	
Life expectancy at birth (years)	48	46	54	54
Under-five mortality rate (per 1,000 live births)	219	235	79	87
Female-headed households (%)	25		28	
Education				
Gross primary enrollment ratio (% of relevant age group)	66	77	144	139
Gross secondary enrollment ratio (% of relevant age group)	12	20	33	36
Gross tertiary enrollment ratio (% of relevant age group)	0	1	1	1
Primary completion rate (% of relevant age group)	24	32	72	70
Youth literacy rate (% of population ages 15–24)	49	70	87	87
Health and related services				
Total fertility rate (births per woman)	6.8		6.0	
Adolescent fertility rate (births per 1,000 women ages 15–19)	..		108	
Women first married by age 18 (% of women ages 20–24)	55		50	
Contraceptive prevalence (% of women ages 15–49)	13		46	
Unmet need for contraception (% of women ages 15–49)	36		26	
Pregnant women receiving prenatal care (%)	90		95	
Births attended by skilled health staff (% of total)	55		71	
Maternal mortality ratio (per 100,000 live births)	1,100		460	
Economic structure, participation, and access to resources				
Labor force participation rate (% of population ages 15+)	76	80	85	81
Wage and salaried workers (% of employed ages 15+)	4	29	..	..
Self-employed workers (% of employed ages 15+)	96	71	..	..
Vulnerable employment (% of employed ages 15+)	96	71	..	..
Unpaid family workers (% of employed ages 15+)	0.4	0.3	..	..
Employment in agriculture (% of employed ages 15+)	..	..	..	..
Employment in industry (% of employed ages 15+)	..	..	..	..
Employment in service (% of employed ages 15+)	..	..	..	..
Women in wage employment in the nonagricultural sector (%)	11		..	
Women's share of part-time employment (% of total)	..		..	
Maternity leave (weeks)	..		8	
Maternal leave benefits (% of wages paid)	..		100	
Female legislators, senior officials and managers (% of total)	..		..	
Employment to population ratio, total (% ages 15+)	69	75	77	77
Employment to population ratio, youth (% ages 15–24)	50	45	55	48
Children in employment (% of children ages 7–14)	..	..	39.4	41.3
Unemployment rate (% of labor force ages 15+)	..	..	..	..
Long-term unemployment rate (% total unemployment)	..	..	..	..
Youth unemployment rate (% of labor force ages 15–24)	..	..	..	..
Account at a formal financial institution (% age 15+)	..	..	17	16
Public life and decision making				
Seats held by women in national parliament (%)	10		22	

Malaysia

East Asia & Pacific	Upper middle income
Population (millions)	28.9
GNI, Atlas ($ billions)	253.0
GNI per capita, Atlas ($)	8,770
Population living below $1.25 a day (%)	<2

	1990		2011	
	Female	Male	Female	Male
Demography				
Sex ratio at birth (boys per girls)	1.06		1.06	
Life expectancy at birth (years)	72	68	77	72
Under-five mortality rate (per 1,000 live births)	16	19	6	7
Female-headed households (%)	..		..	
Education				
Gross primary enrollment ratio (% of relevant age group)	92	93	..	..
Gross secondary enrollment ratio (% of relevant age group)	56	53	72	67
Gross tertiary enrollment ratio (% of relevant age group)	6	7	49	36
Primary completion rate (% of relevant age group)	88	88	..	..
Youth literacy rate (% of population ages 15–24)	95	96	98	98
Health and related services				
Total fertility rate (births per woman)	3.5		2.6	
Adolescent fertility rate (births per 1,000 women ages 15–19)	..		11	
Women first married by age 18 (% of women ages 20–24)	..		..	
Contraceptive prevalence (% of women ages 15–49)	50		..	
Unmet need for contraception (% of women ages 15–49)	..		..	
Pregnant women receiving prenatal care (%)	..		91	
Births attended by skilled health staff (% of total)	93		99	
Maternal mortality ratio (per 100,000 live births)	53		29	
Economic structure, participation, and access to resources				
Labor force participation rate (% of population ages 15+)	43	81	44	77
Wage and salaried workers (% of employed ages 15+)	71	64	78	72
Self-employed workers (% of employed ages 15+)	27	34	21	28
Vulnerable employment (% of employed ages 15+)	25	31	20	23
Unpaid family workers (% of employed ages 15+)	8.1	2.4	7.8	2.6
Employment in agriculture (% of employed ages 15+)	25	26	9	16
Employment in industry (% of employed ages 15+)	28	27	21	31
Employment in service (% of employed ages 15+)	47	46	71	53
Women in wage employment in the nonagricultural sector (%)	35		39	
Women's share of part-time employment (% of total)	..		..	
Maternity leave (weeks)	8		9	
Maternal leave benefits (% of wages paid)	100		100	
Female legislators, senior officials and managers (% of total)	..		25	
Employment to population ratio, total (% ages 15+)	42	78	42	75
Employment to population ratio, youth (% ages 15–24)	38	54	29	41
Children in employment (% of children ages 7–14)	..	..	..	..
Unemployment rate (% of labor force ages 15+)	5.4	4.0	3.6	3.3
Long-term unemployment rate (% total unemployment)	..	..	..	..
Youth unemployment rate (% of labor force ages 15–24)	..	..	12	10
Account at a formal financial institution (% age 15+)	..	..	63	69
Public life and decision making				
Seats held by women in national parliament (%)	5		10	

Maldives

South Asia	Upper middle income
Population (thousands)	320.1
GNI, Atlas ($ billions)	1.8
GNI per capita, Atlas ($)	5,720
Population living below $1.25 a day (%)	<2

	1990		2011	
	Female	Male	Female	Male
Demography				
Sex ratio at birth (boys per girls)	1.07		1.06	
Life expectancy at birth (years)	60	61	78	76
Under-five mortality rate (per 1,000 live births)	101	110	10	12
Female-headed households (%)	..		35	
Education				
Gross primary enrollment ratio (% of relevant age group)	123	123	103	105
Gross secondary enrollment ratio (% of relevant age group)	53	52	..	..
Gross tertiary enrollment ratio (% of relevant age group)	..	..	14	12
Primary completion rate (% of relevant age group)	..	..	103	111
Youth literacy rate (% of population ages 15–24)	98	98	99	99
Health and related services				
Total fertility rate (births per woman)	6.1		1.7	
Adolescent fertility rate (births per 1,000 women ages 15–19)	..		11	
Women first married by age 18 (% of women ages 20–24)	..		4	
Contraceptive prevalence (% of women ages 15–49)	29		35	
Unmet need for contraception (% of women ages 15–49)	..		28	
Pregnant women receiving prenatal care (%)	..		99	
Births attended by skilled health staff (% of total)	90		95	
Maternal mortality ratio (per 100,000 live births)	830		60	
Economic structure, participation, and access to resources				
Labor force participation rate (% of population ages 15+)	20	77	56	77
Wage and salaried workers (% of employed ages 15+)	37	49	45	61
Self-employed workers (% of employed ages 15+)	58	47	54	29
Vulnerable employment (% of employed ages 15+)	57	44	47	20
Unpaid family workers (% of employed ages 15+)	6.6	4.0	22.9	7.9
Employment in agriculture (% of employed ages 15+)	14	28	7	14
Employment in industry (% of employed ages 15+)	39	18	32	20
Employment in service (% of employed ages 15+)	43	50	56	62
Women in wage employment in the nonagricultural sector (%)	16		30	
Women's share of part-time employment (% of total)	..		..	
Maternity leave (weeks)	..		..	
Maternal leave benefits (% of wages paid)	..		..	
Female legislators, senior officials and managers (% of total)	..		14	
Employment to population ratio, total (% ages 15+)	17	71	44	72
Employment to population ratio, youth (% ages 15–24)	14	53	34	51
Children in employment (% of children ages 7–14)	..	..	..	..
Unemployment rate (% of labor force ages 15+)	..	..	23.8	7.9
Long-term unemployment rate (% total unemployment)	..	..	..	..
Youth unemployment rate (% of labor force ages 15–24)	..	..	31	16
Account at a formal financial institution (% age 15+)	..	..	..	..
Public life and decision making				
Seats held by women in national parliament (%)	6		7	

Mali

Sub-Saharan Africa			Low income	
Population (millions)				15.8
GNI, Atlas ($ billions)				9.7
GNI per capita, Atlas ($)				610
Population living below $1.25 a day (%)				50.4

	1990		2011	
	Female	Male	Female	Male
Demography				
Sex ratio at birth (boys per girls)	1.05		1.05	
Life expectancy at birth (years)	45	43	52	50
Under-five mortality rate (per 1,000 live births)	248	267	169	182
Female-headed households (%)	..		12	
Education				
Gross primary enrollment ratio (% of relevant age group)	20	32	76	87
Gross secondary enrollment ratio (% of relevant age group)	4	9	33	46
Gross tertiary enrollment ratio (% of relevant age group)	0	1	4	8
Primary completion rate (% of relevant age group)	6	12	50	61
Youth literacy rate (% of population ages 15–24)	..	..	34	56
Health and related services				
Total fertility rate (births per woman)	7.1		6.2	
Adolescent fertility rate (births per 1,000 women ages 15–19)	..		172	
Women first married by age 18 (% of women ages 20–24)	79		55	
Contraceptive prevalence (% of women ages 15–49)	5		8	
Unmet need for contraception (% of women ages 15–49)	..		31	
Pregnant women receiving prenatal care (%)	31		70	
Births attended by skilled health staff (% of total)	32		49	
Maternal mortality ratio (per 100,000 live births)	1,100		540	
Economic structure, participation, and access to resources				
Labor force participation rate (% of population ages 15+)	38	65	37	70
Wage and salaried workers (% of employed ages 15+)	..	..	4	12
Self-employed workers (% of employed ages 15+)	..	..	89	77
Vulnerable employment (% of employed ages 15+)	..	..	89	77
Unpaid family workers (% of employed ages 15+)	..	..	34.1	18.5
Employment in agriculture (% of employed ages 15+)	..	..	64	68
Employment in industry (% of employed ages 15+)	..	..	3	8
Employment in service (% of employed ages 15+)	..	..	33	24
Women in wage employment in the nonagricultural sector (%)	..		..	
Women's share of part-time employment (% of total)	..		..	
Maternity leave (weeks)	14		14	
Maternal leave benefits (% of wages paid)	100		100	
Female legislators, senior officials and managers (% of total)	..		..	
Employment to population ratio, total (% ages 15+)	35	59	34	63
Employment to population ratio, youth (% ages 15–24)	28	43	28	43
Children in employment (% of children ages 7–14)	..	..	21.6	24.2
Unemployment rate (% of labor force ages 15+)	..	..	..	..
Long-term unemployment rate (% total unemployment)	..	..	..	..
Youth unemployment rate (% of labor force ages 15–24)	..	..	..	..
Account at a formal financial institution (% age 15+)	..	..	7	10
Public life and decision making				
Seats held by women in national parliament (%)	..		10	

Malta

High income

Population (thousands)	415.7
GNI, Atlas ($ billions)	7.7
GNI per capita, Atlas ($)	*18,620*
Population living below $1.25 a day (%)	..

	1990		2011	
	Female	Male	Female	Male
Demography				
Sex ratio at birth (boys per girls)	1.06		1.06	
Life expectancy at birth (years)	78	73	84	80
Under-five mortality rate (per 1,000 live births)	10	13	5	7
Female-headed households (%)	..		..	
Education				
Gross primary enrollment ratio (% of relevant age group)	101	105	*101*	*101*
Gross secondary enrollment ratio (% of relevant age group)	80	86	*95*	*107*
Gross tertiary enrollment ratio (% of relevant age group)	9	12	*41*	*30*
Primary completion rate (% of relevant age group)	97	99	*97*	*96*
Youth literacy rate (% of population ages 15–24)	..	..	..	..
Health and related services				
Total fertility rate (births per woman)	2.1		1.4	
Adolescent fertility rate (births per 1,000 women ages 15–19)	..		13	
Women first married by age 18 (% of women ages 20–24)	..		..	
Contraceptive prevalence (% of women ages 15–49)	86		..	
Unmet need for contraception (% of women ages 15–49)	..		..	
Pregnant women receiving prenatal care (%)	..		..	
Births attended by skilled health staff (% of total)	98		*100*	
Maternal mortality ratio (per 100,000 live births)	14		*8*	
Economic structure, participation, and access to resources				
Labor force participation rate (% of population ages 15+)	27	77	35	67
Wage and salaried workers (% of employed ages 15+)	..	..	94	83
Self-employed workers (% of employed ages 15+)	..	..	6	17
Vulnerable employment (% of employed ages 15+)	..	..	5	12
Unpaid family workers (% of employed ages 15+)	..	..	0.0	0.1
Employment in agriculture (% of employed ages 15+)	..	..	0	2
Employment in industry (% of employed ages 15+)	..	..	13	31
Employment in service (% of employed ages 15+)	..	..	86	67
Women in wage employment in the nonagricultural sector (%)	28		36	
Women's share of part-time employment (% of total)	..		67	
Maternity leave (weeks)	13		*14*	
Maternal leave benefits (% of wages paid)	100		*100*	
Female legislators, senior officials and managers (% of total)	..		23	
Employment to population ratio, total (% ages 15+)	25	72	33	63
Employment to population ratio, youth (% ages 15–24)	56	57	42	48
Children in employment (% of children ages 7–14)	..	..	..	..
Unemployment rate (% of labor force ages 15+)	..	..	7.0	6.1
Long-term unemployment rate (% total unemployment)	..	..	34.7	53.1
Youth unemployment rate (% of labor force ages 15–24)	..	..	14	14
Account at a formal financial institution (% age 15+)	..	..	94	97
Public life and decision making				
Seats held by women in national parliament (%)	3		9	

Marshall Islands

East Asia & Pacific	Lower middle income
Population (thousands)	54.8
GNI, Atlas ($ millions)	214.3
GNI per capita, Atlas ($)	3,910
Population living below $1.25 a day (%)	..

	1990		2011	
	Female	Male	Female	Male
Demography				
Sex ratio at birth (boys per girls)		..		..
Life expectancy at birth (years)	75	70	..	..
Under-five mortality rate (per 1,000 live births)	46	57	23	29
Female-headed households (%)		..		..
Education				
Gross primary enrollment ratio (% of relevant age group)	..	..	101	102
Gross secondary enrollment ratio (% of relevant age group)	..	..	100	97
Gross tertiary enrollment ratio (% of relevant age group)	..	..	..	..
Primary completion rate (% of relevant age group)	..	..	101	94
Youth literacy rate (% of population ages 15–24)	..	..	..	..
Health and related services				
Total fertility rate (births per woman)	5.9		4.5	
Adolescent fertility rate (births per 1,000 women ages 15–19)			..	
Women first married by age 18 (% of women ages 20–24)	..		26	
Contraceptive prevalence (% of women ages 15–49)	37		45	
Unmet need for contraception (% of women ages 15–49)	..		8	
Pregnant women receiving prenatal care (%)	..		81	
Births attended by skilled health staff (% of total)	..		99	
Maternal mortality ratio (per 100,000 live births)	..			
Economic structure, participation, and access to resources				
Labor force participation rate (% of population ages 15+)	..	..	..	..
Wage and salaried workers (% of employed ages 15+)	..	..	..	..
Self-employed workers (% of employed ages 15+)	..	..	..	..
Vulnerable employment (% of employed ages 15+)	..	..	..	..
Unpaid family workers (% of employed ages 15+)	..	..	..	..
Employment in agriculture (% of employed ages 15+)	..	..	..	..
Employment in industry (% of employed ages 15+)	..	..	..	..
Employment in service (% of employed ages 15+)	..	..	..	..
Women in wage employment in the nonagricultural sector (%)	..		..	
Women's share of part-time employment (% of total)	..		..	
Maternity leave (weeks)	..		..	
Maternal leave benefits (% of wages paid)	..		..	
Female legislators, senior officials and managers (% of total)	..		..	
Employment to population ratio, total (% ages 15+)	..	..	..	..
Employment to population ratio, youth (% ages 15–24)	..	..	..	..
Children in employment (% of children ages 7–14)	..	..	..	..
Unemployment rate (% of labor force ages 15+)	13.2	12.2	..	..
Long-term unemployment rate (% total unemployment)	..	..	..	..
Youth unemployment rate (% of labor force ages 15–24)	..	..	..	..
Account at a formal financial institution (% age 15+)	..	..	..	..
Public life and decision making				
Seats held by women in national parliament (%)	..		3	

Mauritania

<table>
<tr><td>Sub-Saharan Africa</td><td colspan="4" align="right">Low income</td></tr>
<tr><td>Population (millions)</td><td colspan="4" align="right">3.5</td></tr>
<tr><td>GNI, Atlas ($ billions)</td><td colspan="4" align="right">3.6</td></tr>
<tr><td>GNI per capita, Atlas ($)</td><td colspan="4" align="right">1,030</td></tr>
<tr><td>Population living below $1.25 a day (%)</td><td colspan="4" align="right">23.4</td></tr>
</table>

	1990		2011	
	Female	Male	Female	Male
Demography				
Sex ratio at birth (boys per girls)	1.05		1.05	
Life expectancy at birth (years)	57	54	60	57
Under-five mortality rate (per 1,000 live births)	115	134	104	120
Female-headed households (%)	..		..	
Education				
Gross primary enrollment ratio (% of relevant age group)	40	54	104	98
Gross secondary enrollment ratio (% of relevant age group)	8	18	25	29
Gross tertiary enrollment ratio (% of relevant age group)	1	5	3	7
Primary completion rate (% of relevant age group)	21	36	72	68
Youth literacy rate (% of population ages 15–24)	..	..	65	71
Health and related services				
Total fertility rate (births per woman)	5.9		4.5	
Adolescent fertility rate (births per 1,000 women ages 15–19)	..		73	
Women first married by age 18 (% of women ages 20–24)	..		35	
Contraceptive prevalence (% of women ages 15–49)	4		9	
Unmet need for contraception (% of women ages 15–49)	..		25	
Pregnant women receiving prenatal care (%)	48		75	
Births attended by skilled health staff (% of total)	40		61	
Maternal mortality ratio (per 100,000 live births)	760		510	
Economic structure, participation, and access to resources				
Labor force participation rate (% of population ages 15+)	19	78	29	79
Wage and salaried workers (% of employed ages 15+)	..	..	..	..
Self-employed workers (% of employed ages 15+)	..	..	..	..
Vulnerable employment (% of employed ages 15+)	..	..	..	..
Unpaid family workers (% of employed ages 15+)	..	..	..	..
Employment in agriculture (% of employed ages 15+)	..	..	..	..
Employment in industry (% of employed ages 15+)	..	..	..	..
Employment in service (% of employed ages 15+)	..	..	..	..
Women in wage employment in the nonagricultural sector (%)	..		..	
Women's share of part-time employment (% of total)	..		..	
Maternity leave (weeks)	14		14	
Maternal leave benefits (% of wages paid)	100		100	
Female legislators, senior officials and managers (% of total)	..		..	
Employment to population ratio, total (% ages 15+)	13	52	20	53
Employment to population ratio, youth (% ages 15–24)	7	28	10	27
Children in employment (% of children ages 7–14)	..	..	18.6	23.9
Unemployment rate (% of labor force ages 15+)	35.8	21.9	44.0	23.9
Long-term unemployment rate (% total unemployment)	..	..	..	..
Youth unemployment rate (% of labor force ages 15–24)	..	..	..	..
Account at a formal financial institution (% age 15+)	..	..	12	23
Public life and decision making				
Seats held by women in national parliament (%)	..		22	

Mauritius

Sub-Saharan Africa			Upper middle income	
Population (millions)				1.3
GNI, Atlas ($ billions)				10.3
GNI per capita, Atlas ($)				8,040
Population living below $1.25 a day (%)				..

	1990		2011	
	Female	Male	Female	Male
Demography				
Sex ratio at birth (boys per girls)	1.04		1.04	
Life expectancy at birth (years)	73	66	77	70
Under-five mortality rate (per 1,000 live births)	21	27	14	16
Female-headed households (%)	..		..	
Education				
Gross primary enrollment ratio (% of relevant age group)	118	117	..	..
Gross secondary enrollment ratio (% of relevant age group)	53	52	91	91
Gross tertiary enrollment ratio (% of relevant age group)	2	4	37	28
Primary completion rate (% of relevant age group)	111	110	..	..
Youth literacy rate (% of population ages 15–24)	92	91	98	96
Health and related services				
Total fertility rate (births per woman)	2.3		1.5	
Adolescent fertility rate (births per 1,000 women ages 15–19)	..		33	
Women first married by age 18 (% of women ages 20–24)	..		..	
Contraceptive prevalence (% of women ages 15–49)	75		..	
Unmet need for contraception (% of women ages 15–49)	..		..	
Pregnant women receiving prenatal care (%)	..		..	
Births attended by skilled health staff (% of total)	91		..	
Maternal mortality ratio (per 100,000 live births)	68		60	
Economic structure, participation, and access to resources				
Labor force participation rate (% of population ages 15+)	38	82	44	76
Wage and salaried workers (% of employed ages 15+)	91	82	86	79
Self-employed workers (% of employed ages 15+)	9	18	15	22
Vulnerable employment (% of employed ages 15+)	7	13	13	16
Unpaid family workers (% of employed ages 15+)	3.1	1.5	4.0	0.6
Employment in agriculture (% of employed ages 15+)	14	18	7	9
Employment in industry (% of employed ages 15+)	50	40	21	32
Employment in service (% of employed ages 15+)	35	42	73	59
Women in wage employment in the nonagricultural sector (%)	37		38	
Women's share of part-time employment (% of total)	..		..	
Maternity leave (weeks)	..		12	
Maternal leave benefits (% of wages paid)	..		100	
Female legislators, senior officials and managers (% of total)	..		23	
Employment to population ratio, total (% ages 15+)	31	76	38	72
Employment to population ratio, youth (% ages 15–24)	26	56	25	39
Children in employment (% of children ages 7–14)	..	..	..	..
Unemployment rate (% of labor force ages 15+)	3.6	3.2	12.3	5.2
Long-term unemployment rate (% total unemployment)	..	..	..	..
Youth unemployment rate (% of labor force ages 15–24)	..	..	28	17
Account at a formal financial institution (% age 15+)	..	..	75	86
Public life and decision making				
Seats held by women in national parliament (%)	7		19	

Mexico

Population (millions)	114.8
GNI, Atlas ($ billions)	1,081.8
GNI per capita, Atlas ($)	9,420
Population living below $1.25 a day (%)	<2

	1990		2011	
	Female	Male	Female	Male
Demography				
Sex ratio at birth (boys per girls)	1.05		1.05	
Life expectancy at birth (years)	74	68	79	75
Under-five mortality rate (per 1,000 live births)	44	53	14	17
Female-headed households (%)	..		..	
Education				
Gross primary enrollment ratio (% of relevant age group)	111	116	112	113
Gross secondary enrollment ratio (% of relevant age group)	55	55	94	88
Gross tertiary enrollment ratio (% of relevant age group)	12	15	28	28
Primary completion rate (% of relevant age group)	91	91	105	104
Youth literacy rate (% of population ages 15–24)	95	96	98	98
Health and related services				
Total fertility rate (births per woman)	3.4		2.3	
Adolescent fertility rate (births per 1,000 women ages 15–19)	..		67	
Women first married by age 18 (% of women ages 20–24)	28		23	
Contraceptive prevalence (% of women ages 15–49)	63		73	
Unmet need for contraception (% of women ages 15–49)	..		..	
Pregnant women receiving prenatal care (%)	78		96	
Births attended by skilled health staff (% of total)	84		95	
Maternal mortality ratio (per 100,000 live births)	92		50	
Economic structure, participation, and access to resources				
Labor force participation rate (% of population ages 15+)	34	84	44	81
Wage and salaried workers (% of employed ages 15+)	80	65	65	67
Self-employed workers (% of employed ages 15+)	16	32	35	33
Vulnerable employment (% of employed ages 15+)	15	29	32	27
Unpaid family workers (% of employed ages 15+)	1.2	2.9	9.1	4.3
Employment in agriculture (% of employed ages 15+)	3	29	4	19
Employment in industry (% of employed ages 15+)	21	30	18	30
Employment in service (% of employed ages 15+)	70	39	78	51
Women in wage employment in the nonagricultural sector (%)	37		39	
Women's share of part-time employment (% of total)	55		57	
Maternity leave (weeks)	12		12	
Maternal leave benefits (% of wages paid)	100		100	
Female legislators, senior officials and managers (% of total)	15		31	
Employment to population ratio, total (% ages 15+)	33	82	42	76
Employment to population ratio, youth (% ages 15–24)	33	68	30	56
Children in employment (% of children ages 7–14)	..	..	4.4	9.1
Unemployment rate (% of labor force ages 15+)	4.2	2.5	5.2	5.3
Long-term unemployment rate (% total unemployment)	..	..	1.4	2.1
Youth unemployment rate (% of labor force ages 15–24)	6	5	10	10
Account at a formal financial institution (% age 15+)	..	..	22	33
Public life and decision making				
Seats held by women in national parliament (%)	12		37	

Micronesia, Fed. Sts.

East Asia & Pacific	Lower middle income
Population (thousands)	111.5
GNI, Atlas ($ millions)	318.6
GNI per capita, Atlas ($)	2,860
Population living below $1.25 a day (%)	*31.2*

	1990		2011	
	Female	Male	Female	Male
Demography				
Sex ratio at birth (boys per girls)	1.07		1.07	
Life expectancy at birth (years)	67	66	70	68
Under-five mortality rate (per 1,000 live births)	48	64	36	47
Female-headed households (%)	..		..	
Education				
Gross primary enrollment ratio (% of relevant age group)	..	..	*111*	*109*
Gross secondary enrollment ratio (% of relevant age group)	..	..	..	..
Gross tertiary enrollment ratio (% of relevant age group)	..	..	..	..
Primary completion rate (% of relevant age group)	..	..	..	..
Youth literacy rate (% of population ages 15–24)	..	..	..	..
Health and related services				
Total fertility rate (births per woman)	5.0		3.4	
Adolescent fertility rate (births per 1,000 women ages 15–19)	..		20	
Women first married by age 18 (% of women ages 20–24)	..		..	
Contraceptive prevalence (% of women ages 15–49)	..		55	
Unmet need for contraception (% of women ages 15–49)	..		..	
Pregnant women receiving prenatal care (%)	..		*80*	
Births attended by skilled health staff (% of total)	..		*100*	
Maternal mortality ratio (per 100,000 live births)	140		*100*	
Economic structure, participation, and access to resources				
Labor force participation rate (% of population ages 15+)	..	..	..	..
Wage and salaried workers (% of employed ages 15+)	..	..	..	..
Self-employed workers (% of employed ages 15+)	..	..	..	..
Vulnerable employment (% of employed ages 15+)	..	..	..	..
Unpaid family workers (% of employed ages 15+)	..	..	..	..
Employment in agriculture (% of employed ages 15+)	..	..	..	..
Employment in industry (% of employed ages 15+)	..	..	..	..
Employment in service (% of employed ages 15+)	..	..	..	..
Women in wage employment in the nonagricultural sector (%)	..		..	
Women's share of part-time employment (% of total)	..		..	
Maternity leave (weeks)	..		..	
Maternal leave benefits (% of wages paid)	..		..	
Female legislators, senior officials and managers (% of total)	..		..	
Employment to population ratio, total (% ages 15+)	..	..	..	..
Employment to population ratio, youth (% ages 15–24)	..	..	..	..
Children in employment (% of children ages 7–14)	..	..	..	..
Unemployment rate (% of labor force ages 15+)	..	..	..	..
Long-term unemployment rate (% total unemployment)	..	..	..	..
Youth unemployment rate (% of labor force ages 15–24)	..	..	..	..
Account at a formal financial institution (% age 15+)	..	..	..	..
Public life and decision making				
Seats held by women in national parliament (%)	..		0	

Moldova

Lower middle income

Population (millions)	3.6
GNI, Atlas ($ billions)	7.1
GNI per capita, Atlas ($)	1,980
Population living below $1.25 a day (%)	<2

	1990		2011	
	Female	Male	Female	Male
Demography				
Sex ratio at birth (boys per girls)	1.06		1.06	
Life expectancy at birth (years)	71	64	73	66
Under-five mortality rate (per 1,000 live births)	30	39	15	17
Female-headed households (%)	..		..	
Education				
Gross primary enrollment ratio (% of relevant age group)	90	90	93	94
Gross secondary enrollment ratio (% of relevant age group)	98	90	89	87
Gross tertiary enrollment ratio (% of relevant age group)	..	..	45	34
Primary completion rate (% of relevant age group)	..		90	92
Youth literacy rate (% of population ages 15–24)	100	100	100	99
Health and related services				
Total fertility rate (births per woman)	2.4		1.5	
Adolescent fertility rate (births per 1,000 women ages 15–19)	..		30	
Women first married by age 18 (% of women ages 20–24)	..		..	
Contraceptive prevalence (% of women ages 15–49)	..		..	
Unmet need for contraception (% of women ages 15–49)	..		..	
Pregnant women receiving prenatal care (%)	..		..	
Births attended by skilled health staff (% of total)	100		100	
Maternal mortality ratio (per 100,000 live births)	62		41	
Economic structure, participation, and access to resources				
Labor force participation rate (% of population ages 15+)	61	74	38	45
Wage and salaried workers (% of employed ages 15+)	..	..	75	66
Self-employed workers (% of employed ages 15+)	..	..	25	34
Vulnerable employment (% of employed ages 15+)	..	..	25	33
Unpaid family workers (% of employed ages 15+)	..	..	4.4	1.8
Employment in agriculture (% of employed ages 15+)	..	..	24	31
Employment in industry (% of employed ages 15+)	..	..	12	25
Employment in service (% of employed ages 15+)	..	..	64	44
Women in wage employment in the nonagricultural sector (%)	..		55	
Women's share of part-time employment (% of total)	..		..	
Maternity leave (weeks)	..		18	
Maternal leave benefits (% of wages paid)	..		100	
Female legislators, senior officials and managers (% of total)	..		38	
Employment to population ratio, total (% ages 15+)	55	64	36	41
Employment to population ratio, youth (% ages 15–24)	38	38	17	21
Children in employment (% of children ages 7–14)	..	..	23.0	34.5
Unemployment rate (% of labor force ages 15+)	..	..	5.6	7.7
Long-term unemployment rate (% total unemployment)	..	..	..	..
Youth unemployment rate (% of labor force ages 15–24)	..	..	16	14
Account at a formal financial institution (% age 15+)	..	..	17	19
Public life and decision making				
Seats held by women in national parliament (%)	..		20	

Monaco

	High income
Population (thousands)	35.4
GNI, Atlas ($ billions)	6.5
GNI per capita, Atlas ($)	183,150
Population living below $1.25 a day (%)	..

	1990 Female	1990 Male	2011 Female	2011 Male
Demography				
Sex ratio at birth (boys per girls)		..		..
Life expectancy at birth (years)	..	..	..	..
Under-five mortality rate (per 1,000 live births)	7	9	3	4
Female-headed households (%)	..			
Education				
Gross primary enrollment ratio (% of relevant age group)	..	..	..	..
Gross secondary enrollment ratio (% of relevant age group)	..	..	..	..
Gross tertiary enrollment ratio (% of relevant age group)	..	..	..	..
Primary completion rate (% of relevant age group)	..	..	..	..
Youth literacy rate (% of population ages 15–24)	..	..	..	..
Health and related services				
Total fertility rate (births per woman)	..		..	
Adolescent fertility rate (births per 1,000 women ages 15–19)	..		..	
Women first married by age 18 (% of women ages 20–24)	..		..	
Contraceptive prevalence (% of women ages 15–49)	..		..	
Unmet need for contraception (% of women ages 15–49)	..		..	
Pregnant women receiving prenatal care (%)	..		..	
Births attended by skilled health staff (% of total)	..		..	
Maternal mortality ratio (per 100,000 live births)	..		..	
Economic structure, participation, and access to resources				
Labor force participation rate (% of population ages 15+)	..	..	..	..
Wage and salaried workers (% of employed ages 15+)	..	..	..	..
Self-employed workers (% of employed ages 15+)	..	..	..	..
Vulnerable employment (% of employed ages 15+)	..	..	..	..
Unpaid family workers (% of employed ages 15+)	..	..	..	..
Employment in agriculture (% of employed ages 15+)	..	..	..	..
Employment in industry (% of employed ages 15+)	..	..	..	..
Employment in service (% of employed ages 15+)	..	..	..	..
Women in wage employment in the nonagricultural sector (%)	..		..	
Women's share of part-time employment (% of total)	..		..	
Maternity leave (weeks)	..		..	
Maternal leave benefits (% of wages paid)	..		..	
Female legislators, senior officials and managers (% of total)	..		..	
Employment to population ratio, total (% ages 15+)	..	..	..	..
Employment to population ratio, youth (% ages 15–24)	..	..	..	..
Children in employment (% of children ages 7–14)	..	..	..	..
Unemployment rate (% of labor force ages 15+)	..	..	..	..
Long-term unemployment rate (% total unemployment)	..	..	..	..
Youth unemployment rate (% of labor force ages 15–24)	..	..	..	..
Account at a formal financial institution (% age 15+)	..	..	..	..
Public life and decision making				
Seats held by women in national parliament (%)	11		19	

Mongolia

East Asia & Pacific

Lower middle income

Population (millions)	2.8
GNI, Atlas ($ billions)	6.5
GNI per capita, Atlas ($)	2,310
Population living below $1.25 a day (%)	..

	1990 Female	1990 Male	2011 Female	2011 Male
Demography				
Sex ratio at birth (boys per girls)	1.03		1.03	
Life expectancy at birth (years)	63	58	73	65
Under-five mortality rate (per 1,000 live births)	91	121	26	35
Female-headed households (%)	..		29	
Education				
Gross primary enrollment ratio (% of relevant age group)	*100*	*100*	118	121
Gross secondary enrollment ratio (% of relevant age group)	*89*	*80*	95	90
Gross tertiary enrollment ratio (% of relevant age group)	..	..	69	46
Primary completion rate (% of relevant age group)	..	..	116	115
Youth literacy rate (% of population ages 15–24)	..	..	97	94
Health and related services				
Total fertility rate (births per woman)	4.1		2.5	
Adolescent fertility rate (births per 1,000 women ages 15–19)	..		19	
Women first married by age 18 (% of women ages 20–24)	..		5	
Contraceptive prevalence (% of women ages 15–49)	57		55	
Unmet need for contraception (% of women ages 15–49)	..		..	
Pregnant women receiving prenatal care (%)	..		99	
Births attended by skilled health staff (% of total)	..		99	
Maternal mortality ratio (per 100,000 live births)	120		63	
Economic structure, participation, and access to resources				
Labor force participation rate (% of population ages 15+)	52	63	54	66
Wage and salaried workers (% of employed ages 15+)	..	..	45	38
Self-employed workers (% of employed ages 15+)	..	..	55	62
Vulnerable employment (% of employed ages 15+)	..	..	54	60
Unpaid family workers (% of employed ages 15+)	..	..	35.1	10.3
Employment in agriculture (% of employed ages 15+)	37	42	39	41
Employment in industry (% of employed ages 15+)	20	22	11	19
Employment in service (% of employed ages 15+)	44	37	50	40
Women in wage employment in the nonagricultural sector (%)	49		53	
Women's share of part-time employment (% of total)	..		..	
Maternity leave (weeks)	14		17	
Maternal leave benefits (% of wages paid)	..		70	
Female legislators, senior officials and managers (% of total)	..		47	
Employment to population ratio, total (% ages 15+)	46	55	52	63
Employment to population ratio, youth (% ages 15–24)	30	39	28	36
Children in employment (% of children ages 7–14)	..	..	8.6	11.4
Unemployment rate (% of labor force ages 15+)	..	..	..	..
Long-term unemployment rate (% total unemployment)	..	..	..	..
Youth unemployment rate (% of labor force ages 15–24)	..	..	..	..
Account at a formal financial institution (% age 15+)	..	..	82	73
Public life and decision making				
Seats held by women in national parliament (%)	25		15	

Montenegro

Europe & Central Asia	Upper middle income
Population (thousands)	632.3
GNI, Atlas ($ billions)	4.5
GNI per capita, Atlas ($)	7,140
Population living below $1.25 a day (%)	<2

	1990		2011	
	Female	Male	Female	Male
Demography				
Sex ratio at birth (boys per girls)	1.08		1.08	
Life expectancy at birth (years)	78	73	77	72
Under-five mortality rate (per 1,000 live births)	16	19	7	8
Female-headed households (%)			..	
Education				
Gross primary enrollment ratio (% of relevant age group)	..	..	118[a]	118[a]
Gross secondary enrollment ratio (% of relevant age group)	..	..	96[a]	95[a]
Gross tertiary enrollment ratio (% of relevant age group)	..	..	53	43
Primary completion rate (% of relevant age group)	..	..	98[a]	99[a]
Youth literacy rate (% of population ages 15–24)	..	..	99	99
Health and related services				
Total fertility rate (births per woman)	1.9		1.6	
Adolescent fertility rate (births per 1,000 women ages 15–19)	..		15	
Women first married by age 18 (% of women ages 20–24)	..		5	
Contraceptive prevalence (% of women ages 15–49)	..		39	
Unmet need for contraception (% of women ages 15–49)	..		26	
Pregnant women receiving prenatal care (%)	..		97	
Births attended by skilled health staff (% of total)	..		100	
Maternal mortality ratio (per 100,000 live births)	8		8	
Economic structure, participation, and access to resources				
Labor force participation rate (% of population ages 15+)	..	..	..	..
Wage and salaried workers (% of employed ages 15+)	..	..	89	80
Self-employed workers (% of employed ages 15+)	..	..	11	20
Vulnerable employment (% of employed ages 15+)	..	..	..	..
Unpaid family workers (% of employed ages 15+)	..	..	0.8	1.0
Employment in agriculture (% of employed ages 15+)	..	..	4	7
Employment in industry (% of employed ages 15+)	..	..	9	27
Employment in service (% of employed ages 15+)	..	..	87	67
Women in wage employment in the nonagricultural sector (%)	39		46	
Women's share of part-time employment (% of total)	..		..	
Maternity leave (weeks)	..		..	
Maternal leave benefits (% of wages paid)	..		..	
Female legislators, senior officials and managers (% of total)	..		31	
Employment to population ratio, total (% ages 15+)	..	..	..	..
Employment to population ratio, youth (% ages 15–24)	..	..	..	..
Children in employment (% of children ages 7–14)	..	..	..	..
Unemployment rate (% of labor force ages 15+)	..	..	20.0	19.5
Long-term unemployment rate (% total unemployment)	..	..	..	..
Youth unemployment rate (% of labor force ages 15–24)	..	..	40	36
Account at a formal financial institution (% age 15+)	..	..	49	52
Public life and decision making				
Seats held by women in national parliament (%)	..		17	

Morocco

Middle East & North Africa	Lower middle income
Population (millions)	32.3
GNI, Atlas ($ billions)	97.6
GNI per capita, Atlas ($)	2,970
Population living below $1.25 a day (%)	2.5

	1990 Female	1990 Male	2011 Female	2011 Male
Demography				
Sex ratio at birth (boys per girls)	1.06		1.06	
Life expectancy at birth (years)	66	62	74	70
Under-five mortality rate (per 1,000 live births)	77	86	30	35
Female-headed households (%)	16		..	
Education				
Gross primary enrollment ratio (% of relevant age group)	55	81	112[a]	118[a]
Gross secondary enrollment ratio (% of relevant age group)	31	44	64[a]	75[a]
Gross tertiary enrollment ratio (% of relevant age group)	8	14	12	14
Primary completion rate (% of relevant age group)	42	61	97[a]	101[a]
Youth literacy rate (% of population ages 15–24)	46	71	72	87
Health and related services				
Total fertility rate (births per woman)	4.0		2.2	
Adolescent fertility rate (births per 1,000 women ages 15–19)	..		12	
Women first married by age 18 (% of women ages 20–24)	18		..	
Contraceptive prevalence (% of women ages 15–49)	42		67	
Unmet need for contraception (% of women ages 15–49)	20		..	
Pregnant women receiving prenatal care (%)	32		77	
Births attended by skilled health staff (% of total)	31		74	
Maternal mortality ratio (per 100,000 live births)	300		100	
Economic structure, participation, and access to resources				
Labor force participation rate (% of population ages 15+)	26	80	26	75
Wage and salaried workers (% of employed ages 15+)	53	48	34	48
Self-employed workers (% of employed ages 15+)	47	53	66	52
Vulnerable employment (% of employed ages 15+)	45	48	65	47
Unpaid family workers (% of employed ages 15+)	29.3	16.8	48.6	15.0
Employment in agriculture (% of employed ages 15+)	3	4	61	32
Employment in industry (% of employed ages 15+)	50	32	13	25
Employment in service (% of employed ages 15+)	47	64	26	43
Women in wage employment in the nonagricultural sector (%)	21		21	
Women's share of part-time employment (% of total)	..		..	
Maternity leave (weeks)	12		14	
Maternal leave benefits (% of wages paid)	100		100	
Female legislators, senior officials and managers (% of total)	..		13	
Employment to population ratio, total (% ages 15+)	23	70	24	68
Employment to population ratio, youth (% ages 15–24)	24	55	16	43
Children in employment (% of children ages 7–14)	..	..	..	..
Unemployment rate (% of labor force ages 15+)	20.4	14.2	10.2	8.4
Long-term unemployment rate (% total unemployment)	..	..	..	..
Youth unemployment rate (% of labor force ages 15–24)	32	31	17	18
Account at a formal financial institution (% age 15+)	..	..	27	52
Public life and decision making				
Seats held by women in national parliament (%)	0		17	

Mozambique

Sub-Saharan Africa			Low income	
Population (millions)				23.9
GNI, Atlas ($ billions)				11.1
GNI per capita, Atlas ($)				460
Population living below $1.25 a day (%)				59.6

	1990		2011	
	Female	Male	Female	Male
Demography				
Sex ratio at birth (boys per girls)	1.03		1.03	
Life expectancy at birth (years)	45	42	51	49
Under-five mortality rate (per 1,000 live births)	218	233	99	107
Female-headed households (%)	..		..	
Education				
Gross primary enrollment ratio (% of relevant age group)	54	72	105	116
Gross secondary enrollment ratio (% of relevant age group)	5	9	24	28
Gross tertiary enrollment ratio (% of relevant age group)	0	1	4	6
Primary completion rate (% of relevant age group)	21	32	52	61
Youth literacy rate (% of population ages 15–24)	..	..	65	79
Health and related services				
Total fertility rate (births per woman)	6.2		4.8	
Adolescent fertility rate (births per 1,000 women ages 15–19)	..		129	
Women first married by age 18 (% of women ages 20–24)	..		56	
Contraceptive prevalence (% of women ages 15–49)	..		12	
Unmet need for contraception (% of women ages 15–49)	..		..	
Pregnant women receiving prenatal care (%)	..		92	
Births attended by skilled health staff (% of total)	..		55	
Maternal mortality ratio (per 100,000 live births)	910		490	
Economic structure, participation, and access to resources				
Labor force participation rate (% of population ages 15+)	85	81	86	83
Wage and salaried workers (% of employed ages 15+)	..	..	..	..
Self-employed workers (% of employed ages 15+)	..	..	..	..
Vulnerable employment (% of employed ages 15+)	..	..	..	..
Unpaid family workers (% of employed ages 15+)	..	..	..	..
Employment in agriculture (% of employed ages 15+)	..	..	..	..
Employment in industry (% of employed ages 15+)	..	..	..	..
Employment in service (% of employed ages 15+)	..	..	..	..
Women in wage employment in the nonagricultural sector (%)	11		..	
Women's share of part-time employment (% of total)	..		..	
Maternity leave (weeks)	8		9	
Maternal leave benefits (% of wages paid)	100		100	
Female legislators, senior officials and managers (% of total)	..		..	
Employment to population ratio, total (% ages 15+)	80	75	81	78
Employment to population ratio, youth (% ages 15–24)	71	62	64	54
Children in employment (% of children ages 7–14)	..	..	27.7	27.2
Unemployment rate (% of labor force ages 15+)	..	..	..	..
Long-term unemployment rate (% total unemployment)	..	..	..	..
Youth unemployment rate (% of labor force ages 15–24)	..	..	..	..
Account at a formal financial institution (% age 15+)	..	..	35	45
Public life and decision making				
Seats held by women in national parliament (%)	16		39	

Myanmar

East Asia & Pacific	Low income
Population (millions)	48.3
GNI, Atlas ($ millions)	..
GNI per capita, Atlas ($)	..
Population living below $1.25 a day (%)	..

	1990		2011	
	Female	Male	Female	Male
Demography				
Sex ratio at birth (boys per girls)	1.03		1.03	
Life expectancy at birth (years)	59	56	67	63
Under-five mortality rate (per 1,000 live births)	96	119	56	69
Female-headed households (%)	..		..	
Education				
Gross primary enrollment ratio (% of relevant age group)	101	107	126	126
Gross secondary enrollment ratio (% of relevant age group)	20	22	56	53
Gross tertiary enrollment ratio (% of relevant age group)	5	4	17	13
Primary completion rate (% of relevant age group)	..	..	106	101
Youth literacy rate (% of population ages 15–24)	..	..	96	96
Health and related services				
Total fertility rate (births per woman)	3.4		2.0	
Adolescent fertility rate (births per 1,000 women ages 15–19)	..		13	
Women first married by age 18 (% of women ages 20–24)	..		..	
Contraceptive prevalence (% of women ages 15–49)	17		46	
Unmet need for contraception (% of women ages 15–49)	..		..	
Pregnant women receiving prenatal care (%)	..		83	
Births attended by skilled health staff (% of total)	46		71	
Maternal mortality ratio (per 100,000 live births)	520		200	
Economic structure, participation, and access to resources				
Labor force participation rate (% of population ages 15+)	72	79	75	82
Wage and salaried workers (% of employed ages 15+)	..	..	..	..
Self-employed workers (% of employed ages 15+)	..	..	..	..
Vulnerable employment (% of employed ages 15+)	..	..	..	..
Unpaid family workers (% of employed ages 15+)	..	..	..	..
Employment in agriculture (% of employed ages 15+)	..	..	..	..
Employment in industry (% of employed ages 15+)	..	..	..	..
Employment in service (% of employed ages 15+)	..	..	..	..
Women in wage employment in the nonagricultural sector (%)	31		..	
Women's share of part-time employment (% of total)	..		..	
Maternity leave (weeks)	..		12	
Maternal leave benefits (% of wages paid)	..		67	
Female legislators, senior officials and managers (% of total)	..		..	
Employment to population ratio, total (% ages 15+)	69	76	72	80
Employment to population ratio, youth (% ages 15–24)	51	52	52	53
Children in employment (% of children ages 7–14)	..	..	..	..
Unemployment rate (% of labor force ages 15+)	8.8	4.7	..	..
Long-term unemployment rate (% total unemployment)	..	..	..	..
Youth unemployment rate (% of labor force ages 15–24)	..	..	..	..
Account at a formal financial institution (% age 15+)	..	..	..	..
Public life and decision making				
Seats held by women in national parliament (%)	..		6	

Namibia

Sub-Saharan Africa			Upper middle income	
Population (millions)				2.3
GNI, Atlas ($ billions)				10.9
GNI per capita, Atlas ($)				4,700
Population living below $1.25 a day (%)				31.9

	1990		2011	
	Female	Male	Female	Male
Demography				
Sex ratio at birth (boys per girls)	1.03		1.03	
Life expectancy at birth (years)	63	59	63	62
Under-five mortality rate (per 1,000 live births)	67	78	38	45
Female-headed households (%)	31		44	
Education				
Gross primary enrollment ratio (% of relevant age group)	123	113	106	108
Gross secondary enrollment ratio (% of relevant age group)	42	34	69	59
Gross tertiary enrollment ratio (% of relevant age group)	4	2	10	8
Primary completion rate (% of relevant age group)	81	67	85	77
Youth literacy rate (% of population ages 15–24)	90	86	95	91
Health and related services				
Total fertility rate (births per woman)	5.2		3.2	
Adolescent fertility rate (births per 1,000 women ages 15–19)	..		58	
Women first married by age 18 (% of women ages 20–24)	12		9	
Contraceptive prevalence (% of women ages 15–49)	41		55	
Unmet need for contraception (% of women ages 15–49)	22		21	
Pregnant women receiving prenatal care (%)	87		95	
Births attended by skilled health staff (% of total)	68		81	
Maternal mortality ratio (per 100,000 live births)	200		200	
Economic structure, participation, and access to resources				
Labor force participation rate (% of population ages 15+)	48	65	59	70
Wage and salaried workers (% of employed ages 15+)	43	65	80	82
Self-employed workers (% of employed ages 15+)	55	33	19	17
Vulnerable employment (% of employed ages 15+)	54	32	16	11
Unpaid family workers (% of employed ages 15+)	31.5	14.5	1.2	1.0
Employment in agriculture (% of employed ages 15+)	52	45	8	23
Employment in industry (% of employed ages 15+)	8	21	9	24
Employment in service (% of employed ages 15+)	40	34	83	53
Women in wage employment in the nonagricultural sector (%)	..		..	
Women's share of part-time employment (% of total)	..		..	
Maternity leave (weeks)	12		12	
Maternal leave benefits (% of wages paid)	..		100	
Female legislators, senior officials and managers (% of total)	..		..	
Employment to population ratio, total (% ages 15+)	38	53	37	50
Employment to population ratio, youth (% ages 15–24)	21	28	9	18
Children in employment (% of children ages 7–14)	..	..	..	..
Unemployment rate (% of labor force ages 15+)	19.0	20.0	43.0	32.5
Long-term unemployment rate (% total unemployment)	..	..	85.8	77.8
Youth unemployment rate (% of labor force ages 15–24)	34	30	64	55
Account at a formal financial institution (% age 15+)	..	..	..	..
Public life and decision making				
Seats held by women in national parliament (%)	7		24	

Nepal

South Asia	Low income
Population (millions)	30.5
GNI, Atlas ($ billions)	16.6
GNI per capita, Atlas ($)	540
Population living below $1.25 a day (%)	*24.8*

	1990		2011	
	Female	Male	Female	Male
Demography				
Sex ratio at birth (boys per girls)	1.05		1.05	
Life expectancy at birth (years)	54	54	70	68
Under-five mortality rate (per 1,000 live births)	133	137	47	49
Female-headed households (%)	..		28	
Education				
Gross primary enrollment ratio (% of relevant age group)	82	136	..	..
Gross secondary enrollment ratio (% of relevant age group)	19	44	*41*	*46*
Gross tertiary enrollment ratio (% of relevant age group)	2	7	5	9
Primary completion rate (% of relevant age group)	*42*	*71*	..	..
Youth literacy rate (% of population ages 15–24)	*33*	*68*	*78*	*88*
Health and related services				
Total fertility rate (births per woman)	5.2		2.7	
Adolescent fertility rate (births per 1,000 women ages 15–19)	..		90	
Women first married by age 18 (% of women ages 20–24)	..		41	
Contraceptive prevalence (% of women ages 15–49)	24		50	
Unmet need for contraception (% of women ages 15–49)	..		28	
Pregnant women receiving prenatal care (%)	15		58	
Births attended by skilled health staff (% of total)	7		36	
Maternal mortality ratio (per 100,000 live births)	770		*170*	
Economic structure, participation, and access to resources				
Labor force participation rate (% of population ages 15+)	80	91	80	88
Wage and salaried workers (% of employed ages 15+)	..	..	..	..
Self-employed workers (% of employed ages 15+)	..	..	..	..
Vulnerable employment (% of employed ages 15+)	..	..	..	..
Unpaid family workers (% of employed ages 15+)	..	..	..	..
Employment in agriculture (% of employed ages 15+)	91	75	..	..
Employment in industry (% of employed ages 15+)	1	4	..	..
Employment in service (% of employed ages 15+)	8	20	..	..
Women in wage employment in the nonagricultural sector (%)	..		..	
Women's share of part-time employment (% of total)	..		..	
Maternity leave (weeks)	7		7	
Maternal leave benefits (% of wages paid)	100		*100*	
Female legislators, senior officials and managers (% of total)	..		..	
Employment to population ratio, total (% ages 15+)	79	89	79	86
Employment to population ratio, youth (% ages 15–24)	77	81	73	73
Children in employment (% of children ages 7–14)	..	..	..	..
Unemployment rate (% of labor force ages 15+)	..	..	2.4	3.1
Long-term unemployment rate (% total unemployment)	..	..	..	..
Youth unemployment rate (% of labor force ages 15–24)	..	..	..	..
Account at a formal financial institution (% age 15+)	..	..	21	30
Public life and decision making				
Seats held by women in national parliament (%)	6		33	

Netherlands

		High income
Population (millions)		16.7
GNI, Atlas ($ billions)		829.0
GNI per capita, Atlas ($)		49,660
Population living below $1.25 a day (%)		..

	1990		2011	
	Female	Male	Female	Male
Demography				
Sex ratio at birth (boys per girls)	1.06		1.06	
Life expectancy at birth (years)	80	74	83	79
Under-five mortality rate (per 1,000 live births)	7	9	4	4
Female-headed households (%)	..		..	
Education				
Gross primary enrollment ratio (% of relevant age group)	105	102	107	108
Gross secondary enrollment ratio (% of relevant age group)	111	120	121	122
Gross tertiary enrollment ratio (% of relevant age group)	32	39	69	62
Primary completion rate (% of relevant age group)	..	..	..	..
Youth literacy rate (% of population ages 15–24)	..	..	..	..
Health and related services				
Total fertility rate (births per woman)	1.6		1.8	
Adolescent fertility rate (births per 1,000 women ages 15–19)	..		4	
Women first married by age 18 (% of women ages 20–24)	..		..	
Contraceptive prevalence (% of women ages 15–49)	76		69	
Unmet need for contraception (% of women ages 15–49)	..		..	
Pregnant women receiving prenatal care (%)	..		..	
Births attended by skilled health staff (% of total)	..		..	
Maternal mortality ratio (per 100,000 live births)	10		6	
Economic structure, participation, and access to resources				
Labor force participation rate (% of population ages 15+)	43	70	58	71
Wage and salaried workers (% of employed ages 15+)	87	88	89	82
Self-employed workers (% of employed ages 15+)	13	12	12	18
Vulnerable employment (% of employed ages 15+)	12	7	10	13
Unpaid family workers (% of employed ages 15+)	5.1	0.3	1.0	0.3
Employment in agriculture (% of employed ages 15+)	3	5	2	3
Employment in industry (% of employed ages 15+)	11	35	6	23
Employment in service (% of employed ages 15+)	84	59	84	61
Women in wage employment in the nonagricultural sector (%)	38		48	
Women's share of part-time employment (% of total)	70		75	
Maternity leave (weeks)	16		16	
Maternal leave benefits (% of wages paid)	100		100	
Female legislators, senior officials and managers (% of total)	18		30	
Employment to population ratio, total (% ages 15+)	40	66	56	68
Employment to population ratio, youth (% ages 15–24)	53	53	64	64
Children in employment (% of children ages 7–14)	..	..	..	..
Unemployment rate (% of labor force ages 15+)	10.9	5.6	4.4	4.5
Long-term unemployment rate (% total unemployment)	44.3	54.3	31.0	34.7
Youth unemployment rate (% of labor force ages 15–24)	12	10	8	8
Account at a formal financial institution (% age 15+)	..	..	98	99
Public life and decision making				
Seats held by women in national parliament (%)	21		39	

New Caledonia

Population (thousands)	254.0
GNI, Atlas ($ billions)	..
GNI per capita, Atlas ($)	..
Population living below $1.25 a day (%)	..

	1990 Female	1990 Male	2011 Female	2011 Male
Demography				
Sex ratio at birth (boys per girls)	1.05		1.05	
Life expectancy at birth (years)	73	68	80	73
Under-five mortality rate (per 1,000 live births)	..	..	..	..
Female-headed households (%)	..		..	
Education				
Gross primary enrollment ratio (% of relevant age group)	..	..	..	..
Gross secondary enrollment ratio (% of relevant age group)	..	..	..	..
Gross tertiary enrollment ratio (% of relevant age group)	..	..	..	..
Primary completion rate (% of relevant age group)	..	..	..	..
Youth literacy rate (% of population ages 15–24)	99	99	100	99
Health and related services				
Total fertility rate (births per woman)	3.2		2.1	
Adolescent fertility rate (births per 1,000 women ages 15–19)	..		20	
Women first married by age 18 (% of women ages 20–24)	..		..	
Contraceptive prevalence (% of women ages 15–49)	..		..	
Unmet need for contraception (% of women ages 15–49)	..		..	
Pregnant women receiving prenatal care (%)	..		..	
Births attended by skilled health staff (% of total)	..		..	
Maternal mortality ratio (per 100,000 live births)	..		..	
Economic structure, participation, and access to resources				
Labor force participation rate (% of population ages 15+)	46	73	47	68
Wage and salaried workers (% of employed ages 15+)	..	..	..	..
Self-employed workers (% of employed ages 15+)	..	..	..	..
Vulnerable employment (% of employed ages 15+)	..	..	..	..
Unpaid family workers (% of employed ages 15+)	..	..	..	..
Employment in agriculture (% of employed ages 15+)	..	..	..	..
Employment in industry (% of employed ages 15+)	..	..	..	..
Employment in service (% of employed ages 15+)	..	..	..	..
Women in wage employment in the nonagricultural sector (%)	..		..	
Women's share of part-time employment (% of total)	..		..	
Maternity leave (weeks)	..		..	
Maternal leave benefits (% of wages paid)	..		..	
Female legislators, senior officials and managers (% of total)	..		..	
Employment to population ratio, total (% ages 15+)	..	..	..	..
Employment to population ratio, youth (% ages 15–24)	..	..	..	..
Children in employment (% of children ages 7–14)	..	..	..	..
Unemployment rate (% of labor force ages 15+)	..	..	..	..
Long-term unemployment rate (% total unemployment)	..	..	..	..
Youth unemployment rate (% of labor force ages 15–24)	..	..	..	..
Account at a formal financial institution (% age 15+)	..	..	..	..
Public life and decision making				
Seats held by women in national parliament (%)	..		..	

New Zealand

	High income
Population (millions)	4.4
GNI, Atlas ($ billions)	127.3
GNI per capita, Atlas ($)	29,140
Population living below $1.25 a day (%)	..

	1990		2011	
	Female	Male	Female	Male
Demography				
Sex ratio at birth (boys per girls)	1.06		1.06	
Life expectancy at birth (years)	78	73	83	79
Under-five mortality rate (per 1,000 live births)	10	12	5	7
Female-headed households (%)	..		..	
Education				
Gross primary enrollment ratio (% of relevant age group)	104	106	101	101
Gross secondary enrollment ratio (% of relevant age group)	89	88	122	116
Gross tertiary enrollment ratio (% of relevant age group)	41	38	99	67
Primary completion rate (% of relevant age group)	..	..	..	..
Youth literacy rate (% of population ages 15–24)	..	..	..	..
Health and related services				
Total fertility rate (births per woman)	2.2		2.1	
Adolescent fertility rate (births per 1,000 women ages 15–19)	..		21	
Women first married by age 18 (% of women ages 20–24)	..		..	
Contraceptive prevalence (% of women ages 15–49)	..		..	
Unmet need for contraception (% of women ages 15–49)	..		..	
Pregnant women receiving prenatal care (%)	95		..	
Births attended by skilled health staff (% of total)	95		..	
Maternal mortality ratio (per 100,000 live births)	18		15	
Economic structure, participation, and access to resources				
Labor force participation rate (% of population ages 15+)	54	74	62	74
Wage and salaried workers (% of employed ages 15+)	87	75	88	80
Self-employed workers (% of employed ages 15+)	13	25	12	20
Vulnerable employment (% of employed ages 15+)	10	15	9	15
Unpaid family workers (% of employed ages 15+)	1.9	0.7	1.3	0.7
Employment in agriculture (% of employed ages 15+)	8	13	4	9
Employment in industry (% of employed ages 15+)	14	33	10	31
Employment in service (% of employed ages 15+)	78	54	86	61
Women in wage employment in the nonagricultural sector (%)	48		51	
Women's share of part-time employment (% of total)	77		73	
Maternity leave (weeks)	14		14	
Maternal leave benefits (% of wages paid)	0		100	
Female legislators, senior officials and managers (% of total)	31		40	
Employment to population ratio, total (% ages 15+)	49	66	58	69
Employment to population ratio, youth (% ages 15–24)	53	56	49	51
Children in employment (% of children ages 7–14)	..	..	..	..
Unemployment rate (% of labor force ages 15+)	7.3	8.1	6.8	6.3
Long-term unemployment rate (% total unemployment)	10.7	17.9	7.1	9.3
Youth unemployment rate (% of labor force ages 15–24)	13	15	16	18
Account at a formal financial institution (% age 15+)	..	..	99	99
Public life and decision making				
Seats held by women in national parliament (%)	14		32	

Nicaragua

Latin America & the Caribbean			Lower middle income	
Population (millions)				5.9
GNI, Atlas ($ billions)				8.9
GNI per capita, Atlas ($)				1,510
Population living below $1.25 a day (%)				11.9

	1990		2011	
	Female	Male	Female	Male
Demography				
Sex ratio at birth (boys per girls)	1.05		1.05	
Life expectancy at birth (years)	67	61	77	71
Under-five mortality rate (per 1,000 live births)	60	72	22	29
Female-headed households (%)	..		..	
Education				
Gross primary enrollment ratio (% of relevant age group)	90	85	116	119
Gross secondary enrollment ratio (% of relevant age group)	42	26	73	66
Gross tertiary enrollment ratio (% of relevant age group)	8	8	..	..
Primary completion rate (% of relevant age group)	56	41	84	78
Youth literacy rate (% of population ages 15–24)	..	..	..	..
Health and related services				
Total fertility rate (births per woman)	4.8		2.6	
Adolescent fertility rate (births per 1,000 women ages 15–19)	..		106	
Women first married by age 18 (% of women ages 20–24)	..		41	
Contraceptive prevalence (% of women ages 15–49)	49		72	
Unmet need for contraception (% of women ages 15–49)	..		8	
Pregnant women receiving prenatal care (%)	72		90	
Births attended by skilled health staff (% of total)	61		74	
Maternal mortality ratio (per 100,000 live births)	170		95	
Economic structure, participation, and access to resources				
Labor force participation rate (% of population ages 15+)	35	83	47	80
Wage and salaried workers (% of employed ages 15+)	51	57	42	49
Self-employed workers (% of employed ages 15+)	49	43	59	51
Vulnerable employment (% of employed ages 15+)	47	40	56	41
Unpaid family workers (% of employed ages 15+)	3.6	5.4	19.7	15.8
Employment in agriculture (% of employed ages 15+)	..	..	15	44
Employment in industry (% of employed ages 15+)	..	..	15	18
Employment in service (% of employed ages 15+)	..	..	70	38
Women in wage employment in the nonagricultural sector (%)	..		38	
Women's share of part-time employment (% of total)	53		59	
Maternity leave (weeks)	12		12	
Maternal leave benefits (% of wages paid)	60		60	
Female legislators, senior officials and managers (% of total)	..		41	
Employment to population ratio, total (% ages 15+)	33	78	45	75
Employment to population ratio, youth (% ages 15–24)	26	68	30	62
Children in employment (% of children ages 7–14)	..	..	..	..
Unemployment rate (% of labor force ages 15+)	14.7	9.0	8.8	7.4
Long-term unemployment rate (% total unemployment)	..	..	..	..
Youth unemployment rate (% of labor force ages 15–24)	15	11	10	8
Account at a formal financial institution (% age 15+)	..	..	13	16
Public life and decision making				
Seats held by women in national parliament (%)	15		40	

Niger

Sub-Saharan Africa	Low income
Population (millions)	16.1
GNI, Atlas ($ billions)	5.8
GNI per capita, Atlas ($)	360
Population living below $1.25 a day (%)	43.6

	1990		2011	
	Female	Male	Female	Male
Demography				
Sex ratio at birth (boys per girls)	1.05		1.05	
Life expectancy at birth (years)	42	41	55	54
Under-five mortality rate (per 1,000 live births)	307	320	122	127
Female-headed households (%)	10		19	
Education				
Gross primary enrollment ratio (% of relevant age group)	20	33	64	77
Gross secondary enrollment ratio (% of relevant age group)	3	9	11	18
Gross tertiary enrollment ratio (% of relevant age group)	0	1	1	2
Primary completion rate (% of relevant age group)	11	22	40	52
Youth literacy rate (% of population ages 15–24)	..	..	..	..
Health and related services				
Total fertility rate (births per woman)	7.8		7.0	
Adolescent fertility rate (births per 1,000 women ages 15–19)	..		196	
Women first married by age 18 (% of women ages 20–24)	83		75	
Contraceptive prevalence (% of women ages 15–49)	4		18	
Unmet need for contraception (% of women ages 15–49)	19		16	
Pregnant women receiving prenatal care (%)	30		46	
Births attended by skilled health staff (% of total)	15		18	
Maternal mortality ratio (per 100,000 live births)	1,200		590	
Economic structure, participation, and access to resources				
Labor force participation rate (% of population ages 15+)	25	92	40	90
Wage and salaried workers (% of employed ages 15+)	..	..	..	..
Self-employed workers (% of employed ages 15+)	..	..	..	..
Vulnerable employment (% of employed ages 15+)	..	..	..	..
Unpaid family workers (% of employed ages 15+)	..	..	..	..
Employment in agriculture (% of employed ages 15+)	..	..	..	..
Employment in industry (% of employed ages 15+)	..	..	..	..
Employment in service (% of employed ages 15+)	..	..	..	..
Women in wage employment in the nonagricultural sector (%)	..		36	
Women's share of part-time employment (% of total)	..		..	
Maternity leave (weeks)	14		14	
Maternal leave benefits (% of wages paid)	50		100	
Female legislators, senior officials and managers (% of total)	..		..	
Employment to population ratio, total (% ages 15+)	25	87	39	85
Employment to population ratio, youth (% ages 15–24)	22	78	33	74
Children in employment (% of children ages 7–14)	..	..	45.0	49.2
Unemployment rate (% of labor force ages 15+)	..	..	..	..
Long-term unemployment rate (% total unemployment)	..	..	..	..
Youth unemployment rate (% of labor force ages 15–24)	..	..	..	..
Account at a formal financial institution (% age 15+)	..	..	1	2
Public life and decision making				
Seats held by women in national parliament (%)	5		13	

Nigeria

Sub-Saharan Africa	Lower middle income
Population (millions)	162.5
GNI, Atlas ($ billions)	207.3
GNI per capita, Atlas ($)	1,280
Population living below $1.25 a day (%)	68.0

	1990		2011	
	Female	Male	Female	Male
Demography				
Sex ratio at birth (boys per girls)	1.06		1.06	
Life expectancy at birth (years)	47	44	53	51
Under-five mortality rate (per 1,000 live births)	205	222	119	129
Female-headed households (%)	14		19	
Education				
Gross primary enrollment ratio (% of relevant age group)	75	95	79	87
Gross secondary enrollment ratio (% of relevant age group)	21	27	41	47
Gross tertiary enrollment ratio (% of relevant age group)	2	6	..	..
Primary completion rate (% of relevant age group)	..	..	70	79
Youth literacy rate (% of population ages 15–24)	62	81	66	78
Health and related services				
Total fertility rate (births per woman)	6.4		5.5	
Adolescent fertility rate (births per 1,000 women ages 15–19)	..		113	
Women first married by age 18 (% of women ages 20–24)	52		39	
Contraceptive prevalence (% of women ages 15–49)	6		15	
Unmet need for contraception (% of women ages 15–49)	21		20	
Pregnant women receiving prenatal care (%)	57		58	
Births attended by skilled health staff (% of total)	31		39	
Maternal mortality ratio (per 100,000 live births)	1,100		630	
Economic structure, participation, and access to resources				
Labor force participation rate (% of population ages 15+)	39	75	48	63
Wage and salaried workers (% of employed ages 15+)	..	..	..	..
Self-employed workers (% of employed ages 15+)	..	..	..	..
Vulnerable employment (% of employed ages 15+)	..	..	..	..
Unpaid family workers (% of employed ages 15+)	..	..	..	..
Employment in agriculture (% of employed ages 15+)	38	51	..	..
Employment in industry (% of employed ages 15+)	4	9	..	..
Employment in service (% of employed ages 15+)	57	38	..	..
Women in wage employment in the nonagricultural sector (%)	..		..	
Women's share of part-time employment (% of total)	..		..	
Maternity leave (weeks)	12		12	
Maternal leave benefits (% of wages paid)	50		50	
Female legislators, senior officials and managers (% of total)	..		..	
Employment to population ratio, total (% ages 15+)	37	69	45	59
Employment to population ratio, youth (% ages 15–24)	21	39	31	36
Children in employment (% of children ages 7–14)	..	..	40.1	41.2
Unemployment rate (% of labor force ages 15+)	4.4	3.7	..	..
Long-term unemployment rate (% total unemployment)	..		..	
Youth unemployment rate (% of labor force ages 15–24)	22	12	..	..
Account at a formal financial institution (% age 15+)	..	..	26	33
Public life and decision making				
Seats held by women in national parliament (%)	..		7	

Northern Mariana Islands

	High income
Population (thousands)	61.2
GNI, Atlas ($ millions)	..
GNI per capita, Atlas ($)	..
Population living below $1.25 a day (%)	..

	1990 Female	1990 Male	2011 Female	2011 Male
Demography				
Sex ratio at birth (boys per girls)	..		..	
Life expectancy at birth (years)	..	..	..	..
Under-five mortality rate (per 1,000 live births)	..	..	..	..
Female-headed households (%)	..		..	
Education				
Gross primary enrollment ratio (% of relevant age group)	..	..	..	..
Gross secondary enrollment ratio (% of relevant age group)	..	..	..	..
Gross tertiary enrollment ratio (% of relevant age group)	..	..	..	..
Primary completion rate (% of relevant age group)	..	..	..	..
Youth literacy rate (% of population ages 15–24)	..	..	..	..
Health and related services				
Total fertility rate (births per woman)	..		..	
Adolescent fertility rate (births per 1,000 women ages 15–19)	..		..	
Women first married by age 18 (% of women ages 20–24)	..		..	
Contraceptive prevalence (% of women ages 15–49)	..		..	
Unmet need for contraception (% of women ages 15–49)	..		..	
Pregnant women receiving prenatal care (%)	..		..	
Births attended by skilled health staff (% of total)	..		..	
Maternal mortality ratio (per 100,000 live births)	..		..	
Economic structure, participation, and access to resources				
Labor force participation rate (% of population ages 15+)	..	..	..	..
Wage and salaried workers (% of employed ages 15+)	..	..	..	..
Self-employed workers (% of employed ages 15+)	..	..	..	..
Vulnerable employment (% of employed ages 15+)	..	..	..	..
Unpaid family workers (% of employed ages 15+)	..	..	..	..
Employment in agriculture (% of employed ages 15+)	0	4	..	..
Employment in industry (% of employed ages 15+)	40	47	..	..
Employment in service (% of employed ages 15+)	58	49	..	..
Women in wage employment in the nonagricultural sector (%)	44		..	
Women's share of part-time employment (% of total)	..		..	
Maternity leave (weeks)	..		..	
Maternal leave benefits (% of wages paid)	..		..	
Female legislators, senior officials and managers (% of total)	..		..	
Employment to population ratio, total (% ages 15+)	..	..	..	..
Employment to population ratio, youth (% ages 15–24)	..	..	..	..
Children in employment (% of children ages 7–14)	..	..	..	..
Unemployment rate (% of labor force ages 15+)	..	..	..	..
Long-term unemployment rate (% total unemployment)	..	..	..	..
Youth unemployment rate (% of labor force ages 15–24)	..	..	..	..
Account at a formal financial institution (% age 15+)	..	..	..	..
Public life and decision making				
Seats held by women in national parliament (%)	..		..	

Norway

High income

Population (millions)	5.0
GNI, Atlas ($ billions)	440.2
GNI per capita, Atlas ($)	88,870
Population living below $1.25 a day (%)	..

	1990		2011	
	Female	Male	Female	Male
Demography				
Sex ratio at birth (boys per girls)	1.06		1.06	
Life expectancy at birth (years)	80	73	84	79
Under-five mortality rate (per 1,000 live births)	7	9	3	3
Female-headed households (%)	..		..	
Education				
Gross primary enrollment ratio (% of relevant age group)	100	100	99	99
Gross secondary enrollment ratio (% of relevant age group)	103	99	110	112
Gross tertiary enrollment ratio (% of relevant age group)	42	35	93	57
Primary completion rate (% of relevant age group)	96	95	99	99
Youth literacy rate (% of population ages 15–24)	..	..	..	..
Health and related services				
Total fertility rate (births per woman)	1.9		1.9	
Adolescent fertility rate (births per 1,000 women ages 15–19)	..		8	
Women first married by age 18 (% of women ages 20–24)	..		..	
Contraceptive prevalence (% of women ages 15–49)	74		..	
Unmet need for contraception (% of women ages 15–49)	..		..	
Pregnant women receiving prenatal care (%)	..		..	
Births attended by skilled health staff (% of total)	100		..	
Maternal mortality ratio (per 100,000 live births)	9		7	
Economic structure, participation, and access to resources				
Labor force participation rate (% of population ages 15+)	55	71	62	70
Wage and salaried workers (% of employed ages 15+)	93	85	96	90
Self-employed workers (% of employed ages 15+)	7	15	4	10
Vulnerable employment (% of employed ages 15+)	..	..	3	7
Unpaid family workers (% of employed ages 15+)	2.6	1.6	0.1	0.2
Employment in agriculture (% of employed ages 15+)	4	8	1	4
Employment in industry (% of employed ages 15+)	11	35	7	31
Employment in service (% of employed ages 15+)	85	56	92	65
Women in wage employment in the nonagricultural sector (%)	47		49	
Women's share of part-time employment (% of total)	83		71	
Maternity leave (weeks)	18		56	
Maternal leave benefits (% of wages paid)	100		100	
Female legislators, senior officials and managers (% of total)	..		31	
Employment to population ratio, total (% ages 15+)	52	65	60	68
Employment to population ratio, youth (% ages 15–24)	48	50	53	52
Children in employment (% of children ages 7–14)	..	..	..	..
Unemployment rate (% of labor force ages 15+)	4.8	5.6	3.1	3.4
Long-term unemployment rate (% total unemployment)	22.5	19.0	8.7	13.1
Youth unemployment rate (% of labor force ages 15–24)	11	12	8	9
Account at a formal financial institution (% age 15+)	..	..	..	..
Public life and decision making				
Seats held by women in national parliament (%)	36		40	

Oman

Population (millions)	2.8
GNI, Atlas ($ billions)	53.6
GNI per capita, Atlas ($)	19,260
Population living below $1.25 a day (%)	..

	1990 Female	1990 Male	2011 Female	2011 Male
Demography				
Sex ratio at birth (boys per girls)	1.05		1.05	
Life expectancy at birth (years)	72	69	76	71
Under-five mortality rate (per 1,000 live births)	46	49	8	9
Female-headed households (%)	..		..	
Education				
Gross primary enrollment ratio (% of relevant age group)	75	83	103	105
Gross secondary enrollment ratio (% of relevant age group)	34	47	103	105
Gross tertiary enrollment ratio (% of relevant age group)	4	4	34	25
Primary completion rate (% of relevant age group)	60	65	108	106
Youth literacy rate (% of population ages 15–24)	..	..	98	98
Health and related services				
Total fertility rate (births per woman)	7.2		2.2	
Adolescent fertility rate (births per 1,000 women ages 15-19)	..		9	
Women first married by age 18 (% of women ages 20–24)	..		..	
Contraceptive prevalence (% of women ages 15–49)	9		24	
Unmet need for contraception (% of women ages 15–49)	..		..	
Pregnant women receiving prenatal care (%)	88		99	
Births attended by skilled health staff (% of total)	87		99	
Maternal mortality ratio (per 100,000 live births)	110		32	
Economic structure, participation, and access to resources				
Labor force participation rate (% of population ages 15+)	17	81	28	82
Wage and salaried workers (% of employed ages 15+)	91	85	..	..
Self-employed workers (% of employed ages 15+)	6	14	..	..
Vulnerable employment (% of employed ages 15+)	..	..	..	..
Unpaid family workers (% of employed ages 15+)	..	..	..	..
Employment in agriculture (% of employed ages 15+)	5	10	..	..
Employment in industry (% of employed ages 15+)	7	8	..	..
Employment in service (% of employed ages 15+)	86	81	..	..
Women in wage employment in the nonagricultural sector (%)	19		22	
Women's share of part-time employment (% of total)	..		..	
Maternity leave (weeks)	..		..	
Maternal leave benefits (% of wages paid)	..		..	
Female legislators, senior officials and managers (% of total)	5		..	
Employment to population ratio, total (% ages 15+)	15	76	24	77
Employment to population ratio, youth (% ages 15–24)	14	42	16	43
Children in employment (% of children ages 7–14)	..	..	..	..
Unemployment rate (% of labor force ages 15+)	..	..	..	..
Long-term unemployment rate (% total unemployment)	..	..	..	..
Youth unemployment rate (% of labor force ages 15–24)	..	..	..	..
Account at a formal financial institution (% age 15+)	..	..	64	84
Public life and decision making				
Seats held by women in national parliament (%)	..		1	

Pakistan

South Asia	Lower middle income
Population (millions)	176.7
GNI, Atlas ($ billions)	198.0
GNI per capita, Atlas ($)	1,120
Population living below $1.25 a day (%)	21.0

	1990		2011	
	Female	Male	Female	Male
Demography				
Sex ratio at birth (boys per girls)	1.05		1.05	
Life expectancy at birth (years)	61	60	66	65
Under-five mortality rate (per 1,000 live births)	118	126	68	76
Female-headed households (%)	7		10	
Education				
Gross primary enrollment ratio (% of relevant age group)	38	72	83	101
Gross secondary enrollment ratio (% of relevant age group)	12	29	30	40
Gross tertiary enrollment ratio (% of relevant age group)	2	4	8	9
Primary completion rate (% of relevant age group)	..		59	74
Youth literacy rate (% of population ages 15–24)	..	..	61	79
Health and related services				
Total fertility rate (births per woman)	6.0		3.3	
Adolescent fertility rate (births per 1,000 women ages 15–19)	..		29	
Women first married by age 18 (% of women ages 20–24)	32		24	
Contraceptive prevalence (% of women ages 15–49)	15		27	
Unmet need for contraception (% of women ages 15–49)	32		25	
Pregnant women receiving prenatal care (%)	26		61	
Births attended by skilled health staff (% of total)	19		43	
Maternal mortality ratio (per 100,000 live births)	490		260	
Economic structure, participation, and access to resources				
Labor force participation rate (% of population ages 15+)	13	85	23	83
Wage and salaried workers (% of employed ages 15+)	..	..	22	40
Self-employed workers (% of employed ages 15+)	..	..	78	61
Vulnerable employment (% of employed ages 15+)	..	..	78	59
Unpaid family workers (% of employed ages 15+)	..	..	65.0	19.7
Employment in agriculture (% of employed ages 15+)	72	48	75	37
Employment in industry (% of employed ages 15+)	14	21	12	22
Employment in service (% of employed ages 15+)	14	31	13	41
Women in wage employment in the nonagricultural sector (%)	8		13	
Women's share of part-time employment (% of total)	..		..	
Maternity leave (weeks)	12		12	
Maternal leave benefits (% of wages paid)	100		100	
Female legislators, senior officials and managers (% of total)	..		3	
Employment to population ratio, total (% ages 15+)	12	81	21	80
Employment to population ratio, youth (% ages 15–24)	11	65	18	63
Children in employment (% of children ages 7–14)	..	..	13.5	12.5
Unemployment rate (% of labor force ages 15+)	0.7	2.8	8.7	4.0
Long-term unemployment rate (% total unemployment)	..	..	..	..
Youth unemployment rate (% of labor force ages 15–24)	1	6	11	7
Account at a formal financial institution (% age 15+)	..	..	3	17
Public life and decision making				
Seats held by women in national parliament (%)	10		23	

Palau

East Asia & Pacific	Upper middle income
Population (thousands)	20.6
GNI, Atlas ($ millions)	134.2
GNI per capita, Atlas ($)	6,510
Population living below $1.25 a day (%)	..

	1990		2011	
	Female	Male	Female	Male
Demography				
Sex ratio at birth (boys per girls)	..		..	
Life expectancy at birth (years)	75	63	..	..
Under-five mortality rate (per 1,000 live births)	24	40	14	23
Female-headed households (%)	..		..	
Education				
Gross primary enrollment ratio (% of relevant age group)	..	..	103	100
Gross secondary enrollment ratio (% of relevant age group)	..	..	..	..
Gross tertiary enrollment ratio (% of relevant age group)	..	..	..	..
Primary completion rate (% of relevant age group)	..	..	..	..
Youth literacy rate (% of population ages 15–24)	..	..	..	..
Health and related services				
Total fertility rate (births per woman)	2.8		..	
Adolescent fertility rate (births per 1,000 women ages 15–19)	..		..	
Women first married by age 18 (% of women ages 20–24)	..		..	
Contraceptive prevalence (% of women ages 15–49)	..		22	
Unmet need for contraception (% of women ages 15–49)	..		..	
Pregnant women receiving prenatal care (%)	..		90	
Births attended by skilled health staff (% of total)	99		100	
Maternal mortality ratio (per 100,000 live births)	..		..	
Economic structure, participation, and access to resources				
Labor force participation rate (% of population ages 15+)	..	..	..	..
Wage and salaried workers (% of employed ages 15+)	..	..	..	..
Self-employed workers (% of employed ages 15+)	..	..	..	..
Vulnerable employment (% of employed ages 15+)	..	..	..	..
Unpaid family workers (% of employed ages 15+)	..	..	..	..
Employment in agriculture (% of employed ages 15+)	..	..	..	..
Employment in industry (% of employed ages 15+)	..	..	..	..
Employment in service (% of employed ages 15+)	..	..	..	..
Women in wage employment in the nonagricultural sector (%)	40		..	
Women's share of part-time employment (% of total)	..		..	
Maternity leave (weeks)	..		..	
Maternal leave benefits (% of wages paid)	..		..	
Female legislators, senior officials and managers (% of total)	..		..	
Employment to population ratio, total (% ages 15+)	..	..	..	..
Employment to population ratio, youth (% ages 15–24)	..	..	..	..
Children in employment (% of children ages 7–14)	..	..	..	..
Unemployment rate (% of labor force ages 15+)	..	..	..	..
Long-term unemployment rate (% total unemployment)	..	..	..	..
Youth unemployment rate (% of labor force ages 15–24)	..	..	..	..
Account at a formal financial institution (% age 15+)	..	..	..	..
Public life and decision making				
Seats held by women in national parliament (%)	..		0	

Panama

Latin America & the Caribbean			Upper middle income	
Population (millions)				3.6
GNI, Atlas ($ billions)				26.7
GNI per capita, Atlas ($)				7,470
Population living below $1.25 a day (%)				6.6

	1990		2011	
	Female	**Male**	**Female**	**Male**
Demography				
Sex ratio at birth (boys per girls)	1.05		1.05	
Life expectancy at birth (years)	75	70	79	74
Under-five mortality rate (per 1,000 live births)	31	36	18	21
Female-headed households (%)	..		..	
Education				
Gross primary enrollment ratio (% of relevant age group)	104	109	106	109
Gross secondary enrollment ratio (% of relevant age group)	63	59	77	71
Gross tertiary enrollment ratio (% of relevant age group)	25	18	56	36
Primary completion rate (% of relevant age group)	87	86	101	101
Youth literacy rate (% of population ages 15–24)	95	95	97	98
Health and related services				
Total fertility rate (births per woman)	3.0		2.5	
Adolescent fertility rate (births per 1,000 women ages 15–19)	..		77	
Women first married by age 18 (% of women ages 20–24)	..		..	
Contraceptive prevalence (% of women ages 15–49)	..		52	
Unmet need for contraception (% of women ages 15–49)	..		..	
Pregnant women receiving prenatal care (%)	..		96	
Births attended by skilled health staff (% of total)	86		89	
Maternal mortality ratio (per 100,000 live births)	100		92	
Economic structure, participation, and access to resources				
Labor force participation rate (% of population ages 15+)	39	79	50	83
Wage and salaried workers (% of employed ages 15+)	80	53	74	64
Self-employed workers (% of employed ages 15+)	20	47	26	36
Vulnerable employment (% of employed ages 15+)	19	44	24	33
Unpaid family workers (% of employed ages 15+)	3.3	7.7	5.5	2.8
Employment in agriculture (% of employed ages 15+)	3	38	7	23
Employment in industry (% of employed ages 15+)	11	16	10	24
Employment in service (% of employed ages 15+)	87	46	83	53
Women in wage employment in the nonagricultural sector (%)	43		43	
Women's share of part-time employment (% of total)	45		48	
Maternity leave (weeks)	14		14	
Maternal leave benefits (% of wages paid)	100		100	
Female legislators, senior officials and managers (% of total)	..		46	
Employment to population ratio, total (% ages 15+)	30	68	45	79
Employment to population ratio, youth (% ages 15–24)	20	47	27	57
Children in employment (% of children ages 7–14)	..	..	5.4	12.1
Unemployment rate (% of labor force ages 15+)	22.6	12.8	4.9	4.2
Long-term unemployment rate (% total unemployment)	26.6	20.9	..	..
Youth unemployment rate (% of labor force ages 15–24)	29	19	15	11
Account at a formal financial institution (% age 15+)	..	..	23	27
Public life and decision making				
Seats held by women in national parliament (%)	8		9	

Papua New Guinea

East Asia & Pacific	Lower middle income
Population (millions)	7.0
GNI, Atlas ($ billions)	10.4
GNI per capita, Atlas ($)	1,480
Population living below $1.25 a day (%)	..

	1990		2011	
	Female	Male	Female	Male
Demography				
Sex ratio at birth (boys per girls)	1.08		1.08	
Life expectancy at birth (years)	59	53	65	61
Under-five mortality rate (per 1,000 live births)	84	92	55	60
Female-headed households (%)	..		..	
Education				
Gross primary enrollment ratio (% of relevant age group)	57	67	57	63
Gross secondary enrollment ratio (% of relevant age group)	8	13	..	..
Gross tertiary enrollment ratio (% of relevant age group)	1	3	..	..
Primary completion rate (% of relevant age group)	41	49	..	..
Youth literacy rate (% of population ages 15–24)	..	..	72	65
Health and related services				
Total fertility rate (births per woman)	4.8		3.9	
Adolescent fertility rate (births per 1,000 women ages 15–19)	..		63	
Women first married by age 18 (% of women ages 20–24)	..		21	
Contraceptive prevalence (% of women ages 15–49)	..		32	
Unmet need for contraception (% of women ages 15–49)	..		..	
Pregnant women receiving prenatal care (%)	..		79	
Births attended by skilled health staff (% of total)	..		53	
Maternal mortality ratio (per 100,000 live births)	390		230	
Economic structure, participation, and access to resources				
Labor force participation rate (% of population ages 15+)	71	74	71	74
Wage and salaried workers (% of employed ages 15+)	..	..	..	..
Self-employed workers (% of employed ages 15+)	..	..	..	..
Vulnerable employment (% of employed ages 15+)	..	..	..	..
Unpaid family workers (% of employed ages 15+)	..	..	..	..
Employment in agriculture (% of employed ages 15+)	..	..	..	..
Employment in industry (% of employed ages 15+)	..	..	..	..
Employment in service (% of employed ages 15+)	..	..	..	..
Women in wage employment in the nonagricultural sector (%)	28		..	
Women's share of part-time employment (% of total)	..		..	
Maternity leave (weeks)	6		6	
Maternal leave benefits (% of wages paid)	0		..	
Female legislators, senior officials and managers (% of total)	..		..	
Employment to population ratio, total (% ages 15+)	68	72	69	73
Employment to population ratio, youth (% ages 15–24)	57	56	55	54
Children in employment (% of children ages 7–14)	..	..	..	..
Unemployment rate (% of labor force ages 15+)	5.9	9.0	1.4	6.6
Long-term unemployment rate (% total unemployment)	..	..	..	..
Youth unemployment rate (% of labor force ages 15–24)	..	..	..	..
Account at a formal financial institution (% age 15+)	..	..	..	..
Public life and decision making				
Seats held by women in national parliament (%)	0		3	

Paraguay

Latin America & the Caribbean			Lower middle income	

Population (millions)				6.6
GNI, Atlas ($ billions)				19.8
GNI per capita, Atlas ($)				3,020
Population living below $1.25 a day (%)				7.2

	1990		2011	
	Female	Male	Female	Male
Demography				
Sex ratio at birth (boys per girls)	1.05		1.05	
Life expectancy at birth (years)	70	66	75	70
Under-five mortality rate (per 1,000 live births)	48	57	20	25
Female-headed households (%)	17		..	
Education				
Gross primary enrollment ratio (% of relevant age group)	102	106	96	100
Gross secondary enrollment ratio (% of relevant age group)	31	30	70	66
Gross tertiary enrollment ratio (% of relevant age group)	10	11	40	29
Primary completion rate (% of relevant age group)	65	65	91	90
Youth literacy rate (% of population ages 15–24)	95	96	99	99
Health and related services				
Total fertility rate (births per woman)	4.5		2.9	
Adolescent fertility rate (births per 1,000 women ages 15–19)	..		68	
Women first married by age 18 (% of women ages 20–24)	24		..	
Contraceptive prevalence (% of women ages 15–49)	48		79	
Unmet need for contraception (% of women ages 15–49)	15		..	
Pregnant women receiving prenatal care (%)	84		96	
Births attended by skilled health staff (% of total)	66		82	
Maternal mortality ratio (per 100,000 live births)	120		99	
Economic structure, participation, and access to resources				
Labor force participation rate (% of population ages 15+)	54	91	58	86
Wage and salaried workers (% of employed ages 15+)	67	69	52	53
Self-employed workers (% of employed ages 15+)	33	31	48	47
Vulnerable employment (% of employed ages 15+)	31	17	46	40
Unpaid family workers (% of employed ages 15+)	0.1	0.4	8.5	9.1
Employment in agriculture (% of employed ages 15+)	1	3	20	31
Employment in industry (% of employed ages 15+)	15	36	9	23
Employment in service (% of employed ages 15+)	84	61	71	46
Women in wage employment in the nonagricultural sector (%)	41		40	
Women's share of part-time employment (% of total)	57		58	
Maternity leave (weeks)	12		12	
Maternal leave benefits (% of wages paid)	50		50	
Female legislators, senior officials and managers (% of total)	..		34	
Employment to population ratio, total (% ages 15+)	50	85	54	83
Employment to population ratio, youth (% ages 15–24)	49	78	42	71
Children in employment (% of children ages 7–14)	..	..	..	..
Unemployment rate (% of labor force ages 15+)	6.3	6.7	7.4	4.4
Long-term unemployment rate (% of total unemployment)	..	..	..	..
Youth unemployment rate (% of labor force ages 15–24)	17	15	18	10
Account at a formal financial institution (% age 15+)	..	..	23	21
Public life and decision making				
Seats held by women in national parliament (%)	6		13	

Peru

Latin America & the Caribbean			Upper middle income	
Population (millions)				29.4
GNI, Atlas ($ billions)				151.4
GNI per capita, Atlas ($)				5,150
Population living below $1.25 a day (%)				4.9

	1990		2011	
	Female	Male	Female	Male
Demography				
Sex ratio at birth (boys per girls)	1.05		1.05	
Life expectancy at birth (years)	68	63	77	71
Under-five mortality rate (per 1,000 live births)	71	79	17	20
Female-headed households (%)	15		23	
Education				
Gross primary enrollment ratio (% of relevant age group)	117	121	105	106
Gross secondary enrollment ratio (% of relevant age group)	65	69	91	92
Gross tertiary enrollment ratio (% of relevant age group)	..	..	45	41
Primary completion rate (% of relevant age group)	..	..	97	97
Youth literacy rate (% of population ages 15–24)	94	97	97	98
Health and related services				
Total fertility rate (births per woman)	3.8		2.5	
Adolescent fertility rate (births per 1,000 women ages 15–19)	..		50	
Women first married by age 18 (% of women ages 20–24)	18		19	
Contraceptive prevalence (% of women ages 15–49)	59		75	
Unmet need for contraception (% of women ages 15–49)	16		8	
Pregnant women receiving prenatal care (%)	64		95	
Births attended by skilled health staff (% of total)	53		85	
Maternal mortality ratio (per 100,000 live births)	200		67	
Economic structure, participation, and access to resources				
Labor force participation rate (% of population ages 15+)	46	78	68	85
Wage and salaried workers (% of employed ages 15+)	53	63	49	59
Self-employed workers (% of employed ages 15+)	47	37	50	41
Vulnerable employment (% of employed ages 15+)	46	30	47	34
Unpaid family workers (% of employed ages 15+)	9.2	2.8	8.7	4.5
Employment in agriculture (% of employed ages 15+)	1	2	1	1
Employment in industry (% of employed ages 15+)	20	32	14	32
Employment in service (% of employed ages 15+)	80	66	86	67
Women in wage employment in the nonagricultural sector (%)	..		38	
Women's share of part-time employment (% of total)	..		61	
Maternity leave (weeks)	12		13	
Maternal leave benefits (% of wages paid)	100		100	
Female legislators, senior officials and managers (% of total)	..		19	
Employment to population ratio, total (% ages 15+)	37	71	64	79
Employment to population ratio, youth (% ages 15–24)	27	44	49	60
Children in employment (% of children ages 7–14)	..	..	39.4	44.8
Unemployment rate (% of labor force ages 15+)	11.5	6.5	10.1	5.8
Long-term unemployment rate (% total unemployment)	..	..	..	..
Youth unemployment rate (% of labor force ages 15–24)	20	13	16	13
Account at a formal financial institution (% age 15+)	..	..	18	23
Public life and decision making				
Seats held by women in national parliament (%)	6		22	

Philippines

East Asia & Pacific **Lower middle income**

Population (millions)	94.9
GNI, Atlas ($ billions)	209.7
GNI per capita, Atlas ($)	2,210
Population living below $1.25 a day (%)	18.4

	1990		2011	
	Female	Male	Female	Male
Demography				
Sex ratio at birth (boys per girls)	1.06		1.06	
Life expectancy at birth (years)	68	62	72	66
Under-five mortality rate (per 1,000 live births)	51	63	22	29
Female-headed households (%)	14		17	
Education				
Gross primary enrollment ratio (% of relevant age group)	108	110	105	107
Gross secondary enrollment ratio (% of relevant age group)	73	71	88	82
Gross tertiary enrollment ratio (% of relevant age group)	31	21	31	25
Primary completion rate (% of relevant age group)	87	86	94	89
Youth literacy rate (% of population ages 15–24)	97	96	98	97
Health and related services				
Total fertility rate (births per woman)	4.3		3.1	
Adolescent fertility rate (births per 1,000 women ages 15–19)	..		48	
Women first married by age 18 (% of women ages 20–24)	14		14	
Contraceptive prevalence (% of women ages 15–49)	36		49	
Unmet need for contraception (% of women ages 15–49)	26		19	
Pregnant women receiving prenatal care (%)	83		78	
Births attended by skilled health staff (% of total)	53		72	
Maternal mortality ratio (per 100,000 live births)	170		99	
Economic structure, participation, and access to resources				
Labor force participation rate (% of population ages 15+)	48	83	50	79
Wage and salaried workers (% of employed ages 15+)	..	..	51	53
Self-employed workers (% of employed ages 15+)	..	..	49	47
Vulnerable employment (% of employed ages 15+)	..	..	46	42
Unpaid family workers (% of employed ages 15+)	..	..	17.4	9.0
Employment in agriculture (% of employed ages 15+)	31	53	23	41
Employment in industry (% of employed ages 15+)	13	16	10	18
Employment in service (% of employed ages 15+)	56	31	68	41
Women in wage employment in the nonagricultural sector (%)	40		42	
Women's share of part-time employment (% of total)			..	
Maternity leave (weeks)	14		9	
Maternal leave benefits (% of wages paid)	100		100	
Female legislators, senior officials and managers (% of total)	..		55	
Employment to population ratio, total (% ages 15+)	43	76	46	74
Employment to population ratio, youth (% ages 15–24)	31	53	30	49
Children in employment (% of children ages 7–14)	..	..	..	..
Unemployment rate (% of labor force ages 15+)	9.8	7.1	6.6	7.4
Long-term unemployment rate (% total unemployment)	..	..	..	..
Youth unemployment rate (% of labor force ages 15–24)	19	13	19	16
Account at a formal financial institution (% age 15+)	..	..	34	19
Public life and decision making				
Seats held by women in national parliament (%)	9		23	

Poland

			High income
Population (millions)			38.5
GNI, Atlas ($ billions)			477.0
GNI per capita, Atlas ($)			12,380
Population living below $1.25 a day (%)			<2

	1990		2011	
	Female	Male	Female	Male
Demography				
Sex ratio at birth (boys per girls)	1.06		1.06	
Life expectancy at birth (years)	76	67	81	73
Under-five mortality rate (per 1,000 live births)	15	19	5	6
Female-headed households (%)	..		..	
Education				
Gross primary enrollment ratio (% of relevant age group)	98	100	98	99
Gross secondary enrollment ratio (% of relevant age group)	90	85	96	98
Gross tertiary enrollment ratio (% of relevant age group)	24	17	87	58
Primary completion rate (% of relevant age group)	..	..	95	96
Youth literacy rate (% of population ages 15–24)	100	100	100	100
Health and related services				
Total fertility rate (births per woman)	2.0		1.3	
Adolescent fertility rate (births per 1,000 women ages 15-19)	..		13	
Women first married by age 18 (% of women ages 20–24)	..		..	
Contraceptive prevalence (% of women ages 15–49)	73		..	
Unmet need for contraception (% of women ages 15–49)	..		..	
Pregnant women receiving prenatal care (%)	..		..	
Births attended by skilled health staff (% of total)	100		..	
Maternal mortality ratio (per 100,000 live births)	17		5	
Economic structure, participation, and access to resources				
Labor force participation rate (% of population ages 15+)	55	72	48	64
Wage and salaried workers (% of employed ages 15+)	71	69	80	75
Self-employed workers (% of employed ages 15+)	29	31	20	25
Vulnerable employment (% of employed ages 15+)	28	28	17	20
Unpaid family workers (% of employed ages 15+)	7.8	5.5	5.2	2.5
Employment in agriculture (% of employed ages 15+)	24	24	13	13
Employment in industry (% of employed ages 15+)	21	41	16	42
Employment in service (% of employed ages 15+)	55	35	71	45
Women in wage employment in the nonagricultural sector (%)	..		48	
Women's share of part-time employment (% of total)	..		67	
Maternity leave (weeks)	16		16	
Maternal leave benefits (% of wages paid)	100		100	
Female legislators, senior officials and managers (% of total)	..		38	
Employment to population ratio, total (% ages 15+)	48	64	43	58
Employment to population ratio, youth (% ages 15–24)	29	39	22	31
Children in employment (% of children ages 7–14)	..	..	..	..
Unemployment rate (% of labor force ages 15+)	14.7	12.2	10.4	9.0
Long-term unemployment rate (% total unemployment)	36.0	33.3	32.5	30.7
Youth unemployment rate (% of labor force ages 15–24)	30	26	29	24
Account at a formal financial institution (% age 15+)	..	..	68	72
Public life and decision making				
Seats held by women in national parliament (%)	14		24	

Portugal

	High income
Population (millions)	10.6
GNI, Atlas ($ billions)	225.6
GNI per capita, Atlas ($)	21,370
Population living below $1.25 a day (%)	..

	1990		2011	
	Female	Male	Female	Male
Demography				
Sex ratio at birth (boys per girls)	1.06		1.06	
Life expectancy at birth (years)	78	71	84	78
Under-five mortality rate (per 1,000 live births)	13	16	3	4
Female-headed households (%)	..		..	
Education				
Gross primary enrollment ratio (% of relevant age group)	118	123	110	113
Gross secondary enrollment ratio (% of relevant age group)	60	60	110	108
Gross tertiary enrollment ratio (% of relevant age group)	26	20	71	60
Primary completion rate (% of relevant age group)	..	..	..	..
Youth literacy rate (% of population ages 15–24)	99	99	100	100
Health and related services				
Total fertility rate (births per woman)	1.4		1.4	
Adolescent fertility rate (births per 1,000 women ages 15–19)	..		13	
Women first married by age 18 (% of women ages 20–24)	..		..	
Contraceptive prevalence (% of women ages 15–49)	..		67	
Unmet need for contraception (% of women ages 15–49)	..		..	
Pregnant women receiving prenatal care (%)	..		..	
Births attended by skilled health staff (% of total)	98		..	
Maternal mortality ratio (per 100,000 live births)	15		8	
Economic structure, participation, and access to resources				
Labor force participation rate (% of population ages 15+)	49	73	57	68
Wage and salaried workers (% of employed ages 15+)	70	72	83	75
Self-employed workers (% of employed ages 15+)	30	28	17	25
Vulnerable employment (% of employed ages 15+)	28	22	14	18
Unpaid family workers (% of employed ages 15+)	4.0	2.0	0.8	0.5
Employment in agriculture (% of employed ages 15+)	21	16	11	11
Employment in industry (% of employed ages 15+)	26	41	16	38
Employment in service (% of employed ages 15+)	53	44	73	51
Women in wage employment in the nonagricultural sector (%)	43		49	
Women's share of part-time employment (% of total)	70		60	
Maternity leave (weeks)	12		17	
Maternal leave benefits (% of wages paid)	100		100	
Female legislators, senior officials and managers (% of total)	37		33	
Employment to population ratio, total (% ages 15+)	48	71	49	60
Employment to population ratio, youth (% ages 15–24)	46	60	24	28
Children in employment (% of children ages 7–14)	..	..	..	..
Unemployment rate (% of labor force ages 15+)	6.8	3.2	13.1	12.4
Long-term unemployment rate (% total unemployment)	49.2	38.0	48.5	47.9
Youth unemployment rate (% of labor force ages 15–24)	13	7	32	29
Account at a formal financial institution (% age 15+)	..	..	78	85
Public life and decision making				
Seats held by women in national parliament (%)	8		29	

Puerto Rico

High income

Population (millions)	3.7
GNI, Atlas ($ billions)	61.6
GNI per capita, Atlas ($)	16,560
Population living below $1.25 a day (%)	..

	1990		2011	
	Female	Male	Female	Male
Demography				
Sex ratio at birth (boys per girls)	1.05		1.05	
Life expectancy at birth (years)	79	70	83	75
Under-five mortality rate (per 1,000 live births)	..	..	..	..
Female-headed households (%)	..		..	
Education				
Gross primary enrollment ratio (% of relevant age group)	..	..	88	84
Gross secondary enrollment ratio (% of relevant age group)	..	..	79	76
Gross tertiary enrollment ratio (% of relevant age group)	..	..	102	70
Primary completion rate (% of relevant age group)	..	..	..	..
Youth literacy rate (% of population ages 15–24)	94	92	87	86
Health and related services				
Total fertility rate (births per woman)	2.2		1.8	
Adolescent fertility rate (births per 1,000 women ages 15–19)	..		51	
Women first married by age 18 (% of women ages 20–24)	..			
Contraceptive prevalence (% of women ages 15–49)	..		..	
Unmet need for contraception (% of women ages 15–49)	..		..	
Pregnant women receiving prenatal care (%)	..		..	
Births attended by skilled health staff (% of total)	..		..	
Maternal mortality ratio (per 100,000 live births)	33		20	
Economic structure, participation, and access to resources				
Labor force participation rate (% of population ages 15+)	31	60	36	55
Wage and salaried workers (% of employed ages 15+)	92	80	92	78
Self-employed workers (% of employed ages 15+)	8	20	8	22
Vulnerable employment (% of employed ages 15+)	..	..	..	..
Unpaid family workers (% of employed ages 15+)	2.1	0.3	0.0	0.0
Employment in agriculture (% of employed ages 15+)	0	6	0	3
Employment in industry (% of employed ages 15+)	21	27	8	18
Employment in service (% of employed ages 15+)	79	68	91	79
Women in wage employment in the nonagricultural sector (%)	47		46	
Women's share of part-time employment (% of total)	..		..	
Maternity leave (weeks)	..		..	
Maternal leave benefits (% of wages paid)	..		..	
Female legislators, senior officials and managers (% of total)	..		43	
Employment to population ratio, total (% ages 15+)	27	50	31	45
Employment to population ratio, youth (% ages 15–24)	13	28	15	22
Children in employment (% of children ages 7–14)	..	..	..	..
Unemployment rate (% of labor force ages 15+)	11.0	17.6	12.8	18.2
Long-term unemployment rate (% total unemployment)	..	..	..	..
Youth unemployment rate (% of labor force ages 15–24)	28	33	25	33
Account at a formal financial institution (% age 15+)	..	..	..	..
Public life and decision making				
Seats held by women in national parliament (%)	..		..	

Qatar

High income

Population (millions)	1.9
GNI, Atlas ($ billions)	150.4
GNI per capita, Atlas ($)	80,440
Population living below $1.25 a day (%)	..

	1990		2011	
	Female	**Male**	**Female**	**Male**
Demography				
Sex ratio at birth (boys per girls)	1.06		1.04	
Life expectancy at birth (years)	75	74	78	79
Under-five mortality rate (per 1,000 live births)	19	22	7	8
Female-headed households (%)	..		..	
Education				
Gross primary enrollment ratio (% of relevant age group)	96	103	104	106
Gross secondary enrollment ratio (% of relevant age group)	92	72	106	98
Gross tertiary enrollment ratio (% of relevant age group)	36	10	31	5
Primary completion rate (% of relevant age group)	76	72	96	96
Youth literacy rate (% of population ages 15–24)	91	89	98	96
Health and related services				
Total fertility rate (births per woman)	4.2		2.2	
Adolescent fertility rate (births per 1,000 women ages 15–19)	..		16	
Women first married by age 18 (% of women ages 20–24)	..			
Contraceptive prevalence (% of women ages 15–49)	32		..	
Unmet need for contraception (% of women ages 15–49)	..		..	
Pregnant women receiving prenatal care (%)	94		100	
Births attended by skilled health staff (% of total)	..		100	
Maternal mortality ratio (per 100,000 live births)	15		7	
Economic structure, participation, and access to resources				
Labor force participation rate (% of population ages 15+)	43	94	52	95
Wage and salaried workers (% of employed ages 15+)	..	..	100	99
Self-employed workers (% of employed ages 15+)	..	..	0	1
Vulnerable employment (% of employed ages 15+)	..	..	0	0
Unpaid family workers (% of employed ages 15+)	..	..	0.0	0.0
Employment in agriculture (% of employed ages 15+)	..	..	0	2
Employment in industry (% of employed ages 15+)	..	..	4	61
Employment in service (% of employed ages 15+)	..	..	96	38
Women in wage employment in the nonagricultural sector (%)	..		12	
Women's share of part-time employment (% of total)	..		..	
Maternity leave (weeks)	8		7	
Maternal leave benefits (% of wages paid)	100		100	
Female legislators, senior officials and managers (% of total)	..		10	
Employment to population ratio, total (% ages 15+)	40	93	50	95
Employment to population ratio, youth (% ages 15–24)	27	68	31	77
Children in employment (% of children ages 7–14)	..	..	..	..
Unemployment rate (% of labor force ages 15+)	..	..	3.3	0.2
Long-term unemployment rate (% total unemployment)	..	..	40.3	35.3
Youth unemployment rate (% of labor force ages 15–24)	..	..	9	0
Account at a formal financial institution (% age 15+)	..	..	62	69
Public life and decision making				
Seats held by women in national parliament (%)	..		0	

Romania

Europe & Central Asia			Upper middle income	
Population (millions)				21.4
GNI, Atlas ($ billions)				174.0
GNI per capita, Atlas ($)				8,140
Population living below $1.25 a day (%)				<2

	1990		2011	
	Female	Male	Female	Male
Demography				
Sex ratio at birth (boys per girls)	1.06		1.06	
Life expectancy at birth (years)	73	67	78	71
Under-five mortality rate (per 1,000 live births)	33	41	11	14
Female-headed households (%)	..		..	
Education				
Gross primary enrollment ratio (% of relevant age group)	92	93	95	96
Gross secondary enrollment ratio (% of relevant age group)	101	104	97	98
Gross tertiary enrollment ratio (% of relevant age group)	8	8	68	50
Primary completion rate (% of relevant age group)	92	92	93	92
Youth literacy rate (% of population ages 15–24)	99	99	97	97
Health and related services				
Total fertility rate (births per woman)	1.8		1.3	
Adolescent fertility rate (births per 1,000 women ages 15–19)	..		29	
Women first married by age 18 (% of women ages 20–24)	..		..	
Contraceptive prevalence (% of women ages 15–49)	57		..	
Unmet need for contraception (% of women ages 15–49)	..		..	
Pregnant women receiving prenatal care (%)	..		..	
Births attended by skilled health staff (% of total)	100		99	
Maternal mortality ratio (per 100,000 live births)	170		27	
Economic structure, participation, and access to resources				
Labor force participation rate (% of population ages 15+)	52	67	49	65
Wage and salaried workers (% of employed ages 15+)	63	75	67	67
Self-employed workers (% of employed ages 15+)	37	25	33	33
Vulnerable employment (% of employed ages 15+)	33	21	32	31
Unpaid family workers (% of employed ages 15+)	5.6	3.5	19.6	7.1
Employment in agriculture (% of employed ages 15+)	34	25	31	29
Employment in industry (% of employed ages 15+)	37	49	20	36
Employment in service (% of employed ages 15+)	29	26	49	35
Women in wage employment in the nonagricultural sector (%)	42		46	
Women's share of part-time employment (% of total)	60		50	
Maternity leave (weeks)	16		18	
Maternal leave benefits (% of wages paid)	..		85	
Female legislators, senior officials and managers (% of total)	27		31	
Employment to population ratio, total (% ages 15+)	49	64	45	60
Employment to population ratio, youth (% ages 15–24)	44	54	20	28
Children in employment (% of children ages 7–14)	..	..	..	..
Unemployment rate (% of labor force ages 15+)	8.7	7.7	6.8	7.9
Long-term unemployment rate (% total unemployment)	51.0	39.6	40.9	42.6
Youth unemployment rate (% of labor force ages 15–24)	23	22	24	24
Account at a formal financial institution (% age 15+)	..	..	41	49
Public life and decision making				
Seats held by women in national parliament (%)	34		13	

Russian Federation

Population (millions)	143.0
GNI, Atlas ($ billions)	1,522.3
GNI per capita, Atlas ($)	10,650
Population living below $1.25 a day (%)	<2

	1990 Female	1990 Male	2011 Female	2011 Male
Demography				
Sex ratio at birth (boys per girls)	1.06		1.06	
Life expectancy at birth (years)	74	64	75	63
Under-five mortality rate (per 1,000 live births)	23	31	10	13
Female-headed households (%)	..		..	
Education				
Gross primary enrollment ratio (% of relevant age group)	107	107	99	99
Gross secondary enrollment ratio (% of relevant age group)	91	89	87	90
Gross tertiary enrollment ratio (% of relevant age group)	58	47	87	65
Primary completion rate (% of relevant age group)	94	93	..	..
Youth literacy rate (% of population ages 15–24)	100	100	100	100
Health and related services				
Total fertility rate (births per woman)	1.9		1.5	
Adolescent fertility rate (births per 1,000 women ages 15–19)	..		25	
Women first married by age 18 (% of women ages 20–24)	..		..	
Contraceptive prevalence (% of women ages 15–49)	63		80	
Unmet need for contraception (% of women ages 15–49)	..		..	
Pregnant women receiving prenatal care (%)	..		..	
Births attended by skilled health staff (% of total)	99		100	
Maternal mortality ratio (per 100,000 live births)	74		34	
Economic structure, participation, and access to resources				
Labor force participation rate (% of population ages 15+)	60	77	56	71
Wage and salaried workers (% of employed ages 15+)	94	90	93	92
Self-employed workers (% of employed ages 15+)	6	10	7	8
Vulnerable employment (% of employed ages 15+)	1	1	5	6
Unpaid family workers (% of employed ages 15+)	0.1	0.1	0.1	0.1
Employment in agriculture (% of employed ages 15+)	..	..	7	11
Employment in industry (% of employed ages 15+)	..	..	19	38
Employment in service (% of employed ages 15+)	..	..	74	51
Women in wage employment in the nonagricultural sector (%)	51		51	
Women's share of part-time employment (% of total)	70		65	
Maternity leave (weeks)	20		20	
Maternal leave benefits (% of wages paid)	100		100	
Female legislators, senior officials and managers (% of total)	..		37	
Employment to population ratio, total (% ages 15+)	52	67	53	66
Employment to population ratio, youth (% ages 15–24)	38	44	34	42
Children in employment (% of children ages 7–14)	..	..	..	..
Unemployment rate (% of labor force ages 15+)	5.2	5.2	6.2	7.0
Long-term unemployment rate (% total unemployment)	13.3	9.1	33.3	32.3
Youth unemployment rate (% of labor force ages 15–24)	13	13	16	15
Account at a formal financial institution (% age 15+)	..	..	48	49
Public life and decision making				
Seats held by women in national parliament (%)	16		14	

Rwanda

Population (millions)	10.9
GNI, Atlas ($ billions)	6.2
GNI per capita, Atlas ($)	570
Population living below $1.25 a day (%)	63.2

	1990		2011	
	Female	Male	Female	Male
Demography				
Sex ratio at birth (boys per girls)	1.01		1.01	
Life expectancy at birth (years)	35	31	57	54
Under-five mortality rate (per 1,000 live births)	148	165	51	57
Female-headed households (%)	21		33	
Education				
Gross primary enrollment ratio (% of relevant age group)	75	76	143	140
Gross secondary enrollment ratio (% of relevant age group)	15	18	37	35
Gross tertiary enrollment ratio (% of relevant age group)	0	1	6	8
Primary completion rate (% of relevant age group)	44	46	74	65
Youth literacy rate (% of population ages 15–24)	..	..	78	77
Health and related services				
Total fertility rate (births per woman)	7.0		5.3	
Adolescent fertility rate (births per 1,000 women ages 15–19)	..		36	
Women first married by age 18 (% of women ages 20–24)	15		8	
Contraceptive prevalence (% of women ages 15–49)	21		52	
Unmet need for contraception (% of women ages 15–49)	39		21	
Pregnant women receiving prenatal care (%)	94		98	
Births attended by skilled health staff (% of total)	26		69	
Maternal mortality ratio (per 100,000 live births)	910		340	
Economic structure, participation, and access to resources				
Labor force participation rate (% of population ages 15+)	89	89	86	85
Wage and salaried workers (% of employed ages 15+)	..	..	..	..
Self-employed workers (% of employed ages 15+)	..	..	..	..
Vulnerable employment (% of employed ages 15+)	..	..	..	..
Unpaid family workers (% of employed ages 15+)	..	..	..	..
Employment in agriculture (% of employed ages 15+)	96	83	..	..
Employment in industry (% of employed ages 15+)	1	5	..	..
Employment in service (% of employed ages 15+)	3	11	..	..
Women in wage employment in the nonagricultural sector (%)	..			
Women's share of part-time employment (% of total)			..	
Maternity leave (weeks)	12		12	
Maternal leave benefits (% of wages paid)	33		100	
Female legislators, senior officials and managers (% of total)	..		..	
Employment to population ratio, total (% ages 15+)	88	88	86	85
Employment to population ratio, youth (% ages 15–24)	81	79	75	71
Children in employment (% of children ages 7–14)	..	..	7.0	8.0
Unemployment rate (% of labor force ages 15+)	0.2	0.6	2.4	2.4
Long-term unemployment rate (% total unemployment)	..	..	..	..
Youth unemployment rate (% of labor force ages 15–24)	1	1	..	..
Account at a formal financial institution (% age 15+)	..	..	28	38
Public life and decision making				
Seats held by women in national parliament (%)	17		56	

Samoa

East Asia & Pacific	Lower middle income
Population (thousands)	183.9
GNI, Atlas ($ millions)	580.5
GNI per capita, Atlas ($)	3,160
Population living below $1.25 a day (%)	..

	1990		2011	
	Female	Male	Female	Male
Demography				
Sex ratio at birth (boys per girls)	1.08		1.08	
Life expectancy at birth (years)	68	62	76	70
Under-five mortality rate (per 1,000 live births)	26	33	16	21
Female-headed households (%)	..		..	
Education				
Gross primary enrollment ratio (% of relevant age group)	*114*	*112*	107	103
Gross secondary enrollment ratio (% of relevant age group)	..	..	88	77
Gross tertiary enrollment ratio (% of relevant age group)	..	..	..	..
Primary completion rate (% of relevant age group)	..	..	103	95
Youth literacy rate (% of population ages 15–24)	*99*	*99*	*100*	*99*
Health and related services				
Total fertility rate (births per woman)	4.8		3.8	
Adolescent fertility rate (births per 1,000 women ages 15–19)	..		26	
Women first married by age 18 (% of women ages 20–24)	..		..	
Contraceptive prevalence (% of women ages 15–49)	..		29	
Unmet need for contraception (% of women ages 15–49)	..		..	
Pregnant women receiving prenatal care (%)	..		93	
Births attended by skilled health staff (% of total)	76		*81*	
Maternal mortality ratio (per 100,000 live births)	260		*100*	
Economic structure, participation, and access to resources				
Labor force participation rate (% of population ages 15+)	40	77	43	78
Wage and salaried workers (% of employed ages 15+)	..	..	..	..
Self-employed workers (% of employed ages 15+)	..	..	..	..
Vulnerable employment (% of employed ages 15+)	..	..	..	..
Unpaid family workers (% of employed ages 15+)	..	..	..	..
Employment in agriculture (% of employed ages 15+)	..	..	..	..
Employment in industry (% of employed ages 15+)	..	..	..	..
Employment in service (% of employed ages 15+)	..	..	..	..
Women in wage employment in the nonagricultural sector (%)	..		..	
Women's share of part-time employment (% of total)	..		..	
Maternity leave (weeks)	..		..	
Maternal leave benefits (% of wages paid)	..		..	
Female legislators, senior officials and managers (% of total)	..		..	
Employment to population ratio, total (% ages 15+)	..	..	..	..
Employment to population ratio, youth (% ages 15–24)	..	..	..	..
Children in employment (% of children ages 7–14)	..	..	..	..
Unemployment rate (% of labor force ages 15+)	..	..	..	..
Long-term unemployment rate (% total unemployment)	..	..	..	..
Youth unemployment rate (% of labor force ages 15–24)	..	..	..	..
Account at a formal financial institution (% age 15+)	..	..	..	..
Public life and decision making				
Seats held by women in national parliament (%)	0		4	

San Marino

Population (thousands)	31.7
GNI, Atlas ($ billions)	1.6
GNI per capita, Atlas ($)	50,400
Population living below $1.25 a day (%)	..

	1990		2011	
	Female	Male	Female	Male
Demography				
Sex ratio at birth (boys per girls)	..		..	
Life expectancy at birth (years)	..	..	86	80
Under-five mortality rate (per 1,000 live births)	12	12	2	2
Female-headed households (%)	..		..	
Education				
Gross primary enrollment ratio (% of relevant age group)	..	..	91	92
Gross secondary enrollment ratio (% of relevant age group)	..	..	96	94
Gross tertiary enrollment ratio (% of relevant age group)	..	..	77	52
Primary completion rate (% of relevant age group)	..	..	95	92
Youth literacy rate (% of population ages 15–24)	..	..	..	..
Health and related services				
Total fertility rate (births per woman)	..		..	
Adolescent fertility rate (births per 1,000 women ages 15–19)	..		..	
Women first married by age 18 (% of women ages 20–24)	..		..	
Contraceptive prevalence (% of women ages 15–49)	..		..	
Unmet need for contraception (% of women ages 15–49)	..		..	
Pregnant women receiving prenatal care (%)	..		..	
Births attended by skilled health staff (% of total)	..		..	
Maternal mortality ratio (per 100,000 live births)	..		..	
Economic structure, participation, and access to resources				
Labor force participation rate (% of population ages 15+)	..	..	..	..
Wage and salaried workers (% of employed ages 15+)	..	..	93	89
Self-employed workers (% of employed ages 15+)	..	..	7	11
Vulnerable employment (% of employed ages 15+)	..	..	..	..
Unpaid family workers (% of employed ages 15+)	..	..	0.0	0.0
Employment in agriculture (% of employed ages 15+)	3	2	0	0
Employment in industry (% of employed ages 15+)	32	52	21	48
Employment in service (% of employed ages 15+)	66	46	79	52
Women in wage employment in the nonagricultural sector (%)	40		44	
Women's share of part-time employment (% of total)	..		..	
Maternity leave (weeks)	..		..	
Maternal leave benefits (% of wages paid)	..		..	
Female legislators, senior officials and managers (% of total)	..		18	
Employment to population ratio, total (% ages 15+)	..	..	..	..
Employment to population ratio, youth (% ages 15–24)	..	..	..	..
Children in employment (% of children ages 7–14)	..	..	..	..
Unemployment rate (% of labor force ages 15+)	9.0	2.0	4.5	1.2
Long-term unemployment rate (% total unemployment)	..	..	..	..
Youth unemployment rate (% of labor force ages 15–24)	..	..	..	..
Account at a formal financial institution (% age 15+)	..	..	..	..
Public life and decision making				
Seats held by women in national parliament (%)	12		17	

São Tomé and Príncipe

Sub-Saharan Africa	Lower middle income
Population (thousands)	168.5
GNI, Atlas ($ millions)	226.9
GNI per capita, Atlas ($)	1,350
Population living below $1.25 a day (%)	28.2

	1990		2011	
	Female	Male	Female	Male
Demography				
Sex ratio at birth (boys per girls)	1.03		1.03	
Life expectancy at birth (years)	62	60	66	63
Under-five mortality rate (per 1,000 live births)	93	99	86	92
Female-headed households (%)	..		39	
Education				
Gross primary enrollment ratio (% of relevant age group)	132	144	125[a]	129[a]
Gross secondary enrollment ratio (% of relevant age group)	34	37	74[a]	65[a]
Gross tertiary enrollment ratio (% of relevant age group)	..	..	4	5
Primary completion rate (% of relevant age group)	71	79	117	112
Youth literacy rate (% of population ages 15–24)	92	96	96	95
Health and related services				
Total fertility rate (births per woman)	5.4		3.6	
Adolescent fertility rate (births per 1,000 women ages 15–19)	..		58	
Women first married by age 18 (% of women ages 20–24)	..		34	
Contraceptive prevalence (% of women ages 15–49)	..		38	
Unmet need for contraception (% of women ages 15–49)	..		37	
Pregnant women receiving prenatal care (%)	..		98	
Births attended by skilled health staff (% of total)	..		82	
Maternal mortality ratio (per 100,000 live births)	150		70	
Economic structure, participation, and access to resources				
Labor force participation rate (% of population ages 15+)	37	78	44	77
Wage and salaried workers (% of employed ages 15+)	69	72	..	..
Self-employed workers (% of employed ages 15+)	30	26	..	..
Vulnerable employment (% of employed ages 15+)	30	26	..	..
Unpaid family workers (% of employed ages 15+)	0.7	0.8	..	..
Employment in agriculture (% of employed ages 15+)	35	42	..	..
Employment in industry (% of employed ages 15+)	3	19	..	..
Employment in service (% of employed ages 15+)	59	36	..	..
Women in wage employment in the nonagricultural sector (%)	32		..	
Women's share of part-time employment (% of total)	..		..	
Maternity leave (weeks)	10		9	
Maternal leave benefits (% of wages paid)	100		100	
Female legislators, senior officials and managers (% of total)	..		..	
Employment to population ratio, total (% ages 15+)	..	..	..	..
Employment to population ratio, youth (% ages 15–24)	..	..	..	..
Children in employment (% of children ages 7–14)	..		..	
Unemployment rate (% of labor force ages 15+)	..	..	24.5	11.0
Long-term unemployment rate (% total unemployment)	..	..	..	..
Youth unemployment rate (% of labor force ages 15–24)	14	6	..	..
Account at a formal financial institution (% age 15+)	..	..	..	..
Public life and decision making				
Seats held by women in national parliament (%)	12		18	

Saudi Arabia

High income

Population (millions)	28.1
GNI, Atlas ($ billions)	500.5
GNI per capita, Atlas ($)	17,820
Population living below $1.25 a day (%)	..

	1990		2011	
	Female	Male	Female	Male
Demography				
Sex ratio at birth (boys per girls)	1.03		1.03	
Life expectancy at birth (years)	70	68	75	73
Under-five mortality rate (per 1,000 live births)	39	46	8	10
Female-headed households (%)	..		..	
Education				
Gross primary enrollment ratio (% of relevant age group)	..	..	106	106
Gross secondary enrollment ratio (% of relevant age group)	..	..	92	103
Gross tertiary enrollment ratio (% of relevant age group)	11	11	42	40
Primary completion rate (% of relevant age group)	..	..	105	107
Youth literacy rate (% of population ages 15–24)	81	94	97	99
Health and related services				
Total fertility rate (births per woman)	5.8		2.7	
Adolescent fertility rate (births per 1,000 women ages 15–19)	..		20	
Women first married by age 18 (% of women ages 20–24)	..		..	
Contraceptive prevalence (% of women ages 15–49)	..		24	
Unmet need for contraception (% of women ages 15–49)	..		..	
Pregnant women receiving prenatal care (%)	..		97	
Births attended by skilled health staff (% of total)	..		97	
Maternal mortality ratio (per 100,000 live births)	44		24	
Economic structure, participation, and access to resources				
Labor force participation rate (% of population ages 15+)	15	80	18	74
Wage and salaried workers (% of employed ages 15+)	..	..	..	..
Self-employed workers (% of employed ages 15+)	..	..	..	..
Vulnerable employment (% of employed ages 15+)	..	..	..	..
Unpaid family workers (% of employed ages 15+)	..	..	..	..
Employment in agriculture (% of employed ages 15+)	..	..	0	5
Employment in industry (% of employed ages 15+)	..	..	2	23
Employment in service (% of employed ages 15+)	..	..	98	72
Women in wage employment in the nonagricultural sector (%)	..		16	
Women's share of part-time employment (% of total)	..		..	
Maternity leave (weeks)	10		10	
Maternal leave benefits (% of wages paid)	50		100	
Female legislators, senior officials and managers (% of total)	..		8	
Employment to population ratio, total (% ages 15+)	13	77	15	72
Employment to population ratio, youth (% ages 15–24)	4	43	4	20
Children in employment (% of children ages 7–14)	..	..	..	..
Unemployment rate (% of labor force ages 15+)	..	..	15.9	3.5
Long-term unemployment rate (% total unemployment)	..	..	..	..
Youth unemployment rate (% of labor force ages 15–24)	..	..	46	24
Account at a formal financial institution (% age 15+)	..	..	15	73
Public life and decision making				
Seats held by women in national parliament (%)	..		0	

Senegal

Sub-Saharan Africa   **Lower middle income**

Population (millions)	12.8
GNI, Atlas ($ billions)	13.7
GNI per capita, Atlas ($)	1,070
Population living below $1.25 a day (%)	29.6

	1990 Female	Male	2011 Female	Male
Demography				
Sex ratio at birth (boys per girls)	1.03		1.03	
Life expectancy at birth (years)	54	52	60	58
Under-five mortality rate (per 1,000 live births)	129	143	60	69
Female-headed households (%)	16		25	
Education				
Gross primary enrollment ratio (% of relevant age group)	47	65	89	83
Gross secondary enrollment ratio (% of relevant age group)	10	20	40	44
Gross tertiary enrollment ratio (% of relevant age group)	..	..	6	10
Primary completion rate (% of relevant age group)	33	53	65	61
Youth literacy rate (% of population ages 15–24)	28	49	56	74
Health and related services				
Total fertility rate (births per woman)	6.6		4.7	
Adolescent fertility rate (births per 1,000 women ages 15–19)	..		93	
Women first married by age 18 (% of women ages 20–24)	48		33	
Contraceptive prevalence (% of women ages 15–49)	7		13	
Unmet need for contraception (% of women ages 15–49)	29		30	
Pregnant women receiving prenatal care (%)	74		93	
Births attended by skilled health staff (% of total)	47		65	
Maternal mortality ratio (per 100,000 live births)	670		370	
Economic structure, participation, and access to resources				
Labor force participation rate (% of population ages 15+)	62	89	66	88
Wage and salaried workers (% of employed ages 15+)	8	14	..	..
Self-employed workers (% of employed ages 15+)	91	78	..	..
Vulnerable employment (% of employed ages 15+)	91	77	..	..
Unpaid family workers (% of employed ages 15+)	32.4	25.3	..	..
Employment in agriculture (% of employed ages 15+)	..	..	33	34
Employment in industry (% of employed ages 15+)	..	..	5	20
Employment in service (% of employed ages 15+)	..	..	42	33
Women in wage employment in the nonagricultural sector (%)	..		..	
Women's share of part-time employment (% of total)	..		..	
Maternity leave (weeks)	14		14	
Maternal leave benefits (% of wages paid)	100		100	
Female legislators, senior officials and managers (% of total)	..		..	
Employment to population ratio, total (% ages 15+)	54	82	58	82
Employment to population ratio, youth (% ages 15–24)	44	73	43	71
Children in employment (% of children ages 7–14)	..	..	14.1	20.9
Unemployment rate (% of labor force ages 15+)	..	..	13.6	7.9
Long-term unemployment rate (% total unemployment)	..	..	..	..
Youth unemployment rate (% of labor force ages 15–24)	..	..	20	12
Account at a formal financial institution (% age 15+)	..	..	5	6
Public life and decision making				
Seats held by women in national parliament (%)	13		43	

Serbia

Population (millions)	7.3
GNI, Atlas ($ billions)	41.3
GNI per capita, Atlas ($)	5,690
Population living below $1.25 a day (%)	<2

	1990		2011	
	Female	Male	Female	Male
Demography				
Sex ratio at birth (boys per girls)	1.08		1.08	
Life expectancy at birth (years)	74	69	77	72
Under-five mortality rate (per 1,000 live births)	27	30	6	8
Female-headed households (%)	..		29	
Education				
Gross primary enrollment ratio (% of relevant age group)	..	..	95	95
Gross secondary enrollment ratio (% of relevant age group)	..	..	92	91
Gross tertiary enrollment ratio (% of relevant age group)	..	..	57	44
Primary completion rate (% of relevant age group)	..	..	99	100
Youth literacy rate (% of population ages 15–24)	..	..	99	99
Health and related services				
Total fertility rate (births per woman)	1.8		1.4	
Adolescent fertility rate (births per 1,000 women ages 15–19)	..		20	
Women first married by age 18 (% of women ages 20–24)	..		5	
Contraceptive prevalence (% of women ages 15–49)	..		61	
Unmet need for contraception (% of women ages 15–49)	..		..	
Pregnant women receiving prenatal care (%)	..		99	
Births attended by skilled health staff (% of total)	..		100	
Maternal mortality ratio (per 100,000 live births)	23		12	
Economic structure, participation, and access to resources				
Labor force participation rate (% of population ages 15+)	..	..	..	..
Wage and salaried workers (% of employed ages 15+)	..	..	73	67
Self-employed workers (% of employed ages 15+)	..	..	27	33
Vulnerable employment (% of employed ages 15+)	..	..	25	28
Unpaid family workers (% of employed ages 15+)	..	..	13.3	4.7
Employment in agriculture (% of employed ages 15+)	..	..	21	23
Employment in industry (% of employed ages 15+)	..	..	16	34
Employment in service (% of employed ages 15+)	..	..	63	43
Women in wage employment in the nonagricultural sector (%)	39		44	
Women's share of part-time employment (% of total)	..		..	
Maternity leave (weeks)	..		52	
Maternal leave benefits (% of wages paid)	..		100	
Female legislators, senior officials and managers (% of total)	..		33	
Employment to population ratio, total (% ages 15+)	..	..	..	..
Employment to population ratio, youth (% ages 15–24)	..	..	..	..
Children in employment (% of children ages 7–14)	..	..	..	..
Unemployment rate (% of labor force ages 15+)	..	..	20.4	18.3
Long-term unemployment rate (% total unemployment)	..	..	70.6	72.4
Youth unemployment rate (% of labor force ages 15–24)	..	..	41	31
Account at a formal financial institution (% age 15+)	..	..	62	62
Public life and decision making				
Seats held by women in national parliament (%)	..		33	

Seychelles

Sub-Saharan Africa	Upper middle income
Population (thousands)	86.0
GNI, Atlas ($ millions)	969.3
GNI per capita, Atlas ($)	11,270
Population living below $1.25 a day (%)	<2

	1990		2011	
	Female	Male	Female	Male
Demography				
Sex ratio at birth (boys per girls)	..		..	
Life expectancy at birth (years)	74	68	77	70
Under-five mortality rate (per 1,000 live births)	15	18	13	15
Female-headed households (%)	..		..	
Education				
Gross primary enrollment ratio (% of relevant age group)	109	112	113	113
Gross secondary enrollment ratio (% of relevant age group)	121	123	131	117
Gross tertiary enrollment ratio (% of relevant age group)	..	..	4	1
Primary completion rate (% of relevant age group)	116	112	127	123
Youth literacy rate (% of population ages 15–24)	98	97	99	99
Health and related services				
Total fertility rate (births per woman)	2.7		2.1	
Adolescent fertility rate (births per 1,000 women ages 15–19)	..		..	
Women first married by age 18 (% of women ages 20–24)	..		..	
Contraceptive prevalence (% of women ages 15–49)	..		..	
Unmet need for contraception (% of women ages 15–49)	..		..	
Pregnant women receiving prenatal care (%)	..		..	
Births attended by skilled health staff (% of total)	..		..	
Maternal mortality ratio (per 100,000 live births)	..		..	
Economic structure, participation, and access to resources				
Labor force participation rate (% of population ages 15+)	..	..	..	..
Wage and salaried workers (% of employed ages 15+)	86	79	..	..
Self-employed workers (% of employed ages 15+)	6	15	..	..
Vulnerable employment (% of employed ages 15+)	..	..	..	..
Unpaid family workers (% of employed ages 15+)	..	..	..	..
Employment in agriculture (% of employed ages 15+)	..	..	..	..
Employment in industry (% of employed ages 15+)	..	..	..	..
Employment in service (% of employed ages 15+)	..	..	..	..
Women in wage employment in the nonagricultural sector (%)	49		..	
Women's share of part-time employment (% of total)	..		..	
Maternity leave (weeks)	14		..	
Maternal leave benefits (% of wages paid)	..		..	
Female legislators, senior officials and managers (% of total)	..		..	
Employment to population ratio, total (% ages 15+)	..	..	..	..
Employment to population ratio, youth (% ages 15–24)	..	..	..	..
Children in employment (% of children ages 7–14)	..	..	..	..
Unemployment rate (% of labor force ages 15+)	12.5	8.6	..	..
Long-term unemployment rate (% total unemployment)	..	..	..	..
Youth unemployment rate (% of labor force ages 15–24)	28	18	..	..
Account at a formal financial institution (% age 15+)	..	..	..	..
Public life and decision making				
Seats held by women in national parliament (%)	16		44	

Sierra Leone

Sub-Saharan Africa	Low income
Population (millions)	6.0
GNI, Atlas ($ billions)	2.8
GNI per capita, Atlas ($)	460
Population living below $1.25 a day (%)	53.4

	1990		2011	
	Female	Male	Female	Male
Demography				
Sex ratio at birth (boys per girls)	1.02		1.02	
Life expectancy at birth (years)	40	37	48	47
Under-five mortality rate (per 1,000 live births)	253	280	176	194
Female-headed households (%)	..		22	
Education				
Gross primary enrollment ratio (% of relevant age group)	42	63	120	129
Gross secondary enrollment ratio (% of relevant age group)	12	23	..	..
Gross tertiary enrollment ratio (% of relevant age group)	..	..	..	..
Primary completion rate (% of relevant age group)	..	..	71	78
Youth literacy rate (% of population ages 15–24)	..	..	50	69
Health and related services				
Total fertility rate (births per woman)	5.7		4.9	
Adolescent fertility rate (births per 1,000 women ages 15–19)	..		112	
Women first married by age 18 (% of women ages 20–24)	..		44	
Contraceptive prevalence (% of women ages 15–49)	3		11	
Unmet need for contraception (% of women ages 15–49)	..		28	
Pregnant women receiving prenatal care (%)	..		93	
Births attended by skilled health staff (% of total)	..		63	
Maternal mortality ratio (per 100,000 live births)	1,300		890	
Economic structure, participation, and access to resources				
Labor force participation rate (% of population ages 15+)	65	67	66	69
Wage and salaried workers (% of employed ages 15+)	..	..	..	..
Self-employed workers (% of employed ages 15+)	..	..	..	..
Vulnerable employment (% of employed ages 15+)	..	..	..	..
Unpaid family workers (% of employed ages 15+)	..	..	..	..
Employment in agriculture (% of employed ages 15+)	..	..	..	..
Employment in industry (% of employed ages 15+)	..	..	..	..
Employment in service (% of employed ages 15+)	..	..	..	..
Women in wage employment in the nonagricultural sector (%)	..		..	
Women's share of part-time employment (% of total)	..		..	
Maternity leave (weeks)	..		..	
Maternal leave benefits (% of wages paid)	..		..	
Female legislators, senior officials and managers (% of total)	..		..	
Employment to population ratio, total (% ages 15+)	63	64	65	66
Employment to population ratio, youth (% ages 15–24)	44	33	47	37
Children in employment (% of children ages 7–14)	..	..	52.5	55.0
Unemployment rate (% of labor force ages 15+)	..	..	..	..
Long-term unemployment rate (% total unemployment)	..	..	..	..
Youth unemployment rate (% of labor force ages 15–24)	..	..	..	..
Account at a formal financial institution (% age 15+)	..	..	13	18
Public life and decision making				
Seats held by women in national parliament (%)	..		12	

Singapore

High income

Population (millions)	5.2
GNI, Atlas ($ billions)	222.6
GNI per capita, Atlas ($)	42,930
Population living below $1.25 a day (%)	..

	1990		2011	
	Female	Male	Female	Male
Demography				
Sex ratio at birth (boys per girls)	1.07		1.07	
Life expectancy at birth (years)	78	73	84	80
Under-five mortality rate (per 1,000 live births)	7	8	2	3
Female-headed households (%)	..		..	
Education				
Gross primary enrollment ratio (% of relevant age group)	..	..	..	..
Gross secondary enrollment ratio (% of relevant age group)	..	..	..	..
Gross tertiary enrollment ratio (% of relevant age group)	..	..	..	..
Primary completion rate (% of relevant age group)	..	..	..	..
Youth literacy rate (% of population ages 15–24)	99	99	100	100
Health and related services				
Total fertility rate (births per woman)	1.9		1.2	
Adolescent fertility rate (births per 1,000 women ages 15–19)	..		6	
Women first married by age 18 (% of women ages 20–24)	..		..	
Contraceptive prevalence (% of women ages 15–49)	65		..	
Unmet need for contraception (% of women ages 15–49)	..		..	
Pregnant women receiving prenatal care (%)	..		..	
Births attended by skilled health staff (% of total)	..		..	
Maternal mortality ratio (per 100,000 live births)	6		3	
Economic structure, participation, and access to resources				
Labor force participation rate (% of population ages 15+)	51	79	57	77
Wage and salaried workers (% of employed ages 15+)	91	82	90	81
Self-employed workers (% of employed ages 15+)	9	18	10	19
Vulnerable employment (% of employed ages 15+)	6	10	7	12
Unpaid family workers (% of employed ages 15+)	2.4	0.4	1.2	0.4
Employment in agriculture (% of employed ages 15+)	0	0	1	2
Employment in industry (% of employed ages 15+)	33	37	17	26
Employment in service (% of employed ages 15+)	67	63	83	73
Women in wage employment in the nonagricultural sector (%)	43		45	
Women's share of part-time employment (% of total)	..		..	
Maternity leave (weeks)	8		12	
Maternal leave benefits (% of wages paid)	100		100	
Female legislators, senior officials and managers (% of total)	17		34	
Employment to population ratio, total (% ages 15+)	50	79	54	74
Employment to population ratio, youth (% ages 15–24)	55	57	33	37
Children in employment (% of children ages 7–14)	..	..	..	..
Unemployment rate (% of labor force ages 15+)	2.0	2.5	3.2	2.6
Long-term unemployment rate (% total unemployment)	..	..	..	..
Youth unemployment rate (% of labor force ages 15–24)	3	3	..	..
Account at a formal financial institution (% age 15+)	..	..	98	98
Public life and decision making				
Seats held by women in national parliament (%)	5		24	

Sint Maarten (Dutch part)

	High income
Population (thousands)	36.6
GNI, Atlas ($ millions)	..
GNI per capita, Atlas ($)	..
Population living below $1.25 a day (%)	..

	1990		2011	
	Female	Male	Female	Male
Demography				
Sex ratio at birth (boys per girls)	..		..	
Life expectancy at birth (years)	..	..	78	73
Under-five mortality rate (per 1,000 live births)	..	..	..	..
Female-headed households (%)	..		..	
Education				
Gross primary enrollment ratio (% of relevant age group)	..	..	..	..
Gross secondary enrollment ratio (% of relevant age group)	..	..	..	..
Gross tertiary enrollment ratio (% of relevant age group)	..	..	..	..
Primary completion rate (% of relevant age group)	..	..	..	..
Youth literacy rate (% of population ages 15–24)	..	..	..	..
Health and related services				
Total fertility rate (births per woman)	..		1.7	
Adolescent fertility rate (births per 1,000 women ages 15–19)	..		..	
Women first married by age 18 (% of women ages 20–24)	..		..	
Contraceptive prevalence (% of women ages 15–49)	..		..	
Unmet need for contraception (% of women ages 15–49)	..		..	
Pregnant women receiving prenatal care (%)	..		..	
Births attended by skilled health staff (% of total)	..		..	
Maternal mortality ratio (per 100,000 live births)	..		..	
Economic structure, participation, and access to resources				
Labor force participation rate (% of population ages 15+)	..	..	..	..
Wage and salaried workers (% of employed ages 15+)	..	..	..	..
Self-employed workers (% of employed ages 15+)	..	..	..	..
Vulnerable employment (% of employed ages 15+)	..	..	..	..
Unpaid family workers (% of employed ages 15+)	..	..	..	..
Employment in agriculture (% of employed ages 15+)	..	..	..	..
Employment in industry (% of employed ages 15+)	..	..	..	..
Employment in service (% of employed ages 15+)	..	..	..	..
Women in wage employment in the nonagricultural sector (%)	..		..	
Women's share of part-time employment (% of total)	..		..	
Maternity leave (weeks)	..		..	
Maternal leave benefits (% of wages paid)	..		..	
Female legislators, senior officials and managers (% of total)	..		..	
Employment to population ratio, total (% ages 15+)	..	..	..	..
Employment to population ratio, youth (% ages 15–24)	..	..	..	..
Children in employment (% of children ages 7–14)	..	..	..	..
Unemployment rate (% of labor force ages 15+)	..	..	..	..
Long-term unemployment rate (% total unemployment)	..	..	..	..
Youth unemployment rate (% of labor force ages 15–24)	..	..	..	..
Account at a formal financial institution (% age 15+)	..	..	..	..
Public life and decision making				
Seats held by women in national parliament (%)	..		..	

Slovak Republic

High income

Population (millions)	5.4
GNI, Atlas ($ billions)	87.4
GNI per capita, Atlas ($)	16,190
Population living below $1.25 a day (%)	<2

	1990		2011	
	Female	**Male**	**Female**	**Male**
Demography				
Sex ratio at birth (boys per girls)	1.05		1.05	
Life expectancy at birth (years)	75	67	80	72
Under-five mortality rate (per 1,000 live births)	15	20	7	9
Female-headed households (%)	..		..	
Education				
Gross primary enrollment ratio (% of relevant age group)	*100*	*100*	*101*	*101*
Gross secondary enrollment ratio (% of relevant age group)	*89*	*86*	*91*	*90*
Gross tertiary enrollment ratio (% of relevant age group)	*16*	*16*	*67*	*43*
Primary completion rate (% of relevant age group)	*96*	*95*	*99*	*98*
Youth literacy rate (% of population ages 15–24)	..	..	..	..
Health and related services				
Total fertility rate (births per woman)	2.1		1.5	
Adolescent fertility rate (births per 1,000 women ages 15–19)	..		17	
Women first married by age 18 (% of women ages 20–24)	..		..	
Contraceptive prevalence (% of women ages 15–49)	74		..	
Unmet need for contraception (% of women ages 15–49)	..		..	
Pregnant women receiving prenatal care (%)	..		..	
Births attended by skilled health staff (% of total)	100		*100*	
Maternal mortality ratio (per 100,000 live births)	15		6	
Economic structure, participation, and access to resources				
Labor force participation rate (% of population ages 15+)	59	72	51	68
Wage and salaried workers (% of employed ages 15+)	97	91	90	79
Self-employed workers (% of employed ages 15+)	3	9	10	21
Vulnerable employment (% of employed ages 15+)	3	6	8	16
Unpaid family workers (% of employed ages 15+)	0.2	0.0	0.1	0.0
Employment in agriculture (% of employed ages 15+)	7	13	2	4
Employment in industry (% of employed ages 15+)	29	48	21	50
Employment in service (% of employed ages 15+)	64	39	77	46
Women in wage employment in the nonagricultural sector (%)	47		49	
Women's share of part-time employment (% of total)	72		62	
Maternity leave (weeks)	..		28	
Maternal leave benefits (% of wages paid)	..		55	
Female legislators, senior officials and managers (% of total)	23		31	
Employment to population ratio, total (% ages 15+)	53	66	44	59
Employment to population ratio, youth (% ages 15–24)	45	48	17	25
Children in employment (% of children ages 7–14)	..	..	..	..
Unemployment rate (% of labor force ages 15+)	11.8	12.5	13.5	13.5
Long-term unemployment rate (% total unemployment)	42.9	40.8	62.5	65.0
Youth unemployment rate (% of labor force ages 15–24)	27	28	34	33
Account at a formal financial institution (% age 15+)	..	..	79	80
Public life and decision making				
Seats held by women in national parliament (%)	..		19	

Slovenia

Population (millions)	2.1
GNI, Atlas ($ billions)	48.5
GNI per capita, Atlas ($)	23,600
Population living below $1.25 a day (%)	<2

	1990		2011	
	Female	Male	Female	Male
Demography				
Sex ratio at birth (boys per girls)	1.05		1.05	
Life expectancy at birth (years)	77	69	83	77
Under-five mortality rate (per 1,000 live births)	9	12	3	3
Female-headed households (%)	..		..	
Education				
Gross primary enrollment ratio (% of relevant age group)	97	97	98	99
Gross secondary enrollment ratio (% of relevant age group)	92	87	97	98
Gross tertiary enrollment ratio (% of relevant age group)	27	22	106	74
Primary completion rate (% of relevant age group)	..	..	96	97
Youth literacy rate (% of population ages 15-24)	100	100	100	100
Health and related services				
Total fertility rate (births per woman)	1.5		1.6	
Adolescent fertility rate (births per 1,000 women ages 15-19)	..		5	
Women first married by age 18 (% of women ages 20-24)	..		..	
Contraceptive prevalence (% of women ages 15-49)	..		..	
Unmet need for contraception (% of women ages 15-49)	..		..	
Pregnant women receiving prenatal care (%)	98		..	
Births attended by skilled health staff (% of total)	100		100	
Maternal mortality ratio (per 100,000 live births)	11		12	
Economic structure, participation, and access to resources				
Labor force participation rate (% of population ages 15+)	47	59	53	65
Wage and salaried workers (% of employed ages 15+)	88	82	87	80
Self-employed workers (% of employed ages 15+)	12	18	13	20
Vulnerable employment (% of employed ages 15+)	10	14	11	15
Unpaid family workers (% of employed ages 15+)	4.6	2.0	5.3	3.4
Employment in agriculture (% of employed ages 15+)	10	11	9	9
Employment in industry (% of employed ages 15+)	36	52	21	43
Employment in service (% of employed ages 15+)	54	37	71	48
Women in wage employment in the nonagricultural sector (%)	48		48	
Women's share of part-time employment (% of total)	..		58	
Maternity leave (weeks)			15	
Maternal leave benefits (% of wages paid)	..		100	
Female legislators, senior officials and managers (% of total)	26		38	
Employment to population ratio, total (% ages 15+)	44	57	49	60
Employment to population ratio, youth (% ages 15-24)	27	30	30	37
Children in employment (% of children ages 7-14)	..	..	..	..
Unemployment rate (% of labor force ages 15+)	6.0	8.1	8.2	8.2
Long-term unemployment rate (% total unemployment)	50.0	57.1	43.1	45.1
Youth unemployment rate (% of labor force ages 15-24)	19	25	17	15
Account at a formal financial institution (% age 15+)	..	..	98	96
Public life and decision making				
Seats held by women in national parliament (%)	..		32	

Solomon Islands

Population (thousands)	552.3
GNI, Atlas ($ millions)	615.2
GNI per capita, Atlas ($)	1,110
Population living below $1.25 a day (%)	..

	1990		2011	
	Female	Male	Female	Male
Demography				
Sex ratio at birth (boys per girls)	1.09		1.09	
Life expectancy at birth (years)	57	56	69	66
Under-five mortality rate (per 1,000 live births)	43	41	22	21
Female-headed households (%)	..		..	
Education				
Gross primary enrollment ratio (% of relevant age group)	82	95	144	146
Gross secondary enrollment ratio (% of relevant age group)	11	17	45	51
Gross tertiary enrollment ratio (% of relevant age group)	..	..	..	..
Primary completion rate (% of relevant age group)	47	60	..	..
Youth literacy rate (% of population ages 15–24)	..	..	..	..
Health and related services				
Total fertility rate (births per woman)	5.9		4.2	
Adolescent fertility rate (births per 1,000 women ages 15–19)	..		66	
Women first married by age 18 (% of women ages 20–24)	..		22	
Contraceptive prevalence (% of women ages 15–49)	..		35	
Unmet need for contraception (% of women ages 15–49)	..		11	
Pregnant women receiving prenatal care (%)	..		74	
Births attended by skilled health staff (% of total)	85		86	
Maternal mortality ratio (per 100,000 live births)	150		93	
Economic structure, participation, and access to resources				
Labor force participation rate (% of population ages 15+)	53	77	53	80
Wage and salaried workers (% of employed ages 15+)	..	..	..	..
Self-employed workers (% of employed ages 15+)	..	..	..	..
Vulnerable employment (% of employed ages 15+)	..	..	..	..
Unpaid family workers (% of employed ages 15+)	..	..	..	..
Employment in agriculture (% of employed ages 15+)	..	..	..	..
Employment in industry (% of employed ages 15+)	..	..	..	..
Employment in service (% of employed ages 15+)	..	..	..	..
Women in wage employment in the nonagricultural sector (%)	..		..	
Women's share of part-time employment (% of total)			..	
Maternity leave (weeks)	12		12	
Maternal leave benefits (% of wages paid)	25		25	
Female legislators, senior officials and managers (% of total)	..		..	
Employment to population ratio, total (% ages 15+)	50	74	51	77
Employment to population ratio, youth (% ages 15–24)	37	51	38	52
Children in employment (% of children ages 7–14)	..	..	..	..
Unemployment rate (% of labor force ages 15+)	..	..	..	..
Long-term unemployment rate (% total unemployment)	..	..	..	..
Youth unemployment rate (% of labor force ages 15–24)	..	..	..	..
Account at a formal financial institution (% age 15+)	..	..	..	..
Public life and decision making				
Seats held by women in national parliament (%)	0		2	

Somalia

Sub-Saharan Africa	Low income
Population (millions)	9.6
GNI, Atlas ($ millions)	..
GNI per capita, Atlas ($)	..
Population living below $1.25 a day (%)	..

	1990		2011	
	Female	Male	Female	Male
Demography				
Sex ratio at birth (boys per girls)	1.03		1.03	
Life expectancy at birth (years)	46	43	53	50
Under-five mortality rate (per 1,000 live births)	170	190	170	190
Female-headed households (%)	..		..	
Education				
Gross primary enrollment ratio (% of relevant age group)	9	18	23	42
Gross secondary enrollment ratio (% of relevant age group)	7	13	5	11
Gross tertiary enrollment ratio (% of relevant age group)	1	4	..	..
Primary completion rate (% of relevant age group)	..	..	..	..
Youth literacy rate (% of population ages 15–24)	..	..	..	..
Health and related services				
Total fertility rate (births per woman)	6.6		6.3	
Adolescent fertility rate (births per 1,000 women ages 15–19)	..		68	
Women first married by age 18 (% of women ages 20–24)	..		45	
Contraceptive prevalence (% of women ages 15–49)	..		15	
Unmet need for contraception (% of women ages 15–49)	..		26	
Pregnant women receiving prenatal care (%)	..		26	
Births attended by skilled health staff (% of total)	..		33	
Maternal mortality ratio (per 100,000 live births)	890		1,000	
Economic structure, participation, and access to resources				
Labor force participation rate (% of population ages 15+)	35	78	38	77
Wage and salaried workers (% of employed ages 15+)	..	..	..	..
Self-employed workers (% of employed ages 15+)	..	..	..	..
Vulnerable employment (% of employed ages 15+)	..	..	..	..
Unpaid family workers (% of employed ages 15+)	..	..	..	..
Employment in agriculture (% of employed ages 15+)	..	..	..	..
Employment in industry (% of employed ages 15+)	..	..	..	..
Employment in service (% of employed ages 15+)	..	..	..	..
Women in wage employment in the nonagricultural sector (%)	22		..	
Women's share of part-time employment (% of total)	..		..	
Maternity leave (weeks)	14		14	
Maternal leave benefits (% of wages paid)	50		50	
Female legislators, senior officials and managers (% of total)	..		..	
Employment to population ratio, total (% ages 15+)	33	73	35	72
Employment to population ratio, youth (% ages 15–24)	30	57	28	52
Children in employment (% of children ages 7–14)	..	..	41.5	45.5
Unemployment rate (% of labor force ages 15+)	..	..	..	..
Long-term unemployment rate (% total unemployment)	..	..	..	..
Youth unemployment rate (% of labor force ages 15–24)	..	..	..	..
Account at a formal financial institution (% age 15+)	..	..	27	35
Public life and decision making				
Seats held by women in national parliament (%)	4		14	

South Africa

Sub-Saharan Africa			Upper middle income	
Population (millions)				50.6
GNI, Atlas ($ billions)				352.0
GNI per capita, Atlas ($)				6,960
Population living below $1.25 a day (%)				13.8

	1990		2011	
	Female	Male	Female	Male
Demography				
Sex ratio at birth (boys per girls)	1.03		1.03	
Life expectancy at birth (years)	65	58	53	52
Under-five mortality rate (per 1,000 live births)	58	66	44	50
Female-headed households (%)	..		..	
Education				
Gross primary enrollment ratio (% of relevant age group)	106	107	100	104
Gross secondary enrollment ratio (% of relevant age group)	71	61	96	92
Gross tertiary enrollment ratio (% of relevant age group)	11	13		
Primary completion rate (% of relevant age group)	80	72	..	..
Youth literacy rate (% of population ages 15–24)	..	..	98	97
Health and related services				
Total fertility rate (births per woman)	3.7		2.4	
Adolescent fertility rate (births per 1,000 women ages 15–19)	..		52	
Women first married by age 18 (% of women ages 20–24)	..		..	
Contraceptive prevalence (% of women ages 15–49)	57		..	
Unmet need for contraception (% of women ages 15–49)	..		..	
Pregnant women receiving prenatal care (%)	..		97	
Births attended by skilled health staff (% of total)	..		..	
Maternal mortality ratio (per 100,000 live births)	250		300	
Economic structure, participation, and access to resources				
Labor force participation rate (% of population ages 15+)	33	64	44	61
Wage and salaried workers (% of employed ages 15+)	..	..	86	83
Self-employed workers (% of employed ages 15+)	..	..	13	16
Vulnerable employment (% of employed ages 15+)	..	..	11	9
Unpaid family workers (% of employed ages 15+)	..	..	1.2	0.5
Employment in agriculture (% of employed ages 15+)	..	..	4	6
Employment in industry (% of employed ages 15+)	..	..	13	33
Employment in service (% of employed ages 15+)	..	..	68	58
Women in wage employment in the nonagricultural sector (%)	..		45	
Women's share of part-time employment (% of total)	..		63	
Maternity leave (weeks)	..		17	
Maternal leave benefits (% of wages paid)	..		60	
Female legislators, senior officials and managers (% of total)	..		31	
Employment to population ratio, total (% ages 15+)	25	49	32	47
Employment to population ratio, youth (% ages 15–24)	12	19	11	15
Children in employment (% of children ages 7–14)	..	..	..	..
Unemployment rate (% of labor force ages 15+)	23.5	17.2	27.7	22.3
Long-term unemployment rate (% total unemployment)	..	..	32.8	33.0
Youth unemployment rate (% of labor force ages 15–24)	..	..	55	45
Account at a formal financial institution (% age 15+)	..	..	51	56
Public life and decision making				
Seats held by women in national parliament (%)	3		42	

South Sudan

Sub-Saharan Africa	Lower middle income
Population (millions)	10.3
GNI, Atlas ($ millions)	..
GNI per capita, Atlas ($)	..
Population living below $1.25 a day (%)	..

	1990		2011	
	Female	Male	Female	Male
Demography				
Sex ratio at birth (boys per girls)			..	
Life expectancy at birth (years)	..	..	61	62
Under-five mortality rate (per 1,000 live births)	215	220	119	122
Female-headed households (%)	..		..	
Education				
Gross primary enrollment ratio (% of relevant age group)	..	..	..	..
Gross secondary enrollment ratio (% of relevant age group)	..	..	..	..
Gross tertiary enrollment ratio (% of relevant age group)	..	..	..	..
Primary completion rate (% of relevant age group)	..	..	..	..
Youth literacy rate (% of population ages 15–24)	..	..	..	..
Health and related services				
Total fertility rate (births per woman)		..	3.9	
Adolescent fertility rate (births per 1,000 women ages 15–19)		..	..	
Women first married by age 18 (% of women ages 20–24)		..	52	
Contraceptive prevalence (% of women ages 15–49)		..	4	
Unmet need for contraception (% of women ages 15–49)		..		
Pregnant women receiving prenatal care (%)		..	40	
Births attended by skilled health staff (% of total)		..	19	
Maternal mortality ratio (per 100,000 live births)		..	..	
Economic structure, participation, and access to resources				
Labor force participation rate (% of population ages 15+)	..	..	..	..
Wage and salaried workers (% of employed ages 15+)	..	..	..	..
Self-employed workers (% of employed ages 15+)	..	..	..	..
Vulnerable employment (% of employed ages 15+)	..	..	..	..
Unpaid family workers (% of employed ages 15+)	..	..	..	..
Employment in agriculture (% of employed ages 15+)	..	..	..	..
Employment in industry (% of employed ages 15+)	..	..	..	..
Employment in service (% of employed ages 15+)	..	..	..	..
Women in wage employment in the nonagricultural sector (%)	..		..	
Women's share of part-time employment (% of total)	..		..	
Maternity leave (weeks)	..		..	
Maternal leave benefits (% of wages paid)	..		..	
Female legislators, senior officials and managers (% of total)	..		..	
Employment to population ratio, total (% ages 15+)	..	..	..	..
Employment to population ratio, youth (% ages 15–24)	..	..	..	..
Children in employment (% of children ages 7–14)	..	..	45.7	45.6
Unemployment rate (% of labor force ages 15+)	..	..	..	..
Long-term unemployment rate (% total unemployment)	..	..	..	..
Youth unemployment rate (% of labor force ages 15–24)	..	..	..	..
Account at a formal financial institution (% age 15+)	..	..	..	..
Public life and decision making				
Seats held by women in national parliament (%)		..	27	

Spain

High income

Population (millions)	46.2
GNI, Atlas ($ billions)	1,428.3
GNI per capita, Atlas ($)	30,930
Population living below $1.25 a day (%)	..

	1990 Female	1990 Male	2011 Female	2011 Male
Demography				
Sex ratio at birth (boys per girls)	1.06		1.06	
Life expectancy at birth (years)	81	73	85	79
Under-five mortality rate (per 1,000 live births)	10	12	4	5
Female-headed households (%)	..		..	
Education				
Gross primary enrollment ratio (% of relevant age group)	105	107	105	106
Gross secondary enrollment ratio (% of relevant age group)	105	99	126	123
Gross tertiary enrollment ratio (% of relevant age group)	37	34	86	70
Primary completion rate (% of relevant age group)	101	102	103	104
Youth literacy rate (% of population ages 15–24)	100	100	100	100
Health and related services				
Total fertility rate (births per woman)	1.3		1.4	
Adolescent fertility rate (births per 1,000 women ages 15–19)	..		11	
Women first married by age 18 (% of women ages 20–24)	..		..	
Contraceptive prevalence (% of women ages 15–49)	..		66	
Unmet need for contraception (% of women ages 15–49)	..		..	
Pregnant women receiving prenatal care (%)	..		..	
Births attended by skilled health staff (% of total)	..		..	
Maternal mortality ratio (per 100,000 live births)	7		6	
Economic structure, participation, and access to resources				
Labor force participation rate (% of population ages 15+)	34	69	52	67
Wage and salaried workers (% of employed ages 15+)	73	74	88	80
Self-employed workers (% of employed ages 15+)	27	26	12	20
Vulnerable employment (% of employed ages 15+)	25	21	9	13
Unpaid family workers (% of employed ages 15+)	10.5	3.0	1.0	0.6
Employment in agriculture (% of employed ages 15+)	10	13	2	6
Employment in industry (% of employed ages 15+)	17	41	9	32
Employment in service (% of employed ages 15+)	73	47	89	62
Women in wage employment in the nonagricultural sector (%)	32		47	
Women's share of part-time employment (% of total)	79		77	
Maternity leave (weeks)	16		16	
Maternal leave benefits (% of wages paid)	75		100	
Female legislators, senior officials and managers (% of total)	30		30	
Employment to population ratio, total (% ages 15+)	26	60	40	53
Employment to population ratio, youth (% ages 15–24)	26	44	22	24
Children in employment (% of children ages 7–14)	..	..	..	..
Unemployment rate (% of labor force ages 15+)	24.5	11.6	22.2	21.2
Long-term unemployment rate (% total unemployment)	58.5	43.3	42.7	40.6
Youth unemployment rate (% of labor force ages 15–24)	40	23	44	48
Account at a formal financial institution (% age 15+)	..	..	92	95
Public life and decision making				
Seats held by women in national parliament (%)	15		36	

Sri Lanka

South Asia			Lower middle income	

Population (millions)	20.9
GNI, Atlas ($ billions)	53.8
GNI per capita, Atlas ($)	2,580
Population living below $1.25 a day (%)	4.1

	1990		2011	
	Female	Male	Female	Male
Demography				
Sex ratio at birth (boys per girls)	1.04		1.04	
Life expectancy at birth (years)	73	66	78	72
Under-five mortality rate (per 1,000 live births)	27	31	11	13
Female-headed households (%)	..		..	
Education				
Gross primary enrollment ratio (% of relevant age group)	108	112	99	99
Gross secondary enrollment ratio (% of relevant age group)	75	69	102	99
Gross tertiary enrollment ratio (% of relevant age group)	3	6	20	11
Primary completion rate (% of relevant age group)	97	97	101	101
Youth literacy rate (% of population ages 15–24)	..	..	99	98
Health and related services				
Total fertility rate (births per woman)	2.5		2.3	
Adolescent fertility rate (births per 1,000 women ages 15–19)	..		22	
Women first married by age 18 (% of women ages 20–24)	14		12	
Contraceptive prevalence (% of women ages 15–49)	66		68	
Unmet need for contraception (% of women ages 15–49)	..		..	
Pregnant women receiving prenatal care (%)	80		99	
Births attended by skilled health staff (% of total)	94		99	
Maternal mortality ratio (per 100,000 live births)	85		35	
Economic structure, participation, and access to resources				
Labor force participation rate (% of population ages 15+)	36	78	35	76
Wage and salaried workers (% of employed ages 15+)	66	58	54	56
Self-employed workers (% of employed ages 15+)	34	42	46	44
Vulnerable employment (% of employed ages 15+)	34	40	45	40
Unpaid family workers (% of employed ages 15+)	18.7	6.7	22.4	4.4
Employment in agriculture (% of employed ages 15+)	43	37	38	30
Employment in industry (% of employed ages 15+)	22	19	25	24
Employment in service (% of employed ages 15+)	32	38	27	28
Women in wage employment in the nonagricultural sector (%)	..		31	
Women's share of part-time employment (% of total)	..		..	
Maternity leave (weeks)	12		12	
Maternal leave benefits (% of wages paid)	100		100	
Female legislators, senior officials and managers (% of total)	..		24	
Employment to population ratio, total (% ages 15+)	28	69	33	74
Employment to population ratio, youth (% ages 15–24)	15	40	20	42
Children in employment (% of children ages 7–14)	..		8.5	13.0
Unemployment rate (% of labor force ages 15+)	21.6	9.7	7.7	3.5
Long-term unemployment rate (% total unemployment)	..	..	..	..
Youth unemployment rate (% of labor force ages 15–24)	..	..	25	16
Account at a formal financial institution (% age 15+)	..	..	67	70
Public life and decision making				
Seats held by women in national parliament (%)	5		6	

St. Kitts and Nevis

	High income
Population (thousands)	53.1
GNI, Atlas ($ millions)	668.9
GNI per capita, Atlas ($)	12,610
Population living below $1.25 a day (%)	..

	1990		2011	
	Female	Male	Female	Male
Demography				
Sex ratio at birth (boys per girls)	..		..	
Life expectancy at birth (years)	70	66	..	..
Under-five mortality rate (per 1,000 live births)	25	32	6	8
Female-headed households (%)	..		..	
Education				
Gross primary enrollment ratio (% of relevant age group)	111	116	91	89
Gross secondary enrollment ratio (% of relevant age group)	85	81	96	93
Gross tertiary enrollment ratio (% of relevant age group)	7	6	25	12
Primary completion rate (% of relevant age group)	104	131	98	88
Youth literacy rate (% of population ages 15–24)	..	..	..	..
Health and related services				
Total fertility rate (births per woman)	2.6		..	
Adolescent fertility rate (births per 1,000 women ages 15–19)	..		..	
Women first married by age 18 (% of women ages 20–24)	..		..	
Contraceptive prevalence (% of women ages 15–49)	..		54	
Unmet need for contraception (% of women ages 15–49)	..		..	
Pregnant women receiving prenatal care (%)	100		100	
Births attended by skilled health staff (% of total)	..		100	
Maternal mortality ratio (per 100,000 live births)	..		..	
Economic structure, participation, and access to resources				
Labor force participation rate (% of population ages 15+)	..	..	..	..
Wage and salaried workers (% of employed ages 15+)	84	81	..	..
Self-employed workers (% of employed ages 15+)	14	17	..	..
Vulnerable employment (% of employed ages 15+)	12	12	..	..
Unpaid family workers (% of employed ages 15+)	1.3	0.7	..	..
Employment in agriculture (% of employed ages 15+)	..	..	..	..
Employment in industry (% of employed ages 15+)	..	..	..	..
Employment in service (% of employed ages 15+)	..	..	..	..
Women in wage employment in the nonagricultural sector (%)	..		..	
Women's share of part-time employment (% of total)	..		..	
Maternity leave (weeks)	..		..	
Maternal leave benefits (% of wages paid)	..		..	
Female legislators, senior officials and managers (% of total)	..		..	
Employment to population ratio, total (% ages 15+)	..	..	..	..
Employment to population ratio, youth (% ages 15–24)	..	..	..	..
Children in employment (% of children ages 7–14)	..	..	..	..
Unemployment rate (% of labor force ages 15+)	..	..	..	..
Long-term unemployment rate (% total unemployment)	..	..	..	..
Youth unemployment rate (% of labor force ages 15–24)	..	..	..	..
Account at a formal financial institution (% age 15+)	..	..	..	..
Public life and decision making				
Seats held by women in national parliament (%)	7		7	

St. Lucia

Latin America & the Caribbean   **Upper middle income**

Population (thousands)	176.0
GNI, Atlas ($ billions)	1.2
GNI per capita, Atlas ($)	6,820
Population living below $1.25 a day (%)	..

	1990		2011	
	Female	**Male**	**Female**	**Male**
Demography				
Sex ratio at birth (boys per girls)	1.03		1.03	
Life expectancy at birth (years)	73	69	77	72
Under-five mortality rate (per 1,000 live births)	20	25	14	17
Female-headed households (%)	..		..	
Education				
Gross primary enrollment ratio (% of relevant age group)	136	142	92	94
Gross secondary enrollment ratio (% of relevant age group)	59	39	94	97
Gross tertiary enrollment ratio (% of relevant age group)	3	3	19	11
Primary completion rate (% of relevant age group)	120	120	93	93
Youth literacy rate (% of population ages 15–24)	..	..	..	..
Health and related services				
Total fertility rate (births per woman)	3.4		2.0	
Adolescent fertility rate (births per 1,000 women ages 15–19)	..		57	
Women first married by age 18 (% of women ages 20–24)	..		..	
Contraceptive prevalence (% of women ages 15–49)	47		..	
Unmet need for contraception (% of women ages 15–49)	..		..	
Pregnant women receiving prenatal care (%)	100		99	
Births attended by skilled health staff (% of total)	..		100	
Maternal mortality ratio (per 100,000 live births)	64		35	
Economic structure, participation, and access to resources				
Labor force participation rate (% of population ages 15+)	58	76	64	77
Wage and salaried workers (% of employed ages 15+)	74	57	..	..
Self-employed workers (% of employed ages 15+)	25	39	..	..
Vulnerable employment (% of employed ages 15+)	21	25	..	..
Unpaid family workers (% of employed ages 15+)	4.1	1.7	..	..
Employment in agriculture (% of employed ages 15+)	15	30	..	..
Employment in industry (% of employed ages 15+)	19	24	..	..
Employment in service (% of employed ages 15+)	64	43	..	..
Women in wage employment in the nonagricultural sector (%)	52		..	
Women's share of part-time employment (% of total)	..		..	
Maternity leave (weeks)	13		13	
Maternal leave benefits (% of wages paid)	60		65	
Female legislators, senior officials and managers (% of total)	50		..	
Employment to population ratio, total (% ages 15+)	..	..	..	..
Employment to population ratio, youth (% ages 15–24)	..	..	..	..
Children in employment (% of children ages 7–14)	..	..	..	..
Unemployment rate (% of labor force ages 15+)	7.0	6.6	18.5	10.0
Long-term unemployment rate (% total unemployment)	..	..	..	..
Youth unemployment rate (% of labor force ages 15–24)	15	15	..	..
Account at a formal financial institution (% age 15+)	..	..	..	..
Public life and decision making				
Seats held by women in national parliament (%)	0		17	

St. Martin (French part)

High income

Population (thousands)	30.6
GNI, Atlas ($ millions)	..
GNI per capita, Atlas ($)	..
Population living below $1.25 a day (%)	..

	1990		2011	
	Female	Male	Female	Male
Demography				
Sex ratio at birth (boys per girls)	..		..	
Life expectancy at birth (years)	..	..	..	..
Under-five mortality rate (per 1,000 live births)	..	..	..	..
Female-headed households (%)	..		..	
Education				
Gross primary enrollment ratio (% of relevant age group)	..	..	..	..
Gross secondary enrollment ratio (% of relevant age group)	..	..	..	..
Gross tertiary enrollment ratio (% of relevant age group)	..	..	..	..
Primary completion rate (% of relevant age group)	..	..	..	..
Youth literacy rate (% of population ages 15–24)	..	..	..	..
Health and related services				
Total fertility rate (births per woman)	2.1		1.8	
Adolescent fertility rate (births per 1,000 women ages 15–19)	..		..	
Women first married by age 18 (% of women ages 20–24)	..		..	
Contraceptive prevalence (% of women ages 15–49)	..		..	
Unmet need for contraception (% of women ages 15–49)	..		..	
Pregnant women receiving prenatal care (%)	..		..	
Births attended by skilled health staff (% of total)	..		..	
Maternal mortality ratio (per 100,000 live births)	..		..	
Economic structure, participation, and access to resources				
Labor force participation rate (% of population ages 15+)	..	..	..	..
Wage and salaried workers (% of employed ages 15+)	..	..	..	..
Self-employed workers (% of employed ages 15+)	..	..	..	..
Vulnerable employment (% of employed ages 15+)	..	..	..	..
Unpaid family workers (% of employed ages 15+)	..	..	..	..
Employment in agriculture (% of employed ages 15+)	..	..	..	..
Employment in industry (% of employed ages 15+)	..	..	..	..
Employment in service (% of employed ages 15+)	..	..	..	..
Women in wage employment in the nonagricultural sector (%)	..			
Women's share of part-time employment (% of total)	..		..	
Maternity leave (weeks)	..		..	
Maternal leave benefits (% of wages paid)	..		..	
Female legislators, senior officials and managers (% of total)	..		..	
Employment to population ratio, total (% ages 15+)	..	..	..	..
Employment to population ratio, youth (% ages 15–24)	..	..	..	..
Children in employment (% of children ages 7–14)	..	..	..	..
Unemployment rate (% of labor force ages 15+)	..	..	..	..
Long-term unemployment rate (% total unemployment)	..	..	..	..
Youth unemployment rate (% of labor force ages 15–24)	..	..	..	..
Account at a formal financial institution (% age 15+)	..	..	..	..
Public life and decision making				
Seats held by women in national parliament (%)	..		..	

St. Vincent and Grenadines

Latin America & the Caribbean	Upper middle income
Population (thousands)	109.4
GNI, Atlas ($ millions)	663.9
GNI per capita, Atlas ($)	6,070
Population living below $1.25 a day (%)	..

	1990		2011	
	Female	Male	Female	Male
Demography				
Sex ratio at birth (boys per girls)	1.03		1.03	
Life expectancy at birth (years)	72	67	74	70
Under-five mortality rate (per 1,000 live births)	24	29	19	23
Female-headed households (%)	..		..	
Education				
Gross primary enrollment ratio (% of relevant age group)	113	114	101	109
Gross secondary enrollment ratio (% of relevant age group)	67	54	109	106
Gross tertiary enrollment ratio (% of relevant age group)	8	4	..	..
Primary completion rate (% of relevant age group)	..	..	92	97
Youth literacy rate (% of population ages 15–24)	..	..		
Health and related services				
Total fertility rate (births per woman)	3.0		2.0	
Adolescent fertility rate (births per 1,000 women ages 15–19)	..		55	
Women first married by age 18 (% of women ages 20–24)	..		..	
Contraceptive prevalence (% of women ages 15–49)	58		48	
Unmet need for contraception (% of women ages 15–49)	..		..	
Pregnant women receiving prenatal care (%)	..		100	
Births attended by skilled health staff (% of total)	..		99	
Maternal mortality ratio (per 100,000 live births)	59		48	
Economic structure, participation, and access to resources				
Labor force participation rate (% of population ages 15+)	44	81	56	78
Wage and salaried workers (% of employed ages 15+)	79	71	..	..
Self-employed workers (% of employed ages 15+)	21	29	..	..
Vulnerable employment (% of employed ages 15+)	17	22	..	..
Unpaid family workers (% of employed ages 15+)	2.7	2.1	..	..
Employment in agriculture (% of employed ages 15+)	14	31	..	..
Employment in industry (% of employed ages 15+)	11	27	..	..
Employment in service (% of employed ages 15+)	75	43	..	..
Women in wage employment in the nonagricultural sector (%)	..		..	
Women's share of part-time employment (% of total)	..		..	
Maternity leave (weeks)	..		13	
Maternal leave benefits (% of wages paid)	..		65	
Female legislators, senior officials and managers (% of total)	..		..	
Employment to population ratio, total (% ages 15+)	..	..	..	..
Employment to population ratio, youth (% ages 15–24)	..	..	..	..
Children in employment (% of children ages 7–14)	..		..	
Unemployment rate (% of labor force ages 15+)	21.4	18.3	..	..
Long-term unemployment rate (% total unemployment)	..	..	..	..
Youth unemployment rate (% of labor force ages 15–24)	43	32	..	..
Account at a formal financial institution (% age 15+)	..	..	..	..
Public life and decision making				
Seats held by women in national parliament (%)	10		17	

Sudan

Sub-Saharan Africa	Lower middle income
Population (millions)	34.3[c]
GNI, Atlas ($ billions)	58.3[d]
GNI per capita, Atlas ($)	1,310[d]
Population living below $1.25 a day (%)	19.8

	1990		2011	
	Female	Male	Female	Male
Demography				
Sex ratio at birth (boys per girls)	1.05		1.05	
Life expectancy at birth (years)	54	51	63	60
Under-five mortality rate (per 1,000 live births)	116[c]	129[c]	81[c]	91[c]
Female-headed households (%)	..		19	
Education				
Gross primary enrollment ratio (% of relevant age group)	42	54	69	76
Gross secondary enrollment ratio (% of relevant age group)	18	23	36	41
Gross tertiary enrollment ratio (% of relevant age group)	2	3	..	..
Primary completion rate (% of relevant age group)	..	..	55	61
Youth literacy rate (% of population ages 15–24)	..	..	84	90
Health and related services				
Total fertility rate (births per woman)	6.0		4.3	
Adolescent fertility rate (births per 1,000 women ages 15–19)	..		55	
Women first married by age 18 (% of women ages 20–24)	27		33[c]	
Contraceptive prevalence (% of women ages 15–49)	9		9	
Unmet need for contraception (% of women ages 15–49)	..		6	
Pregnant women receiving prenatal care (%)	..		56[c]	
Births attended by skilled health staff (% of total)	69		23[c]	
Maternal mortality ratio (per 100,000 live births)	1,000		730	
Economic structure, participation, and access to resources				
Labor force participation rate (% of population ages 15+)	27	79	31	77
Wage and salaried workers (% of employed ages 15+)	..	..	..	..
Self-employed workers (% of employed ages 15+)	..	..	..	..
Vulnerable employment (% of employed ages 15+)	..	..	..	..
Unpaid family workers (% of employed ages 15+)	..	..	..	..
Employment in agriculture (% of employed ages 15+)	..	..	..	..
Employment in industry (% of employed ages 15+)	..	..	..	..
Employment in service (% of employed ages 15+)	..	..	..	..
Women in wage employment in the nonagricultural sector (%)	22		..	
Women's share of part-time employment (% of total)	..		..	
Maternity leave (weeks)	..		8	
Maternal leave benefits (% of wages paid)	..		100	
Female legislators, senior officials and managers (% of total)	..		..	
Employment to population ratio, total (% ages 15+)	23	72	26	72
Employment to population ratio, youth (% ages 15–24)	17	48	19	36
Children in employment (% of children ages 7–14)	..	..	9.5[c]	15.2[c]
Unemployment rate (% of labor force ages 15+)	..	..	..	..
Long-term unemployment rate (% total unemployment)	..	..	..	..
Youth unemployment rate (% of labor force ages 15–24)	..	..	..	..
Account at a formal financial institution (% age 15+)	..	..	4	9
Public life and decision making				
Seats held by women in national parliament (%)	..		25	

Suriname

Latin America & the Caribbean	Upper middle income
Population (thousands)	529.4
GNI, Atlas ($ billions)	4.1
GNI per capita, Atlas ($)	7,840
Population living below $1.25 a day (%)	..

	1990		2011	
	Female	Male	Female	Male
Demography				
Sex ratio at birth (boys per girls)	1.08		1.08	
Life expectancy at birth (years)	71	64	74	67
Under-five mortality rate (per 1,000 live births)	46	57	26	33
Female-headed households (%)	..		..	
Education				
Gross primary enrollment ratio (% of relevant age group)	123	112	112	118
Gross secondary enrollment ratio (% of relevant age group)	63	49	97	74
Gross tertiary enrollment ratio (% of relevant age group)	11	9	..	..
Primary completion rate (% of relevant age group)	96	81	93	82
Youth literacy rate (% of population ages 15–24)	..	..	99	98
Health and related services				
Total fertility rate (births per woman)	2.7		2.3	
Adolescent fertility rate (births per 1,000 women ages 15–19)	..		36	
Women first married by age 18 (% of women ages 20–24)	..		19	
Contraceptive prevalence (% of women ages 15–49)	48		46	
Unmet need for contraception (% of women ages 15–49)	..		..	
Pregnant women receiving prenatal care (%)	..		90	
Births attended by skilled health staff (% of total)	..		90	
Maternal mortality ratio (per 100,000 live births)	84		130	
Economic structure, participation, and access to resources				
Labor force participation rate (% of population ages 15+)	43	72	41	69
Wage and salaried workers (% of employed ages 15+)	..	..	..	..
Self-employed workers (% of employed ages 15+)	..	..	..	..
Vulnerable employment (% of employed ages 15+)	..	..	..	..
Unpaid family workers (% of employed ages 15+)	..	..	..	..
Employment in agriculture (% of employed ages 15+)	2	5	..	..
Employment in industry (% of employed ages 15+)	8	27	..	..
Employment in service (% of employed ages 15+)	87	65	..	..
Women in wage employment in the nonagricultural sector (%)	41		36	
Women's share of part-time employment (% of total)	68		..	
Maternity leave (weeks)	..		..	
Maternal leave benefits (% of wages paid)	..		..	
Female legislators, senior officials and managers (% of total)	..		..	
Employment to population ratio, total (% ages 15+)	34	62	33	63
Employment to population ratio, youth (% ages 15–24)	16	37	8	31
Children in employment (% of children ages 7–14)	..	..	..	..
Unemployment rate (% of labor force ages 15+)	20.1	12.6	..	..
Long-term unemployment rate (% total unemployment)	..	..	..	..
Youth unemployment rate (% of labor force ages 15–24)	47	29	..	..
Account at a formal financial institution (% age 15+)	..	..	..	..
Public life and decision making				
Seats held by women in national parliament (%)	8		12	

Swaziland

Sub-Saharan Africa	Lower middle income
Population (millions)	1.1
GNI, Atlas ($ billions)	3.7
GNI per capita, Atlas ($)	3,470
Population living below $1.25 a day (%)	40.6

	1990 Female	1990 Male	2011 Female	2011 Male
Demography				
Sex ratio at birth (boys per girls)	1.03		1.03	
Life expectancy at birth (years)	61	58	48	49
Under-five mortality rate (per 1,000 live births)	76	91	94	113
Female-headed households (%)	..		48	
Education				
Gross primary enrollment ratio (% of relevant age group)	94	94	109	121
Gross secondary enrollment ratio (% of relevant age group)	..	..	59	61
Gross tertiary enrollment ratio (% of relevant age group)	3	5	6	6
Primary completion rate (% of relevant age group)	66	59	78	76
Youth literacy rate (% of population ages 15–24)	84	83	95	92
Health and related services				
Total fertility rate (births per woman)	5.7		3.3	
Adolescent fertility rate (births per 1,000 women ages 15–19)	..		71	
Women first married by age 18 (% of women ages 20–24)	..		7	
Contraceptive prevalence (% of women ages 15–49)	20		65	
Unmet need for contraception (% of women ages 15–49)	..		24	
Pregnant women receiving prenatal care (%)	..		97	
Births attended by skilled health staff (% of total)	56		82	
Maternal mortality ratio (per 100,000 live births)	300		320	
Economic structure, participation, and access to resources				
Labor force participation rate (% of population ages 15+)	42	74	44	71
Wage and salaried workers (% of employed ages 15+)	..	..	..	..
Self-employed workers (% of employed ages 15+)	..	..	..	..
Vulnerable employment (% of employed ages 15+)	..	..	..	..
Unpaid family workers (% of employed ages 15+)	..	..	..	..
Employment in agriculture (% of employed ages 15+)	..	..	..	..
Employment in industry (% of employed ages 15+)	..	..	..	..
Employment in service (% of employed ages 15+)	..	..	..	..
Women in wage employment in the nonagricultural sector (%)	35		..	
Women's share of part-time employment (% of total)			..	
Maternity leave (weeks)	12		12	
Maternal leave benefits (% of wages paid)	0		..	
Female legislators, senior officials and managers (% of total)	..		..	
Employment to population ratio, total (% ages 15+)	32	58	32	56
Employment to population ratio, youth (% ages 15–24)	22	33	20	31
Children in employment (% of children ages 7–14)	..	..	12.1	14.5
Unemployment rate (% of labor force ages 15+)	..	..	..	..
Long-term unemployment rate (% total unemployment)	..	..	..	..
Youth unemployment rate (% of labor force ages 15–24)	..	..	..	..
Account at a formal financial institution (% age 15+)	..	..	27	30
Public life and decision making				
Seats held by women in national parliament (%)	4		14	

Sweden

	High income
Population (millions)	9.4
GNI, Atlas ($ billions)	502.5
GNI per capita, Atlas ($)	53,170
Population living below $1.25 a day (%)	..

	1990		2011	
	Female	Male	Female	Male
Demography				
Sex ratio at birth (boys per girls)	1.06		1.06	
Life expectancy at birth (years)	80	75	84	80
Under-five mortality rate (per 1,000 live births)	6	7	3	3
Female-headed households (%)	..		..	
Education				
Gross primary enrollment ratio (% of relevant age group)	100	100	101	102
Gross secondary enrollment ratio (% of relevant age group)	92	88	99	100
Gross tertiary enrollment ratio (% of relevant age group)	33	28	90	58
Primary completion rate (% of relevant age group)	96	97	97	97
Youth literacy rate (% of population ages 15–24)	..	..	..	..
Health and related services				
Total fertility rate (births per woman)	2.1		1.9	
Adolescent fertility rate (births per 1,000 women ages 15–19)	..		6	
Women first married by age 18 (% of women ages 20–24)	..		..	
Contraceptive prevalence (% of women ages 15–49)	..		..	
Unmet need for contraception (% of women ages 15–49)	..		..	
Pregnant women receiving prenatal care (%)	..		..	
Births attended by skilled health staff (% of total)	100		..	
Maternal mortality ratio (per 100,000 live births)	6		4	
Economic structure, participation, and access to resources				
Labor force participation rate (% of population ages 15+)	62	71	59	68
Wage and salaried workers (% of employed ages 15+)	95	87	94	86
Self-employed workers (% of employed ages 15+)	5	13	6	15
Vulnerable employment (% of employed ages 15+)	..		4	9
Unpaid family workers (% of employed ages 15+)	0.5	0.2	0.2	0.2
Employment in agriculture (% of employed ages 15+)	2	5	1	3
Employment in industry (% of employed ages 15+)	14	43	8	31
Employment in service (% of employed ages 15+)	84	52	91	66
Women in wage employment in the nonagricultural sector (%)	51		50	
Women's share of part-time employment (% of total)	81		63	
Maternity leave (weeks)	12		69	
Maternal leave benefits (% of wages paid)	90		80	
Female legislators, senior officials and managers (% of total)	..		35	
Employment to population ratio, total (% ages 15+)	60	68	55	63
Employment to population ratio, youth (% ages 15–24)	58	57	40	40
Children in employment (% of children ages 7–14)	..	..	..	..
Unemployment rate (% of labor force ages 15+)	1.8	1.9	7.5	7.6
Long-term unemployment rate (% total unemployment)	11.8	12.3	13.6	17.8
Youth unemployment rate (% of labor force ages 15–24)	5	5	22	24
Account at a formal financial institution (% age 15+)	..	..	99	99
Public life and decision making				
Seats held by women in national parliament (%)	38		45	

Switzerland

High income

Population (millions)	7.9
GNI, Atlas ($ billions)	604.1
GNI per capita, Atlas ($)	76,350
Population living below $1.25 a day (%)	..

	1990		2011	
	Female	Male	Female	Male
Demography				
Sex ratio at birth (boys per girls)	1.05		1.05	
Life expectancy at birth (years)	81	74	85	81
Under-five mortality rate (per 1,000 live births)	7	9	4	5
Female-headed households (%)	..		..	
Education				
Gross primary enrollment ratio (% of relevant age group)	90	89	102	103
Gross secondary enrollment ratio (% of relevant age group)	92	99	94	97
Gross tertiary enrollment ratio (% of relevant age group)	18	33	55	55
Primary completion rate (% of relevant age group)	52	51	97	94
Youth literacy rate (% of population ages 15–24)	..	..	..	..
Health and related services				
Total fertility rate (births per woman)	1.6		1.5	
Adolescent fertility rate (births per 1,000 women ages 15–19)	..		4	
Women first married by age 18 (% of women ages 20–24)	..		..	
Contraceptive prevalence (% of women ages 15–49)	..		..	
Unmet need for contraception (% of women ages 15–49)	..		..	
Pregnant women receiving prenatal care (%)	..		..	
Births attended by skilled health staff (% of total)	..		100	
Maternal mortality ratio (per 100,000 live births)	7		8	
Economic structure, participation, and access to resources				
Labor force participation rate (% of population ages 15+)	56	80	61	75
Wage and salaried workers (% of employed ages 15+)	86	84	87	83
Self-employed workers (% of employed ages 15+)	14	16	13	17
Vulnerable employment (% of employed ages 15+)	11	8	10	9
Unpaid family workers (% of employed ages 15+)	6.4	1.7	2.8	1.5
Employment in agriculture (% of employed ages 15+)	4	5	3	4
Employment in industry (% of employed ages 15+)	18	41	10	31
Employment in service (% of employed ages 15+)	78	54	83	62
Women in wage employment in the nonagricultural sector (%)	43		47	
Women's share of part-time employment (% of total)	82		80	
Maternity leave (weeks)	8		14	
Maternal leave benefits (% of wages paid)	100		80	
Female legislators, senior officials and managers (% of total)	24		33	
Employment to population ratio, total (% ages 15+)	56	80	58	73
Employment to population ratio, youth (% ages 15–24)	69	69	60	64
Children in employment (% of children ages 7–14)	..	..	..	..
Unemployment rate (% of labor force ages 15+)	2.6	1.7	4.5	3.7
Long-term unemployment rate (% total unemployment)	15.6	15.5	39.9	36.6
Youth unemployment rate (% of labor force ages 15–24)	3	3	8	8
Account at a formal financial institution (% age 15+)	..	..	..	..
Public life and decision making				
Seats held by women in national parliament (%)	14		29	

Syrian Arab Republic

Middle East & North Africa	Lower middle income
Population (millions)	20.8
GNI, Atlas ($ billions)	56.3
GNI per capita, Atlas ($)	2,750
Population living below $1.25 a day (%)	<2

	1990 Female	1990 Male	2011 Female	2011 Male
Demography				
Sex ratio at birth (boys per girls)	1.05		1.05	
Life expectancy at birth (years)	72	70	77	74
Under-five mortality rate (per 1,000 live births)	33	39	14	16
Female-headed households (%)	..		..	
Education				
Gross primary enrollment ratio (% of relevant age group)	102	113	121	122
Gross secondary enrollment ratio (% of relevant age group)	43	59	73	73
Gross tertiary enrollment ratio (% of relevant age group)	14	22	..	..
Primary completion rate (% of relevant age group)	86	97	106	105
Youth literacy rate (% of population ages 15–24)	..	..	94	96
Health and related services				
Total fertility rate (births per woman)	5.3		2.9	
Adolescent fertility rate (births per 1,000 women ages 15–19)	..		38	
Women first married by age 18 (% of women ages 20–24)	..		13	
Contraceptive prevalence (% of women ages 15–49)	40		54	
Unmet need for contraception (% of women ages 15–49)	..		11	
Pregnant women receiving prenatal care (%)	51		88	
Births attended by skilled health staff (% of total)	77		96	
Maternal mortality ratio (per 100,000 live births)	240		70	
Economic structure, participation, and access to resources				
Labor force participation rate (% of population ages 15+)	18	80	13	72
Wage and salaried workers (% of employed ages 15+)	..	..	83	60
Self-employed workers (% of employed ages 15+)	..	..	9	38
Vulnerable employment (% of employed ages 15+)	..	..	16	35
Unpaid family workers (% of employed ages 15+)	..	..	8.2	2.4
Employment in agriculture (% of employed ages 15+)	54	23	22	13
Employment in industry (% of employed ages 15+)	8	28	9	36
Employment in service (% of employed ages 15+)	38	49	69	51
Women in wage employment in the nonagricultural sector (%)	15		15	
Women's share of part-time employment (% of total)	..		27	
Maternity leave (weeks)	7		7	
Maternal leave benefits (% of wages paid)	70		70	
Female legislators, senior officials and managers (% of total)	..		9	
Employment to population ratio, total (% ages 15+)	15	76	10	67
Employment to population ratio, youth (% ages 15–24)	14	60	5	42
Children in employment (% of children ages 7–14)	..	..	4.3	8.8
Unemployment rate (% of labor force ages 15+)	14.0	5.2	22.5	5.7
Long-term unemployment rate (% total unemployment)	..	..	..	..
Youth unemployment rate (% of labor force ages 15–24)	..	..	40	15
Account at a formal financial institution (% age 15+)	..	..	20	27
Public life and decision making				
Seats held by women in national parliament (%)	9		12	

Tajikistan

Population (millions)	7.0
GNI, Atlas ($ billions)	6.1
GNI per capita, Atlas ($)	870
Population living below $1.25 a day (%)	6.6

	1990		2011	
	Female	Male	Female	Male
Demography				
Sex ratio at birth (boys per girls)	1.05		1.05	
Life expectancy at birth (years)	66	60	71	64
Under-five mortality rate (per 1,000 live births)	106	122	56	70
Female-headed households (%)	..		..	
Education				
Gross primary enrollment ratio (% of relevant age group)	90	92	98	102
Gross secondary enrollment ratio (% of relevant age group)	..	..	82	94
Gross tertiary enrollment ratio (% of relevant age group)	..	..	16	31
Primary completion rate (% of relevant age group)	..	..	102	106
Youth literacy rate (% of population ages 15–24)	100	100	100	100
Health and related services				
Total fertility rate (births per woman)	5.2		3.2	
Adolescent fertility rate (births per 1,000 women ages 15–19)	..		26	
Women first married by age 18 (% of women ages 20–24)	..		..	
Contraceptive prevalence (% of women ages 15–49)	..		37	
Unmet need for contraception (% of women ages 15–49)	..		..	
Pregnant women receiving prenatal care (%)	..		80	
Births attended by skilled health staff (% of total)	90		88	
Maternal mortality ratio (per 100,000 live births)	94		65	
Economic structure, participation, and access to resources				
Labor force participation rate (% of population ages 15+)	58	76	57	75
Wage and salaried workers (% of employed ages 15+)	..	..	..	..
Self-employed workers (% of employed ages 15+)	..	..	..	..
Vulnerable employment (% of employed ages 15+)	..	..	..	..
Unpaid family workers (% of employed ages 15+)	..	..	..	..
Employment in agriculture (% of employed ages 15+)	..	..	..	..
Employment in industry (% of employed ages 15+)	..	..	..	..
Employment in service (% of employed ages 15+)	..	..	..	..
Women in wage employment in the nonagricultural sector (%)	37		37	
Women's share of part-time employment (% of total)	..		..	
Maternity leave (weeks)	..		20	
Maternal leave benefits (% of wages paid)	..		..	
Female legislators, senior officials and managers (% of total)	..		..	
Employment to population ratio, total (% ages 15+)	51	66	51	67
Employment to population ratio, youth (% ages 15–24)	33	44	31	46
Children in employment (% of children ages 7–14)	..	..	..	..
Unemployment rate (% of labor force ages 15+)	..	..	..	..
Long-term unemployment rate (% total unemployment)	..	..	..	..
Youth unemployment rate (% of labor force ages 15–24)	..	..	..	..
Account at a formal financial institution (% age 15+)	..	..	2	3
Public life and decision making				
Seats held by women in national parliament (%)	..		19	

Tanzania

Sub-Saharan Africa			Low income	

Population (millions)			46.2
GNI, Atlas ($ billions)			24.2
GNI per capita, Atlas ($)			540
Population living below $1.25 a day (%)			67.9

	1990 Female	Male	2011 Female	Male
Demography				
Sex ratio at birth (boys per girls)	1.03		1.03	
Life expectancy at birth (years)	52	49	59	57
Under-five mortality rate (per 1,000 live births)	152	163	65	70
Female-headed households (%)	19		24	
Education				
Gross primary enrollment ratio (% of relevant age group)	69	70	95[a]	92[a]
Gross secondary enrollment ratio (% of relevant age group)	4	6	33[a]	37[a]
Gross tertiary enrollment ratio (% of relevant age group)	0	1	3[a]	5[a]
Primary completion rate (% of relevant age group)	47	48	85[a]	77[a]
Youth literacy rate (% of population ages 15–24)	78	86	76	78
Health and related services				
Total fertility rate (births per woman)	6.2		5.5	
Adolescent fertility rate (births per 1,000 women ages 15–19)	..		129	
Women first married by age 18 (% of women ages 20–24)	37		37	
Contraceptive prevalence (% of women ages 15–49)	10		34	
Unmet need for contraception (% of women ages 15–49)	28		25	
Pregnant women receiving prenatal care (%)	62		88	
Births attended by skilled health staff (% of total)	44		49	
Maternal mortality ratio (per 100,000 live births)	870		460	
Economic structure, participation, and access to resources				
Labor force participation rate (% of population ages 15+)	87	91	88	90
Wage and salaried workers (% of employed ages 15+)	4	13	6	15
Self-employed workers (% of employed ages 15+)	96	87	94	85
Vulnerable employment (% of employed ages 15+)	96	86	93	82
Unpaid family workers (% of employed ages 15+)	0.5	0.6	13.0	9.7
Employment in agriculture (% of employed ages 15+)	90	78	80	73
Employment in industry (% of employed ages 15+)	1	7	2	7
Employment in service (% of employed ages 15+)	8	15	18	21
Women in wage employment in the nonagricultural sector (%)	..		31	
Women's share of part-time employment (% of total)	58		..	
Maternity leave (weeks)	..		12	
Maternal leave benefits (% of wages paid)	..		100	
Female legislators, senior officials and managers (% of total)	..		16	
Employment to population ratio, total (% ages 15+)	76	81	77	81
Employment to population ratio, youth (% ages 15–24)	70	71	69	69
Children in employment (% of children ages 7–14)	..	..	27.1	35.0
Unemployment rate (% of labor force ages 15+)	4.3	2.8	5.8	2.8
Long-term unemployment rate (% total unemployment)	34.3	35.0	..	..
Youth unemployment rate (% of labor force ages 15–24)	8	7	10	7
Account at a formal financial institution (% age 15+)	..	..	14	21
Public life and decision making				
Seats held by women in national parliament (%)	..		36	

Thailand

Upper middle income

Population (millions)	69.5
GNI, Atlas ($ billions)	308.3
GNI per capita, Atlas ($)	4,440
Population living below $1.25 a day (%)	<2

	1990		2011	
	Female	Male	Female	Male
Demography				
Sex ratio at birth (boys per girls)	1.05		1.06	
Life expectancy at birth (years)	76	69	78	71
Under-five mortality rate (per 1,000 live births)	31	39	11	13
Female-headed households (%)	..		30	
Education				
Gross primary enrollment ratio (% of relevant age group)	99	100	90	91
Gross secondary enrollment ratio (% of relevant age group)	29	28	82	76
Gross tertiary enrollment ratio (% of relevant age group)	21	18	54	41
Primary completion rate (% of relevant age group)	..	..	..	..
Youth literacy rate (% of population ages 15–24)	..	..	..	..
Health and related services				
Total fertility rate (births per woman)	2.1		1.6	
Adolescent fertility rate (births per 1,000 women ages 15–19)	..		38	
Women first married by age 18 (% of women ages 20–24)	21		20	
Contraceptive prevalence (% of women ages 15–49)	66		80	
Unmet need for contraception (% of women ages 15–49)	..		..	
Pregnant women receiving prenatal care (%)	80		99	
Births attended by skilled health staff (% of total)	69		100	
Maternal mortality ratio (per 100,000 live births)	54		48	
Economic structure, participation, and access to resources				
Labor force participation rate (% of population ages 15+)	76	87	64	80
Wage and salaried workers (% of employed ages 15+)	26	31	43	45
Self-employed workers (% of employed ages 15+)	74	69	57	55
Vulnerable employment (% of employed ages 15+)	74	67	56	52
Unpaid family workers (% of employed ages 15+)	56.1	27.0	29.7	15.1
Employment in agriculture (% of employed ages 15+)	65	63	37	41
Employment in industry (% of employed ages 15+)	12	16	18	23
Employment in service (% of employed ages 15+)	23	21	45	37
Women in wage employment in the nonagricultural sector (%)	42		46	
Women's share of part-time employment (% of total)	..		..	
Maternity leave (weeks)	12		13	
Maternal leave benefits (% of wages paid)	100		100	
Female legislators, senior officials and managers (% of total)	..		25	
Employment to population ratio, total (% ages 15+)	71	84	63	80
Employment to population ratio, youth (% ages 15–24)	67	72	38	54
Children in employment (% of children ages 7–14)	..	..	..	..
Unemployment rate (% of labor force ages 15+)	2.4	2.0	0.6	0.7
Long-term unemployment rate (% total unemployment)	..	..	..	..
Youth unemployment rate (% of labor force ages 15–24)	4	4	3	3
Account at a formal financial institution (% age 15+)	..	..	73	73
Public life and decision making				
Seats held by women in national parliament (%)	3		16	

Timor-Leste

East Asia & Pacific	Lower middle income
Population (millions)	1.2
GNI, Atlas ($ billions)	3.1
GNI per capita, Atlas ($)	2,730
Population living below $1.25 a day (%)	..

	1990		2011	
	Female	Male	Female	Male
Demography				
Sex ratio at birth (boys per girls)	1.05		1.05	
Life expectancy at birth (years)	47	45	63	62
Under-five mortality rate (per 1,000 live births)	169	190	51	57
Female-headed households (%)	..		12	
Education				
Gross primary enrollment ratio (% of relevant age group)	..	..	122	126
Gross secondary enrollment ratio (% of relevant age group)	..	..	59	57
Gross tertiary enrollment ratio (% of relevant age group)	..	..	14	19
Primary completion rate (% of relevant age group)	..	..	74	71
Youth literacy rate (% of population ages 15–24)	..	..	79	80
Health and related services				
Total fertility rate (births per woman)	5.3		5.5	
Adolescent fertility rate (births per 1,000 women ages 15–19)	..		55	
Women first married by age 18 (% of women ages 20–24)	..		19	
Contraceptive prevalence (% of women ages 15–49)	25		22	
Unmet need for contraception (% of women ages 15–49)	..		31	
Pregnant women receiving prenatal care (%)	..		84	
Births attended by skilled health staff (% of total)	..		29	
Maternal mortality ratio (per 100,000 live births)	1,000		300	
Economic structure, participation, and access to resources				
Labor force participation rate (% of population ages 15+)	41	79	38	74
Wage and salaried workers (% of employed ages 15+)	..	..	..	..
Self-employed workers (% of employed ages 15+)	..	..	..	..
Vulnerable employment (% of employed ages 15+)	..	..	79	66
Unpaid family workers (% of employed ages 15+)	..	..	..	..
Employment in agriculture (% of employed ages 15+)	..	..	..	..
Employment in industry (% of employed ages 15+)	..	..	..	..
Employment in service (% of employed ages 15+)	..	..	..	..
Women in wage employment in the nonagricultural sector (%)	..		..	
Women's share of part-time employment (% of total)	..		..	
Maternity leave (weeks)	..		..	
Maternal leave benefits (% of wages paid)	..		..	
Female legislators, senior officials and managers (% of total)	..		..	
Employment to population ratio, total (% ages 15+)	39	76	37	72
Employment to population ratio, youth (% ages 15–24)	37	55	33	48
Children in employment (% of children ages 7–14)	..	..	17.7	22.2
Unemployment rate (% of labor force ages 15+)	..	..	4.6	3.1
Long-term unemployment rate (% total unemployment)	..	..	..	..
Youth unemployment rate (% of labor force ages 15–24)	..	..	..	..
Account at a formal financial institution (% age 15+)	..	..	..	..
Public life and decision making				
Seats held by women in national parliament (%)	..		39	

Togo

Population (millions)	6.2
GNI, Atlas ($ billions)	3.5
GNI per capita, Atlas ($)	570
Population living below $1.25 a day (%)	28.2

	1990		2011	
	Female	Male	Female	Male
Demography				
Sex ratio at birth (boys per girls)	1.02		1.02	
Life expectancy at birth (years)	55	51	59	56
Under-five mortality rate (per 1,000 live births)	136	158	102	118
Female-headed households (%)	..		..	
Education				
Gross primary enrollment ratio (% of relevant age group)	75	117	133	146
Gross secondary enrollment ratio (% of relevant age group)	11	33	31	60
Gross tertiary enrollment ratio (% of relevant age group)	1	4	..	..
Primary completion rate (% of relevant age group)	24	51	67	86
Youth literacy rate (% of population ages 15-24)	..	..	75	88
Health and related services				
Total fertility rate (births per woman)	6.3		4.0	
Adolescent fertility rate (births per 1,000 women ages 15-19)	..		57	
Women first married by age 18 (% of women ages 20-24)	44		25	
Contraceptive prevalence (% of women ages 15-49)	34		15	
Unmet need for contraception (% of women ages 15-49)	..		41	
Pregnant women receiving prenatal care (%)	43		72	
Births attended by skilled health staff (% of total)	31		59	
Maternal mortality ratio (per 100,000 live births)	620		300	
Economic structure, participation, and access to resources				
Labor force participation rate (% of population ages 15+)	67	84	80	81
Wage and salaried workers (% of employed ages 15+)	..	..	6	17
Self-employed workers (% of employed ages 15+)	..	..	94	83
Vulnerable employment (% of employed ages 15+)	..	..	94	83
Unpaid family workers (% of employed ages 15+)	..	..	28.4	23.1
Employment in agriculture (% of employed ages 15+)	..	..	48	61
Employment in industry (% of employed ages 15+)	..	..	4	10
Employment in service (% of employed ages 15+)	..	..	46	29
Women in wage employment in the nonagricultural sector (%)	41		..	
Women's share of part-time employment (% of total)	..		..	
Maternity leave (weeks)	..		14	
Maternity leave benefits (% of wages paid)	..		100	
Female legislators, senior officials and managers (% of total)	..			
Employment to population ratio, total (% ages 15+)	63	79	75	76
Employment to population ratio, youth (% ages 15-24)	54	63	61	58
Children in employment (% of children ages 7-14)	..	..	47.0	50.3
Unemployment rate (% of labor force ages 15+)	..	..	..	..
Long-term unemployment rate (% total unemployment)	..	..	..	..
Youth unemployment rate (% of labor force ages 15-24)	..	..	..	..
Account at a formal financial institution (% age 15+)	..	..	9	11
Public life and decision making				
Seats held by women in national parliament (%)	5		11	

Tonga

East Asia & Pacific	Lower middle income
Population (thousands)	104.5
GNI, Atlas ($ millions)	399.0
GNI per capita, Atlas ($)	3,820
Population living below $1.25 a day (%)	..

	1990		2011	
	Female	Male	Female	Male
Demography				
Sex ratio at birth (boys per girls)	1.05		1.05	
Life expectancy at birth (years)	71	68	75	69
Under-five mortality rate (per 1,000 live births)	21	28	13	18
Female-headed households (%)	..		..	
Education				
Gross primary enrollment ratio (% of relevant age group)	107	108	108	112
Gross secondary enrollment ratio (% of relevant age group)	98	99	101	101
Gross tertiary enrollment ratio (% of relevant age group)	..	..	..	..
Primary completion rate (% of relevant age group)	120	135	106	102
Youth literacy rate (% of population ages 15–24)	..	..	100	99
Health and related services				
Total fertility rate (births per woman)	4.6		3.9	
Adolescent fertility rate (births per 1,000 women ages 15–19)	..		19	
Women first married by age 18 (% of women ages 20–24)	..		..	
Contraceptive prevalence (% of women ages 15–49)	..		32	
Unmet need for contraception (% of women ages 15–49)	..		..	
Pregnant women receiving prenatal care (%)	..		98	
Births attended by skilled health staff (% of total)	92		98	
Maternal mortality ratio (per 100,000 live births)	67		110	
Economic structure, participation, and access to resources				
Labor force participation rate (% of population ages 15+)	36	76	54	75
Wage and salaried workers (% of employed ages 15+)	..	..	..	..
Self-employed workers (% of employed ages 15+)	..	..	..	..
Vulnerable employment (% of employed ages 15+)	..	..	..	..
Unpaid family workers (% of employed ages 15+)	..	..	..	..
Employment in agriculture (% of employed ages 15+)	..	..	..	..
Employment in industry (% of employed ages 15+)	..	..	..	..
Employment in service (% of employed ages 15+)	..	..	..	..
Women in wage employment in the nonagricultural sector (%)	..		..	
Women's share of part-time employment (% of total)	..		..	
Maternity leave (weeks)	..		..	
Maternal leave benefits (% of wages paid)	..		..	
Female legislators, senior officials and managers (% of total)	..		..	
Employment to population ratio, total (% ages 15+)	..	..	..	..
Employment to population ratio, youth (% ages 15–24)	..	..	..	..
Children in employment (% of children ages 7–14)	..	..	..	..
Unemployment rate (% of labor force ages 15+)	..	..	..	..
Long-term unemployment rate (% total unemployment)	..	..	..	..
Youth unemployment rate (% of labor force ages 15–24)	..	..	..	..
Account at a formal financial institution (% age 15+)	..	..	..	..
Public life and decision making				
Seats held by women in national parliament (%)	0		4	

Trinidad and Tobago

	High income
Population (millions)	1.3
GNI, Atlas ($ billions)	21.3
GNI per capita, Atlas ($)	15,840
Population living below $1.25 a day (%)	..

	1990		2011	
	Female	**Male**	**Female**	**Male**
Demography				
Sex ratio at birth (boys per girls)	1.04		1.04	
Life expectancy at birth (years)	73	65	74	67
Under-five mortality rate (per 1,000 live births)	33	41	24	31
Female-headed households (%)	..		..	
Education				
Gross primary enrollment ratio (% of relevant age group)	97	96	103	107
Gross secondary enrollment ratio (% of relevant age group)	86	84	93	87
Gross tertiary enrollment ratio (% of relevant age group)	6	7	..	..
Primary completion rate (% of relevant age group)	105	99	91	91
Youth literacy rate (% of population ages 15–24)	99	99	100	100
Health and related services				
Total fertility rate (births per woman)	2.4		1.6	
Adolescent fertility rate (births per 1,000 women ages 15–19)	..		32	
Women first married by age 18 (% of women ages 20–24)	34		8	
Contraceptive prevalence (% of women ages 15–49)	53		43	
Unmet need for contraception (% of women ages 15–49)	..		27	
Pregnant women receiving prenatal care (%)	98		96	
Births attended by skilled health staff (% of total)	98		98	
Maternal mortality ratio (per 100,000 live births)	86		46	
Economic structure, participation, and access to resources				
Labor force participation rate (% of population ages 15+)	39	76	55	78
Wage and salaried workers (% of employed ages 15+)	77	73	..	..
Self-employed workers (% of employed ages 15+)	23	26	..	..
Vulnerable employment (% of employed ages 15+)	21	22	..	..
Unpaid family workers (% of employed ages 15+)	6.5	2.5	..	..
Employment in agriculture (% of employed ages 15+)	6	15	2	5
Employment in industry (% of employed ages 15+)	14	34	15	44
Employment in service (% of employed ages 15+)	80	51	82	51
Women in wage employment in the nonagricultural sector (%)	36		..	
Women's share of part-time employment (% of total)	38		..	
Maternity leave (weeks)	13		13	
Maternal leave benefits (% of wages paid)	60		100	
Female legislators, senior officials and managers (% of total)	36		..	
Employment to population ratio, total (% ages 15+)	34	56	51	75
Employment to population ratio, youth (% ages 15–24)	23	44	38	55
Children in employment (% of children ages 7–14)	..	..	2.7	4.1
Unemployment rate (% of labor force ages 15+)	24.2	17.9	6.2	3.5
Long-term unemployment rate (% total unemployment)	36.1	20.2	..	..
Youth unemployment rate (% of labor force ages 15–24)	43	33	13	9
Account at a formal financial institution (% age 15+)	..	..	70	82
Public life and decision making				
Seats held by women in national parliament (%)	17		29	

Tunisia

Middle East & North Africa	Upper middle income
Population (millions)	10.7
GNI, Atlas ($ billions)	42.9
GNI per capita, Atlas ($)	4,020
Population living below $1.25 a day (%)	<2

	1990		2011	
	Female	Male	Female	Male
Demography				
Sex ratio at birth (boys per girls)	1.05		1.05	
Life expectancy at birth (years)	72	69	77	73
Under-five mortality rate (per 1,000 live births)	47	55	15	18
Female-headed households (%)	..		..	
Education				
Gross primary enrollment ratio (% of relevant age group)	104	120	108	112
Gross secondary enrollment ratio (% of relevant age group)	38	50	94	91
Gross tertiary enrollment ratio (% of relevant age group)	6	10	45	29
Primary completion rate (% of relevant age group)	74	86	92	90
Youth literacy rate (% of population ages 15–24)	75	90	96	98
Health and related services				
Total fertility rate (births per woman)	3.6		2.1	
Adolescent fertility rate (births per 1,000 women ages 15–19)	..		5	
Women first married by age 18 (% of women ages 20–24)	10		..	
Contraceptive prevalence (% of women ages 15–49)	50		60	
Unmet need for contraception (% of women ages 15–49)	..		..	
Pregnant women receiving prenatal care (%)	58		96	
Births attended by skilled health staff (% of total)	69		95	
Maternal mortality ratio (per 100,000 live births)	130		56	
Economic structure, participation, and access to resources				
Labor force participation rate (% of population ages 15+)	21	76	26	70
Wage and salaried workers (% of employed ages 15+)	59	69	..	..
Self-employed workers (% of employed ages 15+)	41	30	..	..
Vulnerable employment (% of employed ages 15+)	14	23	..	..
Unpaid family workers (% of employed ages 15+)	21.8	5.7	..	..
Employment in agriculture (% of employed ages 15+)	23	26	..	..
Employment in industry (% of employed ages 15+)	44	31	..	..
Employment in service (% of employed ages 15+)	32	41	..	..
Women in wage employment in the nonagricultural sector (%)	23		..	
Women's share of part-time employment (% of total)	..		..	
Maternity leave (weeks)	4		9	
Maternal leave benefits (% of wages paid)	67		100	
Female legislators, senior officials and managers (% of total)	..		..	
Employment to population ratio, total (% ages 15+)	17	64	21	60
Employment to population ratio, youth (% ages 15–24)	19	38	15	29
Children in employment (% of children ages 7–14)	..	..	..	..
Unemployment rate (% of labor force ages 15+)	21.7	14.7	..	..
Long-term unemployment rate (% total unemployment)	..	..	..	..
Youth unemployment rate (% of labor force ages 15–24)	30	31	..	..
Account at a formal financial institution (% age 15+)	..	..	25	39
Public life and decision making				
Seats held by women in national parliament (%)	4		27	

Turkey

Europe & Central Asia			Upper middle income	
Population (millions)				73.6
GNI, Atlas ($ billions)				766.6
GNI per capita, Atlas ($)				10,410
Population living below $1.25 a day (%)				<2

	1990		2011	
	Female	Male	Female	Male
Demography				
Sex ratio at birth (boys per girls)	1.05		1.05	
Life expectancy at birth (years)	65	61	76	72
Under-five mortality rate (per 1,000 live births)	68	76	14	16
Female-headed households (%)	10		..	
Education				
Gross primary enrollment ratio (% of relevant age group)	98	107	104	105
Gross secondary enrollment ratio (% of relevant age group)	37	63	79	86
Gross tertiary enrollment ratio (% of relevant age group)	9	17	50	61
Primary completion rate (% of relevant age group)	87	97	100	101
Youth literacy rate (% of population ages 15–24)	88	97	97	99
Health and related services				
Total fertility rate (births per woman)	3.0		2.1	
Adolescent fertility rate (births per 1,000 women ages 15–19)	..		32	
Women first married by age 18 (% of women ages 20–24)	23		14	
Contraceptive prevalence (% of women ages 15–49)	63		73	
Unmet need for contraception (% of women ages 15–49)	11		18	
Pregnant women receiving prenatal care (%)	62		95	
Births attended by skilled health staff (% of total)	76		95	
Maternal mortality ratio (per 100,000 live births)	67		20	
Economic structure, participation, and access to resources				
Labor force participation rate (% of population ages 15+)	35	82	28	71
Wage and salaried workers (% of employed ages 15+)	22	47	52	66
Self-employed workers (% of employed ages 15+)	78	54	48	34
Vulnerable employment (% of employed ages 15+)	..	..	47	27
Unpaid family workers (% of employed ages 15+)	69.2	13.0	35.4	4.8
Employment in agriculture (% of employed ages 15+)	76	34	39	18
Employment in industry (% of employed ages 15+)	10	26	15	31
Employment in service (% of employed ages 15+)	14	41	45	51
Women in wage employment in the nonagricultural sector (%)	16		23	
Women's share of part-time employment (% of total)	62		60	
Maternity leave (weeks)	12		16	
Maternal leave benefits (% of wages paid)	67		67	
Female legislators, senior officials and managers (% of total)	..		10	
Employment to population ratio, total (% ages 15+)	32	74	25	65
Employment to population ratio, youth (% ages 15–24)	36	60	21	45
Children in employment (% of children ages 7–14)	..		1.8	3.3
Unemployment rate (% of labor force ages 15+)	8.5	7.8	11.3	9.2
Long-term unemployment rate (% total unemployment)	50.3	43.3	34.2	22.5
Youth unemployment rate (% of labor force ages 15–24)	15	17	21	17
Account at a formal financial institution (% age 15+)	..	..	33	82
Public life and decision making				
Seats held by women in national parliament (%)	1		14	

Turkmenistan

Population (millions)	5.1
GNI, Atlas ($ billions)	24.5
GNI per capita, Atlas ($)	4,800
Population living below $1.25 a day (%)	..

	1990 Female	1990 Male	2011 Female	2011 Male
Demography				
Sex ratio at birth (boys per girls)	1.05		1.05	
Life expectancy at birth (years)	66	59	69	61
Under-five mortality rate (per 1,000 live births)	86	103	48	57
Female-headed households (%)	..		..	
Education				
Gross primary enrollment ratio (% of relevant age group)	..	..	..	..
Gross secondary enrollment ratio (% of relevant age group)	..	..	..	..
Gross tertiary enrollment ratio (% of relevant age group)	..	..	..	..
Primary completion rate (% of relevant age group)	..	..	..	..
Youth literacy rate (% of population ages 15–24)	..	..	100	100
Health and related services				
Total fertility rate (births per woman)	4.3		2.4	
Adolescent fertility rate (births per 1,000 women ages 15–19)	..		17	
Women first married by age 18 (% of women ages 20–24)	..		7	
Contraceptive prevalence (% of women ages 15–49)	..		48	
Unmet need for contraception (% of women ages 15–49)	..		..	
Pregnant women receiving prenatal care (%)	..		99	
Births attended by skilled health staff (% of total)	..		100	
Maternal mortality ratio (per 100,000 live births)	82		67	
Economic structure, participation, and access to resources				
Labor force participation rate (% of population ages 15+)	46	75	46	76
Wage and salaried workers (% of employed ages 15+)	..	..	..	..
Self-employed workers (% of employed ages 15+)	..	..	..	..
Vulnerable employment (% of employed ages 15+)	..	..	..	..
Unpaid family workers (% of employed ages 15+)	..	..	..	..
Employment in agriculture (% of employed ages 15+)	..	..	..	..
Employment in industry (% of employed ages 15+)	..	..	..	..
Employment in service (% of employed ages 15+)	..	..	..	..
Women in wage employment in the nonagricultural sector (%)	..		..	
Women's share of part-time employment (% of total)	..		..	
Maternity leave (weeks)	..		16	
Maternal leave benefits (% of wages paid)	..		100	
Female legislators, senior officials and managers (% of total)	..		..	
Employment to population ratio, total (% ages 15+)	41	65	42	68
Employment to population ratio, youth (% ages 15–24)	25	43	26	46
Children in employment (% of children ages 7–14)	..	..	..	..
Unemployment rate (% of labor force ages 15+)	..	..	..	..
Long-term unemployment rate (% total unemployment)	..	..	..	..
Youth unemployment rate (% of labor force ages 15–24)	..	..	..	..
Account at a formal financial institution (% age 15+)	..	..	1	0
Public life and decision making				
Seats held by women in national parliament (%)	26		17	

Turks and Caicos Islands

				39.2
Population (thousands)				39.2
GNI, Atlas ($ millions)				..
GNI per capita, Atlas ($)				..
Population living below $1.25 a day (%)				..

	1990		2011	
	Female	**Male**	**Female**	**Male**
Demography				
Sex ratio at birth (boys per girls)	..		..	
Life expectancy at birth (years)	..	..	..	..
Under-five mortality rate (per 1,000 live births)	..	..	..	..
Female-headed households (%)	..		..	
Education				
Gross primary enrollment ratio (% of relevant age group)	..	..	..	..
Gross secondary enrollment ratio (% of relevant age group)	..	..	..	..
Gross tertiary enrollment ratio (% of relevant age group)	..	..	0	0
Primary completion rate (% of relevant age group)	..	..	..	..
Youth literacy rate (% of population ages 15–24)	..	..	..	..
Health and related services				
Total fertility rate (births per woman)	..		..	
Adolescent fertility rate (births per 1,000 women ages 15–19)	..		..	
Women first married by age 18 (% of women ages 20–24)	..		..	
Contraceptive prevalence (% of women ages 15–49)	..		..	
Unmet need for contraception (% of women ages 15–49)	..		..	
Pregnant women receiving prenatal care (%)	..		100	
Births attended by skilled health staff (% of total)	..		100	
Maternal mortality ratio (per 100,000 live births)	..		..	
Economic structure, participation, and access to resources				
Labor force participation rate (% of population ages 15+)	..	..	..	..
Wage and salaried workers (% of employed ages 15+)	..	..	96	94
Self-employed workers (% of employed ages 15+)	..	..	4	6
Vulnerable employment (% of employed ages 15+)	..	..	..	..
Unpaid family workers (% of employed ages 15+)	..	..	..	..
Employment in agriculture (% of employed ages 15+)	..	..	..	..
Employment in industry (% of employed ages 15+)	..	..	..	..
Employment in service (% of employed ages 15+)	..	..	..	..
Women in wage employment in the nonagricultural sector (%)	..		38	
Women's share of part-time employment (% of total)	..		..	
Maternity leave (weeks,	..		..	
Maternal leave benefits (% of wages paid)	..		..	
Female legislators, senior officials and managers (% of total)	..		..	
Employment to population ratio, total (% ages 15+)	..	..	..	..
Employment to population ratio, youth (% ages 15–24)	..	..	..	..
Children in employment (% of children ages 7–14)	..	..	..	..
Unemployment rate (% of labor force ages 15+)	..	..	..	..
Long-term unemployment rate (% total unemployment)	..	..	..	..
Youth unemployment rate (% of labor force ages 15–24)	..	..	..	..
Account at a formal financial institution (% age 15+)	..	..	..	..
Public life and decision making				
Seats held by women in national parliament (%)	..		..	

Tuvalu

Upper middle income

Population (thousands)	9.8
GNI, Atlas ($ millions)	48.8
GNI per capita, Atlas ($)	4,950
Population living below $1.25 a day (%)	..

	1990		2011	
	Female	Male	Female	Male
Demography				
Sex ratio at birth (boys per girls)	..		..	
Life expectancy at birth (years)	..	..	..	..
Under-five mortality rate (per 1,000 live births)	52	63	27	33
Female-headed households (%)	..		..	
Education				
Gross primary enrollment ratio (% of relevant age group)	..	..	98	102
Gross secondary enrollment ratio (% of relevant age group)	..	..	..	..
Gross tertiary enrollment ratio (% of relevant age group)	..	..	..	..
Primary completion rate (% of relevant age group)	..	..	109	89
Youth literacy rate (% of population ages 15–24)	..	..	..	..
Health and related services				
Total fertility rate (births per woman)	..		..	
Adolescent fertility rate (births per 1,000 women ages 15–19)	..		..	
Women first married by age 18 (% of women ages 20–24)	..		10	
Contraceptive prevalence (% of women ages 15–49)	39		31	
Unmet need for contraception (% of women ages 15–49)	..		24	
Pregnant women receiving prenatal care (%)	..		97	
Births attended by skilled health staff (% of total)	100		98	
Maternal mortality ratio (per 100,000 live births)	..		..	
Economic structure, participation, and access to resources				
Labor force participation rate (% of population ages 15+)	..	..	..	..
Wage and salaried workers (% of employed ages 15+)	..	..	..	..
Self-employed workers (% of employed ages 15+)	..	..	..	..
Vulnerable employment (% of employed ages 15+)	..	..	..	..
Unpaid family workers (% of employed ages 15+)	..	..	..	..
Employment in agriculture (% of employed ages 15+)	..	..	..	..
Employment in industry (% of employed ages 15+)	..	..	..	..
Employment in service (% of employed ages 15+)	..	..	..	..
Women in wage employment in the nonagricultural sector (%)	..		..	
Women's share of part-time employment (% of total)	..		..	
Maternity leave (weeks)	..		..	
Maternal leave benefits (% of wages paid)	..		..	
Female legislators, senior officials and managers (% of total)	..		..	
Employment to population ratio, total (% ages 15+)	..	..	..	..
Employment to population ratio, youth (% ages 15–24)	..	..	..	..
Children in employment (% of children ages 7–14)	..	..	..	..
Unemployment rate (% of labor force ages 15+)	..	..	..	..
Long-term unemployment rate (% total unemployment)	..	..	..	..
Youth unemployment rate (% of labor force ages 15–24)	..	..	..	..
Account at a formal financial institution (% age 15+)	..	..	..	..
Public life and decision making				
Seats held by women in national parliament (%)	8		7	

Uganda

Sub-Saharan Africa	Low income
Population (millions)	34.5
GNI, Atlas ($ billions)	17.5
GNI per capita, Atlas ($)	510
Population living below $1.25 a day (%)	38.0

	1990		2011	
	Female	Male	Female	Male
Demography				
Sex ratio at birth (boys per girls)	1.03		1.03	
Life expectancy at birth (years)	49	45	55	53
Under-five mortality rate (per 1,000 live births)	164	192	83	97
Female-headed households (%)	..		30	
Education				
Gross primary enrollment ratio (% of relevant age group)	62	77	114	112
Gross secondary enrollment ratio (% of relevant age group)	8	14	26	30
Gross tertiary enrollment ratio (% of relevant age group)	1	2	4	15
Primary completion rate (% of relevant age group)	28	47	54	56
Youth literacy rate (% of population ages 15–24)	63	77	85	90
Health and related services				
Total fertility rate (births per woman)	7.1		6.1	
Adolescent fertility rate (births per 1,000 women ages 15–19)	..		131	
Women first married by age 18 (% of women ages 20–24)	53		40	
Contraceptive prevalence (% of women ages 15–49)	5		30	
Unmet need for contraception (% of women ages 15–49)	..		41	
Pregnant women receiving prenatal care (%)	87		93	
Births attended by skilled health staff (% of total)	38		57	
Maternal mortality ratio (per 100,000 live births)	600		310	
Economic structure, participation, and access to resources				
Labor force participation rate (% of population ages 15+)	82	82	76	80
Wage and salaried workers (% of employed ages 15+)	..	..	..	..
Self-employed workers (% of employed ages 15+)	..	..	..	..
Vulnerable employment (% of employed ages 15+)	..	..	..	..
Unpaid family workers (% of employed ages 15+)	..	..	..	..
Employment in agriculture (% of employed ages 15+)	..	..	..	..
Employment in industry (% of employed ages 15+)	..	..	..	..
Employment in service (% of employed ages 15+)	..	..	..	..
Women in wage employment in the nonagricultural sector (%)	..		..	
Women's share of part-time employment (% of total)	..		..	
Maternity leave (weeks)	8		9	
Maternal leave benefits (% of wages paid)	..		100	
Female legislators, senior officials and managers (% of total)	..		..	
Employment to population ratio, total (% ages 15+)	79	80	72	77
Employment to population ratio, youth (% ages 15–24)	63	60	54	57
Children in employment (% of children ages 7–14)	..	..	36.5	39.8
Unemployment rate (% of labor force ages 15+)	0.6	1.3	5.1	3.1
Long-term unemployment rate (% total unemployment)	..	..	..	..
Youth unemployment rate (% of labor force ages 15–24)	1	3	..	..
Account at a formal financial institution (% age 15+)	..	..	15	26
Public life and decision making				
Seats held by women in national parliament (%)	12		35	

Ukraine

Europe & Central Asia | Lower middle income

Population (millions)	45.7
GNI, Atlas ($ billions)	142.9
GNI per capita, Atlas ($)	3,130
Population living below $1.25 a day (%)	<2

	1990		2011	
	Female	Male	Female	Male
Demography				
Sex ratio at birth (boys per girls)	1.06		1.06	
Life expectancy at birth (years)	75	66	76	66
Under-five mortality rate (per 1,000 live births)	17	22	9	11
Female-headed households (%)	..		49	
Education				
Gross primary enrollment ratio (% of relevant age group)	107	107	100	99
Gross secondary enrollment ratio (% of relevant age group)	97	93	93	95
Gross tertiary enrollment ratio (% of relevant age group)	46	35	88	75
Primary completion rate (% of relevant age group)	99	99	97	96
Youth literacy rate (% of population ages 15–24)	..	..	100	100
Health and related services				
Total fertility rate (births per woman)	1.8		1.5	
Adolescent fertility rate (births per 1,000 women ages 15–19)	..		27	
Women first married by age 18 (% of women ages 20–24)	..		10	
Contraceptive prevalence (% of women ages 15–49)	..		67	
Unmet need for contraception (% of women ages 15–49)	..		10	
Pregnant women receiving prenatal care (%)	..		99	
Births attended by skilled health staff (% of total)	100		99	
Maternal mortality ratio (per 100,000 live births)	49		32	
Economic structure, participation, and access to resources				
Labor force participation rate (% of population ages 15+)	56	71	53	67
Wage and salaried workers (% of employed ages 15+)	..	..	81	83
Self-employed workers (% of employed ages 15+)	..	..	19	17
Vulnerable employment (% of employed ages 15+)	..	..	..	..
Unpaid family workers (% of employed ages 15+)	..	..	0.3	0.4
Employment in agriculture (% of employed ages 15+)	..	..	..	..
Employment in industry (% of employed ages 15+)	..	..	..	..
Employment in service (% of employed ages 15+)	..	..	..	..
Women in wage employment in the nonagricultural sector (%)	47		55	
Women's share of part-time employment (% of total)			..	
Maternity leave (weeks)	..		18	
Maternal leave benefits (% of wages paid)	..		100	
Female legislators, senior officials and managers (% of total)	..		39	
Employment to population ratio, total (% ages 15+)	52	65	49	61
Employment to population ratio, youth (% ages 15–24)	36	37	30	38
Children in employment (% of children ages 7–14)	..	..	..	..
Unemployment rate (% of labor force ages 15+)	..	..	6.8	8.8
Long-term unemployment rate (% total unemployment)	..	..	..	..
Youth unemployment rate (% of labor force ages 15–24)	..	..	19	19
Account at a formal financial institution (% age 15+)	..	..	39	44
Public life and decision making				
Seats held by women in national parliament (%)	..		9	

United Arab Emirates

Population (millions)	7.9
GNI, Atlas ($ billions)	321.7
GNI per capita, Atlas ($)	40,760
Population living below $1.25 a day (%)	..

	1990 Female	1990 Male	2011 Female	2011 Male
Demography				
Sex ratio at birth (boys per girls)	1.05		1.05	
Life expectancy at birth (years)	74	71	78	76
Under-five mortality rate (per 1,000 live births)	20	24	6	7
Female-headed households (%)	..		..	
Education				
Gross primary enrollment ratio (% of relevant age group)	106	110	106	103
Gross secondary enrollment ratio (% of relevant age group)	69	56	93	92
Gross tertiary enrollment ratio (% of relevant age group)	13	3	..	..
Primary completion rate (% of relevant age group)	90	93	101	98
Youth literacy rate (% of population ages 15–24)	..	..	..	..
Health and related services				
Total fertility rate (births per woman)	4.4		1.7	
Adolescent fertility rate (births per 1,000 women ages 15-19)	..		24	
Women first married by age 18 (% of women ages 20-24)	..		..	
Contraceptive prevalence (% of women ages 15–49)	..		..	
Unmet need for contraception (% of women ages 15–49)	..		..	
Pregnant women receiving prenatal care (%)	..		100	
Births attended by skilled health staff (% of total)	..		100	
Maternal mortality ratio (per 100,000 live births)	24		12	
Economic structure, participation, and access to resources				
Labor force participation rate (% of population ages 15+)	25	91	44	92
Wage and salaried workers (% of employed ages 15+)	..	..	99	95
Self-employed workers (% of employed ages 15+)	..	..	1	5
Vulnerable employment (% of employed ages 15+)	..	..	0	1
Unpaid family workers (% of employed ages 15+)	..	..	0.0	0.0
Employment in agriculture (% of employed ages 15+)	..	..	0	5
Employment in industry (% of employed ages 15+)	..	..	7	28
Employment in service (% of employed ages 15+)	..	..	93	66
Women in wage employment in the nonagricultural sector (%)	..		20	
Women's share of part-time employment (% of total)	..		..	
Maternity leave (weeks)	6		6	
Maternal leave benefits (% of wages paid)	100		100	
Female legislators, senior officials and managers (% of total)	..		10	
Employment to population ratio, total (% ages 15+)	24	89	38	90
Employment to population ratio, youth (% ages 15-24)	15	62	24	54
Children in employment (% of children ages 7-14)	..	..	..	..
Unemployment rate (% of labor force ages 15+)	..	..	12.0	2.0
Long-term unemployment rate (% total unemployment)	..	..	..	..
Youth unemployment rate (% of labor force ages 15-24)	..	..	22	8
Account at a formal financial institution (% age 15+)	..	..	47	69
Public life and decision making				
Seats held by women in national parliament (%)	0		18	

United Kingdom

	High income
Population (millions)	62.7
GNI, Atlas ($ billions)	2,370.4
GNI per capita, Atlas ($)	37,780
Population living below $1.25 a day (%)	..

	1990		2011	
	Female	Male	Female	Male
Demography				
Sex ratio at birth (boys per girls)	1.05		1.05	
Life expectancy at birth (years)	79	73	83	79
Under-five mortality rate (per 1,000 live births)	8	10	5	6
Female-headed households (%)	..		..	
Education				
Gross primary enrollment ratio (% of relevant age group)	106	106	107	107
Gross secondary enrollment ratio (% of relevant age group)	85	82	106	105
Gross tertiary enrollment ratio (% of relevant age group)	26	28	70	50
Primary completion rate (% of relevant age group)	..	..	..	..
Youth literacy rate (% of population ages 15-24)	..	..	..	..
Health and related services				
Total fertility rate (births per woman)	1.8		2.0	
Adolescent fertility rate (births per 1,000 women ages 15–19)	..		30	
Women first married by age 18 (% of women ages 20–24)	..		..	
Contraceptive prevalence (% of women ages 15–49)	70		84	
Unmet need for contraception (% of women ages 15–49)	..		..	
Pregnant women receiving prenatal care (%)	..		..	
Births attended by skilled health staff (% of total)	..		..	
Maternal mortality ratio (per 100,000 live births)	10		12	
Economic structure, participation, and access to resources				
Labor force participation rate (% of population ages 15+)	53	75	56	69
Wage and salaried workers (% of employed ages 15+)	92	81	91	81
Self-employed workers (% of employed ages 15+)	7	18	9	18
Vulnerable employment (% of employed ages 15+)	5	12	8	15
Unpaid family workers (% of employed ages 15+)	0.0	0.0	0.5	0.2
Employment in agriculture (% of employed ages 15+)	1	3	1	2
Employment in industry (% of employed ages 15+)	17	44	8	29
Employment in service (% of employed ages 15+)	81	53	91	69
Women in wage employment in the nonagricultural sector (%)	44		47	
Women's share of part-time employment (% of total)	85		75	
Maternity leave (weeks)	14		7	
Maternal leave benefits (% of wages paid)	90		90	
Female legislators, senior officials and managers (% of total)	31		34	
Employment to population ratio, total (% ages 15+)	49	67	52	62
Employment to population ratio, youth (% ages 15–24)	61	66	46	46
Children in employment (% of children ages 7-14)	..	..	..	..
Unemployment rate (% of labor force ages 15+)	6.5	7.0	7.1	8.4
Long-term unemployment rate (% total unemployment)	23.4	41.2	27.5	37.7
Youth unemployment rate (% of labor force ages 15–24)	9	11	18	22
Account at a formal financial institution (% age 15+)	..	..	98	97
Public life and decision making				
Seats held by women in national parliament (%)	6		23	

United States

	High income
Population (millions)	311.6
GNI, Atlas ($ billions)	15,148.2
GNI per capita, Atlas ($)	48,620
Population living below $1.25 a day (%)	..

	1990		2011	
	Female	Male	Female	Male
Demography				
Sex ratio at birth (boys per girls)	1.05		1.05	
Life expectancy at birth (years)	79	72	81	76
Under-five mortality rate (per 1,000 live births)	10	13	7	8
Female-headed households (%)	..		..	
Education				
Gross primary enrollment ratio (% of relevant age group)	104	105	101	102
Gross secondary enrollment ratio (% of relevant age group)	91	91	97	96
Gross tertiary enrollment ratio (% of relevant age group)	79	64	111	79
Primary completion rate (% of relevant age group)	..	..	104	103
Youth literacy rate (% of population ages 15–24)	..	..	..	..
Health and related services				
Total fertility rate (births per woman)	2.1		1.9	
Adolescent fertility rate (births per 1,000 women ages 15–19)	..		30	
Women first married by age 18 (% of women ages 20–24)	..		..	
Contraceptive prevalence (% of women ages 15–49)	71		79	
Unmet need for contraception (% of women ages 15–49)	..		..	
Pregnant women receiving prenatal care (%)	..		..	
Births attended by skilled health staff (% of total)	99		..	
Maternal mortality ratio (per 100,000 live births)	12		21	
Economic structure, participation, and access to resources				
Labor force participation rate (% of population ages 15+)	56	75	58	70
Wage and salaried workers (% of employed ages 15+)	93	90	95	99
Self-employed workers (% of employed ages 15+)	7	11	6	8
Vulnerable employment (% of employed ages 15+)	..	..	..	..
Unpaid family workers (% of employed ages 15+)	0.5	0.1	0.1	0.1
Employment in agriculture (% of employed ages 15+)	1	4	1	2
Employment in industry (% of employed ages 15+)	15	36	7	25
Employment in service (% of employed ages 15+)	84	60	92	72
Women in wage employment in the nonagricultural sector (%)	47		48	
Women's share of part-time employment (% of total)	..		..	
Maternity leave (weeks)	12		12	
Maternal leave benefits (% of wages paid)	0		..	
Female legislators, senior officials and managers (% of total)	..		43	
Employment to population ratio, total (% ages 15+)	53	69	53	63
Employment to population ratio, youth (% ages 15–24)	51	57	42	42
Children in employment (% of children ages 7–14)	..	..	..	..
Unemployment rate (% of labor force ages 15+)	5.5	5.7	8.5	9.4
Long-term unemployment rate (% total unemployment)	3.7	7.0	30.2	32.2
Youth unemployment rate (% of labor force ages 15–24)	11	12	16	19
Account at a formal financial institution (% age 15+)	..	..	84	92
Public life and decision making				
Seats held by women in national parliament (%)	7		18	

Uruguay

Latin America & the Caribbean	Upper middle income
Population (millions)	3.4
GNI, Atlas ($ billions)	40.0
GNI per capita, Atlas ($)	11,860
Population living below $1.25 a day (%)	<2

	1990		2011	
	Female	Male	Female	Male
Demography				
Sex ratio at birth (boys per girls)	1.05		1.05	
Life expectancy at birth (years)	76	69	80	73
Under-five mortality rate (per 1,000 live births)	21	26	9	11
Female-headed households (%)	..		..	
Education				
Gross primary enrollment ratio (% of relevant age group)	108	109	110	114
Gross secondary enrollment ratio (% of relevant age group)	88	74	96	85
Gross tertiary enrollment ratio (% of relevant age group)	..	..	80	47
Primary completion rate (% of relevant age group)	97	92	104	105
Youth literacy rate (% of population ages 15-24)	..	..	99	98
Health and related services				
Total fertility rate (births per woman)	2.5		2.0	
Adolescent fertility rate (births per 1,000 women ages 15-19)	..		59	
Women first married by age 18 (% of women ages 20-24)	..		..	
Contraceptive prevalence (% of women ages 15-49)	83		..	
Unmet need for contraception (% of women ages 15-49)	..		..	
Pregnant women receiving prenatal care (%)	..		96	
Births attended by skilled health staff (% of total)	..		100	
Maternal mortality ratio (per 100,000 live births)	39		29	
Economic structure, participation, and access to resources				
Labor force participation rate (% of population ages 15+)	45	78	56	77
Wage and salaried workers (% of employed ages 15+)	..	..	76	71
Self-employed workers (% of employed ages 15+)	..	..	24	29
Vulnerable employment (% of employed ages 15+)	..	..	21	23
Unpaid family workers (% of employed ages 15+)	..	..	1.6	0.6
Employment in agriculture (% of employed ages 15+)	0	0	5	16
Employment in industry (% of employed ages 15+)	22	40	13	29
Employment in service (% of employed ages 15+)	78	60	83	56
Women in wage employment in the nonagricultural sector (%)	42		46	
Women's share of part-time employment (% of total)	..		65	
Maternity leave (weeks)	12		12	
Maternal leave benefits (% of wages paid)	100		100	
Female legislators, senior officials and managers (% of total)	..		40	
Employment to population ratio, total (% ages 15+)	39	72	51	73
Employment to population ratio, youth (% ages 15-24)	33	57	36	52
Children in employment (% of children ages 7-14)	..	..	5.0	9.4
Unemployment rate (% of labor force ages 15+)	10.9	6.9	7.7	4.5
Long-term unemployment rate (% total unemployment)	..	..	..	..
Youth unemployment rate (% of labor force ages 15-24)	27	21	22	14
Account at a formal financial institution (% age 15+)	..	..	24	23
Public life and decision making				
Seats held by women in national parliament (%)	6		12	

Uzbekistan

Europe & Central Asia	Lower middle income
Population (millions)	29.3
GNI, Atlas ($ billions)	44.2
GNI per capita, Atlas ($)	1,510
Population living below $1.25 a day (%)	..

	1990 Female	1990 Male	2011 Female	2011 Male
Demography				
Sex ratio at birth (boys per girls)	1.05		1.05	
Life expectancy at birth (years)	70	64	71	65
Under-five mortality rate (per 1,000 live births)	68	82	42	55
Female-headed households (%)	..		18	
Education				
Gross primary enrollment ratio (% of relevant age group)	110	111	93	96
Gross secondary enrollment ratio (% of relevant age group)	..	..	104	107
Gross tertiary enrollment ratio (% of relevant age group)	..	..	7	11
Primary completion rate (% of relevant age group)	..	..	92	94
Youth literacy rate (% of population ages 15–24)	..	..	100	100
Health and related services				
Total fertility rate (births per woman)	4.1		2.5	
Adolescent fertility rate (births per 1,000 women ages 15–19)	..		13	
Women first married by age 18 (% of women ages 20–24)	..		7	
Contraceptive prevalence (% of women ages 15–49)	..		65	
Unmet need for contraception (% of women ages 15–49)	..		8	
Pregnant women receiving prenatal care (%)	..		99	
Births attended by skilled health staff (% of total)	..		100	
Maternal mortality ratio (per 100,000 live births)	59		28	
Economic structure, participation, and access to resources				
Labor force participation rate (% of population ages 15+)	46	73	48	75
Wage and salaried workers (% of employed ages 15+)	..	..	..	..
Self-employed workers (% of employed ages 15+)	..	..	..	..
Vulnerable employment (% of employed ages 15+)	..	..	..	..
Unpaid family workers (% of employed ages 15+)	..	..	..	..
Employment in agriculture (% of employed ages 15+)	..	..	..	..
Employment in industry (% of employed ages 15+)	..	..	..	..
Employment in service (% of employed ages 15+)	..	..	..	..
Women in wage employment in the nonagricultural sector (%)	37		39	
Women's share of part-time employment (% of total)	..			
Maternity leave (weeks)	..		18	
Maternal leave benefits (% of wages paid)	..		100	
Female legislators, senior officials and managers (% of total)	..		..	
Employment to population ratio, total (% ages 15+)	41	64	43	67
Employment to population ratio, youth (% ages 15–24)	25	42	26	45
Children in employment (% of children ages 7–14)	..	..	..	..
Unemployment rate (% of labor force ages 15+)	..	..	..	..
Long-term unemployment rate (% total unemployment)	..	..	..	..
Youth unemployment rate (% of labor force ages 15–24)	..	..	..	..
Account at a formal financial institution (% age 15+)	..	..	21	24
Public life and decision making				
Seats held by women in national parliament (%)	..		22	

Vanuatu

East Asia & Pacific	Lower middle income
Population (thousands)	245.6
GNI, Atlas ($ millions)	669.6
GNI per capita, Atlas ($)	2,730
Population living below $1.25 a day (%)	..

	1990		2011	
	Female	Male	Female	Male
Demography				
Sex ratio at birth (boys per girls)	1.07		1.07	
Life expectancy at birth (years)	65	62	73	69
Under-five mortality rate (per 1,000 live births)	36	41	12	14
Female-headed households (%)	..		..	
Education				
Gross primary enrollment ratio (% of relevant age group)	96	98	114	120
Gross secondary enrollment ratio (% of relevant age group)	16	20	55	54
Gross tertiary enrollment ratio (% of relevant age group)	..	..	..	..
Primary completion rate (% of relevant age group)	82	85	83	84
Youth literacy rate (% of population ages 15–24)	85	87	94	94
Health and related services				
Total fertility rate (births per woman)	4.9		3.8	
Adolescent fertility rate (births per 1,000 women ages 15–19)	..		51	
Women first married by age 18 (% of women ages 20–24)	..		27	
Contraceptive prevalence (% of women ages 15–49)	15		38	
Unmet need for contraception (% of women ages 15–49)	..		..	
Pregnant women receiving prenatal care (%)	..		84	
Births attended by skilled health staff (% of total)	87		74	
Maternal mortality ratio (per 100,000 live births)	220		110	
Economic structure, participation, and access to resources				
Labor force participation rate (% of population ages 15+)	79	88	61	80
Wage and salaried workers (% of employed ages 15+)	..	..	23	29
Self-employed workers (% of employed ages 15+)	..	..	76	68
Vulnerable employment (% of employed ages 15+)	..	..	75	67
Unpaid family workers (% of employed ages 15+)	..	..	9.2	8.5
Employment in agriculture (% of employed ages 15+)	..	..	62	59
Employment in industry (% of employed ages 15+)	..	..	3	11
Employment in service (% of employed ages 15+)	..	..	33	29
Women in wage employment in the nonagricultural sector (%)	..		39	
Women's share of part-time employment (% of total)	..		..	
Maternity leave (weeks)	..		13	
Maternal leave benefits (% of wages paid)	..		50	
Female legislators, senior officials and managers (% of total)	..		29	
Employment to population ratio, total (% ages 15+)	..	..	..	..
Employment to population ratio, youth (% ages 15–24)	..	..	..	..
Children in employment (% of children ages 7–14)	..	..	..	..
Unemployment rate (% of labor force ages 15+)	..	..	5.2	4.1
Long-term unemployment rate (% total unemployment)	..	..	..	..
Youth unemployment rate (% of labor force ages 15–24)	..	..	..	..
Account at a formal financial institution (% age 15+)	..	..	..	..
Public life and decision making				
Seats held by women in national parliament (%)	4		0	

Venezuela, RB

Latin America & the Caribbean			Upper middle income	
Population (millions)				29.3
GNI, Atlas ($ billions)				346.1
GNI per capita, Atlas ($)				11,820
Population living below $1.25 a day (%)				6.6

	1990		2011	
	Female	Male	Female	Male
Demography				
Sex ratio at birth (boys per girls)	1.05		1.05	
Life expectancy at birth (years)	74	68	77	71
Under-five mortality rate (per 1,000 live births)	28	34	13	17
Female-headed households (%)	..		..	
Education				
Gross primary enrollment ratio (% of relevant age group)	109	110	101	104
Gross secondary enrollment ratio (% of relevant age group)	62	50	87	80
Gross tertiary enrollment ratio (% of relevant age group)	25	28	99	58
Primary completion rate (% of relevant age group)	86	76	96	94
Youth literacy rate (% of population ages 15–24)	96	95	99	98
Health and related services				
Total fertility rate (births per woman)	3.4		2.5	
Adolescent fertility rate (births per 1,000 women ages 15–19)	..		88	
Women first married by age 18 (% of women ages 20–24)	..		..	
Contraceptive prevalence (% of women ages 15–49)	58		..	
Unmet need for contraception (% of women ages 15–49)	..		..	
Pregnant women receiving prenatal care (%)	..		..	
Births attended by skilled health staff (% of total)	..		..	
Maternal mortality ratio (per 100,000 live births)	94		92	
Economic structure, participation, and access to resources				
Labor force participation rate (% of population ages 15+)	37	81	52	80
Wage and salaried workers (% of employed ages 15+)	71	58	61	55
Self-employed workers (% of employed ages 15+)	29	42	39	45
Vulnerable employment (% of employed ages 15+)	27	34	33	32
Unpaid family workers (% of employed ages 15+)	1.2	1.7	1.1	0.5
Employment in agriculture (% of employed ages 15+)	2	19	2	13
Employment in industry (% of employed ages 15+)	16	30	11	29
Employment in service (% of employed ages 15+)	82	52	87	58
Women in wage employment in the nonagricultural sector (%)	35		42	
Women's share of part-time employment (% of total)	66		62	
Maternity leave (weeks)	18		18	
Maternal leave benefits (% of wages paid)	100		67	
Female legislators, senior officials and managers (% of total)	..		..	
Employment to population ratio, total (% ages 15+)	35	75	47	74
Employment to population ratio, youth (% ages 15–24)	22	54	27	50
Children in employment (% of children ages 7–14)	..	..	3.3	6.9
Unemployment rate (% of labor force ages 15+)	10.0	10.4	9.3	7.7
Long-term unemployment rate (% of total unemployment)	..	..	..	..
Youth unemployment rate (% of labor force ages 15–24)	26	21	22	15
Account at a formal financial institution (% age 15+)	..	..	36	53
Public life and decision making				
Seats held by women in national parliament (%)	10		17	

Vietnam

East Asia & Pacific	Lower middle income
Population (millions)	87.8
GNI, Atlas ($ billions)	111.1
GNI per capita, Atlas ($)	1,270
Population living below $1.25 a day (%)	16.9

	1990		2011	
	Female	Male	Female	Male
Demography				
Sex ratio at birth (boys per girls)	1.05		1.05	
Life expectancy at birth (years)	67	64	77	73
Under-five mortality rate (per 1,000 live births)	43	57	19	25
Female-headed households (%)	..		..	
Education				
Gross primary enrollment ratio (% of relevant age group)	104	113	103	109
Gross secondary enrollment ratio (% of relevant age group)	..	..	81	74
Gross tertiary enrollment ratio (% of relevant age group)	..	..	25	24
Primary completion rate (% of relevant age group)	..	..	..	..
Youth literacy rate (% of population ages 15–24)	93	94	96	97
Health and related services				
Total fertility rate (births per woman)	3.6		1.8	
Adolescent fertility rate (births per 1,000 women ages 15–19)	..		24	
Women first married by age 18 (% of women ages 20–24)	..		9	
Contraceptive prevalence (% of women ages 15–49)	53		78	
Unmet need for contraception (% of women ages 15–49)	..		..	
Pregnant women receiving prenatal care (%)	..		94	
Births attended by skilled health staff (% of total)	..		93	
Maternal mortality ratio (per 100,000 live births)	240		59	
Economic structure, participation, and access to resources				
Labor force participation rate (% of population ages 15+)	76	85	73	81
Wage and salaried workers (% of employed ages 15+)	..	..	..	..
Self-employed workers (% of employed ages 15+)	..	..	..	..
Vulnerable employment (% of employed ages 15+)	..	..	..	..
Unpaid family workers (% of employed ages 15+)	..	..	..	..
Employment in agriculture (% of employed ages 15+)	..	..	54	50
Employment in industry (% of employed ages 15+)	..	..	16	24
Employment in service (% of employed ages 15+)	..	..	30	26
Women in wage employment in the nonagricultural sector (%)	..		..	
Women's share of part-time employment (% of total)	..		..	
Maternity leave (weeks)	..		26	
Maternal leave benefits (% of wages paid)	100		100	
Female legislators, senior officials and managers (% of total)	..		..	
Employment to population ratio, total (% ages 15+)	74	83	71	80
Employment to population ratio, youth (% ages 15–24)	71	76	56	61
Children in employment (% of children ages 7–14)	..	..	13.5	12.5
Unemployment rate (% of labor force ages 15+)	..	..	2.4	1.7
Long-term unemployment rate (% total unemployment)	..	..	..	..
Youth unemployment rate (% of labor force ages 15–24)	..	..	..	..
Account at a formal financial institution (% age 15+)	..	..	19	24
Public life and decision making				
Seats held by women in national parliament (%)	18		24	

Virgin Islands (U.S.)

	High income
Population (thousands)	109.7
GNI, Atlas ($ billions)	..
GNI per capita, Atlas ($)	..
Population living below $1.25 a day (%)	..

	1990		2011	
	Female	Male	Female	Male
Demography				
Sex ratio at birth (boys per girls)	1.06		1.06	
Life expectancy at birth (years)	79	71	82	76
Under-five mortality rate (per 1,000 live births)	..	..	..	..
Female-headed households (%)	..		..	
Education				
Gross primary enrollment ratio (% of relevant age group)	..	..	..	..
Gross secondary enrollment ratio (% of relevant age group)	..	..	..	..
Gross tertiary enrollment ratio (% of relevant age group)	..	..	..	..
Primary completion rate (% of relevant age group)	..	..	..	..
Youth literacy rate (% of population ages 15–24)	..	..	..	..
Health and related services				
Total fertility rate (births per woman)	3.1		1.8	
Adolescent fertility rate (births per 1,000 women ages 15–19)	..		23	
Women first married by age 18 (% of women ages 20–24)	..		..	
Contraceptive prevalence (% of women ages 15–49)	..		..	
Unmet need for contraception (% of women ages 15–49)	..		..	
Pregnant women receiving prenatal care (%)	..		..	
Births attended by skilled health staff (% of total)	..		..	
Maternal mortality ratio (per 100,000 live births)	..		..	
Economic structure, participation, and access to resources				
Labor force participation rate (% of population ages 15+)	51	80	54	72
Wage and salaried workers (% of employed ages 15+)	..	..	..	..
Self-employed workers (% of employed ages 15+)	..	..	..	..
Vulnerable employment (% of employed ages 15+)	..	..	..	..
Unpaid family workers (% of employed ages 15+)	..	..	..	..
Employment in agriculture (% of employed ages 15+)	..	..	..	..
Employment in industry (% of employed ages 15+)	..	..	..	..
Employment in service (% of employed ages 15+)	..	..	..	..
Women in wage employment in the nonagricultural sector (%)	48		..	
Women's share of part-time employment (% of total)	..		..	
Maternity leave (weeks)	..		..	
Maternal leave benefits (% of wages paid)	..		..	
Female legislators, senior officials and managers (% of total)	..		..	
Employment to population ratio, total (% ages 15+)	..	..	..	..
Employment to population ratio, youth (% ages 15–24)	..	..	..	..
Children in employment (% of children ages 7–14)	..	..	..	..
Unemployment rate (% of labor force ages 15+)	..	..	..	..
Long-term unemployment rate (% total unemployment)	..	..	..	..
Youth unemployment rate (% of labor force ages 15–24)	..	..	..	..
Account at a formal financial institution (% age 15+)	..	..	..	..
Public life and decision making				
Seats held by women in national parliament (%)	..		..	

West Bank and Gaza

Middle East & North Africa			Lower middle income	
Population (millions)				3.9
GNI, Atlas ($ billions)				..
GNI per capita, Atlas ($)				..
Population living below $1.25 a day (%)				<2

	1990		2011	
	Female	Male	Female	Male
Demography				
Sex ratio at birth (boys per girls)	1.05		1.05	
Life expectancy at birth (years)	70	67	75	71
Under-five mortality rate (per 1,000 live births)	41	46	21	23
Female-headed households (%)	..		..	
Education				
Gross primary enrollment ratio (% of relevant age group)	..	..	92	92
Gross secondary enrollment ratio (% of relevant age group)	..	..	88	80
Gross tertiary enrollment ratio (% of relevant age group)	..	..	60	43
Primary completion rate (% of relevant age group)	..	..	92	90
Youth literacy rate (% of population ages 15–24)	..	..	99	99
Health and related services				
Total fertility rate (births per woman)	6.5		4.4	
Adolescent fertility rate (births per 1,000 women ages 15–19)	..		49	
Women first married by age 18 (% of women ages 20–24)	..		..	
Contraceptive prevalence (% of women ages 15–49)	..		50	
Unmet need for contraception (% of women ages 15–49)	..		..	
Pregnant women receiving prenatal care (%)	..		99	
Births attended by skilled health staff (% of total)	..		99	
Maternal mortality ratio (per 100,000 live births)	..		..	
Economic structure, participation, and access to resources				
Labor force participation rate (% of population ages 15+)	10	68	15	66
Wage and salaried workers (% of employed ages 15+)	..	..	67	68
Self-employed workers (% of employed ages 15+)	..	..	33	32
Vulnerable employment (% of employed ages 15+)	..	..	32	25
Unpaid family workers (% of employed ages 15+)	..	..	19.5	4.7
Employment in agriculture (% of employed ages 15+)	..	..	21	10
Employment in industry (% of employed ages 15+)	..	..	8	28
Employment in service (% of employed ages 15+)	..	..	71	62
Women in wage employment in the nonagricultural sector (%)	..		17	
Women's share of part-time employment (% of total)	..		..	
Maternity leave (weeks)	..		..	
Maternal leave benefits (% of wages paid)	..		..	
Female legislators, senior officials and managers (% of total)	..		10	
Employment to population ratio, total (% ages 15+)	8	54	13	52
Employment to population ratio, youth (% ages 15–24)	4	35	5	29
Children in employment (% of children ages 7–14)	..	..	..	..
Unemployment rate (% of labor force ages 15+)	..	..	26.8	23.1
Long-term unemployment rate (% total unemployment)	..	..	..	..
Youth unemployment rate (% of labor force ages 15–24)	..	..	50	37
Account at a formal financial institution (% age 15+)	..	..	10	29
Public life and decision making				
Seats held by women in national parliament (%)	..		..	

Yemen, Rep.

Middle East & North Africa	Lower middle income
Population (millions)	24.8
GNI, Atlas ($ billions)	26.4
GNI per capita, Atlas ($)	1,070
Population living below $1.25 a day (%)	17.5

	1990 Female	1990 Male	2011 Female	2011 Male
Demography				
Sex ratio at birth (boys per girls)	1.05		1.05	
Life expectancy at birth (years)	57	55	67	64
Under-five mortality rate (per 1,000 live births)	121	131	73	80
Female-headed households (%)	12		..	
Education				
Gross primary enrollment ratio (% of relevant age group)	..	..	81	100
Gross secondary enrollment ratio (% of relevant age group)	..	..	35	56
Gross tertiary enrollment ratio (% of relevant age group)	2	8	6	14
Primary completion rate (% of relevant age group)	..	..	53	72
Youth literacy rate (% of population ages 15–24)	35	83	74	96
Health and related services				
Total fertility rate (births per woman)	8.7		5.1	
Adolescent fertility rate (births per 1,000 women ages 15–19)	..		69	
Women first married by age 18 (% of women ages 20–24)	49		32	
Contraceptive prevalence (% of women ages 15–49)	10		28	
Unmet need for contraception (% of women ages 15–49)	..		24	
Pregnant women receiving prenatal care (%)	26		47	
Births attended by skilled health staff (% of total)	16		36	
Maternal mortality ratio (per 100,000 live births)	610		200	
Economic structure, participation, and access to resources				
Labor force participation rate (% of population ages 15+)	16	74	25	72
Wage and salaried workers (% of employed ages 15+)	..	..	..	..
Self-employed workers (% of employed ages 15+)	..	..	..	..
Vulnerable employment (% of employed ages 15+)	..	..	..	..
Unpaid family workers (% of employed ages 15+)	..	..	..	..
Employment in agriculture (% of employed ages 15+)	83	44	..	..
Employment in industry (% of employed ages 15+)	2	14	..	..
Employment in service (% of employed ages 15+)	13	38	..	..
Women in wage employment in the nonagricultural sector (%)	6		6	
Women's share of part-time employment (% of total)	..		..	
Maternity leave (weeks)	10		9	
Maternal leave benefits (% of wages paid)	70		100	
Female legislators, senior officials and managers (% of total)	..		..	
Employment to population ratio, total (% ages 15+)	12	67	19	63
Employment to population ratio, youth (% ages 15–24)	9	39	11	39
Children in employment (% of children ages 7–14)	..	..	15.9	20.7
Unemployment rate (% of labor force ages 15+)	3.9	9.3	40.9	11.5
Long-term unemployment rate (% total unemployment)	..	..	..	..
Youth unemployment rate (% of labor force ages 15–24)	10	20	..	..
Account at a formal financial institution (% age 15+)	..	..	1	6
Public life and decision making				
Seats held by women in national parliament (%)	4		0	

Zambia

Sub-Saharan Africa	Lower middle income
Population (millions)	13.5
GNI, Atlas ($ billions)	15.7
GNI per capita, Atlas ($)	1,160
Population living below $1.25 a day (%)	68.5

	1990 Female	1990 Male	2011 Female	2011 Male
Demography				
Sex ratio at birth (boys per girls)	1.03		1.03	
Life expectancy at birth (years)	49	46	49	49
Under-five mortality rate (per 1,000 live births)	186	200	80	86
Female-headed households (%)	16		24	
Education				
Gross primary enrollment ratio (% of relevant age group)	94	103	117	118
Gross secondary enrollment ratio (% of relevant age group)	15	26	..	..
Gross tertiary enrollment ratio (% of relevant age group)	1	3	..	..
Primary completion rate (% of relevant age group)	81	107	108	98
Youth literacy rate (% of population ages 15–24)	66	67	67	82
Health and related services				
Total fertility rate (births per woman)	6.5		6.3	
Adolescent fertility rate (births per 1,000 women ages 15–19)	..		140	
Women first married by age 18 (% of women ages 20–24)	43		42	
Contraceptive prevalence (% of women ages 15–49)	15		41	
Unmet need for contraception (% of women ages 15–49)	31		27	
Pregnant women receiving prenatal care (%)	92		94	
Births attended by skilled health staff (% of total)	51		47	
Maternal mortality ratio (per 100,000 live births)	470		440	
Economic structure, participation, and access to resources				
Labor force participation rate (% of population ages 15+)	74	86	73	86
Wage and salaried workers (% of employed ages 15+)	15	39	..	..
Self-employed workers (% of employed ages 15+)	82	58	..	..
Vulnerable employment (% of employed ages 15+)	81	56	..	..
Unpaid family workers (% of employed ages 15+)	55.7	27.8	..	..
Employment in agriculture (% of employed ages 15+)	56	47	..	..
Employment in industry (% of employed ages 15+)	3	15	..	..
Employment in service (% of employed ages 15+)	18	22	..	..
Women in wage employment in the nonagricultural sector (%)	17		..	
Women's share of part-time employment (% of total)	..		..	
Maternity leave (weeks)	12		12	
Maternal leave benefits (% of wages paid)	100		100	
Female legislators, senior officials and managers (% of total)	..		..	
Employment to population ratio, total (% ages 15+)	62	68	64	71
Employment to population ratio, youth (% ages 15–24)	47	47	51	52
Children in employment (% of children ages 7–14)	..	..	33.3	35.4
Unemployment rate (% of labor force ages 15+)	13.7	11.7	..	..
Long-term unemployment rate (% total unemployment)	..	..	..	..
Youth unemployment rate (% of labor force ages 15–24)	21	21	..	..
Account at a formal financial institution (% age 15+)	..	..	23	19
Public life and decision making				
Seats held by women in national parliament (%)	7		12	

Zimbabwe

Sub-Saharan Africa   **Low income**

Population (millions)	12.8
GNI, Atlas ($ billions)	8.4
GNI per capita, Atlas ($)	660
Population living below $1.25 a day (%)	..

	1990 Female	1990 Male	2011 Female	2011 Male
Demography				
Sex ratio at birth (boys per girls)	1.02		1.02	
Life expectancy at birth (years)	62	59	50	52
Under-five mortality rate (per 1,000 live births)	72	86	61	73
Female-headed households (%)	33		45	
Education				
Gross primary enrollment ratio (% of relevant age group)	100	101	..	..
Gross secondary enrollment ratio (% of relevant age group)	44	50	..	..
Gross tertiary enrollment ratio (% of relevant age group)	4	8	5	7
Primary completion rate (% of relevant age group)	..	..	..	..
Youth literacy rate (% of population ages 15–24)	94	97	100	98
Health and related services				
Total fertility rate (births per woman)	5.2		3.2	
Adolescent fertility rate (births per 1,000 women ages 15–19)	..		56	
Women first married by age 18 (% of women ages 20–24)	33		31	
Contraceptive prevalence (% of women ages 15–49)	43		59	
Unmet need for contraception (% of women ages 15–49)	..		15	
Pregnant women receiving prenatal care (%)	91		90	
Births attended by skilled health staff (% of total)	70		66	
Maternal mortality ratio (per 100,000 live births)	450		570	
Economic structure, participation, and access to resources				
Labor force participation rate (% of population ages 15+)	67	80	83	90
Wage and salaried workers (% of employed ages 15+)	18	53	..	..
Self-employed workers (% of employed ages 15+)	82	47	..	..
Vulnerable employment (% of employed ages 15+)	82	47	..	..
Unpaid family workers (% of employed ages 15+)	20.5	16.4	..	..
Employment in agriculture (% of employed ages 15+)	..	..	..	..
Employment in industry (% of employed ages 15+)	..	..	..	..
Employment in service (% of employed ages 15+)	..	..	..	..
Women in wage employment in the nonagricultural sector (%)	15		..	
Women's share of part-time employment (% of total)	..		..	
Maternity leave (weeks)	12		14	
Maternal leave benefits (% of wages paid)	60		100	
Female legislators, senior officials and managers (% of total)	..		..	
Employment to population ratio, total (% ages 15+)	64	74	80	85
Employment to population ratio, youth (% ages 15–24)	47	48	72	73
Children in employment (% of children ages 7–14)	..	..	..	..
Unemployment rate (% of labor force ages 15+)	7.9	6.5	..	..
Long-term unemployment rate (% total unemployment)	..	..	..	..
Youth unemployment rate (% of labor force ages 15–24)	43	46	..	..
Account at a formal financial institution (% age 15+)	..	..	37	43
Public life and decision making				
Seats held by women in national parliament (%)	11		15	

Notes

a. Data are for 2012.

b. Includes Taiwan, China.

c. Excludes South Sudan.

d. Excludes South Sudan after July 9, 2011.

Glossary

Account at a formal financial institution is the percentage of respondents with an account (self or together with someone else) at a bank, credit union, another financial institution (e.g., cooperative, microfinance institution), or the post office (if applicable) including respondents who reported having a debit card. (World Bank)

Adolescent fertility rate is the number of births per 1,000 women ages 15–19. (United Nations Population Division)

Births attended by skilled health staff are the percentage of deliveries attended by personnel trained to give the necessary care to women during pregnancy, labor, and postpartum; to conduct deliveries on their own; and to care for newborns. (United Nations Children's Fund, ChildInfo, and ICF International)

Children in employment are children ages 7–14 who are involved in any economic activity for at least one hour in the reference week of the survey. (Understanding Children's Work)

Contraceptive prevalence is the percentage of women married or in-union ages 15–49 who are practicing, or whose sexual partners are practicing, any form of contraception. (United Nations Children's Fund and ICF International)

Employment in agriculture is the proportion of employment in agriculture—division 1 (ISIC revision 2) or tabulation categories A and B (ISIC revision 3) and includes hunting, forestry, and fishing—in total employment. (International Labour Organization Key Indicators of Labour Market database)

Employment in industry is the proportion of employment in industry—divisions 2–5 (ISIC revision 2) or tabulation categories C–F (ISIC revision 3) and includes mining and quarrying (including oil production), manufacturing, construction, and public utilities (electricity, gas, and water)—in total employment. (International Labour Organization Key Indicators of Labour Market database)

Employment in service is the proportion of employment in service—divisions 6–9 (ISIC revision 2) or tabulation categories G–P (ISIC revision 3) and include wholesale and retail trade and restaurants and hotels; transport, storage, and communications; financing, insurance, real estate, and business services; and community, social, and personal service—in total employment. (International Labour Organization Key Indicators of Labour Market database)

Employment to population ratio is the proportion of a country's population that is employed. Ages 15 and older are generally considered the working-age population and ages 15–24 are generally considered the youth population. (International Labour Organization Key Indicators of Labour Market database)

Female headed household is the percentage of households with a female head. (ICF International)

Glossary

Female legislators, senior officials and managers refer to the share of legislators, senior officials and managers who are female. (International Labour Organization Key Indicators of Labour Market database)

GNI is the sum of value added by all resident producers plus any product taxes (less subsidies) not included in the valuation of output plus net receipts of primary income (compensation of employees and property income) from abroad. Data are in current U.S. dollars. GNI, calculated in national currency, is usually converted to U.S. dollars at official exchange rates for comparisons across economies, although an alternative rate is used when the official exchange rate is judged to diverge by an exceptionally large margin from the rate actually applied in international transactions. To smooth fluctuations in prices and exchange rates, a special Atlas method of conversion is used by the World Bank. This applies a conversion factor that averages the exchange rate for a given year and the two preceding years, adjusted for differences in rates of inflation between the country, and through 2000, the G-5 countries (France, Germany, Japan, the United Kingdom, and the United States). From 2001, these countries include the Euro area, Japan, the United Kingdom, and the United States. Figures in italics are for years other than 2011. (World Bank)

GNI per capita is gross national income (GNI) converted to U.S. dollars using the World Bank Atlas method divided by midyear population. GNI is the sum of value added by all resident producers plus any product taxes (less subsidies) not included in the valuation of output plus net receipts of primary income (compensation of employees and property income) from abroad. GNI, calculated in national currency, is usually converted to U.S. dollars at official exchange rates for comparisons across economies. The World Bank Atlas method is used to smooth fluctuations in prices and exchange rates. It averages the exchange rate for a given year and the two preceding years, adjusted for differences in rates of inflation between the country and the Euro zone, Japan, the United Kingdom, and the United States. Figures in italics are for years other than 2011. (World Bank)

Gross primary enrollment ratio is the total enrollment in primary level, regardless of age, to the population of the age group that officially corresponds to the primary education. (United Nations Educational, Scientific, and Cultural Organization Institute for Statistics)

Gross secondary enrollment ratio is the total enrollment in secondary level, regardless of age, to the population of the age group that officially corresponds to the secondary education. (United Nations Educational, Scientific, and Cultural Organization Institute for Statistics)

Gross tertiary enrollment ratio is the total enrollment in tertiary level, regardless of age, to the population of the age group that officially corresponds to the tertiary education. (United Nations Educational, Scientific, and Cultural Organization Institute for Statistics)

Labor force participation rate is the proportion of the population ages 15 and older that is economically active: all people who supply labor for the production of goods and services during a specified period. (International Labour Organization Key Indicators of Labour Market database)

Life expectancy at birth is the number of years a newborn infant would live if prevailing patterns of mortality at the time of its birth were to stay the same throughout its life. (World Bank staff estimates from various sources including census reports, the United Nations Population Division's World Population Prospects, national statistical offices, household surveys conducted by national agencies, and ICF International.)

Long-term unemployment rate is the share of people with continuous periods of unemployment extending for a year or longer in the total unemployed. (International Labour Organization Key Indicators of Labour Market database)

Maternal leave benefits are percentage of the wage paid during the maternity leave. (United Nations)

Maternal mortality ratio is a modeled estimate showing the number of women who die from pregnancy-related causes during pregnancy and childbirth per 100,000 live births. (World Health Organization, United Nations Children's Fund, United Nations Population Fund and the World Bank)

Maternity leave is a number of weeks that the benefits are provided. (United Nations)

Population is the de facto definition of population, which counts all residents regardless of legal status or citizenship—except for refugees not permanently settled in the country of asylum, who are generally considered part of the population of their country of origin. Figures in italics are for years other than 2011. (World Bank staff estimates from various sources including census reports, the United Nations Population Division's World Population Prospects, national statistical offices, household surveys conducted by national agencies, and ICF International.)

Population below $1.25 a day is the percentages of the population living on less than $1.25 a day at 2005 international prices. Data are the most recent estimate since 2000. Figures in italics are for years other than 2011. (World Bank)

Pregnant women receiving prenatal care are the percentage of women attended at least once during pregnancy by skilled health personnel for reasons related to pregnancy. (United Nations Children's Fund and ICF International)

Primary completion rate is the percentage of students completing the last year of primary school. It is calculated by dividing the total number of students in the last grade of primary school minus the number of repeaters in that grade by the total number of children of official completing age. (United Nations Educational, Scientific, and Cultural Organization Institute for Statistics)

Glossary

Seats held by women in national parliament is the percentage of parliamentary seats in a single or lower chamber occupied by women. Data listed for 2011 are for 2012 (Inter-Parliamentary Union)

Self-employed workers are those workers who, working on their own account or with one or a few partners or in cooperative, hold the type of jobs defined as a "self-employment jobs." (International Labour Organization Key Indicators of Labour Market database)

Sex ratio at birth refers to male births per female births. (United Nations Population Division)

Total fertility rate is the number of children that would be born to a woman if she were to live to the end of her childbearing years and bear children in accordance with current age-specific fertility rates. (World Bank staff estimates from various sources including census reports, the United Nations Population Division's World Population Prospects, national statistical offices, household surveys conducted by national agencies, and ICF International.)

Under-five mortality rate is the probability that a newborn baby will die before age five if subject to current age-specific mortality rates. (United Nations Children's Fund, World Health Organization, World Bank, and United Nations Population Division)

Unemployment rate is the share of labor force without work but available for and seeking employment. Definitions of labor force and unemployment may differ by country. (International Labour Organization Key Indicators of Labour Market database)

Unmet need for contraception is the percentage of fertile, married women of reproductive age who do not want to become pregnant and are not using contraception. (ICF International)

Unpaid family workers are those who work without pay in a market-oriented establishment operated by a related person living in the same household. (International Labour Organization)

Vulnerable employment is unpaid family workers and own-account workers as a percentage of total employment. (International Labour Organization Key Indicators of Labour Market database)

Wage and salaried workers are those workers who hold the type of jobs defined as "paid employment jobs," where the incumbents hold explicit (written or oral) or implicit employment contracts that give them a basic remuneration that is not directly dependent upon the revenue of the unit for which they work. (International Labour Organization Key Indicators of Labour Market database)

Women first married by age 18 is the percentage of women ages 20–24 who were first married by age 18. (United Nations Children's Fund and ICF International)

Glossary

Women in wage employment in the nonagricultural sector is the share of female workers in the nonagricultural sector (industry and services), expressed as a percentage of total employment in the nonagricultural sector. Industry includes mining and quarrying (including oil production), manufacturing, construction, electricity, gas, and water, corresponding to divisions 2–5 (ISIC revision 2) or tabulation categories C–F (ISIC revision 3). Services include wholesale and retail trade and restaurants and hotels; transport, storage, and communications; financing, insurance, real estate, and business services; and community, social, and personal services— corresponding to divisions 6–9 (ISIC revision 2) or tabulation categories G–P (ISIC revision 3). (International Labour Organization)

Women's share of part-time employment is the female share of total part-time workers. Part-time worker is an employed person whose normal hours of work are less than those of comparable full-time workers. Definition of part-time varies across countries. (International Labour Organization Key Indicators of Labour Market database)

Youth literacy rate is the percentage of people ages 15–24 that can, with understanding, both read and write a short, simple statement about their everyday life. (United Nations Educational, Scientific, and Cultural Organization Institute for Statistics)

Youth unemployment rate is the share of the labor force ages 15–24 without work but available for and seeking employment. Definitions of labor force and unemployment may differ by country. (International Labour Organization Key Indicators of Labour Market database)